## Psychological Aspects of Cyberspace

Hundreds of millions of people across the world use the Internet every day. Its functions vary, from shopping and banking to socializing, dating, and getting help in numerous areas. From a psychological perspective, the Internet has become a major vehicle for interpersonal communication that can significantly affect people's decisions, behaviors, attitudes, and emotions. Moreover, its existence has created a virtual social environment in which people can meet, negotiate, collaborate, and exchange goods and information. Cyberspace is not just a technical device but a phenomenon that has reduced the world to a proverbial global village, fostering collaborations and international cooperations, thus reducing the barriers of geographical distance and indigenous cultures. Azy Barak and a team of prominent social scientists review a decade of scientific investigations into the social, behavioral, and psychological aspects of cyberspace, collating state-of-the-art knowledge in each area. Together they develop emerging conceptualizations and envisage directions and applications for future research.

AZY BARAK is Professor of Psychology in the Department of Education at the University of Haifa, Israel. He is one of the world's leading researchers in the psychology of cyberspace and a founder of important applications in this area.

# Psychological Aspects of Cyberspace

Theory, Research, Applications

**EDITED BY**

AZY BARAK
University of Haifa, Israel

This book is accompanied by a dynamic website (see link at
http://www.cambridge.org/barak) in which the chapter contributors
publish further ideas and additional information. Readers may
ask questions and write comments to which authors respond.

CAMBRIDGE
UNIVERSITY PRESS

PUBLISHED BY CAMBRIDGE UNIVERSITY PRESS
Cambridge, New York, Melbourne, Madrid, Cape Town, Singapore, São Paulo, Delhi

CAMBRIDGE UNIVERSITY PRESS
32 Avenue of the Americas, New York, NY 10013-2473, USA

www.cambridge.org
Information on this title: www.cambridge.org/9780521694643

First published 2008

Printed in the United States of America

*A catalog record for this publication is available from the British Library.*

*Library of Congress Cataloging in Publication Data*

Psychological aspects of cyberspace : theory, research, applications / edited by Azy Barak.
   p.   cm.
Includes bibliographical references and index.
ISBN 978-0-521-87301-7 (hardcover) – ISBN 978-0-521-69464-3 (pbk.)
1. Cyberspace – Psychological aspects.   2. Internet users – Psychology.   I. Barak, Azy.
HM1017.B37   2008
303.48′34–dc22        2007045451

ISBN   978-0-521-87301-7 hardback
ISBN   978-0-521-69464-3 paperback

To my students, from whom I've learned the most

# Contents

# Tables

# Figures

# Preface

The psychology of cyberspace, or cyberpsychology, is a new field of study. Fewer than a handful of universities around the world offer a course in this emerging area, despite the unequivocal fact that many activities today take place online. In this novel social environment, new psychological circumstances project onto new rules governing human experiences, including physiological responses, behaviors, cognitive processes, and emotions. It seems, however, that psychology gradually is acknowledging and accepting this new field of study, as more behavioral scholars have begun to research the field, growing numbers of articles in the area appear in psychology journals, and an increasing number of books related to this domain are being published. This change reflects not only the growing number of professionals who find interest in researching the new field but also the growing number of people – students and laypeople alike – who search for credible and professional answers in this relatively unknown and uninvestigated area of human psychology.

I discovered this exciting direction in psychology mainly because of personal necessity. I was living in London, Ontario, Canada – affiliated with The University of Western Ontario and collaborating with my long-time friend and colleague William (Bill) Fisher, with whom I have thoroughly studied issues of sexuality on the Internet – when the revolutionary computer network, called the Internet, emerged (quite innovative in comparison to the relatively primitive Bitnet we used before). About the same time, Microsoft upgraded to the Windows 95 version and PC screen resolution and colors became more lively and attractive. The geographical distance to my homeland, Israel; the sudden subjectively realistic ability to "be there" while physically in Canada, including more efficient communication with faraway friends and colleagues; and the sensations and activities involved in the new medium led me to a personal insight: The Internet was going to revolutionize humanity in many terms. It took me a while to realize that the field of psychology was going to go through a considerable change, too. I then started to search the Internet for other psychologists who were undergoing a similar experience and similar thoughts. It took a relatively short time to become virtually acquainted with John Suler, John Grohol, Michael Fenichel, Storm King, and several other less conservative psychologists. From a distance, I viewed with much respect Sheizaf Rafaeli's amazing work in implementing the Internet in the Israeli society. Shortly thereafter, I contacted a few more of the leaders in the emerging field, among them

Adam Joinson, Tom Buchanan, Mark Griffiths, Janet Morahan-Martin, Kate Anthony, Jason Zack, and the late Al Cooper. These researchers have become my close colleagues; some of them have contributed to the current collection. Many of my ideas in developing field projects, such as SAHAR – a successful online suicide prevention enterprise (Barak, 2007) – as well as numerous research studies, came into action as a result of continuous online discussions with these and other colleagues.

The idea of putting together the knowledge and creative ideas accumulated by leading world scholars in cyberpsychology emerged after intensive online group communication among most of the contributors to this volume. Though the initial plan was to meet face-to-face and spend two weeks together in an isolated facility to share ideas and visions and to brainstorm on emerging psychological issues, practical constraints, as well as personal priorities, resulted in a written collection of individual essays that form the chapters of this book. Although the unique value of this volume lies in the originality of the thoughts and the creative views of the authors, this anthology – representing a variety of topics about our new field of study – may also serve as an effective sourcebook for professionals who wish to know more about and understand the innovative world that the "information revolution" has brought.

No doubt, "the world is flat," as a well-known columnist stated (Friedman, 2005), and we all share now "a global village," a term coined by Marshall McLuhan (1962) in forecasting the information revolution. What we used to know and believe in – whether psychology, medicine, physics, economics, or meteorology – is falling apart. As a result, we are in the midst of a social revolution. No one knows where it will go or what forms it will take because of such movements and trends as globalization; innovative technologies; fast-growing, synchronous, and limitless communications; and vast and powerful computerization. Psychology has to disconnect from its historical roots and perceptions and adapt to this new world if it desires to stay relevant and influential. Or, as I put it almost a decade ago: "Psychology, on the threshold of a new millennium, is driving on a superhighway that is taking the world to an unknown destination. To avoid potholes in this road, cautious considerations, international brainstorming, and intensive attention to this new, unprecedented development may maximize the social benefits and minimize the costs of the journey" (Barak, 1999, p. 241). It seems that psychology is gradually getting there. But is it going too slowly?

## Acknowledgments

I would like to thank Giuseppe Riva and Tom Buchanan, whose ideas and suggestions have significantly contributed to the depth and scope of this book. I am also grateful to A. M. Goldstein, whose editorial assistance is priceless.

Last but not least, I am indebted to Meyran Boniel-Nissim for her continuous help, support, and encouragement throughout this project.

Azy Barak<br>June 2007

## References

Barak, A. (1999). Psychological applications on the Internet: A discipline on the threshold of a new millennium. *Applied and Preventive Psychology, 8*, 231–246.

Barak, A. (2007). Emotional support and suicide prevention through the Internet: A field project report. *Computers in Human Behavior, 23*, 971–984.

Friedman, T. L. (2005). *The world is flat.* New York: Farrar, Straus and Giroux.

McLuhan, M. (1962). *The Gutenberg galaxy: The making of typographic man.* Toronto, Ontario: University of Toronto Press.

# List of Contributors

**Yair Amichai-Hamburger**

Yair Amichai-Hamburger is the Director of the Research Center for Internet Psychology (CIP) at The Sammy Ofer School of Communications, Interdisciplinary Center (IDC), Herzliya, Israel. His research focuses on Internet use and well-being. He edited *The Social Net: Human Behavior in Cyberspace* (Oxford University Press, 2005) and wrote *Technology and Wellbeing* (Cambridge University Press, 2008). E-mail: yairah@idc.ac.il

**Yaron Ariel**

Yaron Ariel is a Ph.D. candidate at InfoSoc, the Center for the Study of the Information Society, at the University of Haifa, Israel. He received a bachelor's degree in communication studies and political science and a master's degree in communication studies. His research interests, teaching, and previous publications are in online communities, users' motivations in using new media, and the interaction processes associated with information exchange. His personal website is http://yaronariel.com. Email: yaronariel@gmail.com

**Andrea J. Baker**

Andrea J. Baker teaches sociology both online and offline at Ohio University (Lancaster, OH, USA). Her book *Double Click* (Hampton Press, 2005) describes how 89 couples met at dating sites, in chat rooms, and discussion boards, and how they communicated before meeting offline, before presenting a model of successful online relationships. For more on this research and on her study of online and offline activities of a rock fan community, see her website: http://oak.cats.ohiou.edu/~bakera/ or write to bakera@ohiou.edu

**Azy Barak**

Azy Barak is a Professor of Psychology in the Department of Education at the University of Haifa, Israel. He is a Fellow of the International Society for Mental Health Online (ISMHO) and an active member of the International Society for Research on Internet Interventions (ISRII) and other professional organizations. His research interests include the psychological impact of the Internet on individuals, groups, couples, families, and communities, as well as exploitation of the Internet to promote various psychological applications. More information may be found at: http://construct.haifa.ac.il/~azy/azy.htm

## William A. Fisher

William A. Fisher is Professor of Psychology and Professor of Obstetrics and Gynaecology at the University of Western Ontario (London, Canada) and Research Associate at the Center for Health, Intervention, and Prevention at the University of Connecticut (Storrs, CT, USA). His research interests include use of Internet- and software-based interventions to promote sexual and reproductive health and investigation of the impact of pornography on attitudes and behavior. E-mail: fisher@uwo.ca; webpage: http://psychology.uwo.ca/faculty/fisher_res.htm

## Liat Hen

Liat Hen is a doctoral student and a lecturer in the Department of Occupational Therapy at the University of Haifa, Israel. Her research interests include meta-analysis and intervention with children with Developmental Coordination Disorder. E-mail: lhen@univ.haifa.ac.il

## Adam N. Joinson

Adam N. Joinson holds the post of Senior Lecturer in Information Systems at the School of Management, University of Bath. He is author of *Understanding the Psychology of Internet Behavior* (Palgrave, 2003), *Truth, Lies and Trust on the Internet* (with Monica Whitty; Routledge, 2007) and editor of the *Oxford Handbook of Internet Psychology* (with Katelyn McKenna, Tom Postmes, and Ulf-Dietrich Reips; Oxford University Press, 2007). His research interests encompass computer-mediated communication, privacy, trust, and social networking. His website is http://www.joinson.com

## Katelyn Y. A. McKenna (Yael Kaynan)

Katelyn Y. A. McKenna received her Ph.D. in 1998 from Ohio University (Athens, OH, USA). She is currently a Senior Lecturer in the Department of Communications at both the Ben-Gurion University of the Negev and the Interdisciplinary Center Herzliya. She is also a Senior Lecturer within the Department of Psychology at the Interdisciplinary Center Herzliya (Israel), while serving as the Academic Director of the communications program at the Raphael Recanati International School. She has numerous publications in the field of the psychology of the Internet and is one of the editors of *The Oxford Handbook of Internet Psychology* (Oxford University Press, 2007). E-mail: yaeli.kaynan@gmail.com

## Janet Morahan-Martin

Janet Morahan-Martin is Professor of Psychology and Chair of the Department of Applied Psychology at Bryant University (Smithfield, RI, USA), where she can be reached by e-mail at jmorahan@bryant.edu. Dr. Morahan-Martin has published extensively on Internet abuse, personality factors affecting patterns of Internet use, and patterns of online health information retrieval, evaluation, and use. She is a founding member of the International Society for Mental

Health Online and a member of the editorial board of *CyberPsychology & Behavior*.

### Carina B. Paine Schofield

Carina B. Paine Schofield completed a B.Sc. (Hons) in psychology and computing at Bournemouth University (1998) and a Ph.D. in forensic psychology at the Open University (2004) and is currently a research associate at the Institute of Educational Technology, The Open University. She works on the Economic and Social Research Council E-Society–funded Privacy and Self-Disclosure Online (http://www.prisd.net) project. Her research interests include people's privacy concerns when using the Internet, their privacy-related behavior, self-disclosure on the Internet, and children's privacy online. E-mail: carina_paine2002@yahoo.com

### Sheizaf Rafaeli

Sheizaf Rafaeli (http://sheizaf.rafaeli.net, Sheizaf@rafaeli.net) is Director of InfoSoc – the Center for the Study of the Information Society (http://infosoc. haifa.ac.il), and Head of the Graduate School of Management, at the University of Haifa, Israel (http://gsb.haifa.ac.il). He is interested in computers and networks as media. He co-founded and edited the *Journal of Computer Mediated Communication* (*JCMC*, http://jcmc.indiana.edu), co-edited *Network and Netplay* (with Fay Sudweeks and Margaret McLaughlin, MIT Press, 1998), and writes a weekly column about "Online Life" for the *Globes Financial* newspaper. His research touches on individual and organizational aspects and implications of computer-mediated communication (CMC), value of information, and virtual communities.

### Ulf-Dietrich Reips

Ulf-Dietrich Reips (http://www.psychologie.unizh.ch/sowi/reips/reipspers. html; e-mail: u.reips@psychologie.uzh.ch) is an Assistant Professor in the Department of Psychology, University of Zurich, Switzerland. His main research interests are methods, tools, and techniques of Internet-based research, e-learning, online privacy, and self-disclosure; data mining; cognitive, social, and business psychology; and e-health. Reips is founding editor of the *International Journal of Internet Science* and has published more than 60 journal articles, book chapters, and books in the field, including *Dimensions of Internet Science* (with Michael Bosnjak, 2001), *Online Social Sciences* (with Bernad Batinic and Michael Bosnjak, Hogrefe & Huber, 2002), and *The Oxford Handbook of Internet Psychology* (with Adam Joinson, Katelyn McKenna, and Tom Postmes, 2007).

### John Suler

John Suler is a Professor of Psychology at Rider University and author of "The Psychology of Cyberspace" (www.rider.edu/~suler/psycyber/psycyber.html). His current research interests include the development of the online psycho-educational program "eQuest" and research on photographic psychology and imagistic communication in cyberspace.

**Alexander E. Voiskounsky**

Alexander E. Voiskounsky is affiliated with the Psychology Department, Moscow Lomonosov State University (Russia) and lectures on the psychology of cyberspace. He is the first psychologist in Russia to pioneer research in this field. He authored and edited several books in Russian and co-edited two books in English: *States of Mind* (with Diane Halpern; Oxford University Press, 1997) and *Human Perspectives in the Internet Society* (with three more co-editors; WIT Press, 2004). E-mail: vaemsu@gmail.com

**Monica T. Whitty**

Monica T. Whitty is lecturer in the Division of Psychology at Nottingham Trent University (UK). She is the first author of *Cyberspace Romance: The Psychology of Online Relationships* (Palgrave, 2006) and *Trust, Lies and Truth on the Internet* (Routledge, 2007). In recent years, her work has focused on online dating, cyber-relationships, Internet infidelity, misrepresentation of self online, cyberstalking, cyberethics, and Internet and e-mail surveillance in the workplace. E-mail: monica.whitty@ntu.ac.uk

# 1 Reflections on the Psychology and Social Science of Cyberspace

*Azy Barak and John Suler*

Personal computers and computer networks began to take over offices and increasingly the public in the 1980s, but the extensive adoption of the Internet did not come about until the introduction of the first browsers and the overwhelming acceptance of Microsoft Windows and Apple systems – equipped with advanced graphics – both in the mid-1990s. The world changed in many ways for numerous people from that point, as both social institutions and individuals have witnessed and participated in another social revolution: the availability and accessibility of information of all kinds and the dramatic innovation in interpersonal communication. With the assistance and encouragement of governments and many organizations (acting out of a variety of reasons), computers, linked to ever-growing networks, penetrated the general public rather quickly and relatively easily. It did not take long before numerous technological firms around the world, acknowledging significant improvements in a broad array of personal, work-related, social, business-related, and government-related activities, joined a competitive race for this line of business, marked by its creativity and high potential. Accordingly, they advanced and reinforced more intensive use of computers and numerous computer-related activities. This race, in turn, brought about fantastic technological developments that have changed people's world order and lives in many ways, from seeking and using information on any topic to shopping and trading, from communication with acquaintances and with strangers to virtual dating and a love life, from learning and teaching to doing research, from helping others and being helped to improved use of medicine and other facets of health care, from entertainment and leisure to self-expression. These changes in exposure to numerous areas, patterns of behaviors, and priorities are dynamic and continuously emerging, as technology is still developing rapidly and people are not only more open to such changes, but in fact expect them.

Although not all societies or all parts of a society have taken part in this revolution, because of "the digital divide" (see Warschauer, 2003), the Internet era has penetrated homes, workplaces, schools, and communities, as well as public institutions and businesses. No statistical picture of usage may validly be cited to provide an accurate picture of the current state of the art, as statistics relating to computer and Internet use vary rapidly, and data are diverse and highly inconsistent around the world. However, surveys show that in developed countries, such as the United States, Great Britain, Germany, Australia, Japan, and Canada, home penetration of the Internet has exceeded 75 percent. Even in developing countries, such as in Africa, recent years have witnessed a huge increase in computer penetration (see continuously updated figures by Internet World Stats, at http://www.internetworldstats.com/stats.htm). Indeed, the availability and affordability of the Internet have been the cause of personal and social changes. There has been a dramatic increase in the number of human activities that have moved from physical, face-to-face meetings to contacts enabled by online, distant communication (see continuously published surveys by Pew Internet Research, at http://www.pewinternet.org conducted in the United States), thus changing human culture, habits, priorities, governing, parenting, and so on. Other factors have accelerated the rapid and broad adoption of the Internet, such as its growing social acceptability and endorsement (Bargh & McKenna, 2004; Haythornthwaite & Hagar, 2004; King, 1999), as well as its more personally originated motivators, such as anonymity, escapism, perceived privacy, and solitude (Amichai-Hamburger, 2005); the Internet also provides a ready source and outlet for fun and pleasure (Chen, 2006).

Obviously, there are clear psychological aspects to the evolving changes in the widespread use of computers to substitute for what formerly was done face-to-face and in physical ways. It seems that these aspects are twofold. On the one hand, people experience and behave in the new cyberspace environment in a way that requires fresh, innovative psychological conceptualizations, which entails exploiting old psychological knowledge, as well as formulating new ideas, to understand and explain human behavior and experience in cyberspace. On the other hand, using the computer's and Internet's advanced capabilities to enhance various activities traditionally performed offline by psychologists necessitates revolutionary ideas to harness these new psychological applications.

These two major objectives formulate the aim and scope of an emerging field in psychology, still in its embryonic stage: cyberpsychology, or the psychology of cyberspace (Barak, 1999; Sassenberg, Boos, Postmes, & Reips, 2003; Suler, 1996–2007). Research in this field, conducted by investigators from a variety of disciplines – not just psychology (and its various areas) but also from communication, medicine, social work, education, psychiatry, nursing, sociology, management, and others – has been nonsystematic and lacking leadership and direction. Scientific publications dealing with cyberpsychology have appeared in numerous – usually undedicated – online and offline outlets. The first printed books on the subject were published in the late 1990s (e.g., Fink, 1999; Gackenbach, 1998; Wallace, 1999), whereas a dedicated online book made its appearance, too, at this time (Suler, 1996–2007). In this chapter, we will try to lay some foundations to this new and innovative field of psychology.

## Cyberspace as a Psychological Space

With the advance of computers and online networks, a new dimension of human experience emerged: cyberspace. The term has become so commonplace that it may at this point seem trite and commercialized. However, the realm created by the Internet can be understood as a very new and, in many ways, unique psychological space. When they power up their computers, launch a program, write e-mails, or browse a website, people often feel – consciously or subconsciously – that they are entering a "place" that is filled with a wide range of meanings and purposes. For this reason, the online experience involves many expressions that convey the sensation of dimension and place: "worlds, domains, sites, windows, rooms."

On a deep psychological level, people often experience their computers and cyberspace as an extension of their minds and personalities – a "space" that reflects their tastes, attitudes, and interests. In psychoanalytic terms, cyberspace may become a type of "transitional space" (Suler, 1999; Turkle, 1995), that is, an extension of the individual's intrapsychic world. It may be experienced as an intermediate zone between self and other that is part self and part other. As they view the e-mail, webpage, or instant message written by an online companion, some people truly feel that their minds are connected to or even blended with the minds of the others.

The ability of the mind to create and project a realm of meaning and purpose, to shape that realm with spatial/physical metaphors, is powerful. By itself, this ability accounts for much of the universal, perhaps even archetypical experience of cyberspace as a psychologically human space. However, some important features of the Internet have accelerated that process. Its historical transition from a text-only to multimedia environment made it a much more compelling world that encouraged not just the creation of meaning and purpose but also meaning and purpose within a visual and auditory context that resonates with the human experience of the "real" world. Compared with books, radio, or TV, cyberspace is much more interactive. If people can shape their experience of a realm by how they choose to move through it, and if they can alter the appearance of that realm and contribute to it, then that realm becomes all the more powerful as a psychological space. Because the Internet also includes the opportunity to interact with other people, a collective shaping of meaning and purpose elevates cyberspace into a social space that psychologically transcends traditional media.

## Psychology in Cyberspace

As cyberspace has gained prominence, so has the scientific study of it. Because it became a realm for manifesting meaning, behavior, and interpersonal relationships, psychologists naturally and quickly rose to the task of investigating it. A decade ago, psychological publications about the Internet were rare. Sometimes they were viewed in academia as esoteric or frivolous projects. Today, such research is commonplace and more widely accepted. Entire journals are now devoted to it. Many accept "cyberpsychology" as a new field unto itself. This change reveals the undeniable impact of cyberspace as a powerful influence on the psychology of the individual, interpersonal relationships, group behavior, and culture.

Over the course of the past decade, the variety of cyberpsychological studies has expanded in parallel to the rising complexity of cyberspace. Reflecting social anxieties about this surprisingly contagious phenomenon, the early studies that attracted the most attention were those that focused on pathological Internet use and "addiction" (Greenfield, 1999; Kraut et al., 1998; Young, 1998). Dwelling on the frightening aspects of cyberspace has always been a media predilection, but cyberpsychological studies eventually expanded into explorations of the positive as well as the negative aspects of life in cyberspace. The topics that evolved became as diverse as the discipline of psychology. Researchers from all branches of psychology became interested in cyberspace, including cognitive, social, educational, organizational, personality, clinical, and experimental psychologists. After all, asking, "What is psychology in cyberspace?" is like asking, "What is psychology in real life?" All topics in psychology apply: sensation and perception, learning, motivation, personality theory, interpersonal relationships, mental health and illness, group behavior, leadership, and cultural and cross-cultural dynamics.

As psychology delved deeper into cyberspace, some very basic questions quickly became apparent. Will traditional concepts and theories suffice in our understanding of online behavior? Will we have to modify those theories? Will we need to develop new ones?

Such questions developed out of the recognition that cyberspace, as a psychological realm, might be quite different from face-to-face environments. Geographical boundaries are transcended. Almost everything is recordable. The boundaries of "privacy" are more complex. Social interactions can be synchronous, asynchronous, or something in between. Under partial or near complete anonymity, people might become more disinhibited than usual, or they might experiment with different identities. Sensory experience might be reduced to text-only communication or expanded to multimedia experiences, with the sights and sounds of highly creative fantasy.

All of these features of online environments have been mixed and matched and combined in a variety of ways over the past decade. Future designers of cyberspace realms will continue to do so, as well as invent entirely new communication and informational tools. "Cyberspace" or "Internet" is far from being a monolithic entity. Nor is it, by any means, static. It is a multiplicity of environments, all of which are changing and evolving at a seemingly unrelenting and unpredictable pace. To keep up, psychology will need to be equally swift and flexible in its methods of research and theoretical frameworks. It will need to identify the basic psychological building blocks of online environments and social interactions – the core, elemental features of cyberspace experiences that do not change much over time are relevant to all types of psychological studies and form the core foundation for an integrated cyberpsychology. However, it will also need to assimilate and accommodate new developments. To understand the cyberspace worlds of today and tomorrow, psychology must be ready to embrace the unexpected. It must remain open-minded about the strengths and limitations of its methods and theories. Cyberspace is not simply a new topic of research for psychology. It is a new realm of human experience that can transform psychology itself, as quite a few researches and application projects have indeed shown.

Psychology is also challenged to do more than simply study cyberspace. As an applied science, it also faces the task of using cyberpsychological knowledge to address practical issues. How can education be improved with online resources? How can groups and organizations function more effectively? What kinds of online human services can we develop to advance the causes of mental health and social welfare? Psychotherapists are exploring the options of conducting their work via online synchronous and asynchronous communication. Many websites offer information about a variety of social and mental health issues. Online resources now include self-help programs, psychological testing, and various interactive games and programs that address psychological topics. Psychologists are pressed to conduct research to validate these activities and resources, to participate in their development, and to provide education to the public about them. Ideally, the knowledge base of cyberpsychology will become effective to the point where designers in the business sector will employ the expertise of cyberpsychologists in the development of new online environments, communities, and various psychological applications.

## Embracing Cyberspace as a Scientifically Legitimate Social Environment

As mentioned, the scientific study of cyberspace – or a virtual social environment characterized by computer-mediated communication – began over two decades ago. Researchers, at first mostly from the field of communications, sought to apply communication and social psychological models to understand, to explain, and to predict human behavior, while interacting through the mediation of computers. These attempts, however, have been only partially successful, as in quite a few instances findings concerning various types of behaviors could not be described and explained by traditional psychological theory when applied in various online conditions. Examples of such cases include group behavior (e.g., Thatcher & De La Cour, 2003), selling and buying behavior (Galin, Gross, & Gosalker, 2007), or more general social behaviors (Yao & Flanagin, 2006). It seems, therefore, that the new means of communication not only provided a new vehicle for people to interact with one another but also introduced new psychological factors into the formula. For instance, the very ability of users to freely choose between synchronous and asynchronous alternative communication modalities, the combination of text-based communication and anonymity, unidentifiability, and lack of eye-contact, or perceived privacy, are all new components, unknown and unac-counted for by old psychological theoretical approaches. Moreover, the very new, unprecedented experiencing of a virtual environment, which is created in a person's mind and in which people may perform various activities through a computer, led to a feeling – supported by growing research – that tradi-tional psychology had no valid tools to deal with this environment. Thus, new, creative, and innovative conceptualizations, or significant upgrades of older ones, had to be formulated to better account for people's behavior in cyberspace. Cyberpsychology thus attempts to encompass human behavior and experiences in cyberspace by observing psychological phenomena indige-nous to cyberspace and relating them to people experiencing this emerging environment.

Our accumulated knowledge on cyberspace tells us that although some psychological phenomena that exist offline are similar, if not identical, to what happens in the online environment, other phenomena are different and unique to cyberspace. For example, research shows that some important dimensions of self-disclosure in the offline and online environments are very similar: people disclose more personal, intimate, and sensitive information about themselves to those they can relate to (Barak & Gluck-Ofri, 2007; Leung, 2002); that group norms affect the level of self-disclosure (Dietz-Uhler, Bishop-Clark, & Howard, 2005); and that interpersonal self-disclosure is reciprocal (Barak & Gluck-Ofri, 2007; Joinson, 2001; Rollman, Krug, & Parente, 2000; Rollman & Parente, 2001).

However, research has also found that people in cyberspace make more, deeper, and faster disclosures about themselves to others in that environment than in their physical environment (Barak & Bloch, 2006; Beck, 2005; McCoyd & Schwaber Kerson, 2006); this is apparently due to the unique effects of online disinhibition (Suler, 2004). Another example has to do with situation ambiguity and uncertainty: as in the offline environment, ambiguity that characterize the online environment in many cases affects people's behaviors and emotions so that they rely more on their imagination, cognitive processes, and personality dynamics than on actual, valid external information (Barak, 2007; Mantovani, 2002; Suler, 1996; Turkle, 2004). The elevated ambiguous environment typi-fying cyberspace, however, results in more intensive behaviors and emotions, as the role of personal processes becomes more central. This has a direct effect on people's experiences in the particular online environment, especially con-cerning personal engagements, from online dating (Norton, Frost, & Ariely,

2007), online interpersonal relationships (Levine, 2000) to sex (Whitty & Carr, 2006), as well as group behavior (McKenna & Seidman, 2005).

It is important to note that the field of cyberpsychology is not confined to specific *modes* of communication (e.g., e-mail, chat, forum, VoIP [Voice over Internet Protocol], webcam), *purposes* for using the computer and Internet (e.g., playing solitary or group games, learning, shopping, seeking information, undergoing psychotherapy), or *types* of online environment (e.g., information website, social network, chat room). Cyberpsychology, in other words, aims at detecting and understanding specific factors responsible for human behavior in cyberspace across and in interaction with specific dimensions of communication. Identifying psychological rules, as substitutes for or additions to general theories held in regard to human behavior offline, may contribute to a better understanding of people, on the one hand, and better exploitation of cyberspace toward this end, on the other.

## Cyberpsychology – an Evolving Field

Serious consideration has to be given, however, to quite a few factors that significantly affect the development of behavior in cyberspace but – with rapidly developing, sometimes revolutionary, technology – that are impossible to predict. Projecting from the past several years, we now know that the introduction of what is known as Web 2.0 (O'Reilly, 2005), including blogging, podcasting, Wikipedia and other wikis, and photograph and video sharing, all of which emphasize users' creations and communications (as opposed to previously less users' created applications) as one of the major functions of the Internet, has actually had significant impact on cyberspace, in terms of purpose and intensity of use, interpersonal interactions, and the influence of online on offline experiences. Another example: The invention of content syndication through RSS has dramatically changed users' immediacy and mediation of exposure to both publicly and privately created content. This technological innovation, which influences what people are exposed to, has made a significant change in the use of the Internet for many and, naturally, makes online published contents more influential. Yet another example: Wireless Internet has become almost standard in many workspaces, schools, public places, and homes in recent years. This "simple" innovation, providing more flexibility of practical use than ever before, has profoundly changed the way many people communicate. If we add to this collection of advances the rapid, revolutionary development of Internet-enabled cellular phones, we can observe an unpredictable course of social changes. Nobody can yet predict what the open-source movement (see http://www.opensource.org) will bring about (in terms of human behavior), but perhaps it is part of another upcoming revolution. These examples show that cyberpsychology, unlike traditional areas of psychology, must employ hands-on technology and keep up with emerging changes; findings, conclusions, and implications yielded at a certain point in time might be totally erroneous at another point.

Another powerful effect on human behavior in cyberspace might come from a totally different area: the legal arena. Changes in laws concerning computers and the Internet are taking place all over the world, particularly in regard to pedophilia, spamming, phishing, and hacking (Engel, 2006) but also in regard to online gambling and gaming. Consequent to the legislation is its implementation by enforcement agencies. Such moves may affect people's behavior online because, for example, a reduced sense of anonymity, even requirements to identify oneself in many online environments. As anonymity constitutes one of the major factors in determining people's behavior online (e.g., Suler, 2004; Tanis & Postmes, 2007), a lessening of this feature might significantly change online behavior patterns. In addition, probable changes in copyright laws may dramatically change people's use of online music, movies, books, and so on, consequently altering many of their offline behaviors, too.

The significant technological and legal changes, as well as the continued penetration of the Internet into varied aspects of people's lives, will undoubtedly affect their daily experiences and their general behavior, as well as the complexity of cyberpsychology theory. Unlike many other areas of psychology (and contrary to other disciplines), in which the field of study is relatively static and researchers concentrate on deepening its understanding, cyberpsychology is highly dynamic. This aspect creates added scientific challenges; what is considered a pioneering stage might last for many years, as long as new frontiers are established. Moreover, developments in the understanding of cyberspace and its possible exploitation for various psychological applications (Barak, 1999) will affect, in turn, many other fields of psychology, from counseling and therapy, diagnostics and assessment, and the study of cognitive processes to social interactions and relationships, and indeed research methodology.

## The Future of Cyberpsychology

The future of cyberpsychology rests on synergistic collaborations. As a field that expands across all psychological disciplines, cyberpsychology will be most effective when experts from different fields work together. The cyberspace experience is multidisciplinary, drawing on all types of experts in the social sciences, as well as those in the technical fields of human-computer interactions. To join the pioneering of the science of cyberspace, psychologists must embrace the opportunity to work side-by-side with these other disciplines.

The future of cyberpsychology also rests on its understanding of the juxtaposition and interpenetration of online and offline living. How does online behavior affect offline behavior and vice versa? To maximize the well-being of individuals, groups, and societies, how should we balance and integrate online and offline lifestyles? The answers to such questions will do more than just enhance our understanding of cyberspace. They will enhance our understanding of the human experience itself.

## Summary and Conclusions

We have tried to define and characterize a new, evolving field in psychology, cyberpsychology. One of the main issues affecting this field of study has to do with the dynamics and rapid changes that distinguish it and that are caused by its very dependence on fast-growing technology, which in turn affects individuals and society in adopting this technology. This characteristic of cyberpsychology is quite unique compared with other fields of psychology, which typically refer to more static and stable subjects of research. Moreover, although we expect changes and, relying on technological projections and plans, have some clues concerning future developments of computers and the Internet, the past has taught us that even more technological breakthroughs are indeed inevitable. Consequently, cyberpsychology will have to refocus and adjust to these changes, which will likely have further significant effect on human behavior. For example, what is now only in very preliminary stages of development, such as Semantic Web (Antoniou & van Harmelen, 2004), ambient intelligence-embedded agents that operate complicated systems for the sake of the elderly, disabled, and sick people (Weber, Rabaey, & Aarts, 2006), advanced virtual reality (VR) therapeutic applications (Riva, Botella, Légeron, & Optale, 2004; Riva et al., 2007), advanced three-dimensional (3-D) social network systems to provide highly elevated virtual community and live gaming experiences, and the addition of senses of taste and smell into online communication – all such innovations unavoidably will have great effect on people and, hence, on the field of cyberpsychology.

To understand people's behavior in cyberspace and to apply this understanding in introducing actual changes – such as educating netiquette, fostering preventive behaviors, applying e-therapy, and conducting online learning – knowledge from traditional psychology might not be sufficient. In fact, reliance on such knowledge might be misleading in many instances. Exploration of new rules of behavior is needed, together with the formulation of new conceptualizations to more validly account for people's experiences in cyberspace. Although such attempts are in progress (e.g., Suler, 1996–2007), it seems that additional scholars from psychology and related fields who join this emerging field of cyberpsychology will contribute to crystallizing new ideas and conquering a new scientific frontier.

### References

Amichai-Hamburger, Y. (2005). Personality and the Internet. In Y. Amichai-Hamburger (Ed.), *The social net: Human behavior in cyberspace* (pp. 27–55). New York: Oxford University Press.

Antoniou, G., & van Harmelen, F. (2004). *A semantic web primer*. Boston, MA: MIT Press.

Barak, A. (1999). Psychological applications on the Internet: A discipline on the threshold of a new millennium. *Applied and Preventive Psychology, 8*, 231–246.

Barak, A. (2007). Phantom emotions: Psychological determinants of emotional experiences on the Internet. In A. Joinson, K. Y. A. McKenna, T. Postmes, & U. D. Reips (Eds.), *Oxford handbook of Internet psychology* (pp. 303–329). Oxford, UK: Oxford University Press.

Barak, A., & Bloch, N. (2006). Factors related to perceived helpfulness in supporting highly distressed individuals through an online support chat. *CyberPsychology & Behavior, 9*, 60–68.

Barak, A., & Gluck-Ofri, O. (2007). Degree and reciprocity of self-disclosure in online forums. *CyberPsychology & Behavior, 10*, 407–417.

Bargh, J. A., & McKenna, K. Y. A. (2004). The Internet and social life. *Annual Review of Psychology, 55*, 573–590.

Beck, C. T. (2005). Benefits of participating in Internet interviews: Women helping women. *Qualitative Health Research, 15*, 411–422.

Chen, H. (2006). Flow on the net–detecting Web users' positive affects and their flow states. *Computers in Human Behavior, 22*, 221–233.

Dietz-Uhler, B., Bishop-Clark, C., & Howard, E. (2005). Formation of and adherence to a self-disclosure norm in an online chat. *CyberPsychology & Behavior, 8*, 114–120.

Engel, C. (2006). The role of law in the governance of the Internet. *International Review of Law, Computers & Technology, 20*, 201–216.

Fink, J. (Ed.). (1999). *How to use computers and cyberspace in the clinical practice of psychotherapy*. Northvale, NJ: Aronson.

Gackenbach, J. (Ed.). (1998). *Psychology and the Internet*. San Diego, CA: Academic Press.

Galin, A., Gross, M., & Gosalker, G. (2007). E-negotiation versus face-to-face negotiation what has changed – if anything? *Computers in Human Behavior, 23*, 787–797.

Greenfield, D. N. (1999). *Virtual addiction*. Oakland, CA: New Harbinger Publications.

Haythornthwaite, C., & Hagar, C. (2004). The social worlds of the Web. *Annual Review of Information Science and Technology, 39*, 311–346.

Joinson, A. N. (2001). Knowing me, knowing you: Reciprocal self-disclosure in Internet-based surveys. *CyberPsychology & Behavior, 4*, 587–591.

King, S. A. (1999). Internet gambling and pornography: Illustrative examples of the psychological consequences of communication anarchy. *CyberPsychology & Behavior, 2*, 175–193.

Kraut, R., Lundmark, V., Patterson, M., Kiesler, S., Mukopadhyay, T., & Scherlis, W. (1998). Internet paradox: A social technology that reduces social involvement and psychological well-being? *American Psychologist, 53*, 1017–1031.

Leung, L. (2002). Loneliness, self-disclosure, and ICQ ("I Seek You") use. *CyberPsychology & Behavior, 5*, 241–251.

Levine, D. (2000). Virtual attraction: What rocks your boat. *CyberPsychology & Behavior, 3*, 565–573.

Mantovani, G. (2002). Internet haze: Why new artifacts can enhance situation ambiguity. *Culture & Psychology, 8*, 307–326.

McCoyd, J. L. M., & Schwaber Kerson, T. (2006). Conducting intensive interviews using email: A serendipitous comparative opportunity. *Qualitative Social Work, 5*, 389–406.

McKenna, K., & Seidman, G. (2005). You, me, and we: Interpersonal processes in electronic groups. In Y. Amichai-Hamburger (Ed.), *The social net: Human behavior in cyberspace* (pp. 191–217). New York: Oxford University Press.

Norton, M. I., Frost, J. H., & Ariely, D. (2007). Less is more: The lure of ambiguity, or why familiarity breeds contempt. *Journal of Personality and Social Psychology, 92*, 97–105.

O'Reilly, T. (2005). *What is Web 2.0: Design patterns and business models for the next generation of software.* Retrieved March 1, 2007, from http://www.oreillynet.com/pub/a/oreilly/tim/news/2005/09/30/what-is-web-20.html

Riva, G., Botella, C., Légeron, P., & Optale, G. (Eds.). (2004). *Cybertherapy: Internet and virtual reality as assessment and rehabilitation tools for clinical psychology and neuroscience.* Amsterdam: IOS Press.

Riva, G., Gaggioli, A., Villani, D., Preziosa, A., Morganti, F., Corsi, R., Faletti, G., & Vezzadini, L. (2007). NeuroVR: an open source virtual reality platform for clinical psychology and behavioral neurosciences. *Studies in Health Technology and Informatics, 125*, 394–399.

Rollman, J. B., Krug, K., & Parente, F. (2000). The chat room phenomenon: Reciprocal communication in cyberspace. *CyberPsychology & Behavior, 3*, 161–166.

Rollman, B., & Parente, F. (2001). Relation of statement length and type and type of chat room reciprocal communication on the Internet. *CyberPsychology & Behavior, 4*, 617–622.

Sassenberg, K., Boos, M., Pstmes, T., & Reips, U. D. (2003). Studying the Internet: A challenge for modern psychology. *Swiss Journal of Psychology, 62*, 75–77.

Suler, J. (1996). *The black hole phenomenon.* Retrieved March 1, 2007, from http://www.rider.edu/~suler/psycyber/blackhole.html

Suler, J. (1996–2007). *The psychology of cyberspace.* Retrieved March 1, 2007, from http://www.rider.edu/~suler/psycyber/psycyber.html

Suler, J. (1999). *Cyberspace as psychological space.* Retrieved on March 1, 2007, from http://www.rider.edu/~suler/psycyber/psychspace.html

Suler, J. (2004). The online disinhibition effect. *CyberPsychology & Behavior, 7*, 321–326.

Tanis, M., & Postmes, T. (2007). Two faces of anonymity: Paradoxical effects of cues to identity in CMC. *Computers in Human Behavior, 23*, 955–970.

Thatcher, A., & De La Cour, A. (2003). Small group decision-making in face-to-face and computer-mediated environments: the role of personality. *Behaviour & Information Technology, 22*, 203–218.

Turkle, S. (1995). *Life on the screen: Identity in the age of the Internet.* New York: Simon & Schuster.

Turkle, S. (2004). Whither psychoanalysis in computer culture? *Psychoanalytic Psychology, 21*, 16–30.

Wallace, P. (1999). *The psychology of the Internet.* New York: Cambridge University Press.

Warschauer, M. (2003). *Technology and social inclusion: Rethinking the digital divide.* Cambridge, MA: MIT Press.

Weber, W., Rabaey, J. M., & Aarts, E. (Eds.). (2006). *Ambient intelligence.* New York: Springer.

Whitty, T. E., & Carr, A. N. (2006). *Cyberspace romance: The psychology of online relationships.* London, UK: Palgrave Macmillan.

Yao, M. Z., & Flanagin, A. J. (2006). A self-awareness approach to computer-mediated communication. *Computers in Human Behavior, 22,* 518–544.

Young, K. (1998). *Caught in the net.* New York: Wiley.

# 2 Privacy, Trust, and Disclosure Online

*Carina B. Paine Schofield and Adam N. Joinson*

## Introduction

The use of new technology, and particularly the Internet, increasingly requires people to disclose personal information online for various reasons. In computer-mediated communication (CMC), disclosure may serve to reduce uncertainty in an interaction (Tidwell & Walther, 2002) or to establish legitimacy when joining an online group (Galegher, Sproull, & Kiesler, 1998). Disclosure is often a prerequisite to access services (for instance, with the ubiquitous registration form), to make online purchases (Metzger, 2006) or is requested for those same services to be personalized. The increasingly social nature of much web-based software (e.g., social network sites) also places a privacy cost on users due to a heightened requirement for disclosure of personal information as part of the functionality of the system (see BBC News). In addition to this increased need for disclosure, the development of ambient and ubiquitous technologies has raised the possibility that devices will communicate, or even broadcast, personal information without recourse to the user. Moreover, the ability to store information easily and cross-reference databases raises the possibility of unwitting disclosure through information accrual. Perhaps not surprisingly, this has raised a number of privacy concerns, among consumers and privacy advocates (e.g., Jupiter Research, 2002; U.K. Information Commissioner, 2006).

We start this chapter by introducing the existing research literature surrounding privacy and trust online. We then go on to consider how privacy and trust interact in determining online behavior. Finally, the chapter concludes with the description of a number of steps that can be taken to ensure that social software both protects privacy and enables the development of trust.

## Privacy

### What is Privacy?

There have been several attempts to define privacy. In a legal context, privacy has been considered to be largely synonymous with a "right to be let alone" (Warren & Brandeis, 1890). Within psychological literature both Westin's and

Altman's theories figure prominently in the major reviews of privacy in the 1970s. Westin (1967) provides a link between secrecy and privacy and defines privacy as "the claim of individuals, groups, or institutions to determine for themselves when, how and to what extent information about them is communicated to others" (p. 7). Altman (1975) incorporates both social and environmental psychology in understanding the nature of privacy. He defines privacy as "the selective control of access to the self" (p. 24) and believes privacy is achieved through the regulation of social interaction, which can in turn provide us with feedback on our ability to deal with the world and ultimately affect our definition of self. Both Westin's and Altman's theories have stimulated much of the research and theory development of privacy. However, despite many attempts to create a synthesis of the existing literature in this area (e.g., Parent, 1983; Schoeman, 1984), a unified and simple account of privacy has yet to emerge.

## Dimensions of Privacy

The highly complex nature of privacy has resulted in an alternative way of defining it, through its various dimensions. Burgoon, Parrott, LePoire, Kelley, Walther and Perry (1989) and DeCew (1997) have both developed multidimensional definitions of privacy. Burgoon et al. (1989) distinguish four dimensions of privacy and define it using these dimensions as "the ability to control and limit *physical, interactional, psychological* and *informational* access to the self or one's group" (p. 132). DeCew (1997) also reflects the multidimensional nature of privacy in her definition, which distinguishes three dimensions: *informational, accessibility,* and *expressive privacy*. There is much overlap between these multidimensional approaches, and some overlap between the features of each dimension. The broad features for each of the main dimensions are described below:

- *Informational (psychological) privacy* – relates to an individual's right to determine how, when, and to what extent information about the self will be released to another person (Westin, 1967) or to an organization. It covers personal information such as finances, medical details, and so on that an individual can decide who has access to and for what purposes.
- *Accessibility (physical) privacy* – relates to the degree to which a person is physically accessible to others. It "allows individuals to control decisions about who has physical access to their persons through sense perception, observation, or bodily contact" (DeCew, 1997, pp. 76–77). This dimension is grounded within our biological need for personal space.
- *Expressive (interactional) privacy* – "protects a realm for expressing ones self-identity or personhood through speech or activity. It protects the ability to decide to continue or to modify one's behaviour when

the activity in question helps define oneself as a person, shielded from interference, pressure and coercion from government or from other individuals" (DeCew, 1997, p. 77). As such, internal control over self expression and the ability to build interpersonal relationships improves, while external social control over lifestyle choices and so on are restricted (Schoeman, 1992).

## Actual Privacy and Perceived Privacy

Finally, a distinction can also be made between *actual* privacy and *perceived* privacy. These two forms of privacy coexist, and there will often be a mismatch between the two. For example, a person's perceived privacy may be high when they have control over disclosing their personal information to an online store. However, their actual privacy may be low due to the unobtrusive (automatic) collection of their online behavior, and the potential future use of the information they provide by unknown third parties.

More obtrusive invasions of privacy may result in a reduction of perceived privacy alongside actual privacy. For example, in the television program *Big Brother*, a number of housemates live together for several weeks, surrounded by hidden television cameras and microphones. Although housemates may enter the Big Brother house with low levels of perceived privacy (and low levels of actual privacy), over time their perceived privacy will increase (as the cameras are forgotten about), but their actual privacy will remain low.

## The Importance of Privacy

Despite there being no unitary concept of privacy, it is clear that both individuals, and society, attach a level of importance to it. For example, Ingham (1978) states that "man, we are repeatedly told is a social animal, and yet he constantly seeks to achieve a state of privacy" (p. 45). A failure to achieve any level of privacy will result in "costs." For example, by not obtaining privacy, a person will not benefit from the opportunities that the functions of privacy provide, which could result in stress or negative feedback about the self. There are also costs of losing privacy either through privacy invasion (when conditions for privacy are not achieved e.g., being overheard) or privacy violation (when recipients of personal information – intentionally provided by the discloser or gained through a privacy invasion – pass it on to others, e.g., gossip).

In the early privacy research described, invasions and violations were not emphasized. If they were, they were not considered to be an issue for daily life. For example, Ingham (1978) also states, "In everyday social life most individuals are only rarely confronted with an invasion of their privacy, although the number of potential threats is very large" (p. 40). However, since this early research, new technology (and in particular the Internet) has fueled debate and controversy about potential invasions and violations to privacy (Dinev & Hart, 2004) as will be described below.

## Privacy and the Internet

> At no time have privacy issues taken on greater significance than in recent years, as technological developments have led to the emergence of an "information society" capable of gathering, storing and disseminating increasing amounts of data about individuals.     (Schatz Byford, 1996, p. 1)

Over recent years, the Internet has become an important and ubiquitous feature of daily life in the developed world (e.g., online shopping, the sharing of documents, and various forms of online communication). With this increased use of the Internet, the way information is gathered and used has changed. A wide variety of information data is now collected with increasing frequency and in different contexts, making individuals become ever more transparent. The costs of obtaining and analyzing this data are also decreasing with the advances in technology. As recognition of this phenomenon grows, the issue of privacy has increased in salience. There are concerns that the Internet seems to erode privacy (Rust, Kannan, & Peng, 2002) and that offline privacy concerns are magnified online (Privacy Knowledge Base, 2005).

There are a number of specific threats to privacy online. For example, the effect of "ubiquitous" computing (Weiser, 1988) means that we leave data footprints in many areas of our lives that were previously considered "offline." The extremely rapid development of computing power, in terms of greater processing speed, increased storage capacity, wider communication connectivity, and lower machine size all affect privacy (Sparck-Jones, 2003). Specifically, the Internet's feature of *connectivity* (Sparck-Jones, 2003) means that it allows for interactive two-way communication and is woven into people's lives in a more intimate way than some other media as it connects people with places and people with people. Accordingly, it poses unique information privacy threats. These rapid advances mean that information can be efficiently and cheaply collected, stored, and exchanged, even data that may be deemed sensitive by the individuals concerned. As such, massive databases and Internet records of information about individual financial and credit history, medical records, purchases, and so on exist.

Therefore, there are important privacy issues related to online activities (Earp, Anton, Aiman-Smith, & Stufflebeam, 2005) as mundane as buying your weekly groceries over the web (e.g., does the retailer store information on your purchases? Is it sold to third parties so they can send you targeted junk mail?) or as specialized as online psychological research (e.g., is identifying information gathered about participants? Can confidentiality be guaranteed?).

Of course, there are also *benefits* to the technological advances described (personalized service, convenience, improved efficiency). Users can trade off providing valuable information about themselves to take advantage of such benefits. The Pew Internet and American Life Survey (2001) reported that over two-thirds of users are willing to share their personal information under some circumstances. In some situations, expressive privacy may be obtained through the loss of informational privacy to a third party. For example, one may disclose personal details and credit card information to have the convenience of completing an online transaction. In this way, the collection of personal, privacy information can be considered a "double-edged sword" (Malhotra, Kim, & Agarwal, 2004).

## Measuring Privacy

Privacy can be both objective (actual privacy) and subjective (perceived privacy). It is also a dispositional preference (Larson & Chastain, 1990) and a situational characteristic (Margulis, 2003). So, while people might be more or less concerned with their privacy *in general*, situational factors such as the costs and benefits of protecting or revealing information (Acquisti, 2004) combine to determine whether information is disclosed. To complicate matters further, privacy is also dynamic in that it serves to regulate social interaction (Altman, 1975; Derlega & Chaikin, 1977), while at the same time it can highlight uneven power relations (Derlega & Chaikin, 1977) or signify trust (Altman, 1977). Naturally, the complicated nature of privacy poses measurement issues. Generally, the measurement of privacy in online environments focuses on people's privacy concerns (i.e., their subjective attitudes about privacy) or their perceived privacy within a specific interaction.

Several studies have attempted to measure privacy concerns in detail and to identify different types of privacy concern. However, such studies tend to focus on informational privacy, and privacy scales are usually approached with a view of privacy as a one-dimensional construct. The Concern for Information Privacy (CFIP) scale was developed by Smith, Milberg, and Burke (1996). It was the first measure of its kind and measured individuals' concern regarding organizational practices. Later research (e.g., Stewart & Segars, 2002) argued that the CFIP needed to be reevaluated and developed following advances in technology, research, and practice. More recently, Malhotra et al. (2004) operationalized a more multidimensional notion of Internet Users Information Privacy Concerns. Their model (and measuring instrument) recognizes that there are multiple aspects of privacy. However, all of these aspects still lie within the domain of informational privacy, and other dimensions are not addressed.

Harper and Singleton (2001) suggest that one of the main defects of most privacy surveys and studies is that they do not separate out all of the different factors that could be considered privacy issues. It is clear from the definitions of privacy that it is a multifaceted concept, and therefore that scales attempting to measure concern should tap these different facets about which people may be concerned. For instance, Paine, Reips, Stieger, Joinson, and Buchanan (2007) used an automated interview agent to collect Internet users' privacy concerns and report a wide variety of noninformation types of privacy concerns, including viruses and spam.

In addition, following interviews with and observations of Internet users, Viseu, Clement, and Aspinall (2004), suggest that the privacy discourse should be reevaluated to comprise all of the moments involved in online use (the moment of sitting in front of a computer; the moment of interacting with it; and the moment after information has been released).

Furthermore, as well as attitudes and concerns about privacy, it is important to consider behaviors people may adopt to safeguard their privacy. There is a complex relationship between attitude and behavior in this context. For example, a computer virus can be seen as an invasion of privacy. We may be concerned about the possibility of a virus and take steps to prevent it (use of an antivirus software or an operating system less vulnerable to viruses). Concern prompts us to take preventative measures, but knowing that measures have been taken could reduce our level of concern (Paine, Reips, Steiger, Joinson and Buchanan [2007] found that some people reported that they were not concerned about privacy, and when asked why stated that they had taken action to protect their privacy). Therefore, privacy measurements need to measure privacy concerns and privacy-related behaviors to produce a complete picture. Buchanan, Paine, Joinson, and Reips (2007) have recently developed a measure of online privacy concern that covers different dimensions of privacy, as well as including protective behavioral items.

## Trust

### What is Trust?

Bargh and McKenna (2004) describe using the Internet as a "leap of faith." If we contact a potential partner via an online dating site, there is no way of knowing whether they are as they have described themselves in their profile or subsequent communication. When we work in virtual teams, or join virtual communities, we take it on faith that the people we talk to are whom they say. Purchasing online compared with from a bricks-and-mortar store requires a belief that the goods will arrive, that they will be as described on the website, and that your credit card and personal information will not be traded or otherwise misused And, when we seek advice online, we often do not know who the authors of the advice are, and what motivates them to help us.

In these kinds of scenarios, trust is critical in determining people's behavior. Trust has been studied in many different disciplines, and there are a large number of potential definitions (Corritore, Kracher, & Wiedenbeck, 2003; Green, 2007). There is broad agreement, however, that trust is critical when there is a degree of uncertainty (Mayer, Davis, & Schoorman, 1995). This uncertainty also needs to contain an element of risk (Deutsch, 1962). Without any risk, or vulnerability, there is no need for trust (Mayer et al., 1995).

Trust is the "willingness to be vulnerable, based on positive expectations about the actions of others" (Bos, Olson, Gergle, Olson, & Wright, 2002, p. 1). In an interpersonal context, it can be defined as holding "confident expectations of positive outcomes from an intimate partner" (Holmes & Rempel, 1989, p. 188) or "an expectancy held by individuals or groups that the word, promise, verbal, or written statement of another can be relied on" (Rotter, 1967, p. 651). Trust can be a personality trait or disposition, with some people more trusting that others (Mayer et al., 1995). It is also an attitude or belief about the intentions of a specific other (McKnight, Cummings, & Chervany, 1998). It can be generalized (you trust a person or group across all domains) or specific to an interaction (you trust a person only in one domain). There is general agreement that trust is best conceptualized as multidimensional (Bhattacherjee, 2002; Gefen, 2002; Mayer et al., 1995). That is, trust comprises a number of unique aspects that, although interrelated, are also discernable. Bhattacherjee (2002) identifies three main dimensions of trust: *ability*, *integrity*, and *benevolence*.

- *Ability* – refers to the knowledge, skills, and competence of the person trusted to conduct the expected actions. In an e-commerce (electronic commerce) setting, this might be the expectation that an online store has the ability to take an order and process it and will do so without accidentally revealing personal information. According to Bhattacherjee (2002), this dimension of trust is domain specific, that is, trust in one area (e.g., to provide the book we ordered) does not transfer to other domains (e.g., we would not necessarily trust Amazon to provide us with health advice).

- *Integrity* – refers to the belief that the person or institution will act in an honest, reliable, and credible manner (Jarvenpaa, Knoll, & Leidner, 1998). That is, they will adhere to the usual rules or expectations that are perceived as fair to both parties and will not violate the trust placed in them (i.e., you have confidence in the person or organization you are trusting). In an interpersonal context, integrity would reflect your confidence that the person you are trusting will not violate that trust, and it has a strong element of predictability (i.e., you have confidence in how the other person will behave in the future). In e-commerce, integrity would refer to a belief that the organization you are dealing with is honest, reliable, and will keep its promises (Gefen, 2002).

- *Benevolence* – refers to "the extent to which a trustee is believed to intend doing good to the trustor" (Bhattacherjee, 2002, p. 219). In a commercial setting, this might be reflected in beliefs that a company has its customers' best interests at heart (although this does not rule out making a legitimate profit). Benevolent organizations do not make excessive profits or exploit their customers. In an interpersonal setting, benevolence would refer to the belief that the person giving you advice is doing so to help you, not himself/herself (or a third party).

## Trust and the Internet

On the Internet, we often take a leap of faith that the people or organizations we deal with can be trusted. Moreover, lack of trust is a problem for online organizations: "If the web site does not lead the consumer to believe that the merchant is trustworthy, no purchase decision will result" (Ang & Lee, 2000, p. 3). Trust is also essential for cooperation (Deutsch, 1962) and for effective teamwork (whether face-to-face or mediated; Bos et al., 2002). Trust is also critical in understanding when we choose to share with others and when we choose secrecy (Altman, 1977).

### Is trust Reduced Online?

Handy (1995) states that "trust needs touch." This reflects the widely held belief that trust between people is poorly established in lean, mediated environments (e.g., Tanis & Postmes, 2007). To examine whether trust does need touch, Bos et al. (2002) compared trust ratings and cooperation between team members across four different conditions: face-to-face, audio conferencing, videoconferencing, and text chat. The three-person teams were playing a trust game in which cooperation maximized the potential gains for all members, while a competitive strategy reduced the likelihood of a higher gain. Bos et al. predicted that trust would be lowest and performance impeded in the lean media condition. Their results confirmed their predictions: The text chat groups scored the experience lowest in trust and gained the lowest amount of points in the game (signifying a competitive strategy). However, the Bos et al. study may not be strong evidence for trust needing touch. First, the experimenters banned social conversation from the experiment. This immediately placed the "richer" media conditions at an advantage because visual and aural cues normally compensated for in CMC social communication could not be in this sterile environment. Second, and related, such games are artificial in the extreme and have little relationship to how people actually use media. Third, the time given to the experiment was not sufficient for the text-based condition to "catch up" with the media with faster communication exchange (Walther, 1992). Finally, the use of self-reports for trust is unreliable because people tend to rate richer media as higher in trust, despite evidence that communication is more effective without identity cues for experienced users (Tanis & Postmes, 2007).

## Building Trust Online

There are a number of techniques that people engage in to build trust in interpersonal CMC. Researchers have found that on the Internet individuals go about reducing uncertainty by asking more direct, probing questions (Tidwell & Walther, 2002). If this is responded to with heightened self-disclosure (Joinson, 2001a), and reciprocated (Joinson, 2001b), then a cycle of hyperpersonal interaction might occur (Walther, 1996). The use of profiles, and particularly photographs, is also designed to increase the level of trust at an interpersonal level (Tanis & Postmes, 2007; Whitty & Carr, 2006). A further method for increasing trust in interpersonal interaction is media switching. Internet relationships tend to follow a similar pattern of initial contact in a public arena, then to a private domain (e.g., email or AOL messenger), then to the telephone, and then to face-to-face meetings (McKenna, Green, & Gleason, 2002; Parks & Floyd, 1996; Whitty & Gavin, 2001). This movement is not only a signifier of trust (I trust you enough to give you my phone number), but it is also a way that identities can be established, and the *faith* shown earlier on rewarded with *predictability* and, perhaps, *dependability*.

People also use linguistic cues to convey trustworthiness. Galegher et al. (1998) examined the messages of three Usenet support groups and three hobby groups collected for a three-week period to look for clues about how their members established legitimacy and credibility. The group members created legitimacy in a number of ways. They posted messages appropriate to the group, and use snappy headers to make themselves "heard." Galegher et al. note that often posters refer to their own membership of the electronic group, or how long they have lurked for before asking a question/replying to one. Even frequent posters included references to their members of the group 80 percent of the time when asking questions. Posters often signal their membership of the specific problem group (e.g., depression) by introducing information on their diagnosis, prescription, or symptoms. In the support groups Galegher et al. studied, 80 questions received no reply. Most lacked any legitimizing information of the type outlined previously and were generally simply requests for information rather like complex database queries. In the hobby groups, evidence of such legitimacy seeking was much less apparent.

Within pseudonymous environments, reputation systems also provide an important marker for a person's trustworthiness (Resnick, Kuwabara, Zeckhauser, & Friedman, 2000). The most well-known reputation system is that used by eBay. In the eBay system, users leave positive, neutral, or negative feedback, plus a short comment, for each transaction. Resnick and Zeckhauser (2001) studied the eBay reputation system and reported that the feedback given did seem to predict the sellers' future success, including the chances that their goods would be bought.

With the rise of social computing of "Web 2.0" sites, reputation systems have spread, such that it is now common to find community systems with rankings for members based on (among others) longevity, number of postings, and (for the highest ranks) a form of peer review. The ability to "Digg" or "Bury" stories acts as a form of community-derived trust building. Many of the 'blog commenting systems also now incorporate systems for reader rating of comments, and the hiding of poorly ranked comments.

Many e-commerce sites include privacy policies that contain descriptions of their privacy practices for the online collection, use, and dissemination of personal information. Many of these policies address privacy issues in all contexts (i.e., both the primary and secondary use of data). Another development has been the use of web-based seals, for example TRUSTe (see http://www.truste.org/) and Trust UK (see http://www.trustuk.org.uk/). These seals are a visible way to assure customers that online businesses respect an individual's privacy on the Internet and are designed to enable consumers to "buy online with confidence" (Trust UK).

However, there has been mixed research on the use of privacy polices and web-based seals. Liu, Marchewka, Lu, and Yu (2005) found that that levels of trust can be increased by integrating a comprehensive privacy policy into the design of an e-commerce website and that having a privacy policy may lead to a customer returning to a site and making further purchases. However, much research (e.g., Tsai, Cranor, Acquisti, & Fong, 2006) has found that although the majority of users tend to notice the presence of privacy policies, they rarely read them. In addition, using a mock commercial website, Metzger (2006) found that it is the reputation of a company that is important in influencing trust and disclosure of personal information online, not privacy assurances. This finding suggests that despite efforts of online companies to communicate trustworthiness through their strong privacy policies, it is a company's reputation that promotes trust and subsequently disclosure.

Other research has suggested a more far-reaching approach to reducing privacy concerns and gaining trust online in e-commerce. For example, Viseu et al. (2004) suggest websites display their compliance with "fair information practices" prominently (e.g., at the point where users are required to enter their personal information) rather than in "hard to find" and incomprehensible privacy statements. Another approach is suggested by Boyd (2003) who hypothesizes that trust online is built through rhetorical devices such as providing descriptions of websites credentials and competencies, display customer feedback, records of past security performance, and offering simple and clear assessments of risk to potential customers.

## Measuring Trust

Like privacy, trust can be measured at many different levels (Corritore et al., 2003). It can be treated as a disposition or personality trait, or as a specific state associated with a single interaction episode. Most studies of trust online have tended to focus on the latter, more specific aspect of trust. As we also noted,

Table 2.1. *Trust items and factor loading*

| Item | Loading |
| --- | --- |
| I felt comfortable giving my personal information | .43 |
| The data I have provided will be kept secure and not exploited | .70 |
| The intentions of this survey are good | .84 |
| I do not doubt the honesty of this survey or its authors | .81 |
| This survey's authors are a dependable research group | .90 |
| This survey's authors have the appropriate skills and competence to conduct online surveys | .89 |
| This survey is professional | .86 |
| The authors of the survey are trustworthy | .89 |

trust is multidimensional, with each dimension associated with the nature of the specific interaction. For instance, the competence of an online retailer might be related to their ability to deliver a product or service as desired. However, when you trust someone with your secrets, competence might mean believing that they will not accidentally forward your e-mail to the whole department (or print it and forget to collect).

Measures of trust tend to be specific to individual studies, then. For instance, Jarvenpaa, Tractinsky, and Vitale (2000) used seven items to assess trust, ranging from "This store is trustworthy" to, "This store wants to be known as one who keeps promises and commitments," and, "I trust this store keeps my best interests in mind." Gefen (2002) developed a similar scale, based on the three dimensions of integrity, benevolence, and ability. His nine-item scale includes items such as, "Promises made by Amazon.com are likely to be reliable" (Integrity), "I expect that Amazon.com are well meaning" (Benevolence), and "Amazon.com knows how to provide excellent service" (Competence).

Measures of interpersonal trust in CMC research have also tended to use a multidimensional approach. Bos et al. (2002) used an eleven-item scale consisting of items such as, "The other players in the game could be trusted," and "The other players always told me the truth" to measure trust in (competitive) virtual teams. They also used overall payouts as a behavioral measure of trust, on the assumption that high trust would lead to greater cooperation and higher payouts in the game. But, Riegelsberger, Sasse, and McCarthy (2003) question the utility of these kinds of "prisoner's dilemma" games for measuring trust in CMC and recommend it only for specific situations.

In our own research (e.g., Paine, Joinson, Reips, & Buchanan, 2006), we have developed a measure of trust for use in online research that reflects the three different dimensions. Specifically, the measure reflects trust in the competence, benevolence, and integrity of a researcher, enabling us to host materials online easily and assess their trustworthiness. These items are outlined in Table 2.1, alongside their factor loadings using principal components analysis yielding a single factor (without rotation) that explains 65 percent of the variance ($n = 690$). Forcing a two-factor solution yielded a single-item second factor based on the first item. For this reason, it is suggested that all items, except the first ("I felt comfortable giving my personal information"), are used as a single scale to measure trust. In this format, the scale has an internal reliability (Cronbach's alpha) of .93.

## Privacy, Trust, and Online Behaviour

Although we have discussed privacy and trust as separate dimensions, there is considerable evidence that they interact in determining online behavior. Online privacy is often framed as a contributor to trust, rather than as an independent effect on online behavior. For instance, the Google, Inc., privacy counsel for Europe justified the anonymizing of search data by saying, "We believe that privacy is one of the cornerstones of trust" (The Guardian, March 15, 2007). It has also been repeatedly reported that trust is a significant precursor to the disclosure of information online (e.g., Heijden & Verhagen, 2002; Hoffman, Novak, & Peralta, 1999; Jarvenpaa and Tractinsky, 1999; Jarvenpaa et al., 2000; Metzger, 2004). Specifically, Jarvenpaa and Tractinsky (1999) found that trust increases confidence in a company and therefore increases the likelihood of consumers engaging in transactions online. This relationship is borne out in a series of research findings. For instance, Malhotra et al. (2004) examined the links between people's Internet information privacy concerns and their related behavioral intentions. They found that the effect of privacy concerns on behavioral intentions was mediated by trust. Similarly, Chellappa and Sin (2005) studied consumer's intent to use personalization services. They also found that this intent was influenced by both trust and concern for privacy. Metzger (2004) asked participants to evaluate a fictitious commercial website and found that the effect of participants' general concern for privacy and the degree to which they believed e-commerce websites protect their privacy on disclosure was mediated by trust.

In the traditional sense, mediation refers to the effect of an independent variable on a dependent variable being explained by common links to a third variable (i.e., the mediator; Baron & Kenny, 1986). The reported results would therefore suggest that privacy has no direct effect on behavior; instead, any effect could be explained by the links between privacy and trust and between trust and behavior.

Indeed, although many Internet users express privacy-protectionist attitudes, this rarely translates to their actual behavior (Metzger, 2006; Pew Internet and American Life Project, 2000). For instance, Spiekermann, Grossklags, and Berendt (2001) measured the privacy preferences of 171 users and observed their behavior on a mock e-commerce site. On this site, the users were "helped" by a 'bot (short for an automated agent or "robot") that asked a number of purchase-related questions of differing levels of intrusiveness. They found very little evidence that privacy preferences were related to people's actual behavior in response to the 'bot's questions. Similarly, Metzger (2006) found no association between people's privacy concerns and their disclosure to an e-commerce site nor between the content of a privacy policy or presence of a privacy seal and disclosure behavior. The failure of various privacy-enhancing technologies in the marketplace also suggests a disjunction between people's stated attitudes and their actual actions to protect their privacy (Acquisti & Grossklags, 2003).

Liu et al. (2005) propose a "privacy-trust-behavioural intention" model in e-commerce. In their study, they manipulated participants' levels of privacy in fictional websites (by either including a privacy policy or not). They found that privacy has a strong influence on whether someone trusts an e-commerce business. In turn, this level of trust will influence their behavioral intention to purchase from a site.

Recently, our own work has considered whether privacy and trust operate in a mediation or moderator relationship (Joinson, Paine, Buchanan, & Reips, under review). In a series of longitudinal and experimental studies, we found evidence that the effect of perceived privacy on disclosure was mediated by trust at a situational level but also evidence for moderation when privacy and trust were experimentally manipulated. That is, we found evidence that trust and privacy interact to determine disclosure behavior, such that high privacy compensates for low trustworthiness, and high trustworthiness compensates for low privacy. Clearly, privacy and trust are closely related in predicting people's willingness to disclose personal information, and the relationship may be more nuanced than simple mediation.

## Summary and Conclusions

As we have seen earlier in this chapter, issues of privacy and trust are critical not only for the design of computer systems but also in how research is conducted online. We believe that the protection of privacy (in its various forms), alongside mechanisms to promote trust, are critical to both the design of social systems online as well as being important considerations for people aiming to conduct research using the Internet.

However, the rapid development of the e-society poses unique challenges for privacy due to the increased requirement for self-disclosure on an inter-personal and person-organization level. Similarly, using the Internet to collect survey data poses privacy challenges for researchers that can unduly influence response patterns (Joinson, Woodley, & Reips, 2007). There are a number of steps that can be taken to ensure that social software both protects privacy and enables the development of trust.

First, system developers should implement guidelines to limit the amount of personal information collected and privacy policies that require disclosure on a "need-to-know" basis rather than a general assumption that all administrators have full access to users' data. Where possible, identity management solutions should be implemented, even if only at the level of the user interface. For instance, a simple identity management system would be the implementation of pseudonyms within educational virtual learning environments. At the moment, the default option is often to link a publicly accessible learning resource (e.g., a blog or asynchronous conference) directly to the students' real identity. This poses not only an issue as far as informational privacy is concerned but may also limit expressive privacy. By building a simple identity management system that links a pseudonym to the users' real identity, but does not make that link publicly accessible, it is possible to encourage expressive privacy, and with it more effective educational outcomes. Other system design features can be used to protect privacy – for instance, implementing distributed systems rather than centralized data stores tends to be both more secure and less prone to data mining. This can be seen in Internet use too: People who use the same pseudonym across many Internet environments are more easily tracked than those who use various pseudonyms.

Second, trust needs to be built into the design of Internet services, either through the enabling of trust-building activities or the use of trust cues and mechanisms. So, in the case of computer-supported collaborative work, we have seen that trust can be encouraged by allowing users time to exchange socio-emotional messages, rather than forcing them to focus only on task-based communication. Reputation systems also provide a mechanism to develop trust (and to shortcut some of the time taken to build a trusting relationship).

Third, where possible, users should be provided with control over whether to disclose personal information and the use of that personal information once disclosed. In our own research, we have found that the provision of a simple "I prefer not to say" option to sensitive questions in surveys is an effective method for the protection of privacy (Joinson & Reips, 2007) by providing control over whether to disclose. In cases where there is an imperative to collect some information, control can take the form of providing ways for people to disclose information with relatively low diagnosticity. For instance, ambiguity is a well-established mechanism for disclosing information with low information value – if one is asked about a current location, it is possible to "blur" the response by being vague (e.g., "I am in Milton Keynes") rather than precise (e.g., "I am in my office").

We believe that the implementation of these principles to the design of online environments will not only protect privacy for ethical purposes but will also enable much of the rich interaction many people seek when online. The excessive collection of personal information, and loss of trust, poses a challenge to beneficial use of the Internet and threatens to create a surveillance culture lacking in rich social interaction or diverse content. As social scientists, we must promote the development of a socially responsible cyberspace that is of benefit to all its citizens.

## Acknowledgments

The writing of this chapter was supported by funding from the U.K. Economic and Social Research Council E-Society Programme (RES-341-25-0011). We are grateful to Azy Barak and Alexander Voiskownsky for their insightful comments on an earlier draft.

### References

Acquisti, A. (2004). Privacy in electronic commerce and the economics of immediate gratification. In *Proceedings of the ACM Electronic Commerce Conference* (EC 04; pp. 21–29). New York, NY: ACM Press.

Acquisti, A., & Grossklags, J. (2003). *Losses, gains, and hyperbolic discounting: An experimental approach to information security attitudes and behavior.* Second Annual Workshop on "Economics and Information Security."

Altman, I. (1975). *The environment and social behaviour.* Monterey, CA: Brooks/Cole.

Altman, I. (1977). Privacy regulation: Culturally universal or culturally specific? *Journal of Social Issues, 33*, 66–84.

Ang, L., & Lee, B.-C. (2000). Influencing perceptions of trustworthiness in Internet commerce: A rational choice framework. In *Proceedings of Fifth CollECTer Conference on Electronic Commerce* (pp. 1–12). Brisbane.

Bargh, J. A., & McKenna, K. Y. A. (2004). The Internet and social life. *Annual Review of Psychology, 55*, 573–590.

Baron, R. M., & Kenny, D. A. (1986). The moderator-mediator variable distinction in social psychological research: Conceptual, strategic and statistical considerations. *Journal of Personality and Social Psychology, 51*, 1173–1182.

BBC News (2006). *Privacy worried over web's future.* Retrieved June 2006, from http://news.bbc.co.uk/1/hi/technology/5009774.stm.

Bhattacherjee, A. (2002). Individual trust in online firms: Scale development and initial test. *Journal of Management Information Systems, 19*, 211–241.

Bos, N., Olson, J. S., Gergle, D., Olson, G. M., & Wright, Z. (2002). Rich media helps trust development. In *Proceedings of CHI 2002* (pp. 135–140). New York: ACM Press.

Boyd, J. (2003). The rhetorical construction of trust online. *Communication Theory, 13*, 392–410.

Buchanan, T., Paine, C. B., Joinson, A. N., & Reips, U.-D. (2007). Development of measures of online privacy concern and protection for use on the Internet. *Journal of the American Society for Information Science and Technology, 58*, 157–165.

Burgoon, J. K., Parrott, R., LePoire, B. A., Kelley, D. L., Walther, J. B., & Perry, D. (1989). Maintaining and restoring privacy through communication in different types of relationship. *Journal of Social and Personal Relationships, 6*, 131–158.

Chellappa, R. K., & Sin, R. G. (2005). Personalization versus privacy: An empirical examination of the online consumer's dilemma. *Information Technology and Management, 6,* 181–202.

Corritore, C. L., Kracher, B., & Wiedenbeck, S. (2003). On-line trust: Concepts, evolving themes, a model. *International Journal of Human-Computer Studies, 58,* 737–758.

DeCew, J. (1997). *In pursuit of privacy: Law, ethics, and the rise of technology.* Ithaca, NY: Cornell University Press.

Derlega, V. J., & Chaikin, A. L. (1977). Privacy and self-disclosure in social relationships. *Journal of Social Issues, 33,* 102–115.

Deutsch, M. (1962). Cooperation and trust: Some theoretical notes. *Nebraska Symposium on Motivation, 10,* 275–318.

Dinev, T., & Hart, P. (2004). Internet privacy concerns and their antecedents – Measurement validity and a regression model. *Behaviour and Information Technology, 23,* 413–423.

Earp, J. B., Anton, A. I., Aiman-Smith, L., & Stufflebeam, W. H. (2005). Examining Internet privacy policies within the context of user privacy values. *IEEE Transactions on Engineering Management, 53,* 227–237.

Galegher, J., Sproull, L., & Kiesler, S. (1998). Legitimacy, authority and community in electronic support groups. *Written Communication, 15,* 493–530.

Gefen, D. (2002). Reflections on the dimensions of trust and trustworthiness among online consumers. *ACM SIGMIS Database, 33,* 38–53.

Green, M. (2007). Trust and social interaction on the Internet. In A. N. Joinson, K. Y. M. McKenna, T. Postmes, & U.-D. Reips (2007). *Oxford Handbook of Internet Psychology* (pp. 43–52). Oxford, UK: Oxford University Press.

Handy, C. (1995). Trust and the virtual organization. *Harvard Business Review, 73,* 40–50.

Harper, J., & Singleton, S. (2001). *With a grain of salt: What consumer privacy surveys don't tell us.* Retrieved on November 29, 2005, from http://www.cei.org/PDFs/with_a_grain_of_salt.pdf.

Heijden, H. V. D., & Verhagen, T. (2002, January). Measuring and assessing online store image: a study of two online bookshops in the Benelux. In *Proceedings of the 35th Annual Hawaii International Conference on System Sciences,* Honolulu, Hawaii.

Hoffman, D. L., Novak, T. P., & Peralta, M. (1999). Building consumer trust online. *Communications of the ACM, 42,* 80–85.

Holmes, J. G., & Rempel, J. K. (1989). Trust in close relationships. In C. Hendrick (Ed.), *Close relationships* (pp. 187–220). Newbury Park, CA: Sage.

Ingham, R. (1978). Privacy and psychology. In J. B. Young (Ed.), *Privacy* (pp. 35–59). Chichester, UK: Wiley.

Jarvenpaa, S. L., Knoll, K., & Leidner, D. E. (1998). Is anybody out there? Antecedents of trust in global virtual teams. *Journal of Management Information Systems, 14,* 29–64.

Jarvenpaa, S. L., & Tractinsky, N. (1999). Consumer trust in an Internet store: A cross-cultural validation. *Journal of Computer Mediated Communication, 5*(2). Retrieved on October 19, 2007, from http://jcmc.indiana.edu/vol5/issue2/jarvenpaa.html.

Jarvenpaa, S. L., Tractinsky, N., & Vitale, M. (2000). Consumer trust in an Internet store. *Information Management and Technology, 1*, 45–71.

Joinson, A. N. (2001a). Self-disclosure in computer-mediated communication: The role of self-awareness and visual anonymity. *European Journal of Social Psychology, 31*, 177–192.

Joinson, A. N. (2001b). Knowing me, knowing you: Reciprocal self-disclosure on the Internet. *Cyberpsychology & Behavior, 4*, 587–591.

Joinson, A. N., Paine, C. B., Buchanan, T. B, & Reips, U.-R. (under review). *Privacy, trust and self-disclosure online*. Manuscript submitted for publication.

Joinson, A. N., & Reips, U.-D. (2007). Personalized salutation, power of sender and response rates to Web-based survey. *Computers in Human Behavior, 23*, 1372–1383.

Joinson, A. N., Woodley, A., & Reips, U.-D. (2007). Personalization, authentication and self-disclosure in self-administered Internet surveys. *Computers in Human Behavior, 23*, 275–285.

Jupiter Research. (2002). Security and privacy data. Presentation to the Federal Trade Commission Consumer Information Security Workshop. Retrieved on June 20, 2005, from http://www.ftc.gov/bcp/workshops/security/02052011 eathern.pdf.

Larson, D. G., & Chastain, R. L. (1990). Self-concealment: Conceptualization, measurement, and health implications. *Journal of Social and Clinical Psychology, 9*, 439–455.

Liu, C., Marchewka, J. T., Lu, J., & Yu, C.-S. (2005). Beyond concern: A privacy-trust-behavioural intention model of electronic commerce. *Information and Management, 42*, 289–304.

Malhotra, N. K., Kim, S. S., & Agarwal, J. (2004). Internet users' information privacy concerns (IUIPC): The construct, the scale and a causal model. *Information Systems Research, 15*, 336–355.

Margulis, S. T. (2003). On the status and contribution of Westin's and Altman's theories of privacy. *Journal of Social Issues, 59*, 411–429.

Mayer, R. C., Davis, J. H., & Schoorman, F. D. (1995). An integrative model of organizational trust. *Academy of Management Review 20*, 709–734.

McKenna, K. Y. A., Green, A. S., & Gleason, M. E. J. (2002). Relationship formation on the Internet: What's the big attraction. *Journal of Social Issues, 58*, 9–32.

McKnight, D. H., Cummings, L. L., & Chervany, N. L. (1998). Initial trust formation in new organizational relationships. *Academy of Management Review, 23*, 473–490.

Metzger, M. J. (2004). Privacy, trust and disclosure: Exploring barriers to electronic commerce. *Journal of Computer-Mediated Communication, 9*(4). Retrieved on June 20, 2005, from http://jcmc.indiana.edu/vol9/issue4/metzger.html.

Metzger, M. J. (2006). Effects of site, vendor, and consumer characteristics on web site trust and disclosure. *Communication Research, 33*, 155–179.

Paine, C. B., Joinson, A. N., Reips, U.-D., & Buchanan, T. (2006, September). *Privacy, trust, disclosure and the Internet*. Paper presented to the Association of Internet Researchers (AOIR). Internet Research 7.0: Internet Convergences, Brisbane, Australia.

Paine, C. B., Reips, U.-D., Steiger, S., Joinson, A., & Buchanan, T. (2007). Internet users' perceptions of "privacy concerns" and "privacy actions." *International Journal of Human-Computer Studies, 65*, 526–536.

Parent, W. (1983). Privacy, morality and the law. *Philosophy and Public Affairs, 12*, 269–288.

Parks, M. R., & Floyd, K. (1996). Making friends in cyberspace. *Journal of Communication, 46*, 80–97.

Pew Internet and American Life Project (Fox, S., Rainie, L., Horrigan, J., Lenhart, A., Spooner, T., & Carter, C.). (2001).: *Trust and privacy online: Why Americans want to rewrite the rules.* Retrieved on June 15, 2007, from http://www.pewinternet.org/pdfs/PIP_Trust_Privacy_Report.pdf.

Privacy Knowledge Base (2005). Retrieved on June 20, 2005, from http://privacyknowledgebase.com.

Riegelsberger, J., Sasse, M. A., & McCarthy, J. D. (2003). The researcher's dilemma: Evaluating trust in computer mediated communications. *International Journal of Human-Computer Studies, 58*, 759–781.

Resnick, P., Zeckhauser, R. (2001). Trust among strangers in Internet transactions: empirical analysis of eBay's reputation system. Retrieved on June 1, 2007, from http://www.si.umich.edu/~presnick/papers/ebayNBER/RZNBER BodegaBay.pdf.

Resnick, P., Zeckhauser, R., Friedman, E., & Kuwabara, K. (2000). Reputation systems. *Communications of the ACM, 43*, 45–48.

Rotter, J. B. (1967). A new scale for the measurement of interpersonal trust. *Journal of Personality, 35*, 651–665.

Rust, R. T., Kannan, P. K., & Peng, N. (2002). The customer economics of Internet privacy. *Journal of the Academy of Marketing Science, 30*, 455–464.

Schatz Byford, K. (1996). Privacy in cyberspace: Constructing a model of privacy for the electronic communications environment. *Rutgers Computer and Technology Law Journal, 24*, 1–74.

Schoeman, F. (1984). Privacy and intimate information. In F. Schoeman (Ed.), *Philosophical dimensions of privacy* (pp. 403–417). Cambridge, UK: Cambridge University Press.

Schoeman, F. (1992). *Privacy and social freedom.* Cambridge, UK: Cambridge University Press.

Smith, H. J., Milberg, S. J., & Burke, S. J. (1996). Information privacy: Measuring individuals' concerns about organizational practices. *MIS Quarterly, 20*, 167–196.

Sparck-Jones, K. (2003). Privacy: What's different now? *Interdisciplinary Science Reviews, 28*, 287–292.

Spiekermann, S., Grosklags, J., & Berendt, B. (2001, October). *E-privacy in 2nd generation E-commerce: privacy preferences versus actual behavior.* Proceedings of the 3rd ACM Conference on Electronic Commerce, 38–47, Florida, USA.

Stewart, K. A., & Segars, A. H. (2002). An empirical examination of the concern for information privacy instrument. *Information Systems Research, 13*, 36–49.

Tanis, M., & Postmes, T. (2007). Two faces of anonymity: Paradoxical effects of Cues to identity in CMC. *Computers in Human Behaviour, 23*, 955–970.

The Guardian (March 15, 2007). *Google to erase information on billions of internet searches*. Retrieved on October 19, 2007, from http://www.guardian.co.uk/technology/2007/mar/15/news.microsoft.

Tidwell, L. C., & Walther, J. B. (2002). Computer-mediated communication effects on disclosure, impressions, and interpersonal evaluations: Getting to know one another a bit at a time. *Human Communication Research, 28*, 317–348.

Tsai, J., Cranor, L., Acquisti, A., & Fong, C. (2006). *What's it to you? A survey of online privacy concerns and risks*. Working Papers 06-29, NET Institute.

U.K. Information Commissioner. (2006). *A report on the surveillance society* [online]. Retrieved 27 November, 2006, from http://tinyurl.com/ya76db.

Viseu, A., Clement, A., & Aspinall, J. (2004). Situating privacy online: Complex perceptions and everyday practices. *Information, Communication and Society 7*, 92–114.

Walther, J. B. (1996). Computer-mediated communication: Impersonal, interpersonal, and hyperpersonal interaction. *Communication Research, 23*, 3–43.

Walther, J. B. (1992). Interpersonal effects in computer-mediated interaction: A relational perspective. *Communication Research, 19*, 52–90.

Warren, S., & Brandeis, L. D. (1890). The right to privacy. *Harvard Law Review, 4*, 193–220.

Weiser, M. (1988). Ubiquitous computing. Retrieved on June 20, 2005, from http://sandbox.xerox.com/hypertext/weiser/UbiHome.html.

Westin, A. (1967). *Privacy and freedom*. New York: Atheneum.

Whitty, M. T., & Carr, A. N. (2006). *Cyberspace romance: The psychology of online relationships*. Basingstoke, UK: Palgrave Macmillan.

Whitty, M., & Gavin, J. (2001). Age/sex/location: Uncovering the social cues in the development of online relationships. *CyberPsychology & Behavior, 4*, 623–630.

# 3    Internet Abuse: Emerging Trends and Lingering Questions

*Janet Morahan-Martin*

There has been much alarm about Internet abuse in the past decade. Claims of Internet-related crimes such as homicides, suicides, and child neglect have received widespread media attention across the globe ("Chinese Gamer Sentenced to Life," 2005; Spain & Vega, 2005). Many claim that they are or know someone who is addicted to the Internet. Fifteen percent of university students in the United States and Europe and 26 percent of Australian students claim they know someone is addicted to the Internet (Anderson, 1999; Wang, 2001). Almost 10 percent of adult Internet users in a large online study self-identified as Internet addicts (Cooper, Morahan-Martin, Mathy, & Maheu, 2002), while 31 percent of MySpace users (Vanden Boogart, 2006) and 42 percent of online gamers (Yee, 2002) say they are addicted to those Internet applications. In Germany, a camp was established to help children who were addicted to the Internet (Moore, 2003). It is tempting to dismiss these claims as media hype, but clinicians also have reported Internet-related problems and have set up clinics specifically to treat these problems in many countries. In recent years, governments in Asia have established clinics and intervened to reduce Internet use. The first Chinese clinic for Internet addiction in Beijing has expanded from 40 to 300 inpatient beds, and new clinics are being established in other Chinese cities (Griffiths, 2005; Lin-Liu, 2006). The South Korean government established the Korean Center for Internet Addiction Prevention and Counseling "to correct the Internet misuse and to help Internet addicts" (International Telecommunication Union, 2003) and plans to increase the number of treatment centers for Internet addicts from 40 to 100 by 2010 ("South Korea Plans More Centres to Treat Internet Addiction," 2005).

At the same time, there are many who question the concept of Internet addiction. In fact, Ivan Goldberg, who established both criteria for Internet addiction and the online Internet Addiction Support Group in the 1990s, did so as a joke because he did not and still does not believe in Internet addiction (Suler, 2004a). However, research in the past decade has confirmed that some Internet users do develop serious problems from their use of the Internet and has established factors related to problematic Internet use. Some etiological approaches have begun to emerge. This chapter will first discuss varying conceptualizations of Internet abuse and the factors related to it. Questions about the relationship of Internet abuse to other problems will be explored. Models of Internet abuse will be presented, and three types of Internet abuse will be discussed. Finally, research on treatment will be presented.

## What is Internet Abuse?

There is no standard term or definition for Internet abuse. Some of the terms used include *Internet addiction* (Bai, Lin, & Chen, 2001; Chak & Leung, 2004; Li & Chung, 2006; Nalwa & Anand, 2003; Nichols & Nicki, 2004; Pratarelli & Browne, 2002; Simkova & Cincera, 2004; Wei, Zijie, & Daxi, 2004; Yang & Tung, 2007; Yoo et al., 2004; Young, 1998), *Internet dependency* (Chen, Chen, & Paul, 2001; Lin & Tsai, 2002; Scherer, 1997; Wang, 2001; Whang, Lee, & Chang, 2003), *Internet abuse* (Morahan-Martin, 1999, 2001, 2005), *compulsive Internet use* (Greenfield, 1999; Meerkerk, Van Den Eijnden, & Garretsen, 2006), *pathological Internet use* (Davis, 2001; Morahan-Martin & Schumacher, 2000; Niemz, Griffiths, & Banyard, 2005), and *problematic Internet use* (Beard, 2005; Caplan, 2002; Shapira, Goldsmith, Keck, Khosla, & McElroy, 2000; Shapira et al., 2003; Thatcher & Goolam, 2005a, 2005b).

These terms reflect differing conceptualizations of Internet abuse (IA). Some have viewed IA as a clinical entity and have used modified criteria from the *Diagnostic and Statistical Manual of Mental Disorders* (*DSM–IV–TR*) (American Psychiatric Association [APA], 2000) for other disorders to define IA, thus implicitly assuming that IA is a specific disorder or disease. For example, Scherer (1997), Nichols and Nicki (2004), and Li and Chung (2006) define IA using modified criteria for substance abuse (such as withdrawal, and tolerance), whereas Young's (1996, 1998) widely used criteria are adapted from *DSM* criteria for pathological gambling. Others define IA as an impulse control disorder not otherwise specified (NOS) (Orzack, 1999; Shapira et al., 2000; Shapira et al., 2003; Treuer, Fabian, & Furedi, 2001). For example, Shapira et al. (2003) proposed criteria for problematic Internet use that include: "A. Maladaptive preoccupation with Internet use . . . B. Use of the Internet or preoccupation with its use causes clinically significant distress or impairment . . . C. The excessive Internet use does not occur exclusively during periods of hypomania or mania and is not better accounted for by other Axis 1 disorders" (p. 213).

In a similar vein, LaRose, Lin, and Eastin (2003) propose that IA should be viewed as a deficiency in self-regulation. However, they do not view IA from a disease model, but rather as a continuum of deficiencies in self-regulation that includes normal use "that has occasional lapses in self-control [a 'benign problem' . . . ] as well as problematic excessive usage" (LaRose et al., 2003, p. 235).

Other researchers also have approached Internet behaviors not as a clinical disorder but as a continuum from normal to disturbed use (Caplan, 2002, 2003,

2004, 2005a; Davis, Flett, & Besser, 2002; Morahan-Martin & Schumacher, 2000). Terms such as *compulsive, problematic,* or *pathological Internet* use reflect this approach.

Despite differences in how IA is defined and the specific criteria used, there is general agreement that Internet abuse is defined in terms of the negative effect of Internet use; that is, Internet use that causes disturbances in an individual's life. Additionally, most agree that it involves preoccupation with using the Internet, compulsive Internet use, subjective feelings of inability to limit use, and using the Internet to escape or alter negative moods, that is, when down, an anxious (e.g., Aboujaoude, Koran, Gamel, Large, & Serpe, 2006; Caplan, 2002; Davis, 2001; Li & Chung, 2006; Meerkerk et al., 2006; Morahan-Martin, 2001, 2005; Morahan-Martin & Schumacher, 2000; Wang, 2001; Yang & Tung, 2007; Young, 1998). Similar criteria have been established for problematic behaviors related to specific Internet activities such as online interactive games (Parsons, 2005; Yee, 2006b).

Those who develop these disturbed patterns use the Internet more than others, and some have equated Internet abuse with heavy or excessive use of the Internet. However, it is possible to use the Internet heavily without having negative effects. Thus, excessive Internet use alone does not qualify as Internet abuse because Internet abuse is defined in terms of Internet-related disturbances in a person's life.

This chapter uses the term *Internet abuse* except in reference to other authors' terminology. As used here, Internet abuse refers to patterns of using the Internet that result in disturbances in the person's life but does not imply a specific disease process or addictive behavior. The term *excessive Internet use* is used when referring to research using that construct rather than IA.

## Prevalence of Internet Abuse

Studies have been conducted to assess the prevalence of IA in a number of countries. Estimates of the incidence of IA vary widely. Epidemiological studies are limited and have found a low rate of IA: less than 1 percent of U.S. adults over 18 (Aboujaoude et al., 2006) and less than 2 percent of adolescents in Finland and Norway (Johansson & Götestam, 2004; Kaltiala-Heino, Lintonen, & Rimpelä, 2004) had IA. These are far lower than the incidence found in other studies using representative samples. In Taiwan, a study of a representative sample of university students found 5.9 percent with IA (Chou & Hsiao, 2000), while a second study using a cluster sample of high school students reported 11.7 percent had IA (Lin & Tsai, 2002). Leung (2004) reported 37 percent of a representative sample of sixteen- to twenty-four-year-olds in a Hong Kong have IA, which is far higher than other studies. Studies using convenience samples report IA incidence as ranging from 1.8 percent to 18.3 percent (Bai et al., 2001; Chak & Leung, 2004; Kim et al., 2006; Morahan-Martin, 2001; Morahan-Martin & Schumacher, 2000; Niemz et al.,

2005; Scherer, 1997; Thatcher & Goolam, 2005a; Wei et al., 2004; Whang et al., 2003; Yang & Tung, 2007).

Differences in prevalence may represent differences in culture, sampling, age, or criteria used. For example, in South Korea, which has the highest broadband penetration in the world (International Telecommunication Union, 2003), there has been much concern about IA, and online games are enormously popular. Games are televised and professional players have status and salaries similar to top sports players (Chee, 2005; Kosak, 2003). Chee (2005) describes patterns of online game use as embedded in Korean culture. In South Africa, Thatcher and Goolam (2005a) demonstrated that the incidence of IA varied from 1.67 percent to 5.39 percent depending on the ethnic group and criteria used.

Thatcher and Goolam (2005a) substantiated the effect on the choice of criteria on the incidence of IA in a study that compared incidence of IA using three sets of criteria: Young (1996, 1998), Beard and Wolf (2001), and Thatcher and Goolam's (2005b) Problematic Internet Use Questionnaire (PIUQ). To be diagnosed with IA, Young (1996, 1998) requires that an individual exhibit at least five of the eight criteria. These criteria, which were modified from the *DSM* criteria for pathological gambling, include:

1. Is preoccupied with the Internet (think about previous online activity or anticipate next online session).
2. Needs to use the Internet with increasing amounts of time to achieve satisfaction.
3. Has made unsuccessful efforts to control, cut back, or stop Internet use.
4. Is restless, moody, depressed, or irritable when attempting to cut down or stop Internet use.
5. Has stayed online longer than originally intended.
6. Has jeopardized or risked the loss of significant relationship, job, educational or career opportunity because of the Internet.
7. Has lied to family members, therapist, or others to conceal the extent of involvement with the Internet.
8. Uses the Internet as a way of escaping from problems or of relieving a dysphoric mood (e.g., feelings of helplessness, guilt, anxiety, depression) (Young, 1996).

Beard and Wolf (2001) use the same criteria but suggest more stringent requirements for IA. Arguing that a person with IA must indicate impairment from the disorder, they require that to be diagnosed with IA, an individual must fulfill at least one of the last three criteria plus all of the first five criteria. Thatcher and Goolam's (2005b) PIUQ consists of 20 items that are rated on a five-point Likert scale. Factor analysis of this scale found three factors: online preoccupation, adverse effects from Internet use, and preference for online social interactions. Those identified as high risk for IA scored 70–100 on the scale. The incidence of IA in the three groups was 1.67 percent using PIUQ, 1.84

percent using Beard and Wolf's criteria, and 5.29 percent using Young's criteria. All who met Beard and Wolf's stricter criteria also met Young's criteria, but only 35 percent of those who met Young's criteria met Beard and Wolf's criteria. Of those who were classified as having IA using the PIUQ scale, 80 percent were also classified as having IA on Young's scale and 40 percent using Beard and Wolf's scale. The authors highlight that using more lenient criteria results in a significantly higher incidence of IA (Thatcher & Goolam, 2005a).

The lack of a uniform set of criteria for IA that is empirically validated is a weakness that pervades much of the research of IA. Young's criteria for IA (1996, 1998) have been widely used in incidence studies. These criteria are lenient and may overestimate those with IA. Young's criteria have face validity, but other types of validity are not reported. Ultimately, "to determine the accurate prevalence of clinically significant problematic Internet use will require agreement on diagnostic criteria and a study using a clinically validated, structured interview administered to a large and representative sample of the population" (Aboujaoude et al., 2006).

## Questions About IA Research

Critics question whether IA should be considered as a clinical disorder and discount claims such as, "Internet addiction: the emergence of a new clinical disorder" (Young 1998, p. 237). Shaffer, Hall, & Vander Bilt (2000) argue that "empirical support for the construct validity of computer [and Internet] addiction has yet to emerge, (and) . . . defining the construct as a unique psychiatric disorder is therefore premature" (Shaffer et al., 2000, p. 162). LaRose et al. (2003) concur that "many of the 'addicts' and 'pathological Internet users' identified in . . . survey studies . . . of Internet addiction fell well short of the clinical definition that requires a professional assessment of harmful life consequences" (p. 245). Although they acknowledge that true pathology exists at the "extreme end of the spectrum" (p. 245), the authors argue that research on IA has been "studying the relationship between indicators of deficient self-regulation and usage in predominantly non-pathological populations" (p. 245).

### Specific Versus Generalized IA

A second issue is that research on IA does not distinguish between specific applications of Internet use. Those with IA spend more time than others in online activities such as online sexual activities (OSA) and online socially interactive games (Chen et al., 2001; Greenfield, 1999; Meerkerk et al., 2006; Morahan-Martin & Schumacher, 2000; Thatcher & Goolam, 2005a; Wang, 2001; Yang & Tung, 2007; Yoo et al., 2004; Young, 1997), but it is not clear how much these activities contribute to their Internet-related problems. However, evidence suggest that they may be important contributing factors. In a longitudinal study of IA, Meerkerk et al. (2006) found that the only two activities that predicted IA over a year's period were time spent searching for online erotica and playing interactive online games. After two years, searching for erotica was the only online activity that predicted increases in IA. They assert that, "using the Internet for sexual gratification should therefore be regarded as the most important risk factor for the development of (IA)" (p. 98). In factor analytic studies, Pratarelli and his colleagues also found sexual activity an important factor in the development of IA (Pratarelli & Browne, 2002; Pratarelli, Browne, & Johnson, 1999).

Davis (2001) proposes two distinct types of IA: specific and generalized. Specific IA involves abuse of a content-specific function of the Internet such as online sexual behaviors or gambling. When these behaviors become disturbed online, they are technologically enabled variants of established pathologies such as pathological gambling, paraphilias, or compulsive sexuality (Morahan-Martin, 2005). Other Internet activities associated with specific IA such as online interactive games are unique to the Internet. Generalized IA not linked to any specific activity but to Internet abuse that transcends specific applications. It is associated with the unique communication patterns that are available on the Internet (Davis, 2001).

However, there is overlap among these classifications. For example, while playing online socially interactive games, users may engage in online sexual activities. A study of 1,504 U.S. therapists who had treated at least one client with problematic Internet use found considerable overlap among the eleven types of disturbed use that were identified (Mitchell, Becker-Blease, & Finkelhor, 2005).

In this chapter, research on specific applications is distinguished from research that does not differentiate between specific applications. In the latter case, the term IA is used. As will be discussed, there are commonalities across groups.

## Internet Abuse and Other Problems

Individuals with IA are more likely than others to have a number of other problems. These include mood disorders of depression (Kim et al., 2006; LaRose et al., 2003; Thatcher & Goolam, 2005a; Wei et al., 2004; Whang et al., 2003; Yang & Tung, 2007; Young & Rodgers, 1998) and bipolar disorder (Black, Belsare, & Schlosser, 1999; Shapira et al., 2000), substance abuse (Bai et al., 2001; Greenberg, Lewis, & Dodd, 1999), sexual compulsivity (Cooper, Putman, Planchon, & Boies, 1999), and pathological gambling (Greenberg et al., 1999). A study of children found that children with IA were more likely overall to have behavior problems, including attention deficit hyperactivity disorder (ADHD), anxiety/depression, delinquent behavior, and sexual and social problems (Yoo et al., 2004). Personality factors associated with IA include loneliness (Caplan, 2002; Kubey, Lavin, & Barrows, 2001; Morahan-Martin & Schumacher, 2000, 2003; Nalwa & Anand, 2003; Whang et al., 2003), low self-esteem (Niemz et al., 2005; Yang & Tung, 2007), shyness and social anxiety (Caplan, 2002; Chak & Leung, 2004; Pratarelli, 2005; Wei et al., 2004; Yang & Tung, 2007). Research on specific IAs has found similar factors. This suggests a commonality between generalized IA and some forms of specific IA.

## Is Internet Abuse Symptomatic of Other Disorders?

The association of IA with other disorders has raised a number of questions. One interpretation of the co-morbidity of IA with other disorders is that "in most cases, computer (and Internet) use may be symptomatic of other, more primary disorders" (Shaffer et al., 2000, p. 162). Hence, treating IA "as if it were a new diagnostic entity may lead to the misdiagnosis of primary psychiatric disorders for which we have proven therapeutic interventions" (Huang & Alessi, 1997, p. 890).

It is uncertain whether clinicians are using Internet abuse (or any variant of the term) as a primary or even secondary diagnosis. Internet abuse is not listed in *DSM*, which in the United States would affect reimbursement, although it would be possible to use Shapira et al.'s (2003) criteria to diagnose IA as an impulse control disorder NOS. Limited research indicates that clinicians give established diagnoses when treating those with symptoms of IA. In a survey study of eighty mental health counselors in the United States, Parsons (2005) found more than half (55%) had treated someone who met Young's (1998) criteria for IA. Counselors who had treated someone with IA said these clients were also most likely to be diagnosed with depression (40.9%), obsessive-compulsive disorder (34.1%), impulse control disorder (31.8%), relational problems NOS (20.5%), anxiety disorder (15.9%), or adjustment disorder (6.8%).

However, a large-scale study using a systematic sample of 1,504 U.S. psychologists, social workers, and family therapists who had at least one client with an Internet-related problem found that the Internet-related problem frequently was the primary focus of treatment. Excessive overuse of the Internet, either in general or related to specific types of behavior, was the most frequent problem (61%), with frequent overlap with other Internet-related problems. When excessive overuse of the Internet was a presenting problem, it was the primary focus of treatment in 40 percent of cases. Clinicians reported that the Internet-related problem was the primary focus of treatment in 44 percent of cases involving problematic downloading of pornography, 29 percent of cases involving problematic gaming and role-playing behaviors, and 23 percent of cases involving isolative-avoidant use of the Internet. Overall, the likelihood that the Internet-related problem was the primary focus of treatment varied among the eleven categories of Internet-related problems from 23 percent to 48 percent (Mitchell et al., 2005).

## Preexisting Problems and IA

A second issue related to the co-morbidity of IA to other disorders is whether pathology predates IA or whether disturbed Internet use causes Internet-related problems such as depression. Limited evidence that those with IA had preexisting problems is provided by a small-scale study of twenty individuals with IA, defined as impulse control disorder NOS, who were administered face-to-face (F2F) interviews using the Structured Clinical Interview for Diagnostic and Statistical Manual of Mental Disorders (SCID-IV). All twenty participants had at least one lifetime *DSM–IV* Axis 1 diagnosis, with an average of five other diagnoses. Two-thirds (70%) had a lifetime diagnosis of bipolar disorder, 85 percent had received previous mental health treatment, and 75 percent had been treated with psychotropic medications. Participants retrospectively reported moderate to marked reduction in problematic Internet use when given medications appropriate for the co-morbid psychiatric illnesses (Shapira et al., 2000).

Longitudinal studies of Internet use are sparse. However, the HomeNet study (Kraut et al., 1998; Kraut et al., 2002) provides some insight into the effect of Internet use. This study monitored the Internet use of new users in the United States in the mid-1990s. It is one of a limited number of systematic longitudinal studies that followed the antecedents and consequences when a small, select group of users was introduced to the Internet. Users were given a free computer, Internet access, training, and support in exchange for allowing their Internet use to be monitored and for taking part in periodic interviews and testing. In the first follow-up, the researchers found neither loneliness nor depression before beginning Internet use but predicted loneliness or depression after the first twelve to eighteen months of Internet use. However, increased Internet use was associated with higher levels of both loneliness and depression. The researchers ascribe these increases in depression and loneliness to decreases in family communication, social activities, happiness, and the number of individuals in one's social network, which also were associated with increased Internet use (Kraut et al., 1998).

The second wave of the HomeNet study (Kraut et al., 2002) was conducted after participants had been online for two to three years. The results contradicted the results from the first wave. After this amount of time online, loneliness and depression was unrelated to amount of Internet use. However, the researchers found that the effect of Internet use on psychological well-being varied between extroverts and introverts. For introverts, increased use of the Internet was associated with decreases in social involvement as well as decreases in users' sense of well-being as seen in increased levels of loneliness, negative affect and time pressure, and decreased self-esteem. For extroverts, the effects of Internet use were opposite in each of these measures. Separate analyses controlling for previous levels of loneliness and social involvement found increased Internet use associated with increased loneliness and decreased social involvement for introverts and the opposite effects for extroverts. The authors suggest a "rich get richer" hypothesis. That is, for extroverts who already have greater social resources, Internet use enhances their well-being. while the opposite is true for introverts.

These findings highlight not only that that some individuals may be at greater risk of developing Internet-related problems but also that the effect of Internet use depends on characteristics of individual users.

## Is it Appropriate to Apply the Addiction Model to IA?

There is much debate about the appropriateness of applying the addiction model to the Internet. Walther and Reid (2000) argue, "We should not use value-laden terms such as addiction to label something we know so little about" (p. B5). Others question why the Internet has been singled out as addictive. Although people spend more time watching television and talking on the phone than on the Internet, there is little concern that these are addictive (Grohol, 1999; Morahan-Martin, 2005; National Public Radio, 2000), and far less research about them than on IA (Morahan-Martin, 2005). However, like the Internet, when the telephone and television were new technologies, there was much concern about the negative effects of both. The spread of each of these technologies has exposed users to a wider universe, which can fuel fears, especially when children are involved. In the case of the Internet, apprehension can be magnified because users have access to activities that may not be culturally sanctioned, such as speaking to strangers, exploring pornography, and chatting about sexual topics (Bahney, 2006).

Still, many describe themselves as addicted to the Internet or specific applications of the Internet. However, it is unclear what people mean when they describe themselves or anyone else as addicted to the Internet or any other behavior. In a study of Facebook use on four U.S. university campuses, Vanden Boogart (2006) found nearly a third said they were addicted to Facebook; yet there were few negative effects from its use. Higher use of Facebook was associated with lower grades but also with higher social connectedness online. This highlights that self-reports of addiction should not be viewed clinically. The term *addiction* is widely used to describe a number of behaviors, such eating, exercise, gambling, sex, shopping, and television (e.g., Cooper et al., 1999; Jacobs, 1986; Kubey & Csikszentmihalyi, 2002; Milkman & Sunderwirth, 1982). Addiction has even been expanded in medical journals to include "UV (ultra-violet) light tanning as a type of substance-related disorder" (Warthan,

Uchida, & Wagner, 2005), chocolate (Small, Zatorre, Dagher, Evans, & Jones-Gotman, 2001), carrots (Kaplan, 1996), and botox (Singh, Hankins, Dulku, & Kelly, 2006).

This raises a broader, controversial issue of applying the addiction model from substances to any behaviors. Technically, addiction is a lay rather than a clinical term. *DSM* uses the terms abuse and dependence to describe disturbed patterns of substance use, not addiction (APA, 2000). Further, *DSM* does not apply addiction, abuse, or dependence in describing behavioral disturbances. However, as discussed later, some have argued that disturbed patterns of behaviors with characteristics such as withdrawal and tolerance and psychological dependence are similar to substance dependency and view these behaviors as behavioral (Bradley, 1990) and technological addictions (Griffiths, 1995).

Many object to expanding the addiction model to include behaviors. Madras argues, "The word is grossly overused. Addiction is a neurobiological disorder. Clinically, it's a very clear syndrome" (Madras, cited in Lambert, 2000). Others argue that expanding the model of addictions to behaviors trivializes substance-related addictions, undermines acceptance of addictions as illness, and is counterproductive to understanding etiology and treatment approaches for substance-related addictions as well as behaviors that are inappropriately labeled as addictions (Jaffe, 1990; Satel, 1993). Further, Jaffe argues that labeling behaviors as "addictions" results in those behaviors growing, "because it excuses uncontrolled behaviors and predisposes people to interpret their lack of control as the expression of a disease that they can do nothing about" (Peele, as cited in Jaffe, 1990, p. 1426).

## Internet Abuse as an Addictive Behavior

Nevertheless, many mental health professionals believe that the addictive model does encompass both substances and behaviors (e.g., Grant, Brewer, & Potenza, 2006; Marlatt, Baer, Donovan, & Kivlahan, 1988; Pallanti, 2006; Potenza, 2006; Shaffer, 2006; Shaffer et al., 2004). Shaffer et al. (2004) argue for a syndrome model of addiction, which includes both substances and behaviors. Based on "evidence of multiple and interacting biopsychosocial antecedents, manifestations, and consequents – within and among behavioral and substance-related patterns of excess – reflects an underlying addiction syndrome, (they) propose . . . that addiction should be understood as a syndrome with multiple opportunistic expressions" (p. 367). Individual vulnerability to addiction, including shared neurobiological and psychosocial elements, puts individuals at risk for developing problems when exposed to specific objects of addiction. The expression of addiction can vary according to the specific object of addiction, but there are "common manifestations and sequelae (e.g., depression, neuroadaption, and deception)" (p. 368). A summary of the supporting evidence and how it may apply to cases of IA that are clinically significant follows. The term *Internet addiction* is used in this section to differentiate it from *Internet abuse* (IA) which, as used generically in this chapter, does not necessarily imply a mental illness. However, researchers do not necessarily use that term.

Many disorders that have been considered behavioral addictions are listed in *DSM* as impulse-control disorders not otherwise classified. "The essential feature of impulse-control disorders is the failure to resist an impulse, drive, or temptation to perform an act that is harmful to the person or to others" (APA, 2000, p. 609). This group includes pathological gambling, which is a frequent source of problematic online use, and kleptomania. Compulsive sexual behavior also is considered an impulse control disorder NOS. A consensus is growing among those who view IA as a clinical disorder that it should be classified in this group (Aboujaoude et al., 2006; Orzack, 1999; Shapira et al., 2000; Shapira et al., 2003; Treuer et al., 2001). Evidence that there is a relationship between substance and behavioral disorders, including impulse control disorders and other disorders involving poor impulse control such as bulimia, comes from a number of different lines of research. They share a number of clinical symptoms such as

> repetitive or compulsive engagement in a behavior despite adverse consequences, diminished control over the problematic behavior; an appetitive urge or craving state prior to engagement in the problematic behavior, and a hedonic quality during the performance of the problematic behavior (as well as)... repeated unsuccessful attempts to cut back or stop, and impairment in major areas of life functioning.     (Grant et al., 2006)

Additionally, both behavioral and substance abuse show signs of tolerance and withdrawal, which Shaffer et al. (2004) consider a neurobiological adaptation. These symptoms have been found in those with IA.

Furthermore, both chemical and behavioral addictions have similar patterns of co-morbidity and family histories with each other as well as with mood disorders (Grant et al., 2006; Greenberg et al., 1999; Shaffer et al., 2004), and people often go from one object of addiction to another (Shaffer et al., 2004). These suggest possible genetic or neurobiological links between the various types of addiction. Similar patterns have been found with studies of Internet addiction. For example, Greenberg et al. (1999) examined the relationship between behavioral and substance-related addictions. For each of four substance and five behaviors, university students rated the frequency they experienced craving, withdrawal, lack of control, and tolerance. Correlations were performed for the total for each. The Internet addiction scores were significantly correlated with all substances (alcohol, $r = .42$; cigarettes, $r = .34$, caffeine $r = .26$; chocolate, $r = .23$) and behaviors (video games, $r = .64$; television, $r = .57$; gambling, $r = .43$; exercise, $r = .12$; caffeine $r = .12$). All associations are significant at $p = .01$ for all except exercise, with $p = .05$. Overall, those "who reported greater addictive tendencies toward substances... also reported greater addictive tendencies towards... activities $(r \ (127) = .50, \ p < .001)$" (p. 568). The authors conclude that "the overlapping addictions found in the... study do suggest a common core of vulnerability to addictive substances and activities" (p. 570).

Likewise, Yoo et al. (2004), in a study of children in South Korea, found those with Internet addiction were more likely to have a number of addictive behaviors, with disturbed playing of video games the most frequent. Children in this study were more likely to have ADHD, which in turn is a risk factor for substance abuse in adolescence. The authors suggest that ADHD symptoms of inattention and hyperactivity "may be, potentially, important risk factors for Internet addiction" (p. 492). Further, they suggest that "addictive behavior for the Internet may be regarded, in the future, to be on a continuum with other kinds of addictions, especially alcohol and other substances" (p. 493).

"Recent research has raised the possibility of a common biochemical mechanism of addiction to drugs, other chemical substances, or behaviors" (Betz, Mihalic, Pinto, & Raffa, 2000, p. 17). There is evidence that "biochemical, functional neuroimaging, genetic studies and treatment research have suggested a strong neurobiological link between behavioral addictions and substance use disorders" (Grant et al., 2006). Addictive behaviors including "impulse control disorder behaviors may be conceptualized as an imbalance between an overstimulated drive state, an impairment in inhibition or reward processing, or a combination of these factors" (Grant et al., 2006). Several neurotransmitters are believed to be involved: serotonin, dopamine and its pathways, and endogenous opioids. Dysfunction in the serotonin (5-HT) systems have been found in substance abuse and some impulse control disorders. These dysfunctions "may reflect the impairment in frontal inhibition which prevents individuals from controlling their desires" (Grant et al., 2006). The dopaminergic systems have been implicated in both substance and behavioral addictions. This system is involved in the reward system of the brain. Dysfunctions are hypothesized to be involved in what Blum, Cull, Braverman, and Comings (1996) have called a reward deficiency syndrome, which is a "hypothesized hypo-dopaminergic state involving multiple genes and environmental stimuli that puts and individual at high risk for multiple addictive, impulsive and compulsive behaviors [and] is a proposed mechanism of addiction" (Grant et al., 2006). This may be seen in strong craving and urges, which cause individuals to seek the reward from the given behavior or substance despite negative consequences. Endogenous opioids also are involved in processing reward, pleasure, and pain, play a role in the modulation of dopamine neurons, and have been implicated in substance, behavioral, and impulse control disorders. "Individuals with altered opioidergic systems may feel a more intense euphoria after engaging in rewarding behaviors and, thus, have greater difficulty controlling desires to continue the addictive behavior" (Grant et al., 2006).

The role of the brain's reward system has also been found in neuroimaging studies, which "suggest as far as the brain is concerned, a reward's a reward, regardless of whether it comes from a chemical or an experience" (Holden, 2001, p. 980). Neuroimaging studies also indicate similarities between behavioral and substance addiction in decision-making parts of the brain. Decreased activation of the ventromedial prefrontal cortex (vmPFC) has been documented for both substance abuse and impulse control disorders. These abnormalities are "considered important in the disadvantageous decision-making (involving short-term gains vs. long-term losses) central to addiction" (Grant et al., 2006).

Although at this point there are no known biochemical or neuroimaging studies of Internet addiction, research on the commonalities of behavior addictions, particularly impulse control disorders, and substance abuse raises the possibility that Internet addiction also may have a biological basis. Evidence of a link is stronger with specific Internet activities. Much of the research on the biological component of addiction has been conducted with gambling, and similar results would be expected with online gambling. Neuroimaging has found activation of the dopamine system while playing video games (Koepp et al., 1998), which raises the probability that similar results would be found with socially interactive online games that have evolved from video games. Specific IAs involving activities that can create euphoric feeling, such as online sexual behaviors, are likely candidates for confirmation of a biological model of Internet-related behavioral addictions.

## Cognitive Behavioral Model of Addiction and IA

Of course, mere exposure to addictive substances or behaviors will not necessarily lead to addiction, even among vulnerable individuals. Learning is necessary. Cognitive behavioral models have been proposed for substance and behavioral addictions in general (e.g., Marlatt et al., 1998; Shaffer et al., 2004) and for generalized IA (e.g., Caplan, 2002, 2003, 2004, 2005a; Davis, 2001) and specific IAs (e.g., Putnam, 2000; Yee, 2001). Addiction to both substances and behaviors can "be understood as learned adaptive or functional behavior in the context of personal and environmental factors . . . learning factors, such as classical and operant conditioning, observational and social learning, and higher-order cognitive processes such as beliefs, expectancies and attributions are all common to addictive processes" (Marlatt et al., 1988, p. 226). Reinforcing effects are important for the establishment of a habit or pattern of continued behaviors that might lead to addictive behavior. Shaffer et al. (2004) contend that the premorbid stage of any addiction occurs when at-risk individuals "engage in repeated interactions with a specific object or objects of addiction, and . . . the neurobiological or social consequences of these addictions produce a desirable subjective shift that is reliable and robust" (p. 368). The shift in subjective state is "requisite for the development of the addiction syndrome" (p. 368). That is, reinforcement must occur. This reinforcement may be positive (feeling of euphoria) or negative (relief from depression or other negative moods). Conditioned responses to stimuli associated with the object of addiction are learned after repeated association of these cues with unconditioned stimuli. Learned outcome expectancies as well as efficacy beliefs also are important in the acquisition of addictions.

A variant of this model views addiction as a form of self-medication. That is, people use objects of addiction to escape (i.e., negative reinforcement). Khantzian, who has written extensively about addiction as a form of self-medication, says of substance abuse: "The nature of suffering is at times overwhelmingly intense – or elusive … and beyond people's control … the drug user sudden feels some control over what had felt uncontrollable. I do think there's a specificity involved" (cited in Lambert, 2000). This model holds true of a number of impulse control disorders and behavioral addictions. Individuals continue these behaviors because they provide escape or positive feelings. Some have proposed that these disorders may exist "within a broad spectrum of affective (mood) disorders" (Zohar, 2006), which further supports that use may be related to dealing with depression.

There is evidence that many who develop IA use the Internet to modulate moods and as a form of escape. For people suffering from depression, social anxiety, or severe loneliness, using the Internet may provide escape from emotional pain and distress. Like drugs, the Internet offers different types of escape. Those who are lonely can find companionship in chat rooms. Those who are socially anxious can find online interactions are more rewarding or less threatening than offline ones. Those who are depressed can escape into an elaborate fantasy world in online interactive games. Research supports that both those with specific IA and nonspecific IA are more likely than others to use the Internet to modulate negative affect. Those with IA are more likely to use the Internet to escape pressures – when down, anxious, socially isolated – and to control moods (Anderson, 2000; Caplan, 2002; Morahan-Martin & Schumacher, 2000). Similar results are reported in studies of specific forms of IA. Some appear to experience dissociative experiences and flow states (Chou & Ting, 2003), which can both distract an individual from aversive feelings (negative reinforcement) and provide positive experiences (positive reinforcement). Mood modulation also plays a role in the development of specific IAs. Escapism (Parsons, 2005; Yee, 2006b; Zheng et al., 2006) and relief from dissatisfaction (Wan & Chiou, 2006) are predictors of abuse of socially interactive games. Use of the Internet for sexual purposes when stressed is an important predictor of compulsive online sexual behavior (Cooper et al., 1999; Cooper, Griffin-Shelley, Delmonico, & Mathy, 2001).

The following sections will look at theories and research on two specific IAs, online sexual compulsivity and online interactive games, and on generalized IA. Applications of the cognitive behavioral model within each will be provided. Similarities and differences will be highlighted.

## Specific Online Activities and IA

There is a large and growing body of research on specific Internet activities, including online sexual behaviors, gambling, and online interactive games (e.g., Boies, Cooper, & Osborne, 2004; Cooper et al., 1999, Cooper, Delmonico, & Burg, 2000; Griffiths, 2001; Griffiths & Parke, 2002; Ladd & Petry, 2002; Parsons, 2005; Yee, 2006a, 2006b). Although this literature is beyond the scope of this chapter, aspects of research on online sexual behaviors and disturbances and online interactive game use provide insight about IA. The following brief review of selected aspects of compulsive online sexual behaviors and online games highlights similarities and differences between this research and research on IA. There is much overlap between specific IAs and generalized IA.

### Specific Internet Abuses: Online Sexual Compulsion and Problematic Use of Online Pornography

Online sexual activities are an important component in the development of IA. In a longitudinal study of IA, Meerkerk et al. (2006) found that the only two activities that predicted IA over a year's period were time spent searching for online erotica and playing interactive online games. One year later, searching for erotica was the only online activity that predicted increases in IA. The authors conclude that, "using the Internet for sexual gratification should therefore be regarded as the most important risk factor for the development of (IA)" (p. 98). In factor analytic studies, Pratarelli and his colleagues also found sexual activity an important factor in the development of IA (Pratarelli & Browne, 2002; Pratarelli et al., 1999). Online sexual activities (OSA) are some of the most common types of problematic Internet behaviors seen in clinical practice and often are associated with problematic excessive Internet use (Mitchell et al., 2005). Therapists reported that among clients in treatment with Internet-related disturbances, 56 percent involved problematic use of online pornography (defined as leading to guilt or interference with other activities, responsibilities or relationships) and 21 percent involved infidelity (Mitchell et al., 2005).

Cooper et al. (2000), in an online study of people who engaged in OSA found that one-sixth were sexually compulsive, but only 1 percent were what the authors called online sexual compulsives (Cooper et al., 2000). Most who develop problems from their online sexual behaviors have preexisting pathology (Schwartz & Southern, 2000). Putnam (2000) argues that individuals who are vulnerable to developing compulsive sexual behavior may become compulsive when exposed to online sexual activities. Cooper et al. (1999) provides support to this in a study that found some online sexual compulsives had no prior history of sexual compulsivity. They conjecture that these individuals may have been susceptible to sexual compulsivity but "may never have had difficulty with sexual compulsivity if it were not for the Internet" (p. 85) because they had sufficient internal resources and impulse control to resist acting out these impulses until they went online. Those who first became sexually compulsive online were likely to be depressed and to use OSA as an escape or distraction. A second study that compared those who develop problems from their use of OSA were more likely to use OSA to cope with stress and to explore sexual fantasies (Cooper et al., 2001).

A second factor associated with disturbances arising from OSA is being involved in OSA to seek relationships. In a study of OSA among Canadian university students, Boies et al. (2004) conclude that "activities facilitating interpersonal contact were most strongly correlated to Internet-related problems suggesting Internet use is related to a need for affiliation in some individuals" (p. 215). Additionally, there are differences between introverts and extroverts in their use of OSA. Koch and Pratarelli (2004) found introverts more likely than extroverts to use resources intended for adults only, to download or view sexually oriented pictures online, and to be physically aroused while online. Likewise, therapists who had treated clients who used the Internet "to the exclusion of face-to-face social interaction with family, friends, and dating partners" (Mitchell et al., 2005, p. 503) were highly likely to overlap with those who were excessive Internet users (83%) and those with problematic use of Internet pornography (42%) (Mitchell et al., 2005).

Putnam (2000) explains the pathogenesis of the development of online sexual compulsions in terms of operant and classical conditioning. He argues that individuals who are vulnerable to develop compulsive sexual behavior may become compulsive when exposed to online sexual activities. From an operant conditioning model, continuation of online sexual behaviors is both positively reinforced, by sexual arousal and gratification (sometimes accompanied by masturbation and orgasm), and negatively reinforced, by reductions in stress when online. The reinforcing values may be especially strong because reinforcement is on a variable-ratio schedule. Classical conditioning eventually occurs when, with repeated online sexual behavior, computer use is paired with sexual arousal. Thus, the computer may provoke craving to engage in online sexual activities.

These findings are similar to research on IA. Both those with IA and those whose use of OSA is disturbed are more likely than others to be depressed and to use the Internet and to use the Internet to deal with stress. For both, online social interactions are an important factor. Introverts also are more likely to develop IA.

## Specific Internet Abuse: Online Social Interactive Games

Online games have long been associated with the addictive-like behavior. These games date to 1978 when Trubshaw created a computer version of *Dungeons and Dragons* (Bartle, 1996; Kent, 2003). The term used to describe them, MUD, originally meant Multiple User Dungeons although eventually MUD became an acronym for Multiple User Domains and was used generically to describe a wide variety of online games. Turkle (1995) and Rheingold (1993) first brought these games and their addictive appeal to popular attention in the mid-1990s when the Internet began its astronomical growth among the public. MUDs are text-based virtual worlds, run on private servers, free to users, and limited to 250 per game (Kent, 2003). Many are still in use.

Graphical interface began transforming online games in the mid-1990s with the development in 1996 of *Meridian 59*, the first commercially viable Internet-based game that was not limited to a closed circuit, which "incorporate[d] large numbers of players in a single world, a persistent world, and many of the other identifying elements of what later became known as MMOGs" (Massively Multiplayer Online Games) or MMORPGs (Massively Multiplayer Role-Playing Games) (Kent, 2003). *Meridian 59* added a new visual reality by allowing players to experience the fantasy world of the game from the perspective of their characters. In 1999, SONY released one of the most popular MMOGs, *Everquest*, "a fully three-dimensional game that could truly support a massive community" (Kent, 2003), which offered players enhanced opportunities for combat, exploration, and character development. Access to these games is by subscription, usually about US$10–20 per month. Since their inception in 1996, the number of active subscriptions for MMORPGs worldwide is estimated at over 12 million (Mmogchart.com, 2006).

MMORPGs are played in a "fully developed multiplayer universe with an advanced and detailed world [both visual and auditory]" (Griffiths, Davies, & Chappell, 2004). "Different from forms of static entertainment, such as novels, television, cinema, and radio, [MMORPGs] are dynamic and highly interactive allowing players to become mentally immersed within them" (Kurapati, 2004). The result is that players are engrossed "within huge virtual worlds littered with towns, castles and other real life constructs to the point which a player can feel as if living inside a fully functional alternative reality" (Kurapati, 2004). Kurapati referred to this as *immersiveness* and believes it to be an important component of MMORPG abuse.

There may be as many as 2,000 players on a game server at a time. Each player creates his or her own character, or avatar, and then can roam the virtual world, perceive the virtual world through the persona, and act and socialize with others through this persona. Characters gain status and power based on time online and achievement of tasks. The game is continuous; that is, the game continues whether or not an individual is playing. In the virtual world, an individual can play solo or within a group. Players can communicate with each other via on-screen text either privately or between limited or all players in their zone.

## Abuse of Online Interactive Games

MUDs and MMORPGs have been associated with compulsive and addictive behaviors. This is hardly surprising, given the large amount of time that gamers spend online. Overall, MMORPG players are online four times more than other Internet users ("Average MMORPG Gamer," 2005). Yee (2006a), in a large-scale online study of more than 5,000 MMORPG players, found gamers spent an average of 22.71 hours per week in their MMORPG environment ($N = 5,471$, $SD = 14.98$), with a median of twenty hours per week; 8.9 percent spent forty or more hours weekly. Further, three-fifths of players had spent at least ten hours continuously playing a MMORPG at some point. In a second study, adolescent players report playing *EverQuest* 26.25 hours per week ($SD = 16.1$) while adults played report playing 24.7 hours weekly ($SD = 13.34$), with a small group playing over seventy hours (Griffiths et al., 2004). Many play for long periods of a time; three-fifths of players had spent at least ten hours continuously playing a MMORPG at some point in Yee's (2006a) study, while 80 percent of MMORPG players in Ng and Wiemer-Hastings' study (2005) had spent more than eight continuous hours playing in one session.

Anecdotal accounts of addictive MMORPG behavior abound. *Everquest*, one of the most popular MMORPGs, is commonly called Evercrack by gamers. Concerns about MMORPG abuse were the major reason that the South Korean and Chinese governments established Internet addiction centers. In other attempts to limit Internet abuse, the Chinese government initiated a program to restrict the time gamers play online (Taylor, 2006), while the government in Thailand has established an overnight curfew for online games ("Thailand Restricts Online Gamers," 2003).

A significant minority of players self-report being addicted to MMORPGs as well. A twenty-two-year-old male *EverQuest* player describes why he thinks he is addicted.

> I call myself an addict, because I share the same symptoms as someone who's addicted to smoking or alcohol, or some other substance. I think about EQ (*Everquest*) while I'm not playing, I get stressed when I have to go 23 hours without logging on for a fix and I wasn't able to quit when I tried. If that's not an addiction, I don't know what it is.     (Yee, 2002)

Yee (2002) found 40.7 percent of MMORPG players said they consider themselves addicted to the specific MMORPG that they used; the average rate varied between 36.5 and 53.2 percent, depending on the MMORPG played. In a second study, Yee (2006a) reports that about half of MMORPG players self-identified as addicted to the specific MMORPG they used, with differences by age and gender.

Research supports that many MMORPG users report that their game playing interrupts other aspects of their lives. In a study of *EverQuest* players, four-fifths of adults (78.9%) and adolescents (78.4%) reported that they had sacrificed other activities to play the game. Adolescents (22.7%) were more likely than adults (7.3%) to report sacrificing work or education ($X^2 = 19.48$, $df = 1$; $p < .0001$), while adults (20.8%) were more likely than adolescents (12.5%) to report sacrificing socializing with friends, family, or a partner ($\chi = 3.24$, $df = 1$; $p < .0045$). Other activities that were sacrificed to play included: "another hobby or pastime (19.3% adolescents; 27.5% adults) and sleep (19.3% adolescents; 18.5% adults)" (Griffiths et al., 2004). The authors speculate that "some online gamers may be experiencing addictive like experiences similar to findings in other types of video game play" (p. 95), and suggest, based on video game research, that adolescents are more vulnerable.

Other studies of *EverQuest* players have found a significant minority of players exhibit addictive behaviors. Based on an online survey of 3,989 *EverQuest* players, Yee (2002) reported that 15.5 percent had withdrawal symptoms when not playing, 23.8 percent had mood alterations when playing, 28.8 percent played even when they did not enjoy the experience, and 18.4 percent said that playing caused academic, work, health, or financial problems. There were differences by age, as with Griffiths et al. (2004), and by gender. The percentage who had tried unsuccessfully to quit the game was highest among those who were twelve- to seventeen-years-old (males = 30%; females = 18.8%) and decreased steadily with age with about 20 percent of eighteen- to twenty-two-year-olds, 10 percent of twenty-three- to thirty-five-year-olds and 5 percent of those over thirty-five who had been unsuccessful in quitting.

Research on MMORPG abuse is limited. In a study of 513 MMORPG players, Parsons (2005) found 15.3 percent met Young's (1998) criteria for IA, although less than 1 percent had sought professional help. Playing MMORPGs to relieve negative affect (Wan & Chiou, 2006) and as a form escapism (Parsons, 2005; Yee, 2006b; Zheng et al., 2006) are predictors of MMORPG abuse as are having flow experiences while gaming (Chou & Ting, 2003) and sensation seeking (Zheng et al., 2006). Problematic game users also exhibit social disturbances. They are more likely than others to be involved in social interaction (Zheng et al., 2006), but 25 percent have isolated and avoidant patterns of use that involve using the Internet to the exclusion of F2F interactions (Mitchell et al., 2005), which might explain why they are more likely to be lonely (Parsons 2005). Clinicians report that half of those with problematic game use also have problems related to their use of online pornography (Mitchell et al., 2005).

Another predictor of MMORPG abuse, valuing the control and status that the games provided (Chak & Leung, 2004; Yee, 2006b), is unique to MMORPGs. In discussing excessive users of MUDs, Turkle (1995) argued that these games may provide modes of achievement. Some may "prefer the illusory power or pleasure of being able to control the world inside the computer when playing online games" (Chak & Leung, 2004, p. 567). In MMORPGs, the lack of a story line or plot can abet players' feeling of control (Yee, 2001). Yee (2001) describes MMORPGs, notably *Everquest*, as a "virtual Skinner boxes," which

are well designed to promote addiction because they effectively use principles of operant conditioning to promote players spending more and more time
involved in the game by providing tokens of achievement. In the acquisition phase, users are rewarded frequently and are able to quickly move up
to higher levels. During this stage, the tokens of achievement acquire value.
Gradually, however, it takes longer and longer to get to the next level. Shaping
is employed. Gamers also have to perform increasingly elaborate and complex tasks as the games continue. Because the games have "multi-layered and
overlapping goals," players "pursue multiple rewards concurrently," which
fosters motivation to continue because they always feel close to a goal and
reward. Like a slot machine, games also use a variable ratio of reinforcement, which is the most effective way to distribute reinforcement. Ultimately,
one's accomplishments in *Everquest* or other MMORPGs "makes it possible
for Joes and Janes to become heroes...What happens when people can feel
achievement through continuous mouse-clicking...What happens when these
achievements are more rewarding than 'real life' achievements?" (Yee, 2001).
Thus, achievement is an important predictor of MMORPG abuse because it is
conditioned.

## The Role of Online Social Interaction in The Development of Internet Abuse

Research consistently has supported that the unique social interactions
made possible by the Internet are important in the development of both generalized and specific IA (Boies et al., 2004; Caplan, 2002; Davis, 2001; Leung,
2004; Li & Chung, 2006; Morahan-Martin & Schumacher, 2000; Niemz et al.,
2005; Pratarelli & Browne, 2002; Scherer, 1997; Thatcher & Goolam, 2005a;
Weiser, 2001; Young, 1998; Young & Rogers, 1998; Yuen & Lavin, 2004).
Those with IA are more likely than other Internet users to go online to meet
new people, to talk to others with the same interests, and to find emotional
support (Morahan-Martin and Schumacher, 2000). They are more like to use
socially interactive activities such as chat rooms, newsgroups, and socially
interactive games (Chak & Leung, 2004; Chen et al., 2001; Johansson &
Götestam, 2004; Leung, 2004; Lin & Tsai, 2002; Morahan-Martin & Schumacher, 2000; Thatcher & Goolam, 2005a; Weiser, 2001; Whang et al., 2003;
Yoo et al., 2004; Young, 1998). Similar patterns of social interaction also are
related to disturbed patterns of online game use (Mitchell et al, 2005; Zheng
et al., 2006) and sexual behaviors (Boies et al., 2004; Mitchell et al., 2005).

Davis (2001) argues the unique social environment of the Internet is a key
component to the development of IA. Research has confirmed this. Leung
(2004), who studied a representative sample of 976 sixteen- to twenty-four-
year-olds in Taiwan, found social disinhibition on the Internet was an important
predictor of IA. This factor included reporting that "the anonymity of the

Internet allows me to reveal my feelings as much as I like" (p. 228); that it is easier to express inner thoughts online; that the Internet is a more comfortable place to express their view, that they often talk about themselves on the Internet; and that that the Internet "provides a wonderful opportunity to meet new people and sample different cultures" (p. 228). In a second study of U.S. university students, Morahan-Martin and Schumacher (2000) found that the social aspects of Internet use consistently differentiate those with IA from other Internet users and conclude that for those with IA "the Internet can be socially liberating, the Prozac of social communication" (p. 20). In this study, those with IA were more likely than others to report their behaviors online as less socially inhibited. They were more likely to say that they are more themselves online, have more fun with people they know online, share intimate secrets online, and prefer online to F2F communication. Internet abusers consistently reported increased social confidence online, which enhanced their friendship network. They were more likely than others to report that they are friendlier and open up more to people online than in real life, that going online has made it easier to make friends, and that they have a network of online friends. In fact, those with IA were more likely to say that most of their friends they know from being online and that their online friends understand them better than other people. Niemz et al. (2005) replicated these findings in a study of British university students. They found that 44.3 percent of the variance in IA was accounted for by scales that measured increased social confidence and social disinhibition online. Similarly, Leung (2004) found anonymity, social ease online, and social disinhibition were robust predictors of IA, while Whang et al. (2003) found those with IA are more likely to reveal personal concerns to online friends and even to meet online friends F2F. Caplan (2002) hypothesizes that users' preference for the social benefits available online is an important predictor of IA, and, based on his research, concludes that "preference for computer-mediated social interaction, as opposed to face-to-face interaction, plays a role in the etiology, development and outcomes" of generalized IA (p. 555). As noted earlier, social aspects are important as well to the development of specific IA related to disturbances in online sexual behaviors and online interactive games (Boies et al., 2004; Mitchell et al., 2005).

## Loneliness, Social Anxiety, Depression, and Internet Abuse

The preference for online over F2F interaction may be a key factor in the relationship between IA and both loneliness and social anxiety. Those who are chronically lonely and those who are socially anxious share many characteristics, which may predispose them to develop IA. Both are apprehensive in approaching others, fearing negative evaluations and rejection. They tend to be self-preoccupied with their perceived social deficiencies, which leads them to be inhibited, reticent, and withdrawn in interpersonal situations and avoid social interactions (Bruch, Kalfowitz, & Pearl, 1988; Burger, 2004; Leary & Kowalsky, 1995a, 1995b; Morahan-Martin, 1999; Solano & Koesler, 1989).

The Internet is ideally suited for these individuals. Online social interactions are not F2F, often anonymous, less inhibited, and allow increased control, which can alleviate self-defeating behavioral patterns and cognitions. Research supports that social behavior of the socially anxious and lonely is enhanced online (Caplan, 2003; Morahan-Martin & Schumacher, 2003; Shepherd & Edelman, 2005), and they are more likely than others to develop a preference for online over F2F social interaction, which is an important predictor of the development of IA (Caplan, 2003; Ervin, Turk, Heimberg, Fresco, & Hantula, 2004).

Limited research indicates similar changes for those who are depressed. Using data from a representative telephone survey of 1,501 U.S. youths between the ages of ten and seventeen, Ybarra, Alexander, and Mitchell (2005) found strong differences in social uses of the Internet between those who met *DSM–IV* criteria for major depression and others. Although this was not a study of IA, the differences reported are strikingly similar to differences between those with and without IA. The depressed youth used the Internet more than others and were more likely to use chat rooms. They also were more likely to personally self-disclose and use the Internet to interact with people they know only online. The authors suggest that "youth with depressive symptomatology may be replacing in-person engagement with online socializing" (p. 15) and hypothesize that it is possible that youth who are depressed "perceive interaction online as demanding less effort . . . The Internet may offer a safe place for these youth to get the social interaction they need without requiring the social knowledge that in-person interactions demand" (p. 16).

## A Cognitive Behavioral Theory of Generalized Internet Abuse

Cognitive behavioral models of generalized IA focus on the importance of online social interactions in the development of IA. Davis et al. (2002) posit that generalized IA is based on "a more pervasive compulsion to be online and communicate with others" (Davis et al., 2002, p. 332). Davis's (2001) cognitive behavioral model of generalized IA proposes that psychosocial problems such as loneliness and depression predispose some Internet users to develop maladaptive cognitions and behaviors that result in IA. LaRose et al. (2003) suggest that "the transition to problematic usage can begin if the behavior acts as an important or exclusive mechanism to relieve stress, loneliness, depression, or anxiety" (p. 231). This transition also changes expectancies regarding positive result from Internet use.

Caplan, in a series of studies (2002, 2003, 2005a, 2005b), has expanded on Davis's as well as others' theories and research and developed an empirically based model of IA. In this model, a key cognitive component is a preference for online, over F2F, social interaction (POSI), which is defined as "a cognitive individual difference construct characterized by beliefs that one is safer, more efficacious, more confident, and more comfortable with online interpersonal interactions and relationships than with traditional F2F social activities" (Caplan, 2003, p. 629). POSI is a significant mediator between psychosocial problems associated with social anxiety, loneliness, and depression and negative outcomes associated with Internet abuse (2003). A second critical factor is a social skill deficit in perceived social control, which is "an individual's competence at self-presentation, role-taking, and impression management in F2F interpersonal interactions" (Caplan, 2005, p. 725). Drawing on the literature on social anxiety, loneliness and their relationship to Internet use and abuse, this model hypothesizes that those who perceive themselves to have low self-presentational skill are more likely than others "to prefer online social interaction because they perceive their presentational skill in online social interaction to be greater than in F2F interaction" (Caplan, 2005, p. 726). That is, those who lack confidence in their self-control and self-presentational skills experience social anxiety, which leads to their being more likely to turn to communication channels that minimize risks and enhance their capabilities. For them, the Internet provides a "buffer for social interaction" (Davis et al., 2002, p. 332), where their social inhibitions are reduced because they have greater control over their presentation of self and less perceived risk in an anonymous environment. Preference for online social interactions is a predictor for both compulsive Internet use and using the Internet for mood regulation. That is, once POSI is established, individuals may turn to the Internet to mitigate affective distress and their use may become compulsive. In turn, compulsive Internet use mediates the influence of POSI on negative outcomes. All hypotheses have been confirmed in research with U.S. university undergraduates. Although preliminary, this theory provides an important framework for understanding the role of online social interaction in the development of generalized IA. It also provides a model for specific IAs where social use of the Internet is a key factor.

## An Alternative Approach: Psychoanalytic Perspectives on Generalized Internet Abuse

Psychoanalytic interpretations of IA cast an alternative perspective on IA. Focusing mainly on online social interactions and the ability to enact different aspects of self online, psychoanalytic explanations of IA raise questions about normal, even therapeutic, uses versus disturbed use of the Internet and when use may be addictive.

Applications such as online games and chat rooms offer virtual spaces where individuals can experiment with behaviors and aspects of self free of the social constraints of F2F interactions in a relatively anonymous environment. Users can create an online persona and through social interactions construct new selves. These online spaces can become "place[s] for the construction and reconstruction of identity" (Turkle, 1995, p. 14). This is especially true in online games where players specifically develop an online persona through their avatars but is also true in chat rooms and other social areas of the Internet where users consciously and unconsciously project an online persona through their self-presentations, behaviors, and even screen names. Turkle (1995) highlights that this allows for exploration of various parts of self. For example, she asserts that MUDs:

> provide worlds for anonymous social interaction in which one can play a role as close to or as far away from one's "real self" as one chooses.... the anonymity of MUDs ... gives people the chance to express multiple and often unexplored aspects of the self, to play with their identity and try out new ones. MUDs make possible the creation of an identity so fluid and multiple that it strains the limits of the notion.     (p. 12)

These online personae can be highly "evocative objects for thinking about the self" (Turkle, 1995, p. 256). A MUD player observes, "You are the character and you are not the character, both at the same time" (Turkle, 1995, p. 12). Another says, "The persona thing intrigues me ... it's a chance for all of us who aren't actors to play [with] masks. And think about the masks we wear every day" (p. 256). Turkle (1995) compares this to the self that emerges in a psychoanalytic encounter. "It too is significantly virtual, constructed within the space of the analysis, where the slightest shifts come under the most intense scrutiny" (p. 256). "Virtual space is similar to the psychoanalytic notion of transitional space in that it is not truly an internal realm but lies somewhere between an external reality and the internal world" (Allison, Wahlde, Shockley, & Gabbard, 2006, p. 384). As in psychoanalysis, the online world can "operate out of normal time and according to its own rules" (Turkle, 1995, p. 262).

In this sense, online interactions can serve a therapeutic function. As users experiment with aspects of self, they can explore and work through conscious and unconscious conflicts. "Virtual spaces may provide the safety for us to accept what is missing so we can begin to accept ourselves as we are. We can use it as a space for growth. Having literally written our online personae into existence, we are in a position to be more aware of what we project into everyday life (Turkle, p. 263). When the process leads to psychological growth, Internet use, even excessive Internet use that could meet criteria for IA, is "no more addictive than therapy" (Turkle, 1995, p. 13).

However, not all outcomes are positive. Positive outcomes involve working through unresolved issues and integrating them within oneself. Problems occur when individuals act out, sometimes repetitively, existing behaviors and conflicts without working through those issues (Turkle, 1995).

Problems also can occur when individuals dissociate parts of their online selves from the rest of their personality (Suler, 1999, 2004a, 2004b). Many users experience a different, even more positive sense of self online than offline. One user explains:

> "My online persona differs greatly from my persona offline. And in many ways, my online persona is more 'me'." This person, a 37 year old who has stuttered since childhood and says he is "still shy to speak ... [and] out of sync ... [because] I never learned the dynamic of conversation that most people take for granted." However, when communicating on the Internet, "it's completely different: I have a feel for the flow of the conversations, have the time to measure my response, don't have to worry about the balance of conversation space – we all make as much space as we want ... It's been a wonderful liberating experience for me."     (Turkle, 1995, p. 318)

This experience has the potential to be therapeutic if he is able to take these new skills out to his offline life. However, to the extent that he experiences his online self as different from his offline self, he may separate the two, in effect dissociating his online from his offline self. Cooper and Sportolari (1997) observe, "rather than using the Net as a way to work on inhibited or conflictual aspects of the self, people may instead (consciously or not) use online relating to further split off unintegrated parts of themselves, leading to a compulsive and destructive overreliance on their screen personae and relationships."

Suler (2002) contends that "bringing together the various components of online and offline identity into one balanced harmonious whole may be the hallmark of mental health" (p. 456). He argues that "the self does not exist separate from the environment in which that self is expressed ... When a person is shy in person while outgoing online, neither self-presentation is more true. They are two dimensions of that person, each revealed within a different situational context" (Suler, 2004b, p. 325). Further, he proposes that Internet use is pathological or "addicted" when online life is dissociated from in-person life (Suler, 1999, 2004a). A key characteristic of pathological user is that "their cyberspace activity becomes an isolated world into itself ... It becomes a walled-off substitute or escape from their life rather than a supplement to it. Cyberspace becomes a dissociated part of their own mind, a sealed-off intrapsychic zone where conscious and unconscious needs are acted out, but never really understood or satisfied. Reality testing is lost" (Suler, 1999, p. 394). He suggests that alleviating this dissociation should be an important component to therapy.

## Therapy for Clinically Significant Internet Abuse

There is limited research on therapy for those with IA. This reflects the early stage of research on this emerging problem. Most research has been conducted with nonclinical groups, and, as discussed earlier, it is unclear what percentage of those identified as being Internet abusers exhibit clinically significant patterns. However, clinicians increasingly see clients with Internet-related problems, but few have training to treat these problems. A U.S. study of 2,908 mental health professionals in direct practice found that three-fourths (73%) had worked with at least one client with Internet-related problems (Wells, Mitchell, Finkelhor, & Blease, 2006), with excessive problematic use and disturbed patterns of downloading pornography the most frequently encountered problems (Mitchell et al., 2005). There was significant variation in exposure to clients with problematic Internet use and exposure across professional groups. Although over 70 percent of mental health counselors (84%), psychologists (79%), and social workers (73%) had worked with clients with Internet-related problems, only 53 percent of school counselors and 34 percent of school psychologists had. However, less than half of the 1,516 clinicians who had worked with Internet-related problems reported that they asked about "Internet use and/or behavior as part of an initial assessment" (Wells et al., 2006, p. 42). Less than 15 percent of professionals had any training to work with clients with problematic Internet use, with about half of these having training related to Internet addiction and addiction to cybersex. Although about a third of all mental health professionals "had read something in the professional literature on working with clients with problematic internet (use and) experiences" (p. 46), there were variations among professional groups. Marriage and family therapists (51%) were most likely to have read professional literature followed by psychologists (38%), school psychologists (13%), and school counselors (14%). Less than 10 percent of all mental professionals had clinical information regarding the treatment of clients with problematic Internet experiences, but over three quarters were interested in professional development and information related to problematic Internet use (Wells et al., 2006).

Limited research indicates that clinicians' approach to treating clients with IA is generally consistent with their preferred approach to therapy. In a small-scale study of eighty U.S. clinicians, the most commonly used approaches for working with clients with IA were cognitive (43.2%), reality (22.7%), family systems (20.5%), and solution focused therapy (18.2%). All other approaches were less than 10 percent. "There was a shift away from existential and person-centered approaches when dealing with (IA)" (p. 100). Only 2.3 percent of clinicians used an existential approach or online counseling, whereas 4.5 percent used a psychoanalytic approach, and 6.8 percent used group therapy or a person-centered approach (Parsons, 2005).

There is minimal empirical research on treatment of IA and specific IA. The literature has been dominated by case studies (e.g., Allison et al., 2006; Hall & Parsons, 2001; Orzack & Orzack, 1999; Orzack & Ross, 2000; Sattar & Ramaswamy, 2004) or descriptions of approaches to treatment (e.g., Young, 1999). Cognitive behavioral methods are a dominant modality (e.g., Hall & Parsons, 2001; Orzack & Orzack, 1999; Watson, 2005), although other techniques have been suggested.

Clinical reports indicate that IA often is co-morbid with other disorders and presentation can be complex (e.g., Allison et al., 2006; Orzack & Orzack,

1999). Orzack and colleagues advocate treating IA and online sexual addiction like other addictions, particularly food and sex addictions (Orzack & Orzack, 1999; Orzack & Ross, 2000). A team approach using either inpatient or outpatient therapy, depending on the client's needs, is suggested. Multimodal therapy is recommended; this can include cognitive behavioral therapy (CBT), motivational interviewing (Miller & Rollnick, 1991), problem solving, twelve-step groups, peer support, family therapy, appropriate medication, and relapse prevention techniques.

Young (1999) suggests that treatment of IA should focus on moderation and controlled use. She proposes time management techniques, setting concrete goals, providing alternative behaviors, and social support and family therapy.

The Internet has been endorsed as a vehicle for therapy for those with IA (Young, 2005) and as an adjunct to F2F therapy for those with online sexual addiction and compulsivity (Putnam & Maheu, 2000). Although having a person with problematic online behaviors use the Internet as part of therapy "may be akin to having an Alcoholics Anonymous meeting in a bar" (Putnam & Maheu, p. 96), abstinence from the computer and the Internet may not be practical because the Internet has become an integral part of people's professional and social lives. "Therefore, it seems appropriate to include treatment that addresses the problems where it occurs, online" (Putnam & Maheu, 2000, p. 96). Putnam and Maheu (2000) advocate treatment be based on F2F contact with a qualified mental health professional but contend that they can be supplemented with online resources, which "have the advantage of being more accessible than traditional adjuncts to therapy" (p. 94). Online resources are available whenever the client would like to use them and online anonymity fosters less stigmatization and embarrassment.

Although no outcome studies are provided for online counseling for IA, Young (2005) provides information on attitudes to online counseling of forty-eight e-clients who received online counseling for IA from her via a chat room. Reasons for seeking online counseling were anonymity (96%), convenience (71%), not having access to any mental health facilities (38%), cost (27%), and a referral (6%). About half of the e-clients (52%) also cited counselor credentials, that is, "professionals with a background in Internet addiction were not available in their area or that they had previously entered counseling with therapists unfamiliar with Internet addiction" (p. 175). This is consistent with Wells et al.'s (2006) research, which found few therapists with knowledge and experience with IA. Three quarters of clients also expressed concerns about online counseling; these concerns included issues of privacy (52%), security (38%), and fear of being caught while conducting online sessions (31%). Not everyone is sanguine about online therapy. Finn and Banach (2000) argue that online counseling and self-help groups pose many problems, including the lack of standards and regulations, difficulties in ascertaining the credentials and identity of therapists, and loss of privacy.

There are no published studies that systematically evaluate psychopharma-cological treatment of IA. When retrospectively assessing the effect of psy-chotropic medication in fifteen individuals with IA, Shapira et al. (2000) found participants reported moderate to marked reduction in problematic Internet use when given medications appropriate for their co-morbid psychiatric disor-der, with mood stabilizers associated with a higher rate of improvement. This finding should be viewed with caution as the study was small and relied on retrospective self-reports.

Outcome studies of IA treatment are sparse. Fang-ru and Wei (2005) inves-tigated the effect of using an integrated psychosocial intervention of fifty-two adolescents with IA in China. After three months of Solution-Focused Brief Therapy (SFBT) (Hawkes, Marsh, & Wilgosh, 1998), there was a significant reduction in time spent online and a 62 percent reduction in Internet addic-tion symptoms. Additionally, there was an 87 percent reduction in psychiatric symptoms on the symptom checklist (SCL-90); this included reductions in depression, interpersonal sensitivity, anxiety, obsessive-compulsive disorder, hostility, and phobic anxiety, which all had been higher than the domestic norm before treatment.

A study of group treatment for men involved in problematic online sexual behavior indicates that the effect of a treatment program varies according to clients' co-morbid disorders (Orzack, Voluse, Wolf, & Hennen, 2006). In this study, thirty-five men (average age = 44.5), attended one of five closed group programs that met for sixteen weeks. Each of the men was diagnosed with either a sexual paraphilia NOS or impulse control disorder NOS as well as having an anxiety disorder, mood disorder, or ADHD. The program modified a psycho-educational protocol developed by Line and Cooper (2000, cited in Orzack et al., 2006) to treat maladaptive sexual behavior which combined cognitive behavioral and psychodynamnic techniques. The sessions, conducted by a male and female psychologist, included CBT, readiness to change (RtC), and Motivational Interviewing (MI) (Miller & Rollnick, 1991).

> CBT . . . allows participants to identify and then modify maladaptive cogni-tions by providing feedback, coping strategies. The RtC model focuses on an individual's progress through six distinct stages of commitment (Precon-templation, contemplation, determination, action, maintenance and relapse) towards changing unproductive thoughts and behaviors . . . MI revolves around the process of individuals building problem solving strategies to help them change their current situation, with the eventual goal of creating moti-vation to achieve a particular goal.      (Orzack et al., 20006, p. 360)

At the end of this intervention, participants overall had decreased levels of depression (measured with the Beck Depression Index) and increases in quality of life (assessed with the Behavioral and Symptom Scale [BASES-32]), but there was no reduction in participants' inappropriate computer use. There were differences between the three co-morbid groups. Clients who were anxious improved in all three areas, while those with ADHD improved in none. Clients who were depressed were less depressed and improved in quality of life but had no change in their inappropriate computer use.

## Conclusions

Concern about Internet abuse has grown as Internet use has proliferated worldwide. Although some question whether IA exists, clinics have been established to treat those with IA and a growing body of research over the last decade has documented that, worldwide, a small percentage of Internet users develop disturbed patterns of behavior that have been called Internet abuse. People with mood disorders and those who are lonely, socially anxious, or use the Internet to cope with negative feelings are vulnerable to IA. Some researchers conceptualize IA as a continuum of deficient self-regulation that ranges from normal to disturbed use, while others conceptualize IA as a clinical disorder. Even in those cases in which IA reaches clinical significance, there is disagreement about whether IA is a distinct disorder. Some view IA as symptomatic of other, primary disorders that are frequently co-morbid with IA, such as mood disorders or social anxiety.

Among those who contend that IA is a clinical disorder, the consensus is that IA should be considered as an impulse control disorder NOS, that is, individuals' habitual inability to control their Internet use, which causes clinical levels of distress or impairment. Problems with impulse and particularly impulse control disorders have been associated with behavioral addictions. Although behavioral addictions are not universally recognized, there is a growing body of evidence that disturbed patterns of substances and some behaviors – that is, chemical and behavioral addictions – share similar features and etiology. This model may apply to IA. Cognitive behavioral models of IA have also been proposed.

Some users develop IA from problematic use that is specific to a given online application (e.g., MMORPGs) or behavior (e.g., downloading pornography). These are called specific IAs. However, many users develop problems from what has been called a generalized form of IA. These users prefer socially interactive aspects of the Internet. Many are less inhibited in their online social interactions and develop a preference for online over F2F interaction. There is overlap between some specific IAs and generalized IA. In both types, social uses of the Internet or using the Internet to cope with stress become problematic. Future research should focus on the similarities and differences between specific and generalized IA.

Although many clinicians report that they have treated clients with IA or specific IA, few have training in recognizing and treating IA. Research on treatment of IA is limited.

IA is a relatively new area of research, and many areas need further research. The lack of a uniform set of empirically validated criteria for IA is a weakness that pervades much of the research of IA. This is especially pertinent for those who suggest that IA should be accepted as a clinical disorder. Most studies have been surveys of adolescents and university students, which limits generalizability. Future research should use more representative samples of Internet users. Longitudinal research and experimental studies are needed. Empirically based outcome studies and protocols for training clinicians should be high priorities for future research. The Internet is constantly changing and future IA research will reflect these changes.

## References

Aboujaoude, E., Koran, L. M., Gamel, N., Large, M. D., & Serpe, R. T. (2006). Potential markers for problematic internet use: A telephone survey of 2,513 adults. *CNS Spectrums, 11*(10), 750–755. Retrieved June 15, 2007, from http://www.cnsspectrums.com/aspx/articledetail.aspx?articleid=648.

Allison, S. D., Von Wahide, L., Shockley, T., & Gabbard, G. O. (2006). The development of the self in the era of the Internet and role-playing fantasy games. *American Journal of Psychiatry, 163*, 381–385.

American Psychiatric Association. (2000). *Diagnostic and statistical manual of mental disorders* (4th ed., text revision). Washington, DC: Author.

Anderson, K. (1999). Internet dependency among college students: Should we be concerned? Paper presented at the 107th annual convention of the American Psychological Association, Boston, MA. Retrieved February 21, 2000, from http://www.rpi.edu/~anderk4/research.html.

Average MMORPG gamer spends 20–25 hours a week on the game. (2005, March 10). *IT Facts*. Retrieved June 30, 2006, from http://www.itfacts.biz/index.php?id=P2793.

Bahney, A. (2006, March 9). Don't talk to invisible strangers. *New York Times*, pp. E1–E2.

Bai, Y. M., Lin, C. C., & Chen, J. Y. (2001). Internet addiction disorder among clients of a virtual clinic. *Psychiatric Service, 52*(10), 1397.

Bartle, R. (1996). Hearts, clubs, diamonds, spades: Players who suit MUDS, *Journal of MUD Research, 1*(1). Retrieved June 15, 2007, from http://journal.tinymush.org/v1n1/bartle.html.

Beard, K. W. (2005). Internet addiction: A review of current assessment techniques and potential assessment questions. *CyberPsychology & Behavior, 8*, 7–14.

Beard, K. W., & Wolf, E. M. (2001). Modification in the proposed diagnostic criteria for Internet addiction. *CyberPsychology & Behavior, 4*, 377–383.

Betz, C., Mihalic, D., Pinto, M. E., & Raffa, R. B. (2000). Could a common biochemical mechanism underlie addictions? *Journal of Clinical Pharmacy and Therapeutics, 25*, 11–20.

Black, D. W., Belsare, G., & Schlosser, S. (1999). Clinical features, psychiatric comorbidity, and health-related quality of life in persons reporting compulsive computer use behavior. *Journal of Clinical Psychiatry, 60*, 839–844.

Blum, K., Cull, J. G., Braverman, E. R., & Comings, D. E. (1996). Reward deficiency syndrome. *American Scientist, 84*, 132–138.

Boies, A., Cooper, A., & Osborne, C. S. (2004). Variations in Internet-related problems and psychosocial functioning in online sexual activities: Implications for social and sexual development of young adults. *CyberPsychology & Behavior, 7*, 207–230.

Bradley, B. P. (1990). Behavioural addictions: Common features and treatment implications. *British Journal of Addictions, 85*, 1417–1419.

Bruch, M. A., Kalfowitz, N. G., & Pearl, L. (1988). Mediated and unmediated relationships of personality components to loneliness. *Journal of Social and Clinical Psychology, 6*, 346–355.

Burger, J. M. (2004). *Personality*. (6th ed.). Belmont, CA: Wadsworth.

Caplan, S. E. (2002). Problematic Internet use and psychosocial well-being: Development of a theory-based cognitive-behavioral measurement instrument. *Computers in Human Behavior, 18*, 553–575.

Caplan, S. E. (2003). Preference of online social interaction: A theory of problematic Internet use and psychosocial well-being. *Communication Research, 30*, 625–648.

Caplan, S. E. (2004). Refining the cognitive behavioral model of problematic Internet use: A closer look at social skill and compulsive behavior. A paper presented at the annual conference of the National Communication Association, Chicago.

Caplan, S. E. (2005a). A social skill account of problematic Internet use. *Journal of Communication, 55*, 721–736.

Caplan, S. E. (2005b, August). *Refining the cognitive behavioral model of problematic Internet use*. Paper presented at the annual convention of the American Psychological Association, Washington, DC.

Chak, K., & Leung, L. (2004). Shyness and locus of control as predictors of Internet addiction and Internet use. *CyberPsychology & Behavior, 7*, 559–570.

Chee, F. (2005, June). Understanding Korean experiences of online game hype, identity and the menace of the "Wang-ta." Proceedings of the Digital Games Research Association (DiGRA) 2005 Conference, Vancouver, British Columbia. Retrieved December 1, 2006, from http://ir.lib.sfu.ca/retrieve/1645/87614dd3c78bca26f2a1348b3d93.doc.

Chen, K., Chen, I., & Paul, H. (2001). Explaining online behavioral differences: An Internet dependency perspective. *Journal of Computer Information Systems, 41*, 59–63.

Chinese gamer sentenced to life. (2005, June 8). *BBC News*. Retrieved January 13, 2006, from http://news.bbc.co.uk/2/hi/technology/4072704.stm.

Chou, C., & Hsiao, M.-C. (2000). Internet addiction, usage, gratification, and pleasure experience: the Taiwan college students' case. *Computers and Education, 35*, 65–80.

Chou, T.-J., & Ting, D.-D. (2003). The role of flow experience in cyber game addiction. *CyberPsychology & Behavior, 6*, 663–675.

Cooper, A., Delmonico, D., & Burg, R. (2000). Cybersex users, abusers, and compulsives: New findings and implications. In A. Cooper (Ed.), *Cybersex: The dark side of the force* (pp. 5–29). Philadelphia, PA: Brunner Routledge.

Cooper, A., Griffin-Shelley, E., Delmonico, D., & Mathy, R. (2001). Online sexual problems: Assessment and predictive variables. *Sexual Addiction and Compulsivity, 8*, 267–285.

Cooper, A., Morahan-Martin, J., Mathy, R., & Maheu, M. (2002). Toward an increased understanding of user demographics in online sexual activities. *Journal of Sex and Marital Therapy, 28*, 105–129.

Cooper, A., Putman, D., Planchon, L., & Boies, S. (1999). Online sexual compulsivity: Getting tangled in the net. *Sexual Addiction and Compulsivity, 7*, 5–30.

Cooper, A., & Sportolari, L. (1997). Romance in Cyberspace: Understanding online attraction. *Journal of Sex Education and Therapy, 22*, 7–14.

Davis, R. A. (2001). A cognitive-behavioral model of pathological Internet use. *Computers in Human Behavior, 17*, 187–195.

Davis, R. A., Flett, G. L., & Besser, A. (2002). Validation of a new measure of problematic Internet use: Implications for pre-employment screening. *CyberPsychology & Behavior, 5*, 331–346.

Ervin, B. A., Turk, C. L., Heimberg, R. F., Fresco, D. M., & Hantula, D. A. (2004). The Internet: Home to a severe population of individuals with social anxiety disorder? *Journal of Anxiety Disorders, 18*, 629–646.

Fang-ru, Y., & Wei, H. (2005). The effect of integrated psychosocial intervention on 52 adolescents with Internet addiction disorder. *Chinese Journal of Clinical Psychology, 13*, 343–345.

Finn, J., & Banach, M. (2000). Victimization online: The downside of seeking human services for women on the Internet. *CyberPsychology & Behavior, 5*, 785–796.

Grant, J. E., Brewer, J. A., & Potenza, M. N. (2006). The neurobiology of substance and behavioral addictions. *CNS Spectrums, 11*, 924–930. Retrieved December 21, 2006, from http://www.cnsspectrums.com/aspx/articledetail.aspx?articleid=912.

Greenfield, D. (1999). Psychological characteristics of compulsive Internet use: A preliminary analysis. *CyberPsychology & Behavior, 2*, 403–412.

Greenberg, J. L., Lewis, S. E., & Dodd, D. K. (1999). Overlapping addictions and self-esteem among college men and women. *Addictive Behaviors, 24*, 565–571.

Griffiths, D. (2005, October 10). Treating China's online addicts. *BBC News*. Retrieved January 8, 2007, from http://news.bbc.co.uk/2/hi/asia-pacific/4327258.stm.

Griffiths, M. (1995). Technological addictions. *Clinical Psychology Forum, 95*, 32–36.

Griffiths, M. (2001, October). Internet gambling: Preliminary results of the first UK prevalence study. *E-Gambling: The Electronic Journal of Gambling Issues* (Issue 5). Retrieved February 23, 2005, from http://www.camh.net/egambling/issue5/research/griffiths_article.html.

Griffiths, M., Davies, M. N., & Chappell, D. (2004). Online computer gaming: A comparison of adolescent and adult gamers. *Journal of Adolescence, 27*, 87–96.

Griffiths, M., & Parke, J. (2002). The social impact of Internet gambling. *Social Science Computer Review, 20*, 312–320.

Grohol, J. (1999). Too much time online: Internet addiction or healthy social interactions. *CyberPsychology & Behavior, 2*, 395–402.

Hall, A. S., & Parsons, J. (2001). Internet addiction: College student case study using best practices in cognitive behavior therapy. *Journal of Mental Health Counseling, 23*, 312–327.

Hawkes, D., Marsh, T., & Wilgosh, R. (1998). *Solution-focused therapy: A handbook for health care professionals.* Oxford: Butterworth-Heinemann.

Holden, C. (2001). Behavioral addictions: Do they exist? *Science, 294,* 980–982.

Huang, M. P., & Alessi, N. E. (1997). Internet addiction, Internet psychotherapy. *American Journal of Psychiatry, 153,* 890.

International Telecommunication Union. (2003, January 24). Korean Center for Internet Addiction and Counselling. ITU Strategy and Policy Unit Newslog. Retrieved November 3, 2006, from http://www.itu.int/osg/spu/newslog/Korean+Center+For+Internet+Addiction+Prevention+And+Counselling.aspx.

Jacobs, D. (1986). A general theory of addictions. *Journal of Gambling Behavior, 2,* 15–31.

Jaffe, J. (1990). Trivializing dependence. *British Journal of Addiction, 85,* 1425–1427.

Johansson, A., & Götestam, K. G. (2004). Internet addiction: Characteristics of a questionnaire and prevalence in Norwegian youth (12–18 years). *Scandinavian Journal of Psychology, 45,* 223–229.

Kaltiala-Heino, R., Lintonen, T., & Rimpelä, A. (2004). Internet addiction? Potentially problematic use of the internet in a population of 12–18 year old adolescents. *Addiction Research and Theory, 12,* 89–96.

Kaplan, R. (1996). Carrot addiction. *Australian and New Zealand Journal of Psychiatry, 30,* 698–700.

Kent, S. L. (2003). Alternate reality: The history of massively multiplayer online games. Gamespy.com. Retrieved January 1, 2007, from http://archive.gamespy.com/amdmmog/week1/.

Kim, K., Ryu, E., Chon, M.-Y., Yeun, E.-J., Choi, S.-Y., Seo, J.-S., et al. (2006). Internet addiction in Korean adolescents and its relation to depression and suicidal ideation: A questionnaire survey. *International Journal of Nursing Studies, 43,* 185–192.

Koch, W. H., & Pratarelli, M. E. (2004). Effects of intro/extraversion and sex on social internet use. *North American Journal of Psychology, 6,* 371–382.

Koepp, M. J., Gunn, R. N. Lawrence, A. D., Cunningham, V. J., Dagher, A., Jones, T., et al. (1998). Evidence for striatal dopamine release during a video game. *Nature, 393*(6682), 266–268.

Kosak, D. (2003, March 7). Why is Korea the king of multiplayer gaming? *Gamespy.* Retrieved December 12, 2006, from http://archive.gamespy.com/gdc2003/korean/.

Kraut, R., Kiesler, S., Boneva, B., Cummings, J., Helgeson, V., & Crawford, A. (2002). Internet paradox revisited. *Journal of Social Issues, 58,* 49–74.

Kraut, R., Patterson, M., Landmark, V., Kiesler, S., Mukophadhyay, T., & Scherlis W. (1998). Internet paradox: Asocial technology that reduces social involvement and psychological well being? *American Psychologist, 53,* 1017–1031.

Kubey, R., & Csikszentmihalyi, M. (2002). Television addiction is no mere metaphor. *Scientific American, 286,* 79–86.

Kubey, R. W., Lavin, M. J., & Barrows, J. R. (2001). Internet use and collegiate academic performance decrements: early findings. *Journal of Communication, 51,* 366–382.

Kurapati, S. N. (2004). Addiction to massively multi-player on-line games: An ethical analysis. Retrieved December 1, 2006, from http://www.soe.ucsc.edu/~snk/pub/papers/game_addiction.pdf.

Ladd, G. T., & Petry, N. M. (2002). Disordered gambling among university-based medical and dental patients: a focus on Internet gambling. *Psychology of Addictive Behaviors, 16*, 76–79.

Lambert, C. (2000, March–April). Deep cravings. *Harvard Magazine*, 60–68. Retrieved September 14, 2006, from http://www.harvardmagazine.com/print/0300130.html.

LaRose, R., Lin, C. A., & Eastin, M. S. (2003). Unregulated Internet usage: Addiction, habit or deficient self-regulation? *Media Psychology, 5*, 225–253.

Leary, M. R., & Kowalsky, R. M. (1995a). *Social Anxiety*. New York: Guilford.

Leary, M. R., & Kowalsky, R. M. (1995b). The self-presentation model of social phobia. In R. G. Heimberg, M. R. Liebowitz, D. A. Hope, & F. A. Schneier (Eds.), *Social phobia: Diagnosis, assessment, and treatment* (pp. 94–112). New York: Guilford.

Leung, L. (2004). Net-generation attributes and seductive properties of the Internet as predictors of online activities and Internet addiction. *CyberPsychology & Behavior, 7*, 333–348.

Li, S.-M., & Chung, T.-M. (2006). Internet function and Internet addictive behavior. *Computers in Human Behavior, 22*, 1067–1071.

Lin, S., & Tsai, C. C. (2002). Sensation seeking and internet dependence of Taiwanese high school adolescents. *Computers in Human Behavior, 18*, 411–426.

Lin-Liu, J. (2006, February). China's e-junkies head for rehab. *IEEE Spectrum, 43*(2),19.

Marlatt, G. A., Baer, J. S., Donovan, D. M., & Kivlahan, D. R. (1988). Addictive behaviors: Etiology and treatment. *Annual Review of Psychology, 39*, 223–252.

Meerkerk, F.-J., Van Den Eijnden, R. J., & Farretsen, H. F. (2006). Predicting compulsive Internet use: It's all about sex. *CyberPsychology & Behavior, 9*, 95–103.

Milkman, H., & Sunderwirth, S. (1982). Addictive processes. *Journal of Psychoactive Drugs, 14*, 177–192.

Miller, W. R., & Rollnick, S. (1991). *Motivational interviewing: Preparing people to change addictive behavior*. New York: Guilford Press.

Mitchell, K. J., Becker-Blease, K. A., & Finkelhor, D. (2005). Inventory of problematic Internet experiences encountered in clinical practice. *Professional Psychology, 36*, 498–509.

Moore, T. (2003, August 5). Camp aims to beat web addiction. *BBC News*. Retrieved January 8, 2007, from http://news.bbc.co.uk/2/hi/europe/3125475.stm.

Morahan-Martin, J. (1999). The relationship between loneliness and Internet use and abuse. *CyberPsychology & Behavior, 2*, 431–440.

Morahan-Martin, J. (2001). Impact of Internet abuse for college students. In C. Wolfe (Ed.), *Learning and teaching on the World Wide Web* (pp. 191–219). San Diego, CA: Academic Press.

Morahan-Martin, J. (2005). Internet abuse: Addiction? Disorder? Symptom? Alternative explanations? *Social Science Computer Review, 23*, 39–48.

Morahan-Martin, J., & Schumacher, P. (2000). Incidence and correlates of pathological Internet use among college students. *Computers in Human Behavior, 16*, 13–29.

Morahan-Martin, J., & Schumacher, P. (2003). Loneliness and social uses of the Internet. *Computers in Human Behavior, 19*, 659–671.

Nalwa, K., & Anand, A. P. (2003). Internet addiction in students: A cause of concern. *CyberPsychology & Behavior, 6*, 653–656.

National Public Radio/Kaiser/Kennedy School. (NPR). (2000). Survey shows widespread enthusiasm for high technology. Washington, DC: NPR Online. Retrieved September 21, 2003, from http://www.npr.org/programs/specials/poll/technology/index.html.

Ng, B. D., & Wiemer-Hastings, P. (2005). Addiction to the Internet and online gaming. *CyberPsychology & Behavior, 8*, 110–113.

Nichols, L. A., & Nicki, R. (2004). Development of a psychometrically sound Internet addiction scale: A preliminary step. *Psychology of Addictive Behaviors, 18*, 381–384.

Niemz, K., Griffiths, M., & Banyard, P. (2005). Prevalence of pathological Internet use among university students and correlations with self-esteem, the General Health Inventory (GHQ) and disinhibition. *CyberPsychology & Behavior, 8*, 562–570.

Orzack, M. (1999). Computer addiction: Is it real or virtual? *Harvard Mental Health Letter, 15*(7), 8.

Orzack, M., & Orzack, D. S. (1999). Treatment of computer addicts with complex co-morbid psychiatric disorders. *CyberPsychology & Behavior, 2*, 465–473.

Orzack, M., Voluse, A. C., Wolf, D., & Hennen, J. (2006). An ongoing study of group treatment for men involved in problematic Internet-enabled sexual behavior. *CyberPsychology & Behavior, 9*, 348–360.

Orzack, M. H., & Ross, C. J. (2000). Should virtual sex be treated like other sex addictions? *Sexual Addiction & Compulsivity, 7*, 113–125.

Pallanti, S. (2006). From impulse-control disorders toward behavioral addictions. *CNS Sprectrums,11*, 921–922.

Parsons, J. (2005). *An examination of massively multiplayer role-playing games as a facilitator of Internet addiction.* Doctoral thesis, University of Iowa. Retrieved October 1, 2006, from http://etd.lib.uiowa.edu/2005/jparsons.pdf.

Potenza, M. N. (2006). Should addictive disorders include non-substance-related conditions? *Addiction, 101*(Suppl.), 142–151.

Pratarelli, M. E. (2005). *Sex, shyness, and social Internet use.* Paper presented at the 113th Annual Convention of the American Psychological Association, Washington, DC.

Pratarelli, M. E., & Browne, B. L. (2002). Confirmatory factor analysis of Internet use and addiction. *CyberPsychology & Behavior, 5*, 53–64.

Pratarelli, M. E., Browne, B. L., & Johnson, K. (1999). The bits and bytes of computer/Internet addiction: A factor analytic approach. *Behavior Research Methods, Instruments and Computers, 31*, 305–314.

Putnam, D. (2000). Initiation and maintenance of online sexual compulsivity: Implications for assessment and treatment. *CyberPsychology & Behavior, 3*, 553–563.

Putnam, D., & Maheu, M. (2000). Online sexual addiction and compulsivity: Integrating Web resources and behavioral telehealth in treatment. *Sexual Addiction & Compulsivity, 7,* 91–112.

Rheingold, H. (1993). *The virtual community: Homesteading on the electronic frontier.* Reading, MA: Addison-Wesley.

Satel, S. L. (1993). The diagnostic limits of "addiction." *Journal of Clinical Psychiatry, 54,* 237–238.

Sattar, P., & Ramaswamy, S. (2004). Internet gaming addiction. *Canadian Journal of Psychiatry, 49,* 869–870.

Scherer, K. (1997). College life online: Healthy and unhealthy Internet use. *Journal of College Student Development, 38,* 655–665.

Schwartz, M. F., & Southern, S. (2000). Compulsive cybersex: The new tea room. In A. Cooper (Ed.), *Cybersex: The dark side of the force* (pp. 127–144). Philadelphia, PA: Brunner Routledge.

Shaffer, H. J. (2006). *What is addiction? A perspective.* Boston, MA: Harvard Medical School Division of Addictions. Retrieved December 18, 2006, from http://www.divisiononaddictions.org/html/whatisaddiction.htm.

Shaffer, H. J., Hall, M. N., & Vander Bilt, J. (2000). "Computer addiction": A critical consideration. *American Journal of Orthopsychiatry, 70,* 162–168.

Shaffer, H. J., LaPlante, D., LaBrie, R., Kidman, R., Donato, A., & Stanton, M. (2004). Toward a syndrome model of addiction: Multiple expressions, common etiology. *Harvard Review of Psychiatry, 12,* 367–374.

Shapira, N. A., Goldsmith, T. D., Keck, P., Khosla, U., & McElroy, S. (2000). Psychiatric features of individuals with problematic Internet use. *Journal of Affective Disorders, 66,* 283.

Shapira, N., Lessig, M., Goldsmith, T., Szabo, S., Lazoritz, M., Gold, M., et al. (2003). Problematic Internet use: Proposed classification and diagnostic criteria. *Depression and Anxiety, 17,* 207–216.

Shepherd, R., & Edelmann, R. F. (2005). Reasons for Internet use and social anxiety. *Personality and Individual Differences, 39,* 949–958.

Simkova, B., & Cincera, J. C. (2004). Internet addiction disorder and chatting in the Czech Republic. *CyberPsychology & Behavior, 7,* 536–539.

Singh, G. C., Hankins, M. C., Dulku, A., & Kelly, M. B. (2006). Psychosocial aspects of botox in aesthetic surgery. *Aesthetic Plastic Surgery, 30,* 71–76.

Small, D. M., Zatorre, R. J., Dagher, A., Evans, A. C., & Jones-Gotman, M. (2001). Changes in brain activity related to eating chocolate. *Brain, 124,* 1720–1733.

Solano, C. H., & Koester, N. H. (1989). Loneliness and communication problems: Subjective anxiety or objective skills? *Personality and Social Psychology Bulletin, 15,* 126–133.

South Korea plans more centres to treat Internet addiction. (2005, September). Retrieved from Lexis/Nexis database.

Spain, J. W., & Vega, G. (2005). Sony online entertainment: Everquest or EverCrack? *Journal of Business Ethics, 58,* 3–6.

Suler, J. (1999). Healthy and pathological Internet use. *CyberPsychology & Behavior, 2,* 385–394.

Suler, J. (2002). Identity management in cyberspace. *Journal of Applied Psychoanalytic Studies, 4,* 455–460.

Suler, J. (2004a). Computer and cyberspace addiction. *International Journal of Applied Psychoanalytic Studies, 1*, 359–362.

Suler, J. (2004b). The online disinhibition effect. *CyberPsychology & Behavior, 7*, 321–326.

Taylor, R. (2006, April 9). China wrestles with online gamers. *BBC News*. Retrieved January 8, 2007, from http://news.bbc.co.uk/2/hi/programmes/click_online/4887236.stm.

Thailand restricts online gamers. (2003, July 8). *BBC News*. Retrieved January 8, 2007, from http://news.bbc.co.uk/2/hi/asia-pacific/3054590.stm.

Thatcher, A., & Goolam, S. (2005a). Defining the South African Internet addict: Prevalence and biographical profiling of problematic Internet users in South Africa. *South African Journal of Psychology, 35*, 766–792.

Thatcher, A., & Goolam, S. (2005b). Development and psychometric properties of the Problematic Internet Use Questionnaire. *South African Journal of Psychology, 35*, 793–809.

Treuer, T., Fabian, Z., & Furedi, J. (2001). Internet addiction associated with features of impulse control disorder: Is it a real psychiatric disorder? *Journal of Affective Disorders, 66*, 283.

Turkle, S. (1995). *Life on the screen: Identity in the age of the Internet.* New York: Simon and Schuster.

Vanden Boogart, M. R. *Uncovering the social impacts of Facebook on a college campus.* Master's thesis, Kansas State University. Retrieved November 1, 2006, from http://krex.k-state.edu/dspace/handle/2097/181.

Walther, J. B., & Reid, L. D. (2000, February 4). Understanding the allure of the Internet. *Chronicle of Higher Education*, B4–B5.

Wan, C.-H., & Chiou, W.-B. (2006). Psychological motives and online games addition: A test of flow theory and humanistic needs theory for Taiwanese adolescents. *CyberPsychology & Behavior, 9*, 317–324.

Wang, W. (2001). Internet dependency and psychosocial maturity among college students. *International Journal of Human-Computer Studies, 55*, 919–938.

Warthan, M. D., Uchida, T., & Wagner, R. F. (2005). UV light tanning as a type of substance-related disorder. *Archives of Dermatology, 141*, 963–966.

Watson, J. C. (2005). Internet addiction diagnosis and assessment: Implications for counselors. *Journal of Professional Counseling, Practice, Theory and Research, 33*, 17–31.

Wei, L., Zijie, H., & Daxi, L. (2004) Internet use and depression, communication anxiety of medical students. *Chinese Mental Health Journal, 18*, 501–503.

Weiser, E. B. (2001). The functions of Internet use and their social and psychological consequences. *CyberPsychology & Behavior, 4*, 723–743.

Wells, M., Mitchell, K. J., Finkelhor, D., & Becker-Blease, K. A. (2006). Mental health professionals' exposure to clients with problematic Internet experiences. *Journal of Technology in Human Services, 24*, 35–52.

Whang, L. S., Lee, S., & Chang, G. (2003). Internet over-users' psychological profiles: a behavior sampling analysis on Internet addiction. *CyberPsychology & Behavior, 6*, 143–150.

Yang, S. C., & Tung, C.-J. (2007). Comparison of Internet addicts and non-addicts in Taiwanese high school. *Computers in Human Behavior, 23*, 79–96.

Ybarra, M. L., Alexander, C., & Mitchell, K. J. (2005). Depressive symptomomatology, youth Internet use and online interactions: A national survey. *Journal of Adolescent Health, 36*, 9–18.

Yee, N. (2001). The Norrathian scrolls: A study of *Everquest* (version 2.5). Retrieved October 18, 2006, from http://www.nickyee.com/eqt/report.html.

Yee, N. (2002, October). *Ariadne – Understanding MMORPG Addiction.* Retrieved October 18, 2006, from http://www.nickyee.com/hub/addiction/home.html.

Yee, N. (2006a). The demographics, motivations and derived experiences of users of massively-multiuser online graphical environments. *PRESENCE: Teleoperators and Virtual Environments, 15*, 309–329.

Yee, N. (2006b). Motivations for play in online games. *CyberPsychology & Behavior, 9*, 772–775.

Yoo, H. J. Cho, S. C., Ha, J., Yune, S., Kim, S. J., Hwang, J., et al. (2004). Attention deficit hyperactivity symptoms and Internet addiction. *Psychiatry and Clinical Neurosciences, 58*, 487–594.

Young, K. S. (1996, August). *Internet addiction: The emergence of a new clinical disorder.* Paper presented at the 104th annual convention of the American Psychological Association, Toronto, Canada.

Young, K. S. (1997, August). *What makes online usage stimulating: Potential explanations for pathological Internet use.* Paper presented at the 105th annual convention of the American Psychological Association, Chicago, Illinois.

Young, K. S. (1998). Internet addiction: The emergence of a new clinical disorder. *CyberPsychology & Behavior, 1*, 237–244.

Young, K. S. (1999). Internet addiction: Symptoms, evaluation, and treatment. In L. VandeCreek & T. Jackson (Eds.), *Innovations in clinical practice: A sourcebook.* (Vol. 17, pp. 1–13). Sarasota, FL: Professional Resource Press.

Young, K. S. (2005). An empirical examination of client attitudes towards online counseling. *CyberPsychology & Behavior, 8*, 172–177.

Young, K. S., & Rodgers, R. (1998). The relationship between depression and Internet addiction. *CyberPsychology & Behavior, 1*, 25–28.

Yuen, C. N., & Lavin, M. J. (2004). Internet dependence in the collegiate population: The role of shyness. *CyberPsychology & Behavior, 7*, 379–383.

Zheng, H., Ming-Yi, Q., Chun-Li, Y., Jing, N., Jing, D., & Xiao-Yun, Z. (2006). Correlated factors comparison: The trends of computer game addiction and Internet relationship addiction. *Chinese Journal of Clinical Psychology, 14*, 244–247.

Zohar, J. (2006). From obsessive-compulsive spectrum to obsessive-compulsive disorders: The Cape Town consensus statement. *CNS Spectrums, 12*(2, Suppl. 3). Retrieved October 18, 2006, from http://cnsspectrums.com/aspx/article_pf.aspx?articleid=997.

# 4 Flow Experience in Cyberspace: Current Studies and Perspectives

*Alexander E. Voiskounsky*

Cyberspace constitutes a specific environment; the investigations in this field are based either on the original cyberspace-dependent methods and theories, or on universal theories and methods worked out in diverse areas of knowledge, not necessarily closely connected with cyberspace. A psychological theoretical construct (with vast practical perspectives) introduced by Csikszentmihalyi, (2000/1975) known as optimal, or flow experience, alongside the methods of its measurement, basically refer to the universal, that is, nonspecific theoretical and methodological background. This traditional methodology was adapted and accepted within cyberspace; it represents a growing area of the investigators' activity in the field.

Like many other investigations of human behavior in cyberspace, flow-related studies are of both practical and theoretical significance. The practical significance is associated with the challenges deriving from business: a large body of research is stimulated by business expectations of acquiring advantages in the quality of offers to be suggested to customers. The theoretical significance stems from a supposition that optimal experience is an important construct mediating human activity in cyberspace, and thus represents a special level of psychological mediation of mental processes. The mechanisms of multiple mediation and remediation of a previously mediated experience are known to affect human psychic development (Cole, 1996; Vygotsky, 1962).

In this chapter, major research directions are presented and discussed, referring to the optimal, or flow, experience studies conducted within cyberspace environments. The chapter starts with a brief description of optimal experience in the context of positive psychology; the origin and the meaning of a relatively new term *flow* is explained, and several examples are provided. Flow is certainly connected with intrinsic motivation, which is distinguished in the chapter from extrinsic motivation. Some examples are given, and various methods of carrying out flow experience investigations are discussed.

The distinctive characteristics of flow, introduced and validated by Csikszentmihalyi, are presented, alongside several additional characteristics introduced by researchers working in the field of cyberspace-related studies of the optimal experience. Cumulatively, flow characteristics should constitute a valid universal methodological instrument to be used in quantitative measurements. In many cases, though, this is not so, because the sets of flow related characteristics slightly vary in the different empirical studies. In a way, these variations seem reasonable, if one assumes that task specificity is apt to bring fluctuations into a regular presupposed model. The universality of the flow characteristics as discussed in the chapter is a problem area that needs further research.

Numerous research directions are presented in this chapter: well-developed, less well-developed, underdeveloped, and dead-end research directions. The more or less developed areas of research include, for example, the usage of the optimal experience patterns in e-learning, online instruction and distant education; in computer- and Internet-mediated communication, particularly in instant messaging and chatting, in consuming the web media sources and online entertainments; in web marketing, e-shopping, and business applications of web sources; in playing computer games, video gaming, and online gaming, including online multiplayer games; in web navigation, exploratory online behavior, and search of the content items on the web; in illegal penetrations into cyberspace environments, in hacking, for example, and in computer security regulations; in psychological rehabilitation by the means of the high-tech equipment and programs, such as in immersive systems of virtual reality; lastly, in the measurement of the web-site attraction and its friendliness for consumers, as well as in usability testing and in the adaptation of web sources to target populations.

The dead-end direction is in the search for possible correlations between flow and addiction, based on an argument that both promote repetitive actions. There is no likeness between flow and addiction; these processes are opposites from the psychological standpoint. This is a theoretical consideration, and in this chapter, it is shown that the current empirical studies confirm the correctness of this conclusion. Last but not least, the culture-related flow studies in cyberspace environments are evidently underrepresented: there are almost no intercultural projects in the field. The existing ones are described, including the author's cross-cultural project, to prove that this trend, in numerous directions of research, is promising and expected.

This chapter characterizes various directions of research and gives a perspective of flow-related studies within cyberspace environments.

## Flow as a Psychological Construct

The optimal experience, also known as flow experience, is a contribution, made over three decades ago, to what is now called *positive psychology* (Seligman & Csikszentmihalyi, 2000) by one of its leaders, Mihaly Csikszentmihalyi (2000/1975; 1990 and elsewhere). The origin of this new paradigm is described in dozens of Csikszentmihalyi's and his followers' published materials. While interviewing certain professional and amateur dancers, chess players, rock climbers, surgeons, and many others who would express a deep devotion to their preferred sort of activity, Csikszentmihalyi selected the often-reported characteristics of a special feeling common to many of them, which they could estimate very highly. This devotion is undeniably related to what they believe constitute an optimal level of their experience. During the interview sessions, Csikszentmihalyi found that people provide such verbal descriptions, which turned out to be worded almost identically regardless of the particular sort of the preferred activity. Almost everyone mentioned "being in the midst of a flow," or, to express it in a slightly different manner, "flowing from one moment to the next, in which he is in control of his actions, and in which there is a little distinction between self and environment, between stimulus and response, or between past, present, and future" (Csikszentmihalyi, 2000/1975, p. 36). No wonder, Csikszentmihalyi (2000/1975; 1990 and elsewhere) called this sort of the holistic experience flow.

The interviewed people, regardless of their age, gender and culture, professional competence, or marital and income status, reported flow as an enjoyment: They confessed they enjoyed the process of doing even hard work. They further confessed enjoying doing it nonstop, sometimes for long periods, taking risks, or getting painfully tired and sometimes exhausted. They reported they did enjoy it because in return they felt they had been performing to the utmost. No wonder this sort of experience is often called *optimal*, within the positive psychology paradigm.

A flow experience takes place when people are engaged in their chosen activity, including work – "often the most enjoyable part of life," as Csikszentmihalyi (1990, p. 144) puts it – as well as during housework or hobbies and is not likely to occur when the person engaged in the activity is totally relaxed (Csikszentmihalyi, 1990; Massimini & Delle Fave, 2000; Smith & Wilhelm, 2007). Flow cannot be qualified as a regular attribute of one's engagement and involvement in the preferred activity; instead, every time it is a sort of a happening. Before experiencing this specific enjoyment, a person needs to acquire some competence, not necessarily very high, in the preferred activity. Flow happens irrespectively of the nature of the preferred activity, whether it is creative or routine, unique or known to almost everyone, individual or shared with others.

There is not much evidence, registered or oral, of any enjoyment being felt while doing exhaustingly hard backbreaking work with only little chance to survive. Unprecedented valuable evidences from the gulag labor camps, as described by Alexander Solzhenitsyn (1963, 1974–1978), testify to the moments, which not surprisingly are rare, when what the gulag prisoners' experience might be called optimal – psychologically optimal in the abovementioned sense, in no way optimal from the standpoint of economics. Although Solzhenitsyn is a writer, it is widely known that his writings are well-documented, based on someone's (sometimes the author himself) firsthand eyewitness account. It is not accidental that the subtitle of his major book *The Gulag Archipelago* is *An Experiment in Literary Investigation* (Solzhenitsyn, 1974–1978). Contrary to the Csikszentmihalyi's report of "flow in the most dismal captivity" experienced mostly by "specialized intellectuals," masters of the "symbolic world," like mathematicians or poets (Csikszentmihalyi, 2000/1975, p. 193), or such "people of flow" as pilots, polar explorers, designers, and architects (Csikszentmihalyi, 1990, pp. 90–93), Solzhenitsyn gives evidence that poorly educated people may experience flow while performing hard physical work typical for concentration camps (e.g., cutting wood or building up a brick wall), while feeling cold and hungry.

The processes of achieving a desired result are reported, in the optimal experience context, to be much more pleasing and self-rewarding than the result itself, when and if it is gained (Csikszentmihalyi, 1990, 2000/1975). That enjoyment is associated with the process of goal achievement can lead to the conclusion that repetitions – often, lifelong replications – of these goal-seeking processes, consisting of a special mixture of physical and mental actions, are being expected and welcomed. The feelings of flow, or microflow (Csikszentmihalyi, 2000/1975, p. 141), are not restricted to entirely creative sorts of activities, like composing musical pieces or going into favorite exercises: the optimal experience is reported accompanying a lot of less extraordinary activities, such as during daily routines. Thus, flow might neighbor almost every sort of behavior people are genuinely and deeply involved in.

When a process is self-rewarding and its result might be viewed as irrelevant, one is inclined to label such an activity as intrinsically motivated. In fact, the two major classes of motivations should be differentiated: the extrinsic ones depend on bonuses – usually monetary rewards, attractive sex partners, valuable gifts, and all other sorts of a positive feedback; the intrinsic ones depend on particular human beings' interests and pleasures, when tasks and trials are taken for their own sake. The former type of motivation was often overestimated, and reciprocally, the latter was often underestimated. Now and then, some industrial and social practitioners spend huge financial resources and give exceptionally high rewards to their subordinates, managers, or voters in the attempt to achieve their goals. When they lose, they often come to know that their competitors have spent much less resources but have been lucky to gain enthusiastic, that is, intrinsically motivated, low-paid, or even nonpaid supporters.

Within the scope of this chapter, we deal exclusively with the intrinsic motivation. Various types of such motivation are known (Csikszentmihalyi, 2000/1975; Malone & Lepper, 1987; Ryan & Deci, 2000) and used in the practice of self-regulation and education. Csikszentmihalyi and Rathunde classify intrinsically motivated actions as pleasures – "positive responses to food, sex, relaxation, and the stimulation of certain chemical substances" (Csikszentmihalyi & Rathunde, 1993, p. 58) and enjoyments that refer to the optimal experience, which we will discuss in more details.

The major difference between extrinsic and intrinsic motivation is that pleasure is a somewhat passive and relaxing feeling, while enjoyment accompanies nonstop efforts to achieve something worth being strived for. Pleasure is associated with an equilibrium: "let it be as it is," while prolongation of enjoyment means a long-term activity. Ironically, because of the possibility of getting tired, which is a likely result of being active, enjoyment might be and often is or seems to be less pleasing than pleasure itself. In the life span, however, people tend to remember – and feel proud of – mostly the active styles of behavior they used to practice and the concomitant enjoyments (Csikszentmihalyi, 1990). Of course, any classification in the field should not be taken for granted too rigidly. Csikszentmihalyi and Rathunde do not forget to mention that the alternatively classified motivations cannot be fully and entirely expected to substitute one another: "Pleasure and enjoyment, and indeed intrinsic and extrinsic motivation, are not mutually exclusive, and they can be present in consciousness at the same time" (Csikszentmihalyi & Rathunde, 1993, p. 58). Those who practice transcendent techniques (meditation, yoga, Zen, and the like) find fewer problems, compared with nonpracticing people, in acquiring a kind of optimal experience and enjoyment.

Flow represents one of the two most elaborated theories of intrinsic motivation, developed within the positive psychology (Seligman & Csikszentmihalyi, 2000) paradigm; the other theory was worked out and presented by Deci and Ryan (1985). In fact, the theory of an optimal, or flow, experience is not exclusively motivational. Csikszentmihalyi and his collaborators undertook serious efforts to present a flow experience in a manifold manner: as a cognitive (the starting point is the focus of attention) artifact applied to the holistic description of a personal development (Csikszentmihalyi, 1978, 2000/1975); as a major factor of the biocultural evolution and selection (Csikszentmihalyi, 1990; Massimini & Delle Fave, 2000); as a theory of creativity, good work, and development of talented adolescents (Csikszentmihalyi, 1996; Csikszentmihalyi, Rathunde, & Whalen, 1993; Gardner, Csikszentmihalyi, & Damon, 2001); as a developmental psychology theory (Csikszentmihalyi, 1990; Csikszentmihalyi & Larson, 1984); as a basis for the psychological rehabilitation practice (Delle Fave & Massimini, 2004, 2005); and as a high-level methodological construct applicable within the field of psychology, as well as outside this field (Csikszentmihalyi, 1990, 1993, 2004). In this chapter, despite the variety of interpretations, a flow experience is discussed as a motivational paradigm.

Theoretically and empirically, Csikszentmihalyi (1990, 2000/1975 and elsewhere) selected the following major characteristics of flow: clear and distinct objectives; temporary loss of self-consciousness; distorted sense of time; actions merging with awareness; immediate feedback; high concentration on the task; high level of control over it; balance (precise matching) between the available skills and the task challenges; lastly, experiences bring full satisfaction and are worth doing for their own sake. The importance of the latter point is marked by the special term coined from Greek: *autotelic* (self + goal), which means that the only goal of doing something is just the act of doing it, regardless of whether external rewards will follow. One may add that doing it brings enjoyment, unlike most of the activities that are exotelic: the meaning of doing them is not enjoyment but pursuing some other objectives with external rewards. The majority of human beings' actions are extrinsically motivated, and processes of goal setting result in a well-established and well-stimulated hierarchy of the goals to be achieved.

According to the standpoint and argumentation presented by Csikszentmihalyi (1990 and elsewhere), a lifestyle that includes a limited number of the exotelic types of activities and is not too restrictive in performance of autotelic types of behavior, has all the reasons to be named among the best ways to feel happy. In a recent web research project – to be discussed in more detail next – the respondents were questioned about the real or imaginable positive effects associated with being online, and an intended causality was formulated in the following words: "Positive affects are not only highly correlated with flow symptoms but also caused by flow symptoms." A comment is nevertheless made that "further research is needed to verify this declaration" (Chen, 2006, p. 231).

## Theoretical and Practical Reasons for Psychological Studies in the Cyberspace

The originator of the "flow experience" theory, Mihaly Csikszentmihalyi, refrains from discussing the possible applications of an optimal experience within cyberspace environments, with the exception of several brief interviews, popular papers (Kubey & Csikszentmihalyi, 2002), and the following statement:

> Certain technologies become successful at least in part because they provide flow and thus motivate people to use them. A good example is the Internet . . . This technology has been adapted to all sorts of unexpected uses, and has made possible an enormous variety of unpredicted experiences. It partly accounts, for instance, for the spectacular success of the Linux open system software, where tens of thousands of amateur and professional programmers work hard to come up with new software for the sheer delight of solving a problem, and for being appreciated by respected peers. In the process, Linux has been making headway against much more formidable competitors such as Microsoft who have to pay their programmers to write software – a clear example of emergent intrinsic rewards actually trumping extrinsic rewards.        (Csikszentmihalyi, Abuhamdeh, & Nakamura, 2005)

This statement gives a psychologically adequate explanation of a well-known situation on the software market. A recent work by Luthiger and Jungwirth (2007) shows that open source programmers report fun, or enjoyment, as we have called it, to be inherent to their work, and they provide such reports significantly more often as compared with the developers of commercial software. Luthiger and Jungwirth suggest that programmers engaged in commercial software projects have a good chance, nevertheless, to get involved in projects that provide both extrinsic benefits and fun – the fun represents a characteristic closely connected with intrinsic motivation and the flow experience. The employers too should be aware of this fact because a programmer's fun is likely to increase his or her productivity (Luthiger & Jungwirth, 2007). In an earlier study of the open source programmers' motivation, the researchers report that "an interplay between extrinsic and intrinsic motivations: neither dominates or destroys the efficacy of the other" (Lakhani & Wolf, 2005, p. 19).

To the best of the author's knowledge, there are no further Csikszentmihalyi's statements in the field. Csikszentmihalyi's close follower Delle Fave recently co-authored an article in which she thoroughly discusses some actual perspectives of the optimal experience methodology in the design and use of top-level information technologies related to virtual reality environments (Gaggioli, Bassi, & Delle Fave, 2003). The variety of flow related research in cyberspace environments is certainly much broader. We can suggest three major explanations – from practical to theoretical – to support this fact.

First, the business challenge, coming primarily from the high-tech field: Numerous companies and enterprises are competing in the quality of offers and services they suggest to their consumers. Because of this reason, the expectations of gaining at least the slightest advantages by the application of well-developed psychological measures are a good reason to intensify investigations or applied work to produce certain special services with a potential to determine the optimal forms of the customers' experience. This challenge stimulates both the marketing research and applied work in the field of flow experience.

Second, the methodology of the optimal experience research matches the framework of the cyberspace studies. Indeed, computers, the Internet, and the World Wide Web provide support to the flow-related fieldwork, which is often rather laborious and time consuming when administered offline but is much less laborious and time consuming when the computer and online facilities are used. As a result, a well-planned online flow-measuring study may be effectively fulfilled within a short period of time and requires a reasonably low budget; what is no less important, it is based on hundreds of publications and teaching courses. Such studies are being administered within numerous samples, including, for example, experts and students in information technologies, as well as the users of diverse social services, that is, e-shoppers, online gamers, chatters, mobbers, web surfers, e-learners, and so on.

Third, the theoretical significance of the investigations of the optimal forms of human behavior within cyberspace environments derives from the importance of mediation and remediation for human psychic development. Because the most important psychic processes, or the higher mental functions, in Vygotsky's (1962) terminology, are mediated and internalized, their further development is dependent on the effectiveness of the mechanisms of remediation; the latter means acquiring newer and newer ways of mediation – each rests on the multitude of previously internalized sign systems. The importance of remediation processes for current psychological theory and practice is specially marked by Cole (1996). Thus, a research into the human use of the components of cyberspace, including, for example, personal meanings and connotations, step-by-step objectives, motivated actions, and optimal experience, is at the same time a study of the human psychic development (Arestova, Babanin, & Voiskounsky, 1999; Cole, 1996; Voiskounsky, 1998) and has a "futurological" quality. Many of the novel dimensions of the remediation processes will become, in due course, a common attribute of future generations.

## Characteristics of Flow as Used in Empirical Research

In this section, we discuss characteristics referring to the optimal experience. The prior set of characteristics, known from Csikszentmihalyi's works, were often empirically tested and thoroughly discussed in cyberspace environments. Although some scholars consider this set of characteristics, which were introduced and described by Csikszentmihalyi and his followers, as nonpredictive and lacking rigorous operationalizations, there are other investigators who administered surveys and semistructured interviews within the samples of the frequent cyberspace visitors. After they coded, sorted, and analyzed the narratives, they were able to confirm that the characteristics of flow described by Csikszentmihalyi were close to what the competent respondents expressed (Chen, 2006; Chen, Wigand, & Nilan, 1999; Novak, Hoffman, & Duhachek, 2003; Pace, 2004). As a result, the diverse "flow models" are based on the slightly different sets of characteristics, which are sometimes defined differently. Some additional task-dependent characteristics were suggested and validated: for example, "intention to return" (to an e-shop site; Koufaris, 2002). Several authors have discussed the variety of characteristics introduced by numerous researchers, including Csikszentmihalyi, and have presented them in table form (Finneran & Zhang, 2005; Novak & Hoffman, 1997; Siekpe, 2005).

In an influential study (Hoffman & Novak, 1996; Novak & Hoffman, 1997), a model of flow experience in cyberspace was introduced, and it included such characteristics as vividness and interactivity, which cumulatively induce the parameter of "presence," or "(tele)presence," formulated as "mediated perception of an environment" (Hoffman & Novak, 1996, p. 61). In subsequent publications (Novak, Hoffman, & Yung, 2000; Novak et al., 2003), the authors empirically validated the inclusion of some of these characteristics (for example, presence and interactivity) into the model, which they developed and later revised. The inclusion of media-specific characteristics referring to the mediated environments seems a reasonable thing to do; moreover, "presence," or a feeling such as being in a somewhat different place, possibly sharing this place with other people was not once named by respondents in interviews or surveys, among other characteristics (Chen et al., 1999; Pace, 2004; Skadberg & Kimmel, 2004).

The meanings of many terms related to the cyberspace update quickly, some connotations change, and some new ones are acquired. The term *presence* is an example of such a developing parameter with multiple meanings that keep acquiring new connotations. We can readily state it this way, because at the webpage "About Presence" (http://ispr.info) placed by the International Society for Presence Research, this term is explicated in twelve points, with several subpoints. A biocultural view on the multilayer evolution of presence in diverse environments, including the mediated ones, and particularly in cyberspace, has been introduced recently (Riva, Waterworth, & Waterworth, 2004).

The term *interactivity* is often used to distinguish new media from traditional media. Its analysis was first presented by several authors, including Rafaeli (1988). Since that time, the concept of interactivity has not once been investigated in the contexts of sociology, communication science, and psychology (Chung & Zhao, 2004; Sohn & Lee, 2005), nor discussed in the context of the flow experience in cyberspace (Chen et al., 1999; Finneran & Zhang, 2005; Liao, 2006; Nakatsu, Rauterberg, & Vorderer, 2005; Novak & Hoffman, 1997; Novak et al., 2000). The two terms, *presence* and *interactivity*, are probably the best terms to characterize the specifics of flow experienced in cyberspace environments.

Scholars often accept that flow dimensions can be more or less variable, dependent on the particular type of cyberspace-related experience human beings are engaged in. "Not all of them are needed . . . to give users the experience of Flow" (Chen, 2007, p. 32). This is a reasonable argument. To qualify an experience as optimal, one does not necessarily need every particular characteristic that has been introduced by Csikszentmihalyi or his followers. In an analytical article, it is reasonably stated: "These factors may not be the only ones that contribute to flow, but Csikszentmihalyi identifies them as the most commonly exhibited ones" (Finneran & Zhang, 2005, p. 83).

Indeed, the flow patterns inherent in cyberspace-related types of behavior may differ a lot: a sensation of flow experienced while shopping online might be described using a set of characteristics that only partly match the parameters describing flow experienced while gaming online or navigating the web. Rettie states that "while respondents recognized most of Csikszentmihalyi's dimensions, the merging of action and awareness and loss of self-consciousness were not really relevant" (Rettie, 2001, p. 111). Chen et al. (1999) also report that they faced some problems placing the parameter "actions and awareness become merged" exclusively into the "antecedents of flow" group because this parameter might have partly fallen into several groups. One can easily conclude that possible classifications in the field should not be considered entirely predictable.

It is tempting to admit that the sets of characteristics differ, taken for example less competent (in a particular type of activity) and more competent (in the same type of activity) respondents; with a change of activity, the level of personal competence for the same respondents may turn out to be the opposite, as is often the case. Taking all the arguments into consideration, there are possibly numerous sets of flow characteristics (sometimes called *dimensions*, or *parameters*), which can be informally called *flow dialects*, and these "dialects" are strongly dependent on the task specificity, personal competence in this or that task, emotional state, quality of computer or web interfaces, particular software applications, type of prior instruction, and many other parameters that have not yet become obvious.

One of the most useful of Csikszentmihalyi's findings is that flow may be expected and indeed happens when and if the available skills balance – or, better, tightly match – the task challenges a person chooses in his or her activity, provided of course that both the challenges and the tasks are high enough and close to the person's utmost. Flow is placed at the cutting edge of the person's skills, and it is a moving target. An increase of the acquired skills leads to an appropriate extension of the challenges, to save the precise matching – and the concomitant enjoyment, too. Reciprocally, any choice of the greater challenges demands an update of the available skills.

As a result, a congruence or a balance of the skills and the task challenges is very often accepted as a major antecedent of flow (Hoffman & Novak, 1996; Pearce & Howard, 2004); some authors, however, report a failure to report this ratio as a significant parameter (Skadberg & Kimmel, 2004). In these empirical studies, the participants often get confused when requested to classify the standard of the skills they possess or the level of the task challenges they choose (Chen et al., 1999; Shin, 2006). The more vaguely the applied activity (related to the use of computers and the web sources) is formulated, the greater the participants' confusion is, which is probably the reason most of the current research projects in the field refer to the specialized, that is, nonuniversal tasks performed in cyberspace.

The empirical rule that flow (and enjoyment) occurs when and if the task challenges match the skills means that there is a fine and positively estimated perspective for personal growth. Numerous studies held outside the cyberspace field have proved this is true. The mechanism of balance/matching between the task challenges and the skills is fairly easy to investigate and to check. Indeed, the researchers of the optimal experience within cyberspace environments use the tasks/challenge ratio intensely.

## Data Collection Methods in the Optimal Experience Studies Related to Cyberspace

The methods of collecting data related to the flow experience in cyberspace environments do not differ too much from the methods practiced outside cyberspace. In general, the data collection methods include mostly surveys, especially online surveys that are becoming intensely used, as well as interviews and semistructured interviews, discussions of narratives describing certain flow-related cases, open-ended questionnaires, focus groups and group discussions, subjective estimations of the frequency of occurrence of the selected parameters of the optimal forms of experience (Chen et al., 1999; Manssour, 2003; Novak et al., 2000; Pace, 2004; Pearce, Ainley, & Howard, 2005; Pilke, 2004; Rettie, 2001; Shoham, 2004).

The survey is usually qualified as a regular method of measuring the optimal forms of experience. Surveys are administered within particular populations, for example, the subscribers to a special group of online services, visitors of some website(s), learners of a certain software product (Ghani & Deshpande, 1994; Harvey, Loomis, & Bell, 1998; Heidman & Sharafi, 2004; Konradt, Filip, & Hoffmann, 2003; Koufaris, 2002; Skadberg & Kimmel, 2004; Trevino & Webster, 1992; Webster, Trevino, & Ryan, 1993). This style of surveying can be called *retrospective* because it refers to a habitual behavior, related to the cyberspace, to a favorite type of web source, or to a known software product (Huang, 2006; Korzaan, 2003; Montgomery, Sharafi, & Heidman, 2004; Sharafi, Heidman, & Montgomery, 2006). Most often, the questionnaires measuring flow and nonflow parameters are administered in parallel to separate the flow characteristics from the more traditional behavior patterns.

The Experience Sampling Method (ESM) is believed to be the most accurate method of collecting data in naturalistic environments. Since the ESM has been introduced and validated (Csikszentmihalyi & Larson, 1987), it has been widely used within the positive psychology studies, as well as outside of this field, such as in studies of well-being, stress, time management, coping, and emotional experience. Originally, the ESM procedure involved a pager beeping at randomly selected moments several times a day, often over several weeks: Each time the signal is an invitation to fill in an experience sampling sheet. One advantage of this methodology is that the participant self-reports the characteristics of the actual experience. Thus, it is a dynamic instrument, adapted for administering in natural settings: The self-reports are collected exactly at the moments when the daily experiences take place or just shortly after that. The ESM procedure is not limited to the use of the telephone or e-mail pagers: The preprogrammed electronic wristwatches, randomly sent out Short Message Service (SMS) messages, palm-top computers, PDAs, as well as diverse commercial, or open source, software packages, including the programs that dynamically adapt to the previously provided responses, are widely used in the field (Barrett & Barrett, 2001; Conner Christensen, Feldman Barrett, Bliss-Moreau, Lebo, & Kaschub, 2003; Scollon, Diener, Oishi, & Biswas-Diener, 2005).

The newest step in the application of the ESM methodology in cyberspace environments has been undertaken by Hsiang Chen, who started to survey online participants in 1990s (Chen et al., 1999) and recently reported (Chen, 2006) that he has constructed, tested, and applied the web version, which substitutes the random-time beeper and the ESM booklet to fill in. Specifically, at random moments, a window will pop up at the upper left side of a participant's computer screen, activating the questionnaire items. Immediately after the questionnaire is filled in, the record is sent to the researcher's remote database (Chen, 2006). To acquire a reasonable amount (i.e., no less than three sampling forms filled in) of the flow-related characteristics pertaining to a particular person while he or she stays online, the random-time interval, Chen (2006) reports, is scheduled during a short period, only five to ten minutes, so that even the short-term cyberspace visitors can get at least three signals and thus three runs of the sampling form to fill in. This forethought seems to be reasonable: Some respondents, for example, elementary school students, report extremely short periodic occurrences of flow during the game sessions (Inal & Cagiltay, 2007). As a result, "the on-line ESM tool proved to be reliable and valid" (Chen, 2006, p. 232). This methodology will foster greater cyberspace-related investigations of the optimal experience.

Although the sets of characteristics and the content of the questions related to the optimal forms of experience will vary only slightly, the procedural component of the studies, including the usage of the hardware and software pieces, is likely to be the subject of methodological innovations in the coming years.

## Flow in Diverse Cyberspace-Related Activities

The beginning of the optimal experience research in the cyberspace field dates back to the time when the term *cyberspace* had not yet been fully accepted in the academic glossary. The participants in the earliest studies were competent in the "human-computer interaction," "computer-mediated communication," or "computerized exploratory behavior" (Ghani & Deshpande, 1994; Trevino & Webster, 1992; Webster et al., 1993), which is rather general. Participants were also proficient in the use of some particular types of the information technologies, for example, "online gaming," or "marketing" (Hoffman & Novak, 1996; McKenna & Lee, 1995). Both directions of studies are present in the current publications: the former ("activities involving information technology," "Internet/Web use," or "computer-mediated environment") in the lesser proportion (Finneran & Zhang, 2005; Montgomery et al., 2004; Pace, 2004; Rettie, 2001; Sharafi et al., 2006; Siekpe, 2005) and the latter in the greater proportion – these works are briefly characterized in this section.

A large and growing body of studies is on the online consumer and marketing applications of the optimal experience theory and practice. Researchers are doing their best to find out certain dependencies between the flow characteristics, the behavioral and marketing parameters, and indicators of the computer/web-based skills to develop a hierarchy of the first-order and the higher-order dimensions in the field (Hoffman & Novak, 1996; Huang, 2006; Korzaan, 2003; Koufaris, 2002; Rettie, 2001; Siekpe, 2005; Smith &

Sivakumar, 2004). This direction of research and practice seems to be accelerating, especially with the practice of e-shopping on the rise. The currently available experience leads to useful recommendations aimed at avoiding some possibly restrictive decisions as well as lessening the negative influences on the visitors and customers of the existing e-shops and at perfecting the design and the usability of the would-be e-marketing sites (Pace, 2004; Rettie, 2001; Siekpe, 2005).

The educational applications of the optimal experience methodology have always been thoroughly investigated, and the cyberspace field is not an exception (Chan & Ahem, 1999; Konradt & Sulz, 2001; Konradt et al., 2003; Pearce et al., 2005; Shin, 2006). A flow experience is a significant predictor of the learners' satisfaction with the teaching courses (Shin, 2006). But the positive effects of the flow experience on a learner's task, Pearce and Howard (2004) state, need to be differentiated from the possibly interfering effects originating in the use of cyberspace-related artifacts that compete for a learner's attention (such as webpages, simulation models, etc.). A flow experience in distance education and in individuation of the learning and teaching practice is of growing interest for researchers. For example, Liao (2006) investigated the possible effect of the types of interactions of the distance learners (i.e., learner-learner, learner-instructor, and learner-interface) on their reported flow experience. O'Broin and Clarke (2006) developed a mobile teaching assistant tool that helps plan learning sessions for individual students: when one or more conditions of flow are absent, the tool can suggest modifications to the session so that the conditions may once again be present. More and more advanced applications of the optimal experience theory in the educational practice of the hypermedia use can be expected to follow (Konradt & Sulz, 2001; Konradt et al., 2003).

The practice of playing computer, video, and online games is also a growing area of flow-related investigations (Chen, 2007; Chen & Park, 2005; Chiou & Wan, 2006; Choi & Kim, 2004; Chou & Ting, 2003; Hsu & Lu, 2004; Inal & Cagiltay, 2007; Jegers, 2006; Kim, Oh, & Lee, 2005; McKenna & Lee, 1995; Sweetser & Wyeth, 2005; Voiskounsky, Mitina, & Avetisova, 2004, 2005; Wan & Chiou, 2006). Characteristics of flow have been found usefully realized in a gaming environment for the computer-learning courses adapted for the students of a primary and secondary school (Andersen & Witfelt, 2005). Such parameters as a design for a game, including well-organized feedback, and the appropriateness of the gamers' goals have been found to be important for the occurrence of flow (Choi & Kim, 2004). A kind of enjoyment related to a flow experience is introduced to explain that certain text-only games have remained attractive for players over several decades (Voiskounsky et al., 2004; Voiskounsky et al., 2005). Flow is one of the reliable predictors of the players' acceptance of a new online game (Hsu & Lu, 2004); Jenova Chen (2007) proposes an adaptive strategy of a game design, which would let diverse players experience flow in their own personal way and thus enjoy the game. Many studies involve multiuser games such as MMORPGs (Massively Multiplayer Online Role-Playing Games) and MUDs (Multi User Dungeons): a flow experience is found to correlate inherently with the social interactions taking place within the playing sessions (Chen & Park, 2005; Kim et al., 2005; McKenna & Lee, 1995; Voiskounsky et al., 2004; Voiskounsky et al., 2005). Sweetser and Wyeth (2005) and Jegers (2006) introduce a GameFlow. This model of computer gaming is presumably based on the characteristics of flow and includes such constructs as "social interaction" and "immersion" – the latter is an advanced version of the abovementioned parameter "presence." Wan and Chiou (2007) find the flow theory useful for advanced studies, to be carried out in the future, of the MMORPG gamers' intrinsic and extrinsic motivation. In general, it would not be incorrect to state that the flow experience is essential for the immersive style of playing and that the flow-related approach to the study of the gamers' behavior has proved to be important and fruitful.

The investigations of the optimal experience in the mediated forms of communication and interaction in the cyberspace are not numerous. Few studies refer to the practice of chatting, journalistic work, and web-media enjoyment (Luna, Peracchio, & de Juan, 2002; Manssour, 2003; Nakatsu et al., 2005; Sherry, 2004; Shoham, 2004). Scholars' lack of interest in this area has no obvious reason, especially taking into account that the interactive services are the earliest in the cyberspace (e.g., Fido, e-mail, or Usenet) and are developing intensely (e.g., blogging, instant messaging, Internet telephony, or webcasting). Moreover, enjoyment is a frequent companion feeling to the processes of the media consuming, or mediated, interaction; it is well known that flow is intimately connected to enjoyment (Sherry, 2004). The problem is that the enjoyment felt while consuming media is often passive and addictive; thus, it needs to be distinguished from the optimal forms of experience (Kubey & Csikszentmihalyi, 2002). "TV watching . . . leads to the flow condition very rarely" (Csikszentmihalyi, 1990, p. 83). There are relatively numerous studies analyzing – in the context of the flow experience – the patterns of the mediated social interactions between the online gamers. These works may be thought of as a counterpoint to the shortage of studies referring to the flow experienced while interacting in the cyberspace.

The publications on the flow experience pertinent to an illicit use of the information technologies, and in particular to hacking (taken, probably not quite correctly, as a generic term combining cracking, carding, phreaking, dissemination of viruses and trojans, and sometimes spamming or phishing), are not numerous. Although various computer security issues are nowadays universally believed to be critically important, the valuable theoretical classifications (Beveren, 2001) or empirical studies (Lakhani & Wolf, 2005; Voiskounsky, Babaeva, & Smyslova, 2000; Voiskounsky & Smyslova, 2003a, 2003b) in the field are rather few, possibly because of the difficulties in collecting relevant data. Computer programmers are sometimes called hackers (probably not quite correctly, without any connotation to an illegal performance), if they voluntarily develop an open source software; they report they feel enjoyment and experience flow (Luthiger & Jungwirth, 2007). It has been proposed recently (Voiskounsky, 2004, 2005, 2006) to teach adolescents the fundamentals of computer ethics in order to help the younger generations, including the talented young computer geeks/nerds (Babaeva & Voiskounsky, 2002), to overcome a temptation of joining the communities of computer criminals. This proposal rests on the existing studies of the patterns of the flow experience within the hackers' community and on the psychological theories of human moral development

Quite a humane direction for research in cyberspace is the application of the flow experience methodology for the psychological rehabilitation of the disabled and traumatized (Gaggioli et al., 2003; Miller & Reid, 2003; Reid, 2004; Riva, Castelnuovo, & Mantovani., 2006). Although the theory and methodology of such rehabilitation is still under discussion (Gaggioli et al., 2003) and far from being perfectly qualified – no full clinical records are available at the moment – the practice leads to certain valuable recommendations, especially about the ways of providing help for children with cerebral palsy using virtual reality systems (Miller & Reid, 2003; Reid, 2004). Moreover, the Virtual Reality Play Intervention Program has proved to be useful in engaging disabled children in enjoyable experiences and thus making the quality of their lives better (Miller & Reid, 2003). The virtual reality–related approach to research and rehabilitation seems to be parallel, as it has been recently stated (Gaggioli, 2005; Riva et al., 2006), to the ambient intelligence approach – within both of them the investigators combine the cognitive (referring to the resources of attention) and the emotional (referring to enjoyment) parameters of behavior into a unified conception. Some specialists are planning to use widely, among others, the psychological mechanism of "transformation of flow," which means "optimal experiences to identify and exploit new and unexpected resources and sources for development" (Riva et al., 2006, p. 240).

Finally, we should mention the perspectives of the use of the optimal experience characteristics for the development of the web usability methods, for the design and testing of interfaces (Bederson, 2004; Johnson & Wiles, 2003; Mistry & Agrawal, 2004; Pilke, 2004; Smyslova & Voiskounsky, 2005). The "perceived ease of use" of a technology is a factor that is believed to affect flow experience (Phau & Gan, 2000). Some practical steps, both technological and motivational, have been worked out, aimed to ensure the design and maintenance of a user-friendly technology, which would promote the use of various computer applications and the navigation within a particular web site and over the World Wide Web in general. "It is expected that our understanding of the flow phenomenon would guide . . . designers to be able to design a product that will lead users to flow experiences" (Finneran & Zhang, 2005, p. 83). This is an extremely competitive direction of research. Any reasonable recommendation targeted, for instance, on the perfecting of a game interface design, of a web or software usability checking procedure, promises excellent opportunity for both academics and practitioners alike.

## Optimal Experience and Psychological Addiction: the Two Opposites

The meaning of the optimal experience is that of a principally positive psychological phenomenon. Within the positive psychology school, flow is universally understood as an enjoyable experience, with a strong positive effect on lifestyle and quality of life. Contrary to that, there is a tendency in the field of cyberspace studies to associate the flow experience with addictive types of behavior and to investigate the dimensions and parameters of this prospective interconnection (Chen & Park, 2005; Chiou & Wan, 2006; Chou & Ting, 2003; Tzanetakis & Vitouch, 2002; Wan & Chiou, 2006). In this chapter, we will not discuss the nature, phenomenology, genesis, and status of cyberspace-related addictions and dependencies, also known as problematic/pathological/heavy/excessive Internet use/abuse/overuse or disorder. The publications on this theme will not be reviewed either, because in the current section we take *addictions* as a generic term, covering the majority of the possible or reported misuses of the Internet taken as a whole or of its particular services, such as online gaming, online pornography, online communication, online romance, online surfing, online gambling, online exploratory behavior, or online shopping.

An addiction is a sort of escape from personal problems and a decrease in the quality of life, which are opposite of feelings associated with positive psychological phenomena, including the flow experience. Thus, any analogy between flow and addiction is inadequate and correlating the symptoms of the optimal experience and the Internet addiction will hardly seem justified. Most often, attempts to establish such correlations refer to the parameters of the online/video/computer gaming experience. Indeed, gaming is probably the most addictive of the various cyberspace-related behaviors, partly because game developers and providers try hard to hook the devoted addicts to their newest products, using, for instance, the "principles in behavioral conditioning" (Yee, 2006, p. 70).

In their theoretical article, Chen and Park (2005) discriminate between the two close types of online games – MUDs and MMORPGs; rich in visual stimuli, the latter evolution emerged from the text-only-mode MUDs (Castronova, 2005). Chen and Park (2005) believe that MUDs (both adventurous and social) are best suited for the social interaction, while MMORPGs, which supposedly provide the gamers with more levels to match their challenges and their skills, are best suited for experiencing the flow. Though this argument sounds reasonable, it is nevertheless not true because of these two main reasons.

First, recent studies state that people play MUDs to experience flow and also to achieve, to interact, and to cognate: these factors are shared by the participants in samples of the Russian and French gamers (Voiskounsky et al., 2004; Voiskounsky, Mitina, & Avetisova, 2006a; Voiskounsky et al., 2005). Second, Bartle (2003), Castronova (2005), and others convincingly describe the full multitude of the within-game and outside-of-game channels that those adept at MMORPGs use for intensive social interactions. Thus, the discrimination that is so important for Chen and Park (2005) is not in fact strongly discriminating. When they state that the MMORPG addicts seek the flow, while the MUD addicts seek the social interaction, the former statement cannot be accepted, taking into account the abovementioned psychological inequality in the enjoyments inherent in flow and in the addictive types of behavior. The addicts may try to seek flow, but unless they recover from the addiction, they can hardly reach it.

The opposite idea, that flow causes addiction, is stated in an empirical article by Chou and Ting (2003). They provide a logically reasonable but psychologically insufficient sequence of arguments, namely, that "people who enjoy flow experience during an activity may develop a tendency to repeat the activity . . . Repetition of a particular activity may eventually develop into a tendency toward addiction. . . . Flow experience is the precondition that actually activates addiction" (Chou & Ting, 2003, p. 665). Moreover, they empirically testify to this sequence of statements. Chou and Ting (2003) have testified that the repetitive behavior, not necessarily the flow experience, may activate the addictive activity.

The replication of behaviors intimately associated with flow, often resulting in the lifelong repetitions of the selected, and necessarily enjoyable, activities, is indeed characteristic of optimal forms of experience. However, the replications and repetitions are the outer, visible actions taken apart from the inner meaning of such behaviors. The reduction of the flow experience to repetitive actions is psychologically inadequate and disagrees with the essence of positive psychology. From the biocultural perspective, the psychological meaning of a well-known tendency toward the repetitions of the enjoyable activity is totally opposite of any sort of the addictive behavior. Massimini and Delle Fave (2000) introduce the term *mimetic flow* for the activities that "turn out to be poor in complexity potential, which is an essential feature of authentic flow activities and a prerequisite for individual development. Moreover, such activities do not foster the participant's constructive integration in the culture" (p. 28). On the contrary, they foster a human being's marginalization. Examples of the mimetic flow include the intake of drugs and psychoactive substances, stealing, passive leisure activities such as watching TV, abuse of technological artifacts (cars, computers, weapons, etc.): "In most cases, there is a misinterpretation of risk behavior as challenging behavior. No connections with individual development and integration in the social context can be found in such practices" (Massimini & Delle Fave, 2000, p. 29).

Within positive psychology, to preserve the enjoyment, repetitive actions should undergo a continuous update of both skills and challenges to their highest possible (utmost) level of matching. The psychological mechanism of a mismatch between the skills and the challenges is described in the study of the specifics of the flow-related experience in hacking (Voiskounsky & Smyslova, 2003a, 2003b). Such a mismatch, when either an update of the skills does not follow an increase of the challenges or vice versa, means indeed a danger of losing the optimality of experience. As a result, a person may turn to a repetitive and possibly addictive type of behavior. But the processes of parallel, step-by-step increase of both the skills and the challenges, though not easily attained while hacking, should not raise problems while gaming: the level structure of the popular well-designed games and the abundance of the goals to pursue guarantee that the players save good and continuous chances to experience flow.

An important and theoretically valuable study (Chiou & Wan, 2006; Wan & Chiou, 2006) shows empirically that the flow experience is negatively correlated to Internet addiction. The authors' further analysis differentiates satisfactions from dissatisfactions inherent in the online gaming experience and provide well-justified evidences that in the process of gaming the addicts seek a kind of relief from their dissatisfaction. Thus, the flow experience and the addictive states have little in common, though the repetitions of certain actions do happen, but their psychological nature is entirely incompatible and dissimilar. This result, we believe, hinders further attempts to validate that the cyberspace-related addictions and the optimal forms of experience are of the same psychological background.

## Cross-Cultural Studies of Flow Experience

The optimal experience research field has traditionally included cross-cultural comparative studies. Csikszentmihalyi's and his colleagues' books very often include culture-related chapters. Useful examples are the special issue (2004) of the *Journal of Happiness Studies*, with an introductory article "The Flow Experience across Cultures" by Moneta (2004), and the special issue (2000) of the *American Psychologist*, with an introduction by Seligman and Csikszentmihalyi (2000).

The situation is different with the flow-related research in cyberspace environments. Rather little can be said about the populations of the habitual cyberspace visitors speaking languages other than English or Chinese (particular research has been done mostly in Taiwan). Some investigations have also been carried out within populations of German-speaking students (Konradt & Sulz, 2001; Konradt et al., 2003; Tzanetakis & Vitouch, 2002; Vollmeyer & Rheinberg, 2006), within Russian gamers (Voiskounsky et al., 2004; Voiskounsky et al., 2005) and hackers (Voiskounsky & Smyslova, 2003a, 2003b), within Korean online gamers (Choi & Kim, 2004), and within all the Scandinavian populations of information technologies users – the speakers of Norwegian (Heidman & Sharafi, 2004), Swedish (Montgomery at al., 2004; Sharafi et al., 2006), and Finnish (Pilke, 2004). Pioneer studies have also been carried out in Israel within the groups chatting in Hebrew (Shoham, 2004), within a population of Brazilian journalists actively using information technologies (Manssour, 2003), and within the Turkish children playing social games (Inal & Cagiltay, 2007).

The list of empirical studies made in a number of countries may sound impressive, but the problem is that none of these works is comparative and neither can be qualified as a cross-cultural study. This situation is in no way satisfactory because cyberspace is global and intercultural by its nature. One can easily remember many other cyberspace-related research areas (for example, the digital divide, the gender issues in e-shopping, the attitudes toward the information technologies, the computer anxiety, etc.) in which the intercultural comparisons are of paramount interest.

Thus, both in the field of the optimal experience studies and in the field of cyberspace studies, there is a tendency to carry out cross-cultural projects. Because of this, we stress the necessity and actuality of performing such projects in the area of the flow experience studies related to the cyberspace environments. Such studies have a good chance of becoming internationally accepted. In this section, we describe the research projects that are going along with the aforementioned tendency.

First, we should mention a comparative investigation of the flow patterns displayed while navigating through a marketing website; bilingual speakers of Spanish and English participated in the study (Luna et al., 2002). One of the researchers' goals is to create a cross-cultural model of a web-related flow experience and to trace the effect of several cultural factors (including, for example, a within-site navigation using the first or the second language verbal skills) on the attitudes toward the website and on the participants' actual cognitive schemes. Besides, some marketing parameters are of special interest, namely, the purchases from the e-shop and the intention to visit it again. This study is being done in the context of psycholinguistics and sociolinguistics and is a part of an ongoing project.

The second project will be described in more detail; it is a study carried out by the author and his collaborators Dr. Olga Mitina and Ph.D. student Anastasiya Avetisova (both are affiliated with the Psychology Department, Moscow State University). It is targeted at the culture-specific aspects of a flow experience within samples of Russian and French online gamers. The project has been initially planned as cross cultural; it consists of two empirical online studies administered under the same methodology and procedure and a comparative study. The published reports include the analysis of the Russian-speaking gamers (Voiskounsky et al., 2004; Voiskounsky et al., 2005), of the French-speaking gamers (Voiskounsky et al., 2006a), and the comparative analysis (Voiskounsky, Mitina, & Avetisova, 2006b). Since the work is published, we are not going into the details of methodology and are not discussing the full results. Instead, we disclose the reasons for carrying out this project; the results are presented in a brief form and put in a relatively new context that has not been emphasized in the publications.

The study was held within the communities of the MUD gamers – MUDs represent a text-only version of the class of online games called MMORPG. MUDs have been played continuously since 1978 (Bartle, 2003). It is a global activity; nobody knows how many nonnative speakers of English were engaged in MUDding when there were no options to use a language other than English. With years passing, various national-language scripts became available. According to the plan, the two relatively new populations, namely, the French and the Russian, of MUD players have been compared as a whole, that is, any single player had a chance to be questioned irrespective of the particular MUD-type game he or she used to play. The reasons for comparing the French and the Russian MUD gamers are as follows (Voiskounsky et al., 2006a).

First, both in Russia and in France, there are MUD servers and MUD players; the two cultures do not exhibit either prejudices or sympathies toward online gaming; that is, the proportions of these two antagonistic processes would not be called unequal for the two cultures. No prior research of flow experienced while playing MUDs is known in any of these two countries.

Second, the online speakers of French as well as the online speakers of Russian partly include the citizens of the countries other than the two metropolitan states. Besides France, the speakers of French (francophones) are also located in Canadian Quebec, in European countries neighboring France, and in French-speaking African countries. Besides Russia, speakers of Russian are also located in post-Soviet countries (including the Ukraine, the population of which is close to France), as well as in the United States, Israel, Germany, Australia, and many other countries. Since the speakers of the two languages are distributed over the globe, it is reasonable to suppose that the respective online populations of the MUD gamers are also distributed. Moreover, it is reasonable to assume that the distributions are equally uneven: rather few French-speaking Africans and rather few speakers of Russian from the post–Soviet Central Asian states are expected to be regular, frequent visitors to the MUD servers.

Third, we find some parallels in the ways the two metropolitan countries are late in acquiring the global access to the Internet: the Russians due to the totalitarian nature of the Soviet state for which the idea of a free exchange of views has always been totally alien (Voiskounsky, 2001) and the French due to the pioneer development of the videotex system Minitel, which has been used more widely than its analogs (Prestel in the United Kingdom, Bildschirmtext in Germany, CAPTAIN in Japan, etc.). With time passing, the wide penetration of the Minitel seems to be a sort of a barrier to the advance of the Internet:

"France was the first to develop a public telematic system . . . Minitel became a symbol of France," but "the French telematic system now appears outmoded." (Lemos, 1996, p. 37).

Fourth, the two online audiences seem to be comparable in the approximate number of cyberspace visitors. Because no direct statistics for the MUD players is known, we assume that the two supposedly comparable online audiences contain a supposedly comparable number of the online gamers and finally a supposedly comparable number of the MUD players. After we compared the audiences at the time when the research was held, in 2003 (Russian part) and in 2004 (French part), we estimated (Voiskounsky et al., 2006a) that the francophone audience outscored the audience of Russian speakers by approximately 10 percent. We assume that the populations of the MUD players in the two countries are comparable in approximately the same proportion.

The cross-cultural methodology included the adaptation of the prior (Russian) questionnaire of forty questions (including eight questions on demography, on longevity and frequency of playing sessions) to make the French questionnaire culturally and linguistically identical. The procedure is described elsewhere (Voiskounsky et al., 2006a). The analysis of the results included explorative and confirmatory factor analyses, comparative analysis of the questionnaires' items, and qualitative analysis of the factor models allocated to the Russian and the French samples. Because the current chapter is not a full report of the comparative study, we proceed to the description of the two resulting factor models and of the correlations between the factors and the particular questionnaires' items.

The total number of participants in the study was 347 Russian speakers Russian and 203 francophones. As we anticipated, both samples included noncitizens of Russia and France, respectively. The explorative factor analysis provided a six-factor model for the Russian-speaking sample (Voiskounsky et al., 2004; Voiskounsky et al., 2005) and a three-factor model for the francophone sample (Voiskounsky et al., 2006a). The factors can be viewed in Figure 4.1, which provides correlations between the factors and the questionnaire items (nondemographic ones) which were loosely translated into English. Both factor models include the *flow* factor. The two factor models are statistically important, the intercorrelations between the factors are reasonably high (Voiskounsky et al., 2004; Voiskounsky et al., 2006a). We proceed to a brief comparative discussion of the factor models (Voiskounsky et al., 2006b).

Six factors in the right part of the Figure 4.1 characterize the Russian-speaking sample, three factors in the left part – the francophone sample. The former includes all the factors characterizing the latter: *Flow*, *Achievement*, *Cognition*, and *Interaction*. The latter means social (user-to-user) interaction, not personal interaction between the user and the system – the distinction between the two types of interaction within the gaming environments was introduced by Choi and Kim (2004). Hence, the factor models characterizing the Russian-speaking and the francophone samples are partly similar. The factor

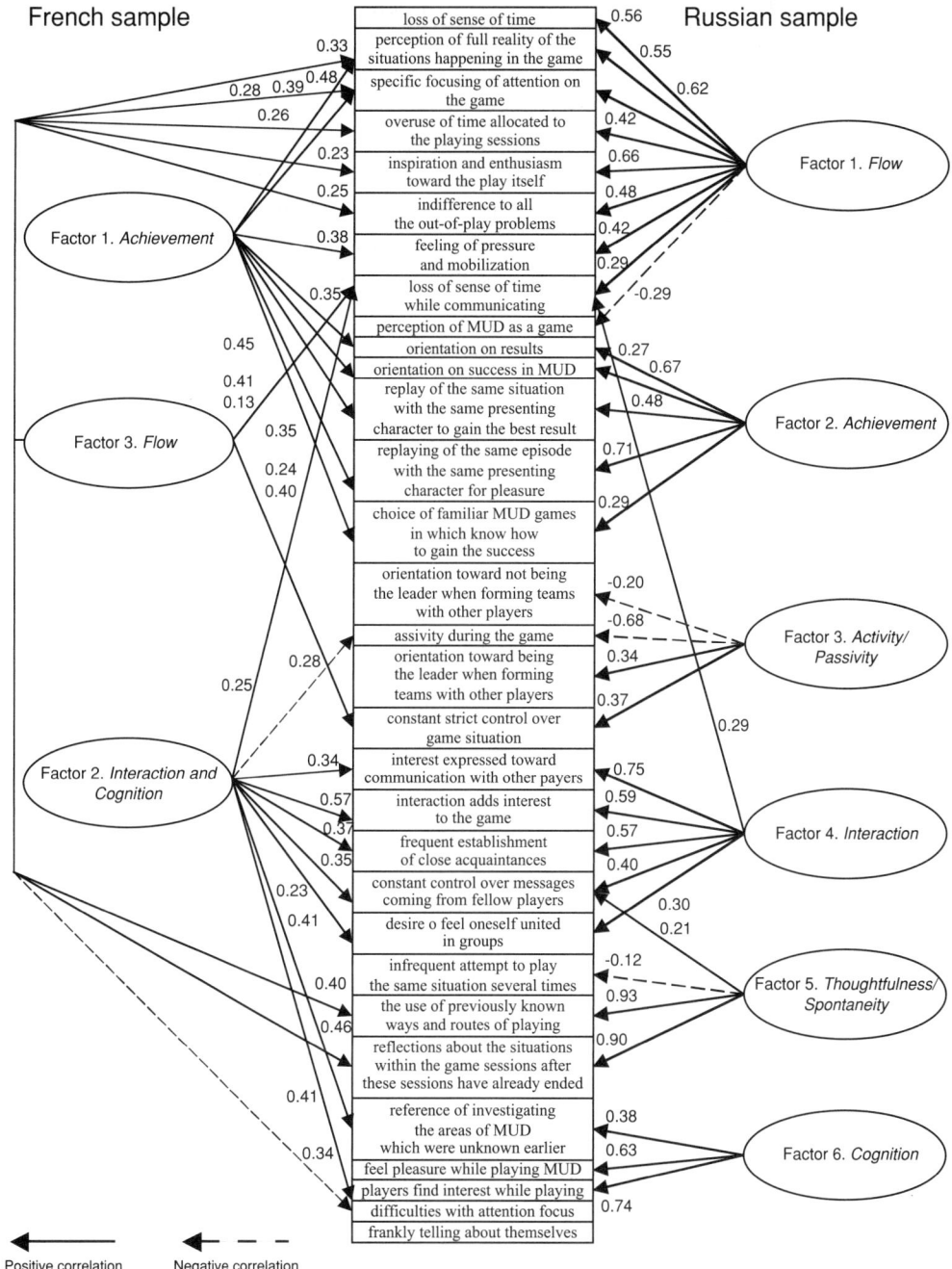

Figure 4.1. *Correlations between the factors and the questions: the Russian and the French samples.*

model characterizing the Russian-speaking, but not the Francophone sample, includes two more factors, namely, *Activity/Passivity* and *Thoughtfulness/ Spontaneity*. The factors *Interaction* and *Cognition* merge in the francophone sample, while for the speakers of Russian they represent independent factors. In a way, the factor structure characterizing the speakers of Russian is quite logical: the four factors common for the two samples and characterizing the prevalent game styles do not merge, unlike the factor structure of the francophone sample. On the other side, the latter might be called logical because in the multiplayer games *Cognition* presupposes *Interaction* in the form of social perception, that is, gaining knowledge about other fellow players; thus, the merger of the two factors can be reasonably interpreted.

The information in Figure 4.1 presents a different perspective, which is not presented in Voiskounsky et al. (2006b). Notice that the major factor for the Francophone sample, that is, *Achievement*, includes all the questionnaire items referring to the Russian-speaking sample factor *Achievement* plus several items referring to the *Flow* factor (partly common to the Russian-speaking and the francophone samples). Thus, for the francophones, *Achievement* includes certain elements of *Flow*: "focused attention," "pressure and mobilization," and "perception of reality of the game situations" (the latter is close to "presence") – all rather heavily loaded. In other words, the desire for *Achievement*, characteristic for the francophone sample, includes some standard characteristics of *Flow*. The *Achievement* for the Russian-speaking sample does not include any characteristics alien to this desire. For the speakers of Russian *Achievement* is not the first factor, unlike the francophones.

To conclude, the flow experience is indeed an important component of online multiplayer games, either as the major factor (the Russian-speaking sample) or as one of the factors expanded by several characteristics of flow participating in the structure of the major factor (as in the francophone sample). This outcome seems to be important in the cross-cultural context. Of course, the qualitative comparison of the factor models is not the final point in interpretation and discussion. New cultural and intercultural studies as well as further analysis of the empirical results are needed to advance our knowledge of the role of a flow experience in gaming behavior and in cyberspace-related behavior in general. We believe the importance of cross-cultural investigations in the field will be constantly increasing, and the projects described in this section give certain grounds for an optimistic prognosis.

## Conclusion

The optimal experience studies form a small sector in the full scope of research of the patterns of human behavior in cyberspace environments. These studies rely on a well-developed flow experience theory and methodology.

Cyberspace-related studies, reciprocally, enrich the optimal experience field providing some worthwhile characteristics pertinent to flow, for example, "presence." No less important, cyberspace presents new directions for scholarly and applied work within the optimal experience paradigm. With time and with further influential investigations, this sector has a good chance to occupy a special position within the flexible, not yet ossified, area of cyberspace psychology. The advanced studies in the field are of great theoretical and practical importance.

The role of various cyberspace environments is perhaps the most significant in the procedural component of flow research. The flow studies have never depended on specific hardware units: pagers, programmable wristwatches, and personal computers are universal, and as such provide excellent options to realize this experience sampling methodology. With progress in information technologies, a hardware hurdle is likely to disappear gradually from the procedural design of the optimal experience studies. Over time, a software component will be its substitute, and data collecting will be performed online more often, that is, in cyberspace. Procedural innovations are major contributions of cyberspace-related technologies to the optimal experience paradigm.

The diversity of the flow studies within cyberspace environments embraces human-computer interaction and computer-mediated communication in problem-specific areas such as flow experiences in e-shopping, business applications of web sources and web marketing, online instruction, e-learning and distance education, computer/video/online playing and online entertainment, mediated interactions and online media consuming, web design and web usability, online navigation and web exploratory behavior, computer security and illicit online behavior, psychological rehabilitation supported by the use of the virtual reality systems, and more specified areas. Among others, there is a tendency to correlate the parameters of flow and addiction, arguing that both promote repetitive actions. This tendency is theoretically false: flow is positive, means enjoyment, and signifies an utmost behavior, and addiction means escape from the personal problems and asocial marginalization and signifies a totally negative psychological condition. Thus, flow and addiction are opposites, and current empirical studies prove this conclusion.

Both the optimal experience field and the cyberspace field are entirely global activities, and there are many culture-related research projects in both of these fields. But the area of optimal experience studies in the cyberspace environments is almost an exception. Serious efforts are needed to change this situation, and the two ongoing cross-cultural projects described in this chapter (namely, flow experienced by bilinguals while they navigate through a marketing website, and the role of flow in the playing activity of the French and Russian gamers) provide potential for optimism. Further studies are expected in all the aforementioned directions, and particularly in the intercultural direction.

## Acknowledgments

Research was supported by Russian Foundations for Humanities, project 06-06-00342a. The author thanks Professor Sheizaf Rafaeli for helpful comments on an earlier version of this chapter, and Professor Diane Halpern and Mr. Patrick Williams for friendly support in editing the text.

### References

Andersen, K., & Witfelt, C. (2005). Educational design: Bridging the gap between computer-based learning and experimental learning environments. *International Journal of Continuing Engineering Education and Life-long Learning, 15*, 5–18.

Arestova, O. N., Babanin, L. N., & Voiskounsky, A. E. (1999). Psychological research of computer-mediated communication in Russia. *Behaviour & Information Technology, 18*, 141–147.

Babaeva, J. D., & Voiskounsky, A. E. (2002). IT-giftedness in children and adolescents. *Educational Technology & Society, 5*, 154–162. Retrieved September 4, 2002, from http://ifets.ieee.org/periodical/vol_1_2002/babaeva.pdf.

Barrett, L. F., & Barrett, D. J. (2001). An introduction to computerized experience sampling in psychology. *Social Science Computer Review, 19*, 175–185.

Bartle, R. (2003). *Designing virtual worlds*. Indianapolis, IN: New Riders Publishing.

Bederson, B. B. (2004). Interfaces for staying in the flow. *Ubiquity*, 5(27). Retrieved July 16, 2006, from http://www.acm.org/ubiquity/views/v5i27_bederson.html.

Beveren, J. V. (2001). A conceptual model for hacker development and motivations. *Journal of E-Business*, 1.2. Retrieved April 2, 2002, from http://www.ecob.iup.edu/jeb/December2001-issue/Beveren%20article2.pdf.

Castronova, E. (2005). *Synthetic worlds. The business and culture of online games*. Chicago: University of Chicago Press.

Chan, T. S., & Ahem, T. C. (1999). Targeting motivation – adapting flow theory to instructional design. *Journal of Educational Computing Research, 21*, 151–163.

Chen, H. (2006). Flow on the net – detecting web users' positive affects and their flow states. *Computers in Human Behavior, 22*, 221–233.

Chen, H., Wigand, R. T., & Nilan, M. S. (1999). Optimal experience of web activities. *Computers in Human Behavior, 15*, 585–608.

Chen, J. (2007). Flow in games (and everything else). *Communications of the ACM, 50*(4), 31–34.

Chen, J. V., & Park, Y. (2005). The difference of addiction causes between massive multiplayer online game and multi user domain. *International Review of Information Ethics, 4*(12), 53–60.

Chiou, W.-B., & Wan, C.-S. (2006). A further investigation of the motives of online games addiction. Paper presented at the National Educational Computing Conference (San Diego, July 5–7, 2006). Retrieved August 23, 2006, from http://center.uoregon.edu/ISTE/uploads/NECC2006/KEY_12738686/Chiou_NECC06ChiouWenBin_RP.pdf.

Choi, D., & Kim, J. (2004). Why people continue to play online games: In search of critical design factors to increase customer loyalty to online contents. *CyberPsychology & Behavior, 7*, 11–24.

Chou, T.-J., & Ting, C.-C. (2003). The role of flow experience in cyber-game addiction. *CyberPsychology & Behavior, 6*, 663–675.

Chung, H., & Zhao, X. (2004). Effects of perceived interactivity on web site preference and memory: Role of personal motivation. *Journal of Computer-Mediated Communication, 10*(1). Retrieved May 10, 2007, from http://jcmc.indiana.edu/vol10/issue1/chung.html.

Cole, M. (1996). *Cultural psychology: A once and future discipline*. Cambridge, MA: Harvard University Press.

Conner Christensen, T., Feldman Barrett, L., Bliss-Moreau, E., Lebo, K., & Kaschub, C. (2003). A practical guide to experience-sampling procedures. *Journal of Happiness Studies, 4*, 53–78.

Csikszentmihalyi, M. (1978). Attention and the holistic approach to behavior. In K. S. Pope, & J. L. Singer (Eds.), *The stream of consciousness* (pp. 335–359). New York: Plenum Press.

Csikszentmihalyi, M. (1990). *Flow: The psychology of optimal experience*. New York: Harper and Row.

Csikszentmihalyi, M. (1993). *The evolving self: A psychology for the third millennium*. New York: HarperCollins.

Csikszentmihalyi, M. (1996). *Creativity: Flow and the psychology of discovery and invention*. New York: HarperPerennial.

Csikszentmihalyi, M. (2000/1975). *Beyond boredom and anxiety: Experiencing flow in work and play*. San Francisco, CA: Jossey-Bass.

Csikszentmihalyi, M. (2004). Materialism and the evolution of consciousness. In T. Kasser & A. D. Kanner (Eds.), *Psychology and consumer culture: The struggle for a good life in a materialistic world* (pp. 91–106). Washington, DC: American Psychological Association.

Csikszentmihalyi, M., Abuhamdeh, S., & Nakamura, J. (2005). Flow. In A. Elliot & C. S. Dweck (Eds.), *Handbook of competence and motivation* (pp. 598–608). New York: Guilford Press.

Csikszentmihalyi, M., & Larson, R. (1984). *Being adolescent: Conflict and growth in the teenage years*. New York: Basic Books.

Csikszentmihalyi, M., & Larson, R. (1987). Validity and reliability of the Experience Sampling Method. *Journal of Nervous and Mental Disease, 175*, 526–536.

Csikszentmihalyi, M., & Rathunde, K. (1993). The measurement of flow in everyday life: Toward a theory of emergent motivation. In *Nebraska Symposium on Motivation: Vol 40. Developmental perspectives on motivation* (pp. 57–97). Lincoln: University of Nebraska Press.

Csikszentmihalyi, M., Rathunde, K. R., & Whalen, S. (1993). *Talented teenagers: The roots of success and failure*. New York: Cambridge University Press.

Deci, E., & Ryan, R. (1985). *Intrinsic motivation and self-determination in human behavior*. New York: Plenum Press.

Delle Fave, A., & Massimini, F. (2004). Bringing subjectivity into focus: Optimal experiences, life themes, and person-centered rehabilitation. In P. A. Linley & S. Joseph (Eds.), *Positive psychology in practice* (pp. 581–597). Hoboken, NJ: Wiley & Sons.

Delle Fave, A., & Massimini, F. (2005). The relevance of subjective well-being to social politics: Optimal experience and tailored intervention. In F. A. Huppert, N. Baylis, & B. Keverne (Eds.), *The Science of well-being* (pp. 379–402). New York: Oxford University Press.

Finneran, C. M., & Zhang, P. (2005). Flow in computer-mediated environments: Promises and challenges. *Communications of the Association for Information Systems, 15*, 82–101.

Gaggioli, A. (2005). Optimal experience in ambient intelligence. In G. Riva, F. Vatalaro, F. Davide, & M. Alcaniz (Eds.), *Ambient intelligence* (pp. 35–43). Amsterdam, The Netherlands: IOS Press.

Gaggioli, A., Bassi, M., & Delle Fave, A. (2003). Quality of experience in virtual environments. In G. Riva, F. Davide, & W. A. IJsselsteijn (Eds.), *Being there: Concepts, effects and measurement of user presence in synthetic environments* (pp. 122–135). Amsterdam, The Netherlands: IOS Press.

Gardner, H., Csikszentmihalyi, M., & Damon, W. (2001). *Good work: When excellence and ethics meet.* New York: Basic Books.

Ghani, J. A., & Deshpande, S. P. (1994). Task characteristics and the experience of optimal flow in human-computer interaction. *Journal of Psychology, 128*, 381–391.

Harvey, M., Loomis, R. J., & Bell, P. A. (1998). The influence of museum exhibit design on immersion and psychological flow. *Environment and Behavior, 30*, 601–627.

Heidman, L., & Sharafi, P. (2004). Early use of Internet-based educational resources: Effects on students' engagement modes and flow experience. *Behaviour & Information Technology, 23*, 137–146.

Hoffman, D. L., & Novak, T. P. (1996). Marketing in hypermedia computer-mediated environments: Conceptual foundations. *Journal of Marketing, 60*(3), 50–68.

Hsu, C., & Lu, H. (2004). Why do people play on-line games? An extended TAM with social influences and flow experience. *Information and Management, 41*, 853–868.

Huang, M.-H. (2006). Flow, enduring, and situational involvement in the web environment: A tripartite second-order examination. *Psychology and Marketing, 23*, 383–411.

Inal, Y., & Cagiltay, K. (2007). Flow experiences of children in an interactive social game environment. *British Journal of Educational Technology, 38*, 455–464.

Jegers, K. (2006). Pervasive GameFlow: Understanding player enjoyment in pervasive gaming. In Th. Strang, V. Cahill, & A. Quigley (Eds.), *Pervasive 2006 Workshop Proc. Pervasive 2006.* Retrieved July 16, 2006, from http://www.ipsi.fraunhofer.de/ambiente/pergames2006/final/PG_Jegers_GameFlow.pdf.

Johnson, D., & Wiles, J. (2003). Effective affective user interface design in games. *Ergonomics, 46*, 1332–1345.

Kim, Y.-Y., Oh, S., & Lee, H. (2005). What makes people experience flow? Social characteristics of online games. *International Journal of Advanced Media and Communication, 1*, 76–92.

Konradt, U., Filip, R., & Hoffmann, S. (2003). Flow experience and positive affect during hypermedia learning. *British Journal of Educational Technology, 34*, 309–327.

Konradt, U., & Sulz, K. (2001). The experience of flow interacting with a hypermedia learning environment. *Journal of Educational Multimedia and Hypermedia, 10*, 69–84.

Korzaan, M. (2003). Going with the flow: Predicting online purchase intentions. *Journal of Computer Information Systems, 43*(4), 25–31.

Koufaris, M. (2002). Applying the technology acceptance model and flow theory to online consumer behavior. *Information Systems Research, 13*, 205–223.

Kubey, R., & Csikszentmihalyi, M. (2002). Television addiction is no mere metaphor. *Scientific American, 286*, 74–80.

Lakhani, K. R., & Wolf, R. G. (2005). Why hackers do what they do. Understanding motivation and effort in free/open source software projects. In J. Feller, B. Fitzgerald, S. A. Hissam, & K. R. Lakhani (Eds.), *Perspectives on free and open source software* (pp. 3–22). Cambridge, MA: MIT Press.

Lemos, A. (1996). The labyrinth of Minitel. In R. Shields (Ed.), *Cultures of Internet: Virtual spaces, real histories, living bodies* (pp. 33–48). London: Sage.

Liao, L.-F. (2006). A flow theory perspective on learner motivation and behavior in distance education. *Distance Education, 27*, 45–62.

Luna, D., Peracchio, L. A., & de Juan, M. D. (2002). Cross-cultural and cognitive aspects of web site navigation. *Journal of the Academy of Marketing Science, 30*, 397–410.

Luthiger, B., & Jungwirth, C. (2007). Pervasive fun. *First Monday, 12*(1). Retrieved May 21, 2007, from http://firstmonday.org/issues/issue12_1/luthiger/index. html.

Malone, T., & Lepper, M. (1987). Making learning fun: A taxonomy of intrinsic motivation for learning. In R. E. Snow & M. J. Farr (Eds.), *Aptitude learning and instruction. Vol. 3. Conative and affective process analysis* (pp. 111–140). Hillsdale, NJ: Lawrence Erlbaum.

Manssour, A. B. B. (2003). Flow in journalistic telework. *CyberPsychology & Behavior, 6*, 31–39.

Massimini, F., & Delle Fave, A. (2000). Individual development in a bio-cultural perspective. *American Psychologist, 55*, 24–33.

McKenna, K., & Lee, S. (1995). *A love affair with MUDs: Flow and social interaction in Multi-User Dungeons.* Retrieved October 2, 2002, from http://www. fragment.nl/mirror/various/McKenna_et_al.nd.A_love_affair_with_muds.html.

Miller, S., & Reid, D. (2003). Doing play: Competency, control, and expression. *CyberPsychology & Behavior, 6*, 623–632.

Mistry, P., & Agrawal, G. (2004). Functional metaphoric approach to be "in the flow" with computer interfaces. *Indian Human Computer Interaction (IHCI) Proc.* Retrieved March 3, 2006, from http://web.media.mit.edu/~pranav/research/stayingintheflow/functional-metaphoric-approach.pdf.

Moneta, J. B. (2004). The flow experience across cultures. *Journal of Happiness Studies, 5*, 115–121.

Montgomery, H., Sharafi, P., & Heidman, L. R. (2004). Engagement in activities involving information technology: Dimensions, modes, and flow. *Human Factors, 46*, 334–348.

Nakatsu, R., Rauterberg, M., & Vorderer, P. (2005). A new framework for entertainment computing: From passive to active experience. In F. Kishino, Y. Kitamura,

H. Kato, & N. Nagata (Eds.), *Entertainment Computing – ICEC 2005. Fourth International Conference on Entertainment Computing. Lecture Notes in Computer Science*, 3711, 1–12. Retrieved May 30, 2007, from http://www.idemployee.id.tue.nl/g.w.m.rauterberg/publications/ICEC2005(1)paper.pdf.

Novak, T. P., & Hoffman, D. L. (1997). *Measuring the flow experience among web users.* Retrieved April 2, 2006, from http://sloan.ucr.edu/blog/uploads/papers/Measuring%20the%20Flow%20Experience%20Among%20Web%20Users%20%5BHoffman,%20Novak%20-%20July%201997%5D.pdf.

Novak, T. P., Hoffman, D. L., & Duhachek, A. (2003). The influence of goal-directed and experiential activities on online flow experiences. *Journal of Consumer Psychology, 13*, 3–16.

Novak, T. P., Hoffman, D. L., & Yung, Y.-F. (2000). Measuring the customer experience in online environments: A structural modeling approach. *Marketing Science, 19*, 22–42.

O'Broin, D., & Clarke, S. (2006). *INKA: Using flow to enhance the mobile learning experience.* Retrieved August 24, 2006, from http://www.cs.tcd.ie/publications/tech-reports/reports.06/TCD-CS-2006-42.pdf.

Pace, S. (2004). A grounded theory of the flow experiences of web users. *International Journal of Human-Computer Studies, 60*, 327–363.

Pearce, J. M., Ainley, M., & Howard, S. (2005). The ebb and flow of online learning. *Computers in Human Behavior, 21*, 745–771.

Pearce, J. M., & Howard, S. (2004). Designing for flow in a complex activity. *Lecture Notes in Computer Science, 3101*, 349–358.

Phau, I., & Gan, J. S. (2000). Effects of technological and individual characteristics on flow experience. An Agenda of Hypotheses. In S. Chetty, & B. Collins (Eds.), *Visionary marketing for the 21st century: Facing the challenge. Proc., ANZMAC 2000 Conference* (pp. 981–984). Retrieved August 23, 2006, from http://smib.vuw.ac.nz:8081/www/ANZMAC2000/CDsite/papers/p/Phau1.pdf.

Pilke, E. M. (2004). Flow experiences in information technology use. *International Journal of Human-Computer Studies, 61*, 347–357.

Rafaeli, S. (1988). Interactivity: From new media to communication. In R. P. Hawkins, J. M. Wiemann, & S. Pingree (Eds.), *Sage annual review of communication research: Advancing communication science. Vol. 16* (pp. 110–134). Beverly Hills, CA: Sage.

Reid, D. (2004). A model of playfulness and flow in virtual reality interactions. *Presence: Teleoperators & Virtual Environments, 13*, 451–462.

Rettie, R. (2001). An exploration of flow during Internet use. *Internet Research: Electronic Networking Applications and Policy, 11*(2), 103–113.

Riva, G., Castelnuovo, G., & Mantovani, F. (2006). Transformation of flow in rehabilitation: The role of advanced communication technologies. *Behavior Research Methods, 38*, 237–244.

Riva, G., Waterworth, J. A., & Waterworth, E. L. (2004). The layers of presence: A bio-cultural approach to understanding presence in natural and mediated environments. *CyberPsychology & Behavior, 7*, 402–416.

Ryan, R. M., & Deci, E. L. (2000). Self-determination theory and the facilitation of intrinsic motivation, social development, and well-being. *American Psychologist, 55*, 68–78.

Scollon, C. N., Diener, E., Oishi, S., & Biswas-Diener, R. (2005). An experience sampling and cross-cultural investigation of the relation between pleasant and unpleasant affect. *Cognition and Emotion, 19*, 27–52.

Seligman, M. E. P., & Csikszentmihalyi, M. (2000). Positive psychology: An introduction. *American Psychologist, 55*, 5–14.

Sharafi, P., Heidman, L., & Montgomery, H. (2006). Using information technology: Engagement modes, flow experience, and personality orientations. *Computers in Human Behavior, 22*, 899–916.

Sherry, J. L. (2004). Flow and media enjoyment. *Communication Theory, 14*, 328–347.

Shin, N. (2006). Online learner's "flow" experience: An empirical study. *British Journal of Educational Technology, 37*, 705–720.

Shoham, A. (2004). Flow experiences and image making: An on-line chat rooms ethnography. *Psychology and Marketing, 21*, 855–882.

Siekpe, J. S. (2005). An examination of multidimensionality of flow construct in a computer-mediated environment. *Journal of Electronic Commerce Research, 6*, 31–43.

Skadberg, Y. X., & Kimmel, R. (2004). Visitors' flow experience while browsing a web site: Its measurement, contributing factors and consequences. *Computers in Human Behavior, 20*, 403–422.

Smith, D. N., & Sivakumar, K. (2004). Flow and Internet shopping behavior: A conceptual model and research propositions. *Journal of Business Research, 57*, 1199–1208.

Smith, M. W., & Wilhelm, J. D. (2007). Going with the flow. In Sh. Carter (Ed.), *Literacies in context* (pp. 134–167). Southlake, TX: Fountainhead Press.

Smyslova, O. V., & Voiskounsky, A. E. (2005, July). *The importance of intrinsic motivation in usability testing.* Paper presented at the HCI International Conference, Las Vegas, Nevada.

Sohn, D., & Lee, B.-K. (2005). Dimensions of interactivity: Different effects of social and psychological factors. *Journal of Computer-Mediated Communication, 10*(3). Retrieved May 10, 2007, from http://jcmc.indiana.edu/vol10/issue3/sohn.html.

Solzhenitsyn, A. (1963). *One day in the life of Ivan Denisovich.* New York: Bantam.

Solzhenitsyn, A. (1974–1978). *The Gulag archipelago (1918–1956): An experiment in literary investigation.* (3 vols.). London: Collins-Harvill.

Sweetser, P., & Wyeth, P. (2005). GameFlow: A model for evaluating player enjoyment in games. *ACM Computers in Entertainment (CIE), 3* (3). Retrieved November 2, 2006, from http://www.itee.uq.edu.au/~penny/_papers/Sweetser-CIE.pdf.

Trevino, L. K., & Webster, L. (1992). Flow in computer-mediated communication. *Communication Research, 19*, 539–573.

Tzanetakis, R., Vitouch, P. (2002). Flow-experience, the Internet and its relationship to situation and personality. Abstract of a paper presented at the Internet Research 3.0: Net/ Work/Theory (Maastricht, The Netherlands). Retrieved January 24, 2004, from http://aoir.org/2002/program/tzanetakis.html.

Voiskounsky, A. (2001). Internet culture in Russia. In W. Frindte, T. Koehler, P. Marquet, & E. Nissen (Eds.), *Internet-based teaching and learning (IN-TELE) 99. Proceedings of IN-TELE 99 Conference* (pp. 36–44). Frankfurt a/M: Peter Lang.

Voiskounsky, A. (2004). Current problems of moral research and education in the IT environment. In K. Morgan, C. A. Brebbia, J. Sanchez, & A. Voiskounsky (Eds.), *Human perspectives in the Internet society: Culture, psychology and gender* (pp. 33–41). Southampton, UK: WIT Press.

Voiskounsky, A. E. (1998). Telelogue speech. In F. Sudweeks, M. McLaughlin, & Sh. Rafaeli (Eds.), *Network and netplay: Virtual groups on the Internet* (pp. 27–40). Menlo Park, CA, Cambridge, MA: AAAI Press/MIT Press.

Voiskounsky, A. E. (2005). Virtual environments: The need of advanced moral education. In Ph. Brey, F. Grodzinsky, & L. Introna (Eds.), *Ethics of new information technology. Proceedings of the Sixth International Conference of Computer Ethics: Philosophical enquiry* (pp. 389–395). Enshede, The Netherlands: CTIT.

Voiskunsky, A. E. (2006). Ethical behavior in virtual environments. In K. von Knop, H. Neisser, A. A. Salnikov, & B. Ganor (Eds.), *Security, terrorism and privacy in information society* (pp. 399–414). Bielefeld: W. Bertelsmann Verlag.

Voiskounsky, A. E., Babaeva, J. D., & Smyslova, O. V. (2000). Attitudes towards computer hacking in Russia. In D. Thomas & B. Loader (Eds.), *Cybercrime: Law enforcement, security and surveillance in the information age* (pp. 56–84). New York: Routledge.

Voiskounsky, A. E., Mitina, O. V., & Avetisova, A. A. (2004). Playing online games: Flow experience. *Psychology Journal*, 2(3), 259–281. Retrieved November 2, 2004, from http://www.psychnology.org/PSYCHNOLOGY_JOURNAL_2_3_VOISKOUNSKY.pdf.

Voiskounsky, A. E., Mitina, O. V., & Avetisova, A. A. (2005). Communicative patterns and flow experience of MUD players. *International Journal of Advanced Media and Communication, 1*, 5–25.

Voiskounsky, A. E., Mitina, O. V., & Avetisova, A. A. (2006a). Flow experience and interaction: Investigation of Francophone online gamers. In F. Sudweeks, H. Hrachovec & Ch. Ess (Eds.), *Cultural attitudes towards technology and communication. Proceedings, 5th International Conference* (pp. 385–396). Murdoch, Australia: School of Information Technology, Murdoch University.

Voiskounsky, A. E., Mitina, O. V., & Avetisova, A. A. (2006b). Cross-cultural investigation of online gaming: Models of flow experience and interaction in samples of Russian and French gamers. In *Reality and Game & Game and Reality. Papers of the 37th Annual Conference of the International Simulation and Gaming Association* (pp. 64–86). St. Petersburg, Russia: ENGECON Publ.

Voiskounsky, A. E., & Smyslova, O. V. (2003a). Flow-based model of computer hackers' motivation. *CyberPsychology & Behavior, 6*, 171–180.

Voiskounsky, A. E., & Smyslova, O. V. (2003b). Flow in computer hacking: A model. In C.-C. Chung, C.-K. Kim, W. Kim, T.-W. Ling, & K.-H. Song (Eds.), *Web and communication technologies and Internet-related social issues – HSI 2003. Proc., Second International Conference on Human.Society@Internet (Seoul, Korea, June 2003). Lecture Notes in Computer Science, 2713*, 176–186.

Vollmeyer, R., & Rheinberg, F. (2006). Motivational effects on self-regulated learning with different tasks. *Educational Psychology Review, 18*, 239–253.

Vygotsky, L. S. (1962). *Thought and language*. Cambridge, MA: MIT Press.

Wan, C.-S., & Chiou, W.-B. (2006). Psychological motives and online games addiction: A test of flow theory and humanistic needs theory for Taiwanese adolescents. *CyberPsychology & Behavior, 9*, 317–324.

Wan, C.-S., & Chiou, W.-B. (2007). The motivations of adolescents who are addicted to online games: A cognitive perspective. *Adolescence, 42*, 179–198.

Webster, J., Trevino, L. K., & L. Ryan. (1993). The dimensionality and correlates of flow in human-computer interaction. *Computers in Human Behavior, 9*(4), 411–426.

Yee, N. (2006). The labor of fun: How video games blur the boundaries of work and play. *Games and Culture, 1*, 68–71.

# 5  Cybertherapeutic Theory and Techniques

*John Suler*

A new and rather surprising door in the history of the mental health field has opened. Professionals have begun to explore methods for using online environments to help people. How do these methods compare to in-person interventions? Although face-to-face approaches may be advantageous in many cases, there are some advantages to computer-mediated and online interventions. One obvious and frequently cited benefit that applies to all forms of online work is the opportunity to reach people who are unable to visit the professional for geographical, physical, or lifestyle reasons. Computer-mediated work also may be an important initial step in the establishment of what could become an ongoing, in-person treatment. Other advantages, as I'll discuss later, are specific to particular types of online interventions.

In writing this chapter, I decided not to organize it around the concept of *psychotherapy*. After all, what do we mean by that term? If we assembled a group of psychotherapists to discuss this question, we would be lucky if they came to any agreement other than a very general definition about psychotherapy as a service in which a professional helps a person with a problem. That controversy exists even before we toss cyberspace into the debate. Whether we call it *psychotherapy* or not, there have been many approaches over the past 100 years for applying psychological principles to the delivery of mental health services. Now cyberspace offers even more possibilities – many never dreamed of in the past. Because there is easy access to people, information, and activities in cyberspace, some of these clinical possibilities involve an intersection of individual and group psychotherapy, community psychology, and a wide variety of educational and personal growth activities. In the future, we may choose not to define these forms of clinical work as "psychotherapy," or we may modify our concepts about what psychotherapy is.

Psychotherapeutic processes can be conceptualized in at least three ways in cyberspace. We can think of computers as handy tools to be incorporated into preexisting theories of clinical work. The old ideas remain basically the same; we simply deliver them within cyberspace environments. In a second approach, we can define and develop a variety of new computer-mediated intervention systems, such as "e-mail therapy" and "chat therapy" in which we explore the unique therapeutic aspects of that particular communication pathway, without necessarily considering other online communication modalities.

In the third approach, which I will emphasize in this chapter, we can conceptualize online psychotherapeutic activities according to a framework that identifies the elemental components of online communication (Suler, 2000, 2006). These components can be controlled, combined, and modified in various ways to address the needs of different people as well as the changing needs of a particular person. Each component can facilitate certain types of psychotherapeutic change. Some of them may have been overlooked in more traditional forms of clinical work. In a sense, computer-mediated communication deconstructs the psychotherapeutic process (similar to how it deconstructs human "relationships"), not only revealing its elemental components but also offering the opportunity to understand and develop their potential for therapeutic change.

In this chapter, I will outline this conceptual framework, which I will call Cybertherapeutic Theory. I will use it to place into context the variety of online individual psychotherapies that are currently being conducted, as well as those that might be attempted in the future. I will apply the theory to understanding online group and community work. Lastly, I will use the theory as a springboard to propose a new type of online clinical work in which the professional serves as a consultant to a person's online therapeutic activities, rather than as that individual's personal "therapist" – a type of professional work that I have described previously in the eQuest project (Suler, 2005, 2006).

## Cybertherapeutic Theory

Some people say that in psychotherapy it is the relationship between the professional and the client that heals. If this is true, then might cyberspace offer different types of therapeutic relationships based on the different types of communication it offers? As compared to in-person psychotherapy, online clinical work is unique in how it provides the opportunity to interact with clients via different pathways, each one having its unique pros and cons; each one being a slightly different type of relationship.

In the sections that follow, I will explore six components of the communication pathway between mental health professionals and clients within a cyberspace environment. Each of these components may be considered a dimension containing a gradient of differences in a particular quality. The five dimensions also overlap and interact. Any given communication modality can be classified on each of the six dimensions.

### 1.  Synchronous/asynchronous

Unlike in-person encounters, cyberspace offers the choice of meeting in or out of "real time." In synchronous communication, the client and professional are sitting at their computer at the same moment, interacting with each other in that same time frame. Some examples include text-only and avatar chat, Internet telephoning, and videoconferencing. Technical factors, especially transmission speeds, will determine just how closely a synchronous meeting approaches the temporal pace of an in-person encounter. "Lag" may slow down conversation so that there are seconds, or even minutes, between exchanges.

In asynchronous meetings, the professional and client do not have to be sitting at their computers at the same time. Usually this means there is a disconnection of the time frames in which the interaction occurs. Examples of asynchronous encounters include e-mail, discussion boards, and delayed viewing of audio and video transmissions. However, some modalities typically classified as asynchronous (e.g., e-mail, discussions boards) could be used in a synchronous fashion. The distinction between synchronous and asynchronous communication should not be defined in terms of particular software or hardware tools but rather in terms of people's experience of being in the same continuous time frame with each other. In particular, during synchronous communication the unit of time for interacting has a more distinct beginning and ending.

Some of the pros and cons of synchronous versus asynchronous communication revolve around this element of a distinct unit of time for meeting (i.e., an "appointment"). In asynchronous communication, there are no difficulties in scheduling or making an appointment, and being in different time zones is irrelevant. However, setting aside these convenience factors, there are several disadvantages associated with losing the practical and psychological significance of the boundaries implicit in an appointment. Because there are no widely accepted standards in our culture about interacting asynchronously with a professional, the professional must create them in a practical and effective way. Making the effort to be with a person for a specific meeting time also may be interpreted as a sign of commitment and dedication. There may even be some loss of the sense of commitment that "meeting with me right now" can create. Coming late to a session and no-shows are lost as a psychologically significant indices, although pacing and length of replies in asynchronous communication may serve as meaningful cues. In defense of asynchronous communication, some might claim that in the mind of the client "therapy" may become associated specifically with the appointment and be less perceived as an ongoing, daily process.

The psychological significance of "presence" must be considered when comparing synchronous and asynchronous styles. Some people may experience the in-the-moment or here-and-now connection to the professional as a higher degree of mutual presence, which may be a critical factor in therapies that emphasize the healing qualities of the professional relationship, as in humanistic theories and psychoanalytic self-psychology. Synchronous interactions may be more spontaneous, resulting in more revealing, uncensored disclosures by the client. Changes in the rhythm of the asynchronous exchange of messages may be psychologically meaningful, but unlike the moment-by-moment presence of synchronous communication, subtle pauses in conversation go undetected. For people who have difficulty coping with the emotional or verbal demands of here-and-now interactions – as in severe social anxieties or cognitive disorders that impair verbal interaction – asynchronous communication may be the preferred modality.

The distinct advantage of asynchronous modalities rests in the opportunity afforded by the "zone for reflection" (Suler, 2000). Choosing one's time to respond is not only convenient, especially for those with busy lifestyles; it also creates an opportunity to think about the message received and more carefully compose a reply. For the client, this might have important implications for issues concerning impulsivity, stimulating an observing ego, and the process of working through. For the professional, interventions can be planned more precisely and effectively, including the opportunity to consult one's colleagues and resources before responding, while countertransference reactions may be managed with more care. According to the twenty-four-hour rule" in text communication such as e-mail, one can compose a reply immediately as an exercise in spontaneity and catharsis, then wait twenty-four hours to review and possibly modify the message before sending it (Suler, 2000). Such write-wait-revise exercises may therapeutically stimulate cognitive and emotional changes.

## 2. Text/sensory

Most of the interactions occurring on the Internet are typed text. Examples are instant messaging, chat, e-mail, discussion boards, and blogs. Currently, e-mail and chat are the methods frequently used by mental health professionals. Most reports in the literature focus on clinical interventions using text, even though these reports often refer to this work with such generic terms as "online counseling" and "Internet psychotherapy." Other reports specifically identify the unique aspects of text-based clinical work and the therapeutic aspects of writing (Anthony, 2004; Chechele & Stofle, 2003; Childress, 1999; Goss & Anthony, 2004; Murphy & Mitchell, 1998; Stofle, 2002; Suler, 2004b; Wright, 2002).

Lacking sounds and images, text conversations are not robust sensory encounters. Internet telephoning and videoconferencing attempt to re-create the more sensory-rich sights and sounds of an in-person encounter. Some research has begun to explore the use and effectiveness of such online audiovisual interventions (Day & Schneider, 2002; Glueckauf et al., 2002; Manchanda & Mclaren, 1998; Rees & Stone, 2005; Simpson, 2003). In this category of sensory-rich communication, we may also include the more imaginary multimedia environments in which the therapeutic process takes place in an artificially constructed scene or "virtual reality" – in some cases including visual icons called *avatars* that clients use to represent themselves within that environment (Gaggioli, Mantovani, Castelnuovo, Wiederhold, & Riva, 2003; Glantz,

Rizzo, & Graap, 2003; Riva, 2000, 2003; Schuemie, Van der Straaten, Krijn, & Van der Mast, 2001; Wiederhold & Wiederhold, 1998). These multimedia environments may simulate real situations, as in virtual reality (VR) treatments for phobias, or they may be purely imaginative and even fantasy-based scenes.

Even though I am distinguishing text from sensory communication, there indeed is a visual component to typed text conversations, for example, in the creative use of smileys, spacing, capital letters, punctuation marks, and ASCII art. Also, the tools for embedding graphics and sounds into e-mail and discussion boards are becoming more common.

Some of the advantages of text interventions are determined by technical factors. Multimedia communication, such as videoconferencing, requires extra equipment, more technical know-how, and fast connections to work smoothly. Because text files are small, it is much easier to save permanent records of the therapeutic encounter, which gives the professional as well as the client an opportunity to review and to evaluate their work together. At the same time, it creates complications concerning the confidentiality of those records. The entire therapeutic process as well as the relationship between the professional and client could be preserved. As multimedia tools become more widely used, and as storage and connection speed capabilities increase, the recording advantage of text communication will be less significant, although analyses of text interactions may still be more easily quantified and standardized than analyses of auditory or visual records.

A more enduring issue involves the differences between reading/writing and hearing/speaking, as well as individual differences in cognitive skills for these types of communication. Compared with reading and writing, hearing and speaking are usually more quick and efficient. Because of poor reading or writing skills, some people will have difficulty expressing themselves and understanding others via text communication. However, some people, because of cognitive or interpersonal style, may naturally communicate better through reading and writing. The process of writing may also tap therapeutic cognitive processes and encourage an observing ego, self-reflection, insight, working through, and the therapeutic construction of a personal narrative, as in journal writing and bibliotherapy. Some of these therapeutic effects will tend to be more pronounced in asynchronous, rather than synchronous, text communication.

Some of the advantages of text communication may be attributed to the effects of absent face-to-face cues, increased anonymity, and the Online Disinhibition Effect (Suler, 2004a). Some people who may balk at seeing a therapist in-person – because of anxiety about self-disclosure, the stigma of being a "patient," and so – and may be more willing to seek text-based help because of the anonymity it offers. Clients may be less expressive when confronted with a face-to-face encounter or may feel more uncomfortable with too many visual/auditory cues. The absence of face-to-face contact may encourage them to be more honest and revealing.

However, in-person contact has some obvious advantages. Without face-to-face cues, a person's identity is not as easily determined, which may present complications concerning confidentiality. Multiple sensory cues provide valuable information for understanding the client, such as visual appearance, body language, and vocal expression.

For some clients, the feeling of the presence will be more powerful when meeting in-person, which can enhance the effect of the therapist's interventions, the therapist's self-object functions, the sense of intimacy, and the client's commitment to the therapy. Typed text may feel "formal" and lack a supportive, empathic tone. Rather than encouraging productive self-disclosures, the Online Disinhibition Effect might result in the client regressing or acting out in ways that disrupts the therapeutic process. Because text communication tends to be more ambiguous due to the lack of visual and auditory cues that confirm meaning, there will be a tendency for more misunderstandings, projections, and transference reactions. Although enhanced transference may be useful to psychoanalytic clinicians, it may pose unnecessary complications for other types of therapists.

One of the most important challenges in exploring psychotherapeutic processes in cyberspace will be our understanding people's preferences for auditory, text, and visual communication, how those preferences relate to cognitive and personality styles, and what combinations of these modalities are therapeutic for different people and problems. In this exploration, we may draw on clinical and empirical research concerning the differences between verbal and imagistic processes in psychotherapy (Suler, 1989).

## 3. Imaginary/realistic

One of the most fascinating and potentially powerful aspects of cyberspace is its flexibility for recreating reality-oriented experiences as well as those that are highly imaginative. Cyberspace is filled with fantasy-based communities, some purely textual and others more graphic. Although some people prefer the flight of pure imagination that is activated by text-only encounters in role-playing scenarios, others prefer imaginary visual and multimedia environments. When designing mental health interventions, professionals can consider the therapeutic potentials of experiences for clients that are lifelike versus those that are more inventive. The imaginary environment could be provided by the professional, or the client might be encouraged to seek out one that already exists online.

There are a wide variety of possible therapeutic applications of imaginary environments. A client's interpersonal experimentation in an imaginary online community may provide very valuable material to be discussed with a mental health professional. Well-known techniques such as interpersonal role-playing, psychodrama, implosion, the development of relaxation scenes, generating imaginative intrapsychic resources, and the exploration of dreams, fantasies, and childhood memories could thrive in imaginary environments designed with the help of a mental health professional. In the case of multimedia scenarios, these therapeutic experiences might involve the use of avatars, which are imaginative visual representations of oneself, often within an imaginative visual scene. Avatar psychotherapy might involve both the client and psychotherapist experimenting with various visual representations of themselves to help clients explore their self-concepts, as well as understand transference and countertransference dynamics.

The disadvantages of imaginary scenarios must be considered when planning therapeutic experiences for clients. Some forms of psychopathology may not respond well to imaginary environments or may be exacerbated by them, as in psychotic conditions. An excessive focus on imaginary encounters and identities could become a form of defense and acting out, a diversion from true psychotherapeutic work, or it may destructively magnify projections and transference reactions. Although some clients may be more anxious and less expressive when dealing with a realistic face-to-face situation, others will feel more comfortable in that situation and in being who they "really" are. The client's sense of the therapist's presence may be more grounded when the therapist appears real, which can enhance the impact of the therapist's interventions, the therapist's selfobject functions, the sense of intimacy, and the client's commitment to the therapy.

## 4. Automated/interpersonal

The basic purpose of the computer is to automate tasks we cannot do, do not want to do, or would take much longer to do. In mental health interventions, the computer could automate specific tasks or even conduct interventions by itself with varying degrees of supervision by a human professional. Programs such as Eliza have simulated a fully automated psychotherapy (Suler, 1987).

There are a variety of advantages and applications of automation. Computer programs may be efficient, objective, and accurate tools in the assessment, testing, and diagnostic phases of treatment (Barak & Buchanan, 2004; Epstein & Klinkenberg, 2001). They may work well in helping clients make decisions about entering psychotherapy and what type of psychotherapy. Some people may at first be more comfortable and expressive with a nonhuman therapist. In turn, computers do not have feelings and can be programmed to minimize countertransference reactions, making them potentially much more objective and neutral in their work. Diagnostic as well as treatment protocols that are very specific and programmatic may be particularly amenable to automation, resulting in a cost-effective treatment. Computers, in some respects, possess a superior memory than humans and may be better at detecting thematic patterns that surface in the dialogue with a client. They might even be capable of detecting changes in voice and body language, as they are capable of detecting psychophysiological changes, such as heart rate, skin conductance, and blood pressure – biological cues that therapists usually cannot perceive.

Of course, completely eliminating the professional's human presence from any intervention will be a mistake in many cases. The complexities and subtleties of some mental health interventions may be impossible to re-create in a computer program. Computer programs do not reason or learn nearly as well as humans and therefore may be very limited in their ability to adapt to changing, complex, or unique psychotherapeutic situations. Some clients will not feel comfortable or expressive with a nonhuman relationship. Those who believe "it's the relationship that heals" in psychotherapy may question whether such a relationship is even possible with a machine. Can the curative power of empathy be simulated by a computer program? Does a machine's elimination of emotion and countertransference eliminate the opportunity to use these personal reactions as tools for understanding and better helping the client?

Despite their advantages, computers mostly will be inferior to human professionals in understanding and therefore discussing and working with, the human condition. Nevertheless, the goal is not to eliminate automation but to decide when it is appropriate, with whom, and with how much interpersonal involvement by the professional.

## 5. Invisible/present

The potential invisibility of the professional afforded by computers overlaps with the automated/interpersonal dimension. If a mental health intervention with clients is automated, then it is possible for human professionals to watch over the machine's work. They can adjust programs or, if necessary, step in to intervene themselves. Other variations of invisibility might include a professional unobtrusively observing a client's behavior in some therapeutic online environment, or "listening in" on a colleague's individual or group work, for example, silently overseeing an e-mail list, perhaps to supervise or back-up the colleague through private communications. It is also possible for clients to be invisible. They can observe others in individual or group sessions or in an online community, either with or without the knowledge of the professional and the other participants, resulting in vicarious learning and therapeutic gains.

There are several benefits of invisibility. Some clients may be more comfortable and expressive when they believe a professional is not present. Some invisible clients may greatly prefer and benefit significantly from a vicarious learning experience. Being an invisible client also can reduce or eliminate the cultural stigma of undergoing mental health treatment.

However, there are a variety of disadvantages. The curative effects of a healing human relationship are lost when either the client or therapist are not present. The client's or therapist's commitment to the therapy may be greatly reduced when his or her counterpart is not present. Obviously, the client's unawareness that a professional is listening or secretly intervening raises an ethical red flag. With informed consent, the invisible professional then becomes more present in the mind of the client. Over time, some clients will forget that there is someone observing, allowing the professional to slip more into invisibility. Other clients may never feel comfortable in what becomes a self-conscious, even paranoid, environment. However, the idea of being completely invisible also could lull a therapist or client into a false sense of security. With enough technical know-how, an outsider can detect or observe one's participation in any type of online meeting.

A useful aspect of computer-mediated communication is that the degree of presence of the professional or client can be regulated. In text-based groups, one can lurk, periodically communicate, or maintain an ongoing participation. The presence of the client or therapist can be maximized when the communication is synchronous and sensory. Here and now, seeing and hearing the actual person – as in videoconferencing – will make that person feel more real, alive, and present for many people. Although the "interpersonal" and "present" factors overlap, it is possible to have an interpersonal intervention that lacks a present professional (e.g., a professional pretending to be an automated system), as well as an automated intervention with a present professional (e.g., a client working with a computer program while knowing that a professional is silently observing).

## 6.  Individual/group

As in other types of mental health interventions, cyberspace offers opportunities for both a one-on-one relationship between the professional and client and group experiences. With group activities, the professional might play a variety of roles: provide information to clients about online group opportunities, advise clients about their group experiences, offer consultation to online groups and communities, or design and facilitate online groups and communities.

One very important feature of the Internet is its ability to bring together people who are experiencing similar problems – people who are geographically distant as well as those who struggle with unusual issues. Thousands of online support groups address many social and mental health topics. These groups may serve as valuable adjuncts to clients in psychotherapy or as stand-alone therapeutic experiences. Similarly, there are thousands of online communities of all shapes and sizes. A client's lifestyle in one or more of them may be the perfect social microcosm for exploring psychological issues. Given the nature of the client's problems, a professional might recommend a particular community or a behavioral assignment within a community. The online community might then serve as a setting for the development of new interpersonal skills and psychotherapeutic change.

Even psychotherapists who are not actively involved in online clinical work will benefit greatly from understanding what online resources are available for their clients. In this age of the Internet, all mental health professionals need at least a basic knowledge of online behavior, relationships, communities, and especially support groups (Chang, 2005; Davison, Pennebaker, & Dickerson, 2000; Finn, 1995; Godin, Trushel, & Singh, 2005; Hsiung, 2000; King & Moreggi, 1998; Madara, 1997; Tichon & Shapiro, 2003; Weinberg, 2001; Zuckerman, 2003). Professionals who expressly focus on online activities when working with clients, or who consult with, design, and manage online groups, will need to cultivate a specialized knowledge of relationships and group dynamics in cyberspace.

Some of the factors in deciding whether a client might benefit from individual and group experiences in cyberspace overlap with those in evaluating the pros and cons of in-person individual and group work. However, online group experiences may raise some unique issues. How will clients cope with text and synchronous versus asynchronous communication? How will they manage their online identities in the group, and how might they respond to how other members manage and "experiment" with their identities? How might they need to integrate the lifestyle they develop online with their in-person lifestyle?

Professionals who consult with, design, and manage online groups will need to address the same questions, as well as consider a variety of other issues: the group's membership, purpose, value system, rules of conduct, leadership structure, and communication infrastructure. This work involves a mixture of concepts and techniques from traditional group therapy, community psychology, and organizational psychology, as well as ideas unique to online communities (Kim, 2000; Rheingold, 2000). Maximizing the well-being of an online group also involves more than just remedial interventions. Following the principles of secondary and primary prevention in community psychology, it requires an early detection of small problems before they escalate into big ones, as well as a sensible design of the community so that some problems can be avoided from the start. Some of these interventions will be aimed at the purely psychological and social dimensions of the group, while others will involve software changes in the media for communicating and interacting.

The boundaries, structure, and definition of "group" can be quite different online than in-person. Various combinations of the five previously discussed dimensions of online communication will significantly alter group dynamics, thereby providing a variety of potentially therapeutic experiences for clients. Clinicians have begun to explore traditional communication options for synchronous and asynchronous work with couples, families, and groups (Bellafiore, Colòn, & Rosenberg, 2004; Jencius & Sager, 2001; King, Engi, & Poulos, 1998; Ouellette & Sells, 2001; Pollock, 2006; Sander, 1999; Weinberg, 2001).

However, a wide range of other options might be explored. Using layered interactions a group could function at two different levels using two different channels of communication, with one channel perhaps functioning as a meta-discussion of the other. For example, a group could meet via synchronous text or videoconferencing. Then, using a saved transcript or recording of this meeting as a reference, the group discusses this session via e-mail. Essentially, this is a computer-mediated enhancement of the "self-reflective loop" in group psychotherapy, as described by Yalom (1995). The group process becomes layered, with a core, spontaneous, synchronous experience and a superimposed meta-discussion. Such layered interactions may be especially useful when the core experience involves role-plays with a reality-oriented meta-discussion.

Other interesting possibilities arise from the use of invisibility. In a nested group, people could communicate with one another while also being able to invisibly communicate with one or more people within that group. Although such private messaging could create subgrouping and conflict, it also could be useful in enabling group members, as well as the professional, to offer hidden coaching and support that ultimately enhances the whole group. In overlapping groups, individuals or subgroups within one group can communicate with individuals or subgroups from a sibling group, which enables a comparison of experiences across groups. Professionals also might create a meta-group that silently observes the interaction of a second group and then offer its feedback to that group, or privately to individual members, either during or after the online meeting.

Group strategies may involve environments that are one-to-many, many-to-one, and many-to-many. In a webpage or blog, a person may therapeutically express himself to a group of people. If the group can provide feedback to that person, those replies might also be beneficial. Communities of weblogs and social network systems enable people to find and communicate with other people who share similar backgrounds and interests. Innovative mental health professionals will find ways to assist clients in exploring and optimally benefiting from these opportunities.

## Clinical Implications of Cybertherapeutic Theory

Psychotherapists from different perspectives may evaluate these dimensions of Cybertherapeutic Theory quite differently. Those who rely more on specific procedures and protocols – as in some behavioral and cognitive approaches – may find automated interventions very useful. Psychoanalytic and behavioral clinicians who work with fantasy-based material (dream work, exposure, flooding, implosion) or invented role-plays may be enticed by the imaginary dimension of computer-mediated therapy. Asynchronous text communication may be useful to psychotherapists who emphasize the construction of a personal narrative, as in some psychoanalytic therapies and bibliotherapies. Some psychoanalytic workers also will be intrigued by the heightened transference and countertransference that occurs in text-based interactions.

However, those therapists – especially humanistic thinkers – who uphold the therapeutic power of a face-to-face, authentic relationship may reject any type of computer-mediated intervention. They will likely prefer a fully present interpersonal encounter. Surely, clinicians who work closely with body cues and body contact (e.g., Thought Field Therapy, Somatic Experiencing Therapy, Eye Movement Desensitisation and Reprocessing [EMDR]) will find cyberspace very limiting.

From a practical standpoint, however, it's hard to imagine any clinician who wouldn't find e-mail useful as a way to maintain contact with the client, just as telephone calls have become routine. In Cybertherapeutic Theory, such communications would be conceptualized as features of a multimodality clinical intervention, and therefore subject to analysis according to the six dimensions of the theory.

There are numerous ways the various dimensional elements can be combined and sequenced to design a therapeutic encounter that addresses the needs of clients. People who can benefit from in-depth psychotherapeutic work (e.g., those who are higher functioning, educated, or artistically inclined) may fare well in rich imaginary scenarios, coordinated with a text-based evaluation of the experience. Trauma that needs to be mastered gradually can begin with text-based explorations, then slowly incorporate actual sensory re-creations to assist in the assimilation of the trauma. Some therapies (e.g., EMDR) also may invent imaginary text or sensory resources to counteract the trauma. Developing the social skills needed to mastering specific difficult interpersonal situations can progress from imaginary/automated/asynchronous scripted role-plays with minimal sensory cues (and perhaps an invisible therapist to evaluate and coach) to more challenging spontaneous role-plays that are synchronous, interpersonal, and sensory enriched. To grapple with issues concerning intimacy and interpersonal anxiety, schizoid and socially phobic clients may benefit from a therapeutic program that begins with encounters that are text based, asynchronous, and perhaps even automated and then moving toward more synchronous, sensory, present, and ultimately in-person encounters.

An important aspect of Cybertherapeutic Theory is that we are evaluating mental health interventions based on the types of communication pathways between clients and professionals. This approach differs from the more traditional method of defining a psychotherapeutic intervention, which is more closely linked to one's theory of psychopathological causes. It is even possible that our understanding of how different communication pathways affect the therapeutic process may lead to new frameworks for conceptualizing psychological problems. Psychological health may be assessed according to the person's ability to move among as well as integrate the dimensional features of computer-mediated and in-person communication.

As the technology of cyberspace advances, the methods for computer-mediated interventions will also change. A critical component of this change will be a careful evaluation – and perhaps reinterpretation – of the ethical issues associated with the practice of psychotherapy. The foremost concern in the clinician's mind should always be the welfare and rights of the client as outlined by the evolution of professional guidelines.

## Cybertherapeutic Activities and Programs

There is a trend nowadays to think of the Internet as a place where we can take a particular style of individual psychotherapy and translate it into an online mode, as in a chat or e-mail version of a psychodynamic or cognitive therapy. However, relying on Cybertherapeutic Theory, professionals also can begin exploring ways to shape the wide variety of therapeutic activities in cyberspace into new interventions that aren't necessarily an online adaptation of preexisting clinical theories or techniques. Such personal growth and psycho-educational activities in cyberspace can serve as supplements to individual psychotherapy or as stand-alone activities.

They also can be integrated into a comprehensive and integrated program, such as "eQuest" (Suler, 2005). A person enters the program with some specific personal issue in mind that is related to mental health. Almost any issue can be explored and possibly resolved in the program (divorce, anxiety attacks, eating disorders, etc.). In the form of a website, the program consists of instructions that guide the person through a variety of online activities and exercises that address the personal issue. The program's philosophy advocates the merit of developing one's online skills, activities, and relationships as assets to resolve life difficulties. It emphasizes the importance of experimenting with different types of online activities and communication modalities, exploring personal expression and identity in cyberspace, and developing an online lifestyle that can be effectively integrated with one's in-person lifestyle. The person's specific goal is to address the personal problem or issue that he or she brings to the program, but the more encompassing goal is to become a knowledgeable user of online resources and to develop an online lifestyle as a psycho-educational, therapeutic process. These two goals go hand-in-hand.

When designing, prescribing, and implementing these online therapeutic activities – especially in comprehensive programs – the professional may not play the same central role in the transformative process as they do in traditional psychotherapies. Instead, the professional may empower clients by guiding them through their own process of educational and personal growth, by acting as a consultant in that process rather than a psychotherapist per se. Although clients might benefit from undertaking such cybertherapeutically designed activities and programs on their own, the outcomes no doubt will be more effective when the professional serves in this consulting role. In the sections that follow, I will describe some of the components that might be integrated into a cybertherapeutic program, as well as the possible functions of the professional consultant. However, because we live in an age when many psychotherapy clients are online, even traditional psychotherapists could benefit from understanding these features of cybertherapeutic endeavors.

## 1.  Goal Setting and Assessment

Before clients attempt a cybertherapeutic activity or program, the professional should help them clarify the specific issue or goal they have in mind. What exactly do they hope to learn or resolve? In developing eQuest (Suler, 2005), I encourage participants to pick an issue that is personally meaningful, an issue that is important in the person's life. Although some have difficulty in deciding which of several possible goals to choose, they rarely if ever are unable to identify an issue they wish to explore. Sometimes they need help in focusing an otherwise vague or broad goal. Sometimes they choose one that appears to be, at first glance, abstract and academic rather than personal. However, even a cursory discussion usually clarifies the personal significance of the issue they selected.

The professional should assess the person's computer abilities. Strategies for such an assessment could be adapted from those created by the ISMHO Clinical Case Study Group (2001) for determining a person's suitability for online psychotherapy, including such issues as writing and keyboarding skills, knowledge about computers and the Internet, and prior experience with online activities. Basic skills in web browsing and e-mail would probably be necessary but a well-designed activity or program should be effective even for people with intermediate and advanced knowledge of cyberspace, particularly in the feedback offered by the consultant.

In this assessment stage, the consultant should take care to assess any contraindicated vulnerabilities in personality, as well as the possibility that a particular person might choose an issue to explore that is too emotionally charged or inappropriate in some way. For example, because of the possibility of acting out and intense transference reactions in online relationships, people with severe personality disorders, impulse disorders, and psychotic conditions might not benefit from online social activities or might require detailed consultation. Some issues – like online sexual perversions and crime – might be explored via readings but perhaps should not be investigated via social contacts.

The consultant might develop structured tools for assessment purposes. In the eQuest program (Suler, 2005), an Assessment Profile and Interview is used to conduct pre- and postassessments, as well as to track participants through the program. During a preassessment interview with the participant, the consultant uses rating scales and checklists to assess a person's self-reported computer and Internet skills, prior online activities, knowledge and experience concerning the personal issue being explored in the program, and social/cognitive preferences related to online activities. Ratings of these social/cognitive preferences are based on the six dimensions of Cybertherapeutic Theory, that is, preferences for text, visuals, synchronous versus asynchronous communication, and so on. A graphical profile, which visually summarizes these aspects of the person, is used by the professional as a reference for consulting the person during the cybertherapeutic activities. After the participant completes the program, the assessment tool is used to obtain a self-reported evaluation of progress made within the program.

## 2.   Utilizing Online Information

Any cybertherapeutic program should encourage clients to take advantage of the vast amount of information online about mental health issues. However, current research recognizes the varying quality of such information and the importance of educating people in the assessment of it (Casteel, 2003; Griffiths & Christensen, 2000; Morahan-Martin, 2000; Morahan-Martin & Anderson, 2000; Palmiter & Renjilian, 2003). Guidelines for helping clients use online information should include criteria for objectively evaluating the quality of that information; that is, what are the credentials of the person who wrote that web article, is it a reputable organization that created the website, what do reviews of that site say about it, how many and what other sites link to that information. The consultant also should encourage the client to explore the subjectively experienced validity of the resource. Why does the information feel or not feel "right" to the person? How can the person make sense out of that information and apply it to his or her situation? In eQuest (Suler, 2005), participants evaluate an online resource with a seven-point rating system based on such objective and subjective criteria.

Among the many online resources are the professionally created sites intended for people who are looking for help with a variety of behavioral and mental health problems, such as smoking, alcoholism, depression, post-traumatic stress disorder, eating disorders, self-injurious behaviors, and social phobias. These sites may offer information about the causes, symptoms, and professional treatments for these problems, as well as self-help and self-management strategies that people can try on their own. Such sites are the most widely used mental health resources in cyberspace.

Given all the information that a client might discover, it can be very helpful to understand why a particular piece of information catches a person's eye. Conscious as well as unconscious needs may be reflected in the information people choose to examine. For every webpage that presents some idea or "fact," there will be another page that proposes contrary ideas and "facts." The consultant must encourage the client to be aware of the tendency to seek out information that confirms one's preexisting beliefs about some social or mental health issue and to understand the psychological and emotional underpinnings of that bias.

## 3. Participating in Online Groups

As the size and social complexity of cyberspace has expanded tremendously, it is hard to imagine any social or mental health issue that is not being addressed by an online group. Some may be small and casual discussion groups, but others, including a wide variety of self-help organizations, offer sophisticated psychotherapeutic and psychoeducational support (King & Moreggi, 1998; Madara, 1997; Salem, Bogat, & Reid, 1997). Gathering useful information, learning vicariously from observing people interacting, sharing, and seeking advice from others, and providing assistance to others – as the "helper therapy principle" suggests (Riessman, 1965) – can all enhance the process of personal growth.

However, there is a learning curve in understanding the culture of online groups and knowing how to participate in them effectively. When consulting with clients and designing cybertherapeutic programs, the professional can offer practical suggestions about how to find and join online groups, what to say or not to say when creating a personal profile, the importance of observing the group's culture before participating, how to introduce oneself, and what to expect as a newcomer. Because some groups are something less than useful and benign, even hurtful or blatantly pathological, a cybertherapeutic program should contain a set of guidelines about how to evaluate whether a group is helpful; for example, how active is the group; how do members react to newcomers; what are the conversations like; how does the group handle disagreement and conflict; what are the components of the groups ideology concerning the issue it addresses; is this ideology amenable to the client's belief system, and how might the ideology be therapeutically beneficial to the participant, perhaps even serving as a "cognitive antidote" for the participant's maladaptive beliefs (Suler, 1984). Recognizing universality – that your problem isn't unusual and you aren't alone in having to deal with it – is a powerful therapeutic aspect of a group experience. Because cyberspace enables people with even rare problems to join together, it excels in its opportunity to offer group camaraderie and mutual understanding.

As in eQuest (Suler, 2005), a client may be encouraged to read the literature about the pros and cons of online groups and social relationships. Of special interest are the ways that a person might behave in online groups compared with in-person groups, including how one might react to online disinhibition. The consultant's attempts to help the client understand such reactions can lead to important insights into the client's personality as well as the issue being addressed in the cybertherapeutic program.

## 4. One-on-One Relationships

Although many people form relationships with others they meet on the Internet, they may not be as familiar with the pros and cons of online relationships as they need to be. The professional can assist them in this goal. In a cybertherapeutic program where clients are exploring some specific personal issue, the professional may encourage and guide them in establishing relationships with people who share that issue or are knowledgeable about it. The relationship that forms may involve mentoring or peer help and support, in some cases evolving into a friendship. Clients might privately contact a few people they encounter in the online groups they have joined, people with whom they sense the possibility of a rewarding relationship.

Because online text-based relationships can be quite unique compared with in-person relationships, the eQuest program offers suggestions, readings, and exercises to assist the participant in maximizing the benefits of these relationships while avoiding the pitfalls of miscommunication with text. In an exercise involving expressive keyboarding techniques, such as the use of caps, parenthetical expressions, trailers, rich text, and emoticons (Suler, 2006), the participant composes a practice text message to a real or imaginary person online using as many keyboarding techniques as possible. Transference reactions due to the ambiguity of text conversations is a common problem in cyberspace, so the program also includes an exercise in which a person mentally imagines the online companion and then compares that mental representation to images of significant others in the person's life. Another exercise involves reading out loud one's text message, using different vocal tones and speech patterns, to evoke the various meanings and emotions that the online companion might perceive in the message. To get a "big picture" of what a relationship has been like – and to understand the development of that relationship over time – another exercise encourages the person to scan the titles of e-mail messages in the archive for that relationship, and then reread some of those past e-mails.

As part of their education in online relationships, the consultant might encourage clients to explore how they perceive and react to the consultant via online communication. If the consultant and client interact face-to-face as well as online, then comparing these two modes of communication can be especially helpful in clients realizing how they react and behave differently in cyberspace versus in-person. The relationship between the client and the consultant can become a safe place for people to openly discuss self-expression, distortions in interpersonal perceptions, the disinhibition effect, and transference reactions. Clients sometimes perceive and react to the professional very differently online than in-person. Understanding that discrepancy can lead them to important insights into the nature of online communication, and into their own personality dynamics.

## 5.  Online Tests and Interactive Programs

Although online people can sample a variety of personality tests, aptitude tests, interest inventories, and other types of interactive programs. Whatever the issue a person brings to psychotherapy or a cybertherapeutic program, there is almost always some online test or questionnaire related to it. In eQuest, participants are encouraged to browse through websites that offer such resources and complete any tests that look useful or interesting to them. Sometimes they select tests that are obviously related to their personal issue, but often they try a test simply because it catches their eye. They are encouraged to discuss the results of these tests with the consultant.

Professionals should advise clients about how most of these tests are not valid psychometric instruments, that the results should be viewed with some healthy skepticism. This alone is a significant lesson in cyberspace, where such tests proliferate as commercial endeavors or simple entertainment. Nevertheless, it also can be a valuable learning experience to experiment with these tests and determine for oneself whether they are accurate. In the eQuest guidelines – and especially in the discussions with the consultant – participants are encouraged to use these questionnaires as springboards for thinking about themselves and the personal issue being explored. It can be very valuable to see which particular tests or programs people choose, to understand why the person wanted to experiment with them. The choice often reflects underlying concerns, wishes, and needs that may be related to the personal issue being explored in the program.

## 6.  Free-Form Browsing

When people go online, often they are searching for specific resources or intending to go to a specific place. The destination is predetermined. That mental set tends to narrow one's field of view. It can prevent people from discovering other resources that they did not know existed in cyberspace. Sometimes that agenda even imposes a kind of linear intention into one's movement through cyberspace that defeats the purpose and beauty of the hypertext, associational structure of the World Wide Web.

The free-form browsing component of eQuest attempts to reverse that mental set, to get people to explore more freely, to revive the playful and creative attitude of discovery that arises from divergent thinking. Several types of free-form browsing exercises are within the program, but they all encourage the person to devote a few online sessions to simply wandering around cyberspace with no specific agenda. People might use a random link generator that launches them onto a webpage somewhere on the Internet, as an arbitrary starting point to begin their wandering. Or, they may start their journey on a familiar page, then begin clicking on links, sometimes choosing those links randomly and sometimes clicking ones that catch their eye. The exercise works best when people do not rely on a conscious analysis or evaluation of where they are going but instead rely on intuition and "gut feeling."

For some people, the process involves a contemplative form of free association. It becomes a fascinating kind of projective test in which people allow unconscious needs and feelings to direct their path. How the person experiences the process of free-form browsing, as well as what the person discovers online, are both revealing. For people with compulsive tendencies or rigid lifestyle patterns, free-form browsing can be a therapeutic challenge. Although many people do not, at first, realize the psychological significance of how they undertake and experience free-form browsing, the consultant often can provide feedback that stimulates such insights.

## 7. Creating an Online Presence

Many online environments and communities offer people the opportunity to create a personal profile or webpage in which people present information about their background and interests. Blogs and photography sharing communities have become a popular way to express oneself. The professional can help the client engage these tasks as a valuable therapeutic, self-reflective exercise. Many important questions can be considered: What do you think is important about you and your life? What do you want others to know about you? What might be the reactions of others to how you present yourself? How people choose to present and in a sense create their online identity is an intriguing aspect of life in cyberspace. That identity may not correspond exactly to one's in-person behavior.

In eQuest, the guidelines for creating a personal webpage suggest that people say something about their lives, personalities, backgrounds, and interests as well as describe what they have learned about the personal issues they are exploring in the program and hence about themselves. With the help of the consultant, they are encouraged to experiment with fonts, backgrounds, colors, graphics, and photographs, to be as creative and self-expressive as they wish. Links to online indexes of thousands of personal webpages, as well as pages of previous eQuest participants, gives them the opportunity to examine how other people decided to present themselves.

Because self-awareness and personal identity revolve around how others perceive us, the consultant and cybertherapeutic program can encourage the client to think about "audience." How might clients create their webpage, profile, or blog differently, depending on who read it: friends, family, coworkers, people who are familiar with their issue being explored in the cybertherapeutic program, or almost anyone online? Clients might be instructed to ask family or friends for their feedback on their webpage or profile. After experimenting with different versions, the client can decide which would be most appropriate to upload to their particular online groups.

## 8. Assisting With Media Transitions, Anxiety, and Mental Set

Because the philosophy of a cybertherapeutic program maintains that people can benefit therapeutically from experimenting with different communication modalities, the program will encourage and guide people to become involved in a various online environments that include text, visuals, audio, synchronous and asynchronous communication, imaginary versus real environments, and varying degrees of invisibility and presence. The theory behind this multiple modality emphasis is that a communication environment shapes the expression of personal identity and social interaction. Because each environment can offer a different form of expression, exploring new ones may enhance interpersonal learning as well as the cohesion and development of one's identity.

However, when seeking computer-mediated help, people will tend to try those services that operate via communication modalities with which they are already familiar and comfortable. Those particular services and modalities may not necessarily be the best option. The person may need to explore new environments, to make a *media transition*. In some cases, the change might be a small one, while in other situations, the transition might be quite dramatic. One function of the online mental health professional would be to help a person make such transitions.

Confronting the possibility of change stirs apprehension. In the case of moving to a new type of communication modality, we may call this *media transition anxiety*. Although the degree of that anxiety will vary depending on one's personality and the magnitude of the change required, several factors generally contribute to it in most people. Some may feel stressed by the amount of time and energy they must devote to mastering a different modality. To avoid feelings of incompetence and possible failure, people may wish to remain in an old environment that they have mastered rather than make the challenging transition to a new one that they may not understand. A fear of the unknown may prove to be an obstacle, especially in new social environments where one must figure out how the social system works, how to behave appropriately within it, and how to present one's identity. It is always possible that others might be critical or rejecting. For some people, the anxiety arises from the fear that installing new software or entering a new environment might result in problems with one's computer. Trying to make things a little better can sometimes make what you already had a lot worse, so a "If it ain't broke, don't fix it" philosophy prevails. The consultant might consider exploring the psychological issues that possibly underlie these attitudes of the client.

Resistance to exploring new environments also may be the result of *media mental set*, a narrow and rigid pattern of thinking about communication modalities that fails to consider new information or perspectives. People can become so accustomed and loyal to one type of communication environment that they refuse to consider others. They approach issues, including psychological and social ones, strictly in terms of that particular environment, while failing to see alternative solutions offered by other types of environments. Their thinking gets mentally stuck within that media. Personal limitations in imagination, curiosity, or learning and problem-solving abilities may result in a media mental set, but even people without such limitations can slip into such a state of mind. They idealize their particular modality. Their self-esteem and identity are invested in it. They harbor nostalgic memories about being there. They may feel the need to protect those feelings, memories, and identity, which can lead to a rationalized defense of their media that resembles territorial behavior. Sometimes media mental set becomes the norm for an entire online community, so a person's status within it can become jeopardized if a change to another modality is undertaken or even considered. To avoid cognitive dissonance, people devalue other modalities that might indeed appear valuable, but which they are not trying.

The professional working with an online client may need to address media transition anxiety and media mental set on several levels. To stimulate cognitive development, they may assist clients in realizing how they previously made communication manageable and predictable by relying on familiar assumptions and in then making the leap into assimilating alternative methods of communication. The professional may need to help the client understand the personality and attitudinal factors that contribute to media transition anxiety and mental set, which often turns out to be psychotherapeutic work that overlaps with other issues in the client's life, including the issue the person brings to the cybertherapeutic program. The professional also can stimulate media transition motivation by inspiring the clients' sense of necessity, accomplishment, pride, delight, and even adventure in making a change. That motivation can be conceptualized in terms of Maslow's hierarchy of needs, including the needs to acquire information, establish social bonds, acquire mastery and self-esteem, and self-actualize through creative self-expression.

When assisting clients in media transitions, the professional can offer practical suggestions. Minimize cost and maximize benefits by only attempting big changes when they are necessary. Expect a period of adaptation when entering a new online environment. Depending on how different the modality is, anticipate a learning curve in which new perceptual, motor, cognitive, and interpersonal skills will need to be developed. Accept confusion, the necessity of making small steps, and the fact that even excellent media have some design flaws. Sometimes confusion and frustration is justified. In a new social environment, you will need to learn the software first before you can fully attend to the people there. Try to understand the norms of the group – what is considered acceptable and unacceptable behavior – before you start to participate. Accept the role of newbie, seek out the advice of those who are familiar with the environment but also recognize and leave a hostile community. Investigate the new modality while recognizing that mental sets developed from a previous one might prevent you from realizing some of the resources in this new environment. Recognize when it is a good idea to stretch your particular set of cognitive, perceptual, and social skills by engaging a new environment, and when an environment simply does not match your skills and interests.

## 9. Integration

In a cybertherapeutic program, the consultant must help the client integrate the various activities and experiences generated by the program. Rather than allowing the program to become a miscellaneous collection of things to do online, the consultant assists the client in developing a "big picture" by identifying significant themes and patterns in how the client progresses through the program. The client's experiences are like pieces of a puzzle that need to be compared, contrasted, and assembled to arrive at that bigger picture. Because the overarching goal of the program is to help clients understand the factual information concerning the personal issue being explored, the subjective effect of that issue in their lives, and what it means to develop a lifestyle in cyberspace, the consultant encourages them to realize that these three learning objectives are not separate, but intertwined. Even advanced Internet users, who already may be familiar with the basic cyberspace information provided in the program, can benefit from this more psychologically sophisticated integrative process that requires the objective assistance of a professional consultant.

Dissociating online and offline activities – immersing oneself in cyberspace as an experience isolated from the rest of one's life – can be a problem for some people. It is one of the classic features of Internet addiction (Greenfield, 1999; Suler, 1999; Young, 1998). Therefore, one of the integrative functions of a cybertherapeutic program and its consultant is to help people bring their online and in-person living together. In eQuest, the suggestions are deceptively simple: discuss your offline life with your online companions; contact online companions on the phone or in-person; talk with family and friends about online experiences; interact online with the people you know in-person. As simple as they seem, these activities are essential for gaining new perspectives, preventing misperceptions of online experiences, and discovering different dimensions of the client's lifestyle and personality.

Although online, people also tend to dissociate from their body. Cyberspace is a sedentary activity that easily becomes a disembodied experience. Although some advocates of online living praise the value of minds connecting directly without the "distraction" of physical presence, it is a mistake to think that our bodies play no role in our sense of self or in our online encounters. Using felt-sense exercises (Gendlin, 1982), eQuest encourages people to become aware of body sensations while online and to understand how those sensations inform our experience of what we encounter in cyberspace. Aching backs and necks are common symptoms of excessive and perhaps compulsive computing – a bodily warning that it's probably time to stop – but much more subtle sensations reveal underlying emotional reactions to online activities, especially concerning online relationships. Often these reactions are unconscious. The consultant can further enhance such explorations into unconscious responses to cyberspace by encouraging clients to remember and understand their dreams about computers and the Internet. In fact, many of the consultant's attempts at integration – at reading between the lines to detect hidden patterns and themes – are explorations of the unconscious not unlike the interventions of the psychodynamic psychotherapist.

## The context of Cybertherapeutic Theory

The effectiveness of Cybertherapeutic Theory will be determined by the professional and political context in which it develops. A widespread implementation of the theory will require the interdisciplinary efforts of such fields as clinical and cognitive psychology, communications, human-computer interaction, and Internet technology. The software and hardware possibilities, the psychological research on the six factors underlying Cybertherapeutic Theory, and the clinical implications of such possibilities and factors must develop hand-in-hand. The most effective model for a cybertherapy program might involve an interdisciplinary team that helps decide what psychotherapeutic approach, with which clinician, in what type of online environment, would work best for a particular client. A cybertherapeutic program for a client might involve a package of several types of online activities, with the package designed and conducted by the interdisciplinary team. Although assessments based on Cybertherapeutic Theory would serve as the overarching structure for designing interventions, the wide variety of possible interventions would require the development of specializations in online clinical work, training programs, and perhaps even certifications.

For cybertherapeutic systems to succeed, the complex ethical, professional, and legal issues related to online clinical work that are currently being debated must be resolved (Anthony & Goss, 2003; Barnett & Scheetz, 2003; Hsiung, 2002; Kraus, 2004; Ragusea & VandeCreek, 2003). These issues include the development of standards for specialized training, verification of the client's identity, the insurance of privacy, and clinical work across political boundaries.

A successful and widespread implementation of Cybertherapeutic Theory would require the development of online networks that integrate consumer information, referral systems, assessment strategies, the interdisciplinary teams, and the cybertherapeutic environments. One important feature of these networks will be linking online and in-person services, as well as providing consultation to clients on how to navigate them. Ideally, the result will be networked services in which technicians, researchers, cybertherapeutic consultants, and clinicians work together to empower clients in making effective decisions about optimizing mental health.

### References

Anthony, K. (2004). Therapy online – the therapeutic relationship in typed text. In G. Bolton, S. Howlett, C. Lago, & J. K. Wright (Eds.), *Writing cures: An introductory handbook of writing in counselling and psychotherapy* (pp. 133–141). Hove, East Sussex, UK: Brunner-Routledge.

Anthony, K., & Goss, S. (2003). Ethical thinking in online therapy. In D. Hill (Ed.), *Forms of ethical thinking in therapeutic practice* (pp. 50–66). London, UK: Open University Press.

Barak, A., & Buchanan, T. (2004). Internet-based psychological testing and assessment. In R. Kraus, J. Zack, & G. Stricker (Eds.), *Online counseling: A handbook for mental health professionals* (pp. 217–239). San Diego, CA: Elsevier Academic Press.

Barnett, J. E., & Scheetz, K. (2003). Technological advances and telehealth: Ethics, law, and the practice of psychotherapy. *Psychotherapy: Theory, Research, Practice, Training, 40*, 86–93.

Bellafiore, D. R., Colòn, Y., & Rosenberg, P. (2004). Online counseling groups. In R. Kraus, J. Zack, & G. Stricker (Eds.), *Online counseling: A handbook for mental health professionals* (pp. 197–216). San Diego, CA: Elsevier Academic Press.

Casteel, M. A. (2003). Teaching students to evaluate Web information as they learn about psychological disorders. *Teaching of Psychology, 30*, 258–260.

Chang, T. (2005). Online counseling: Prioritizing psychoeducation, self-help, and mutual help for counseling psychology research and practice. *Counseling Psychologist, 33*, 881–890.

Chechele, P. J., & Stofle, G. (2003). Individual therapy online via email and Internet relay chat. In S. Goss & K. Anthony (Eds.), *Technology in counselling and psychotherapy: A practitioner's guide* (pp. 39–58). Houndmills, UK: Palgrave Macmillan.

Childress, C. A. (1999). Interactive e-mail journals: A model of providing psychotherapeutic intervention using the Internet. *CyberPsychology & Behavior, 2*, 213–221.

Davison, K. P., Pennebaker, J. W., & Dickerson, S. S. (2000). Who talks? The social psychology of illness support groups. *American Psychologist, 55*, 205–217.

Day, S. X., & Schneider, P. L. (2002). Psychotherapy using distance technology: A comparison of face-to-face, video, and audio treatment. *Journal of Counseling Psychology, 49*, 499–503.

Epstein, J., & Klinkenberg, W. D. (2001). From Eliza to Internet: A brief history of computerized assessment. *Computers in Human Behavior, 17*, 295–314.

Finn, J. (1995). Computer-based self-help groups: A new resource to supplement support groups. *Social Work with Groups, 18*, 109–117.

Gaggioli, A., Mantovani, F., Castelnuovo, G., Wiederhold, B., & Riva, G. (2003). Avatars in clinical psychology: A framework for the clinical use of virtual humans. *CyberPsychology & Behavior, 6*, 117–125.

Gendlin. E. (1982). *Focusing*. New York: Bantam Books.

Glantz, K., Rizzo, S. A., & Graap, K. (2003). Virtual reality for psychotherapy: Current reality and future possibilities. *Psychotherapy: Theory, Research, Practice, Training, 40*, 55–67.

Glueckauf, R. L., Fritz, S. P., Ecklund-Johnson, E. P., Liss, H. J., Dages, P., & Carney, P. (2002). Videoconferencing-based family counseling for rural teenagers with epilepsy: Phase 1 findings. *Rehabilitation Psychology, 47*, 49–72.

Godin, S., Truschel, J., & Singh, V. (2005). Assessing quality assurance of self-help sites on the Internet. *Journal of Prevention & Intervention in the Community, 29*, 67–84.

Goss, S., & Anthony, K. (2004). Ethical and practical dimensions of online writing cures. In G. Bolton, S. Howlett, C. Lago, & J. K. Wright (Eds.), *Writing cures: An introductory handbook of writing in counselling and psychotherapy* (pp. 170–178). Hove, East Sussex, UK: Brunner-Routledge.

Greenfield, D. (1999). *Virtual addiction*. Oakland, CA: New Harbinger.

Griffiths, K. M., & Christensen, H. (2000). Quality of web based information on treatment of depression: Cross sectional survey. *British Medical Journal, 321*, 1511–1519.

Hsiung, R. C. (2000). The best of both worlds: An online self-help group hosted by a mental health professional. *CyberPsychology & Behavior, 3*, 935–950.

Hsiung, R. C. (2002). Suggested principles of professional ethics for e-therapy. In R. C. Hsiung (Ed.), *e-Therapy: Case studies, guiding principles and the clinical potential of the Internet* (pp. 150–165). New York: Norton.

ISMHO Clinical Case Study Group. (J. Suler, lead author). (2001). Assessing a person's suitability for online therapy. *CyberPsychology and Behavior, 4*, 675–680.

Jencius, M., & Sager, D. E. (2001). The practice of marriage and family counseling in cyberspace. *The Family Journal: Counseling and Therapy for Couples and Families, 9*, 295–301.

Kim, A. J. (2000). *Community building on the web*. Berkeley, CA: Peachpit Press.

King, S. A., Engi, S., & Poulos, S. T. (1998). Using the Internet to assist family therapy. *British Journal of Guidance and Counseling, 26*, 43–52.

King, S. A., & Moreggi, D. (1998). Internet therapy and self-help groups: The pros and cons. In J. Gackenbach, (Ed.), *Psychology and the Internet: Intrapersonal, interpersonal, and transpersonal implications* (pp. 77–109). San Diego, CA: Academic Press.

Kraus, R. (2004). Ethical and legal considerations for providers of mental health services online. In R. Kraus, J. Zack, & G. Stricker (Eds.), *Online counseling: A handbook for mental health professionals* (pp. 123–144). San Diego, CA: Elsevier Academic Press.

Madara, E. J. (1997). The mutual-aid self-help online revolution. *Social Policy, 27*(3), 20–26.

Manchanda, M., & Mclaren, P. (1998). Cognitive behaviour therapy via interactive video. *Journal of Telemedicine and Telecare, 4*(Suppl. 1), 53–55.

Morahan-Martin, J. M. (2000). How Internet users find, evaluate, and use online health information: A cross-cultural review. *CyberPsychology & Behavior, 7*, 497–510.

Morahan-Martin, J., & Anderson, C. D. (2000). Information and misinformation online: Recommendations for facilitating accurate mental health information retrieval and evaluation. *CyberPsychology & Behavior, 3*, 731–746.

Murphy, L. J., & Mitchell, D. L. (1998). When writing helps to heal: E-mail as therapy. *British Journal of Guidance and Counseling, 26*, 21–32.

Ouellette, P. M., & Sells, S. (2001). Creating a telelearning community for training social work practitioners working with troubled youth and their families. *Journal of Technology in Human Services, 18*, 101–116.

Palmiter, D., Jr., & Renjilian, D. (2003). Clinical web pages: Do they meet expectations? *Professional Psychology: Research & Practice, 34*, 164–169.

Pollock, S. L. (2006). Internet counseling and its feasibility for marriage and family counseling. *Family Journal: Counseling and Therapy for Couples and Families, 14*, 65–70.

Ragusea, A. S., & VandeCreek, L. (2003). Suggestions for the ethical practice of online psychotherapy. *Psychotherapy: Theory, Research, Practice, Training, 40*, 94–102.

Rees, C. S., & Stone, S. (2005). Therapeutic alliance in face-to-face versus videoconferenced psychotherapy. *Professional Psychology: Research and Practice, 36*, 649–653.

Rheingold, H. (2000). *The virtual community: Homesteading on the electronic frontier.* Cambridge, MA: MIT Press.

Riessman, F. (1965). The helper therapy principle. *Social Work 10*, 26–32.

Riva, G. (2000). From telehealth to e-health: Internet and distributed virtual reality in health care. *CyberPsychology & Behavior, 3*, 989–998.

Riva, G. (2003). Virtual environments in clinical psychology. *Psychotherapy: Theory, Research, Practice, Training, 40*, 68–76.

Salem, A. D., Bogat, G. A., & Reid, C. (1997). Mutual help goes on-line. *Journal of Community Psychology, 25*, 189–207.

Sander, F. M. (1999). Couples group therapy conducted via computer-mediated communication: A preliminary case study. *Computers in Human Behavior, 12*, 301–312.

Schuemie, M. J., Van der Straaten, P., Krijn, M., & Van der Mast, C. A. P. G. (2001). Research on presence in virtual reality: A survey. *CyberPsychology & Behavior, 4*, 183–201.

Simpson, S. (2003). Video counselling and psychotherapy in practice. In S. Goss & K. Anthony (Eds.), *Technology in counselling and psychotherapy: A practitioner's guide* (pp. 109–128). Houndmills, UK: Palgrave Macmillan.

Stofle, G. S. (2002). Chat room therapy. In R. C. Hsiung (Ed.), *e-Therapy: Case studies, guiding principles and the clinical potential of the Internet* (pp. 92–135). New York: Norton.

Suler, J. (1984). The role of ideology in self-help groups. *Social Policy 12*, 29–36.

Suler, J. (1987). Computer-simulated psychotherapy as an aid in teaching clinical psychology. *Teaching of Psychology, 14*, 37–39.

Suler, J. (1989). Mental imagery in psychoanalytic treatment. *Psychoanalytic Psychology, 6*, 343–366.

Suler, J. (1999). To get what you need: Healthy and pathological Internet use. *CyberPsychology and Behavior 2*, 385–394.

Suler, J. (2000). Psychotherapy in cyberspace: A 5-dimension model of online and computer-mediated psychotherapy. *CyberPsychology and Behavior 3*, 151–160.

Suler, J. (2004a). The online disinhibition effect. *CyberPsychology and Behavior 7*, 321–326.

Suler, J. (2004b). The psychology of text relationships. In R. Kraus, J. Zack, & G. Stricker (Eds.), *Online counseling: A handbook for mental health professionals* (pp. 19–50). San Diego, CA: Elsevier Academic Press.

Suler, J. (2005). eQuest: Case study of a comprehensive online program for self-study and personal growth. *CyberPsychology and Behavior, 8*, 379–386.

Suler, J. (2006). *The psychology of cyberspace.* Retrieved on June 1, 2007, from www.rider.edu/users/suler/psycyber/psycyber.html (originally published 1995).

Tichon, J. G., & Shapiro, M. (2003). The process of sharing social support in cyberspace. *CyberPsychology & Behavior, 6*, 161–170.

Weinberg, H. (2001). Group process and group phenomena on the Internet. *International Journal of Group Psychotherapy, 51*, 361–378.

Wiederhold, B. K., & Wiederhold, M. D. (1998). A review of virtual reality as a psychotherapeutic tool. *Cyber psychology & Behavior, 1*, 45–52.

Wright, J. (2002). Online counselling: learning from writing therapy. *British Journal of Guidance & Counselling, 30*, 285–298.

Yalom, I. (1995). *The theory and practice of group psychotherapy.* New York: Basic Books.

Young, K. (1998). *Caught in the net.* New York: Wiley.

Zuckerman, E. (2003). Finding, evaluating, and incorporating Internet self-help resources into psychotherapy practice. *Journal of Clinical psychology, 59*, 217–225.

# 6 Exposure in Cyberspace as Means of Enhancing Psychological Assessment

*Azy Barak and Liat Hen*

## Introduction

For those who regularly surf through cyberspace and experience it as a parallel and not unusual social environment – whether this takes the form of online forums, chat rooms, or personal communication through instant messaging (IM) – it is customary to encounter various types and exhibitions of human behavior. Many Internet surfers, in the beginning, are convinced that most other surfers impersonate, lie, cheat, or at the very least attempt to pull your leg; later, however, it occurs to them that this basic premise is generally wrong. After spending much time in virtual communities, publicly and privately interacting with numerous anonymous individuals, many people start to realize that their behavior in cyberspace reflects their actual personalities or mood states. To their astonishment, as they observe over time other people's gestures, behavioral patterns, writing styles, frequency and intensity of involvement in group situations, personal associations, vocabulary, choice of verbal expressions, netiquette, and other features of their online behavior – all based on textual communication – laypeople realize that they can learn a great amount about themselves and about others. Moreover, it occurs to them that under these circumstances, they could learn *even more* about many people's personality dispositions, attitudes, moral values, sensitivities, habits, needs, and preferences than in an offline, face-to-face (F2F) environment. This intuitive recognition by many Internet users is consistent with what behavioral theorists and researchers of cyberspace have argued in regard to the emergence of self in cyberspace. That is, in contrast to common belief, we now know that many people, when immersed in cyberspace, remove their everyday, offline masks and games and expose their more authentic selves, revealing their longer-term personality dispositions and traits or their current mood and emotional state (McKenna, 2007; also see McKenna, Chapter 10).

This chapter takes another step in this knowledge direction. Under the assumption that people not only tend to express and reflect themselves in online situations but also usually feel comfortable doing so, the idea advanced here is that the online environment may constructively be used to assess and evaluate people in professional terms. Because psychologists so widely use and need assessment and evaluation activities – for clinical, educational, vocational, and other purposes – cyberspace may be professionally exploited to enhance traditional methods of assessment and evaluation. This, in turn, might increase the level of assessment validity or, at least, expand its perspectives, on the one hand, and generate improvements in location convenience (i.e., assessment from a distance) and perhaps even time elasticity (i.e., asynchronous assessment), on the other. This chapter attempts to provide this new approach with some firm grounding and offers examples of its possible application. It should be noted that the emphasis of this chapter is on Internet-based assessment rather than stand-alone computer-assisted testing; for elaboration of the distinctions between these procedures, see Reips (2002, 2006).

## Psychological Assessment

Psychological assessment is considered a regular activity conducted by psychologists for various clinical assessments and diagnostic purposes involving the need to measure, compare, characterize, and evaluate clients. Assessment is normally based on psychological testing, professional interviewing, and behavioral observation. Traditionally, these three major approaches require F2F contact between professional and client to enable the implementing of a certain assessment procedure. The methods conducted for assessment – though prevalent and highly standard – usually yield reasonable to mediocre assessments in terms of criterion-related validity.

In recent years, psychological assessment has been conducted through online instruments and procedures for many purposes, among them clinical diagnostics of a variety of problems and concerns (e.g., Andersson, Carlbring, Kaldo, & Strom, 2004; Carlbring et al., 2007; Emmelkamp, 2005; Hyler, Gangure, & Batchelder, 2005; Luce et al., 2007); neuropsychological and rehabilitation assessment needed to enhance a therapeutic technique (e.g., Erlanger et al., 2003; Medalia, Lim, & Erlanger, 2005; Schatz & Browndyke, 2002); educational assessment needed to evaluate learning, school-related adjustment, and the selection of candidates for specific study programs (Wu & He, 2004); vocational, organizational, and career-related assessments needed for job selection work-related assessment among applicants or employees (e.g., Bartram, 2004; Konradt, Hertel, & Joder, 2003; Whitaker, 2007); career counseling assessment for identifying personal abilities, interests, values, and personality characteristics relevant for choosing and developing specific career paths (Barak & Cohen, 2002; Jones, 2004; Kleiman & Gati, 2004); group and social assessment to identify and detect specific factors at work in the group, focus group, community, or organization (Bartram, 2004; Reid & Reid, 2005); family assessment conducted to identify interpersonal patterns that might interfere with family relations and functioning (Bischoff, 2004); and the like. In this regard, a recent meta-analysis performed by Hyler et al. (2005) found no differences between assessment conducted by telepsychiatry and in-person psychiatric assessment.

## Problems in Traditional Psychological Assessment

Conventional psychological assessment has more than a few limitations and drawbacks. Although scholars educate for and foster valid assessment procedures, it is no secret that even in the best-case scenario, most assessment tools reach but a mediocre level of criterion-related measurement validity. It seems that many practitioners are impressed more by the face validity of a test, especially when it is accompanied by impressive theory and good marketing (e.g., Rorschach Inkblot Test; Draw a Tree) than by rigorous empirical research and complicated statistics, particularly if findings prove inconsistent with beliefs. In many cases, moreover, psychologists adopt an assessment method they are familiar with, have in their possession, or learned and became accustomed to using rather than what meets basic psychometric and methodological requirements and, consequently, professional and ethical expectations. Likewise, many practitioners tend to ignore (or downplay) that their interviews are, in principle, biased, thus leading to invalid impressions of interviewees in many cases. Many practitioners also disregard "contaminating" factors or do not give them significant weight when assessing people. Therefore, they may come away with erroneous evaluations just because a person undergoing assessment may at the time be anxious, nervous, depressed, tired, or distracted by personal issues. Although textbooks and study programs teach and emphasize this crucial possible error, it seems that in reality, an assessment does become invalidated because of it.

A comprehensive review of the numerous problems and limitations of traditional psychological assessment would be too exhaustive to cover in the framework and context of this chapter. Its weaknesses are many, however, despite the natural unwillingness of professionals to admit to it. Traditional, paper-and-pencil psychological testing is a typical example. Although standard textbooks (e.g., Aiken, 2003; Anastasi & Urbina, 1996) list numerous serious threats to the quality of measurement in this type of assessment, practitioners in the field disregard them in many cases as though diagnostics based on such tests are fully valid and reflect people accurately. Among these threats to quality are the use of invalid or inappropriate tests, use of obsolete versions of tests (now even sold through online auctions; LoBello & Zachar, 2007), the lack of the use of updated test norms; uneasiness and anxiety that many people experience when taking tests, especially in public; unreliable scoring; and more. These problems not only limit the validity of test results but also, in many cases, cause a highly invalid assessment.

Another major vehicle with which to conduct psychological assessment is interviewing. Although an interview enables direct contact with and impressions of a person – in the context of psychiatric evaluation, clinical diagnostics, job application, or screening applicants for study program – and therefore offers an added value over written psychological tests, personal interviews suffer from many weaknesses, too (e.g., Eder & Harris, 2005; Sommers-Flanagan &

Sommers-Flanagan, 2002). These range from the inconvenience of scheduling personal appointments, the need to travel (sometimes for very long distances), many interviewers' unavoidable biases pertaining to certain personal characteristics of interviewees, rehearsal by interviewees to improve their impression, to the inevitable significant effects of the interview setting and atmosphere.

A third major tool in psychological assessment has to do with situation testing, usually as part of an assessment center (AC), where people – in individual, dyad, or group settings – are asked to perform certain tasks because some of their personality characteristics are reflected in their behavior and are evaluated by professional, trained observers (Thornton & Rupp, 2005). Although this approach may overcome major limitations of paper-and-pencil tests and allow trained raters to observe actual behaviors in challenging situations, it has the disadvantages of inconvenience, high cost, and possibly biased raters' judgments.

Most applications of psychological assessment take part in certain locations and facilities. Exploiting the Internet in this regard enables independence from this binding conception and the adoption of an innovative approach, one that calls for disconnection from the preconception of a common physical *place*, and sometimes *time*, in the context of assessment. The first rule of this new approach states that a person undergoing assessment does not have to be in the same physical location as the assessor. The possible, and highly probable, result is that client and therapist (or assessor) does not have to be in a F2F situation. The second rule states that these two people do not have to interact with each other at a given time but may each operate on his or her own time schedule. If this rule is known and accepted in advance, along with certain guidelines pertaining to it, then communication might not only be uninterrupted but even lively and more immersive. This is not the typical manner in which psychological practitioners are trained to interact with clients, nor is common in typical, normal, and close human interaction. However, perhaps *because* of its atypicality, the new conception may enhance and elevate assessment to new, much-improved levels.

The following sections will make an attempt to show how the Internet can be harnessed to overcome some of the shortcomings of the three main methods of psychological assessment: testing, interviewing, and situation testing. It is important to note that the use of the Internet is being advocated not only for what is now obvious, namely, convenience, availability, affordability, and acceptability of computers and the Internet as a prevalent means of communication. Beyond these important advantages, the unique psychological environment created by the Internet enables professional psychological assessment to advance to a new level and attain *greater validity*, not just more efficiency. The contention here is that applying assessment procedures in cyberspace, given that they are executed in a way that is consistent with recent scientific knowledge and understanding about cyberspace as a social environment and given people's experiences in it, will result in a significantly improved means of assessing and diagnosing people for a variety of purposes.

## Cyberspace as a Social Environment

The Internet was first thought to provide a convenient and efficient communication network. With its innovative technical developments and the public's awareness of the capabilities and advantages of this technology, the Internet has become much more than a communication device (such as the telephone); it is effectively a virtual social environment. We may refer to it as such, since people can – and do – behave through it (or "in" it) in a parallel way to almost everything they do in their physical ("offline") environment, whether socializing, learning, shopping, dating, playing games, discussing, making love, selling, watching movies, listening to radio or any music they like, doing research, participating in conferences, stealing, sharing opinions, voting and electing, gossiping, fighting, or just wandering around. The virtual environment – often termed *cyberspace* – thus provides an alternative social environment for those who will not or cannot, for any reason, use their physical environment for the same purposes. Research shows that this is not only an option for many people but has become an actual, normal way of life (Bargh & McKenna, 2004; Haythornthwaite & Hagar, 2004; Joinson, McKenna, Postmes, & Reips, 2007; McMillan & Morrison, 2006; Selwyn, Gorard, & Furlong, 2005; see also Barak & Suler, Chapter 1).

It is not only that people use the Net massively and intensively for a variety of social and professional activities, but also they behave in this online environment in ways that we have only recently begun to comprehend. The study of online behavior, though not new – it goes back more than two decades, when more primitive, text-only computer-mediated communication networks were in use – has actually been upgraded with the introduction of new technologies, such as fast, broadband, and wireless Internet connection; much more sophisticated, colorful, larger computer screens; the emergence of blogs and blogging, these virtual soapboxes ushering in a considerable personal and social change; and significantly upgraded browsing and online communication software. These innovations have made "old" research of the 1980s and 1990s almost obsolete, as they have been accompanied by behavioral and social changes. The cumulative research available strongly indicates that at least a part of people's behavior online is similar in many ways to their offline behaviors. As a result, we can legitimately adopt models of behavior determined and constructed in the context of F2F physical social situations and apply them to cyberspace, using various theoretical frameworks, from psychoanalysis (e.g., Turkle, 2004) to social psychological theory of planned behavior (e.g., Hsu, Yen, Chiu, & Chang, 2006), for example. However, it is also known that this adoption of a theory is not simple or direct. For example,

the effects of deindividuation in explaining various online behaviors, originally developed in the context of offline behaviors in F2F groups and crowds
(e.g., Festinger, Pepitone, & Newcomb, 1952; Prentice-Dunn & Rogers, 1982),
though once thought to be highly relevant in computer-mediated communication (e.g., Spears & Lea, 1992), has only partially been supported and often
much refuted, in more recent research of online environments (Joinson, 2001;
Moral-Toranzo, Canto-Ortiz, Gómez-Jacinto, 2007; Yao & Flanagin, 2006).

   To understand psychological aspects in cyberspace more accurately, we
apparently need more specific, relevant theoretical approaches. Several such
models and viewpoints have been postulated in recent years, some of which
will be noted here. One of the phenomena characterizing cyberspace is that a
highly inducing environment is created in terms of *flow* and *presence*. "Flow"
refers to the feeling of a complete, energized focus on an activity, characterized
by a high level of enjoyment and fulfillment (Csikszentmihalyi, 1990; see also
Voiskownsky, Chapter 4). By "presence" is meant the subjective experience of
"being there" in an immersive, computer-mediated environment, such as virtual reality and simulators (Jacobson, 2001). These two special psychological
processes create a new sense of existence, in which one disconnects (to different
degrees) from the physical reality and experiences emotions and a state of mind
different from the offline environment in which one is engaged at the same time
(Barak, 2007b). This unique psychological state has several important implications. In the context of this chapter, the situation creates a special opportunity
to observe and evaluate people in a relatively "purer" state of being, relatively
less distracted by and defensive of stimuli existing in their physical environment, on the one hand, and more directly, closely connected to their selves, on
the other. Because of certain characteristics of online interpersonal communication and subsequent relationships, such as anonymity and unidentifiability,
McKenna and her associates have argued – and provided research and numerous examples in support of this argument – that people in cyberspace reveal
their "true selves" (Bargh, Fitzsimons, & McKenna, 2003; Bargh, McKenna,
& Fitzsimons, 2002; McKenna, 2007; McKenna & Bargh, 1998, 1999; 2000;
McKenna & Green, 2002; McKenna, Green, & Gleason, 2002; McKenna &
Seidman, 2005a, 2005b; see also McKenna, Chapter 10). According to this
view, while people offline behave and express themselves in ways that are
filtered, censored, fabricated, and acted – following several dynamic reasons,
such as social norms and sanctions, shame, and guilt feelings – people online
feel freer to be closer to their basic personality structure, express their "real
me," and actualize psychological and social needs, frequently those that go
unsatisfied in their offline environment. According to this approach – and
in great contrast to common belief – not only are people in cyberspace not
looking to impersonate and fabricate, their anonymity enabling them to cheat,
fake, lie, and be phony at will, but just the opposite is true: they generally
behave in a more truthful, frank, authentic, honest, candid, and transparent
manner, so that their basic, true needs and values are revealed. Thus, in the

context of this chapter, according to McKenna's point of view, the personal pattern of behavior online is a more direct and more valid way to assess and evaluate a person because significant psychological parts of an individual are revealed in his or her online behavior that might be concealed, or distorted, in the offline environment.

The approach outlined above is related to one of the major psychological processes existing in cyberspace, known as the *online disinhibition effect*. Although attention to this phenomenon was given a while ago in studies of computer-mediated communication (e.g., Kiesler, Siegel, & McGuire, 1984; Spears & Lea, 1994; Walther, 1996), the online disinhibition effect, including its positive as well as negative aspects, has become a primary theme in understanding human behavior in cyberspace with the emergence of the Internet (e.g., Joinson, 1998, 2001; Suler, 2004a). The online disinhibition effect is assumed to be a product of several psychological factors that operate in cyberspace and have a great impact on people's behavior. The main factors are considered to be anonymity, invisibility, lack of eye contact, neutralization of people's status, asynchronicity as a major mode of communication, and textuality of communication. As a result of these factors, expressed dynamically but whose relative powers and directions are still to be empirically determined, an individual goes through a disinhibition process, whereby behaviors (including verbal expressions) not normally displayed in the physical environment, or not as intensively or prevalently, are expressed and become more frequent on the Internet. Consequences of disinhibition are negative and positive; typical negative behavior outcomes of the online disinhibition effect ("toxic disinhibition"; Suler, 2004a) include expressions of aggression, acting out, defamation, flaming, emotional blackmailing, interference, impersonation, flooding, and sabotaging. Such negative behaviors are typical in virtual communities (including online support groups) and other online interpersonal contacts (e.g., Alonzo & Aiken, 2004; Harman, Hansen, Cochran, & Lindsey, 2005; Lee, 2005; Malamuth, Linz, & Yao, 2005; Suler, & Phillips, 1998; Thompson, 2003). Positive behavioral outcomes of the online disinhibition effect ("benign disinhibition"; Suler, 2004a) include expressions of self-awareness and self-understanding, pro-social activities (such as advice and information giving), volunteering, emotional sharing and positive self-disclosures, philanthropic behaviors and donation giving, and emotional support (Barak, 2007a; Barak & Bloch, 2006; Barak & Dolev-Cohen, 2006; Joinson, 2001, 2003; Joinson & Paine, 2007; McKenna et al., 2002; Meier, 2004; Sillence & Briggs, 2007; Tichon & Shapiro, 2003).

The combination of the three phenomena mentioned previously – the intensive psychological effects of flow and presence, the emergence of "true self," and the online disinhibition effect – make cyberspace a psychologically unique social environment. People, in general, behave in it more freely and more openly than in their offline, physical environment. Moreover, if we add to these powerful psychological phenomena that cyberspace is generally a less clear, less comprehensible environment, in which ambiguity and vagueness prevail. This ironically allows users – owing to inherent psychological mechanisms – to produce dynamically thoughts, beliefs, attributions, and assumptions to close cognitive gaps and make situations more meaningful and clearer (Barak, 2007b; Suler, 2002; Turkle, 2004). These psychological mechanisms cause people to project inner needs, expectations, wishes, and perceptions so that their overt behavior reflects their personality characteristics.

Thus, in the context of accurate assessment of self, which is the focus of the current chapter, it seems that behavior in an online environment offers an innovative approach to knowing people. That is, professionals can take the advantage of online social environments and exploit them for assessment purposes, thus achieving the fundamental aim of knowing and understanding a person in a more valid way. Anderson (2003) suggested, in the context of organizational selection, that the area of online testing is opportunistic and lacks theory and rationale. The psychological conception that we have presented here thus seems to close this gap, as it adds the missing theoretical framework to the practice of assessment performed online.

The relationships among type of use (and abuse) of the Internet, online behavioral patterns, writing content and style in various online channels, and individual differences have been found and replicated in numerous empirical observations. For example, both Barak and Miron (2005) and Mandrusiak et al. (2006) found clear indications of suicidality in online writing content and style. Quayle, Vaughan, and Taylor (2006), among others, showed how personal values were related to Internet use in the context of sexual offenders. Harman et al. (2005) reported on relationships between children's faking and impersonation and a number of relevant personal dispositions. In a series of studies, Amichai-Hamburger and his associates (e.g., Amichai-Hamburger, Fine, & Goldstein, 2004; Amichai-Hamburger, Wainapel, & Fox, 2002) found clear connections between various Internet-usage behaviors and relevant personal traits. Cooper, Griffin-Shelley, Delmonico, and Mathy (2001) and Chaney and Chang (2005) supplied evidence for a clear relationship between some personality characteristics and compulsive use of online sex. Caplan (2005) showed how one's level of social skills is related to problematic Internet use (see also Morahan-Martin, Chapter 3). This selection of research findings in different areas strongly supports the notion that much can indeed be learned about people when observing their online behavior. In the context of this chapter, the implications are clear: The psychological mechanisms and processes that interact and operate in influencing a person in cyberspace expose and reveal the user's personality characteristics.

Despite the existence of a large amount of evidence concerning the interrelationship of personal characteristics and online behavior, this subject has yet to be projected onto current psychological assessment. That is, cyberspace as a social environment has not sufficiently been exploited to follow, observe, and diagnose people. If we combine the significant factors noted previously – the self online, online disinhibition effect, flow and presence, psychological effects on people's experiences, and the expression of personal dispositions in one's behavior in the cyberspace environment – together with notable practical advantages of using online assessment (i.e., availability, convenience, low cost, easily logged sessions), the opportunity for more valid and more efficient assessment becomes clear. Add to this that assessors (e.g., raters, examiners, evaluators) can be invisible online and hardly intrusive (Fritsche & Linneweber, 2006) and that evaluations may be performed at a time of one's choice and in cases even be automated, the adoption of the online environment for assessment purposes becomes compelling.

In the sections to follow, we will review, speculate, and propose ideas relating to online assessment. Some of these ideas have already been in use, at least to some degree; we will try to promote the notion that psychological assessment may be upgraded to another level completely by effectively using the emerging area of the psychology of cyberspace.

## Opportunities for Online Testing

Online psychological testing has been in use for a decade. In the beginning, online tests were used mainly for free self-testing. Perhaps for that reason, many of these tests were amateur and far from following professional standards, often created by nonprofessionals who exploited the new, exciting medium for fun and entertainment and much less for pure professional purposes. The intrusion of the Internet into society, on the one hand, and improved technology, on the other, encouraged professionals to enter this field in acknowledgment of the advantages that computers and the Internet offer in delivering different kinds of psychological tests. Whereas doubts and suspicions characterized the early stages of online testing – mainly in regard to the questionable quality of measurement under new conditions and the moderating of contaminating factors (e.g., computer skills) – cumulative research evidence (see reviews by Barak & Buchanan, 2004; Barak & English, 2002; Naglieri et al., 2004) has convinced even the most skeptical that this was a legitimate and, in many cases, apparently an even preferred, psychological testing procedure. The field is still under development, and basic standards and procedures are still being investigated, constructed, and proposed (see Bartram, 2006; International Test Commission, 2006; Lumsden, 2007; Sale, 2006).

### Methods and Possible Applications

*Online testing* is a generic term that refers to numerous types of testing procedures and techniques. First, it includes not only tests, in terms of testing domains of achievements, skills, abilities, and specific aptitudes but also the measuring of a variety of traits and personality dispositions, attitudes, values, preferences and interests, perceptions, feelings, evaluations, and more. The general idea is to replace traditional paper-and-pencil tests and questionnaires with computerized versions that are administered on a computer screen, used by test-takers anywhere and at any time, and centrally maintained and assessed by professionals (occasionally through certain agencies). Second, in taking advantage of the computer's sophisticated capabilities, such tests are not necessarily static; though their questions or items are printed and respondents write or mark their answers, these tests are potentially *dynamic*. This means they can do the following: (a) exploit the convenient, easy, and immediate means of being *updated and edited*; (b) use *multimedia* components, including sound, color pictures, animations, and video, to enrich and allow a broader spectrum of senses to take part in the test; (c) use *interactive* components, so that respondents may actively interact with stimuli provided, such as moving objects, coloring, fill-out puzzles, drawing, and so on; (d) use an *online clock* to track and control test-takers' performance or implicit attitudes (Nosek, Banaji, & Greenwald, 2002); (e) easily *save* test materials, answers, or results (depending on option availability and permission) for sharing or future use; (f) obtain scores or assessments *quickly and accurately* by using the most up-to-date methods and norms. Other special advantages include (a) the ability to take the test (in most cases) at a *location and time of ones choice*, thus saving travel time, parking, and other nuisances; (b) avoiding the use of wasted and *environmentally unfriendly materials* (e.g., paper); and (c) easy use of the test and the results for statistics and *research*.

## Online Testing Methods

Although this chapter employs the general term *online testing*, there are quite a few diverse testing techniques and approaches. The simple and most common procedure entails publishing an interactive test on the web, where respondents can freely mark (or fill in) their responses on a multiple-choice form. Once respondents, by a click, submit the test to the server, a preassigned software program calculates scores and provides feedback to the test-takers. There are numerous variations of this general procedure: for instance, scores may not be provided to test-takers but to a professional or to an assessment agency; scores might be converted to, or accompanied by, a written text that provides interpretations and, at times, recommendations. As mentioned, many tests on the Internet do not go through any process of professional supervision; however, there are quite a few professional tests online, many of these protected, with site access and test-taking available only to those authorized to enter.

To use online tests for professional purposes –for clinical assessment or job selection – closer supervision of both the test-takers and the testing procedure and environment should take place. Various options exist to fulfill this requirement, including preauthorization for test-takers and taking the test from preassigned, closely monitored computers (usually, supervised by local personnel in a testing agency).

In terms of professional needs and expectations, however, allowing at least preliminary clinical assessment or initial screening of job applicants to be done by computer is quite innovative and has many advantages. Recent studies by Bartram and Brown (2004); Chuah, Drasgow, and Roberts (2006); and Herrero and Meneses (2006) showed that even under circumstances of possible cheating on the tests or biasing test scores or manipulating them to make a better impression, the results remained consistent between paper-and-pencil and online versions. However, Bauer and McCaffrey (2006) argued that coaching might significantly damage assessment validity for many psychological tests and listed several ways to cope with this threat. However, coaching is possible – and may actually make a difference – with offline tests, too, though Johnson (2005) found that web users were more likely to manipulate their responses than paper-and-pencil personality test-takers. In the context of assessment for the selection of employees, Tippins et al. (2006) listed problems of unprotected online psychological tests and provided several ideas on coping with the issue.

## Testing in a Virtual Social Environment

Although the main advantage of online testing might be viewed as distance test-taking, it may be argued that another advantage – psychological rather than technical in nature – of this technology occurs in the virtual social environment of test-taking. That is, when a test-taker connects to a computer and becomes immersed in a virtual environment, which is created by a computer's numerous capabilities, the surfer to a great degree disconnects from the physical environment in which he or she is physically engaged. A person so disconnecting experiences a unique psychological process that is usually nonexistent in other, more realistic environments. This experience is characterized by faster, deeper, and broader opening-up, authenticity, and disclosure. These factors are considered ideal for assessment purposes because people reveal more quantity online, as well as more accurate information about themselves. In the areas of personality, attitudes, values, needs, and emotional assessment, this phenomenon may become a crucial factor because many people typically tend to avoid disclosure, or to manipulate it, fearing that full (or extensive) exposure might harm them in some way or that they are less self-focused when offline. Exploiting online communication for testing, then, might be beneficial not only for the sake of convenience and cost but also to for the very validity of the assessment desired. Indeed, a recent study by Hanna, Weinberg, Dant, and Berger (2005) found that respondents to an online survey showed higher sense of self-awareness, were more thoughtful, and disclosed deeper feelings than paper-and-pencil survey, regardless of level of anonymity.

Most research into online testing and assessment conducted to date has examined their similarity to and consistency with the same tests or procedures administered with paper and pencil. Almost all research has revealed highly *correlated* results between offline and online testing. In many cases, however, online test scores were *elevated* (though Carlbring et al. [2007] showed no level differences) relative to the scores of the very same offline tests. The question then becomes: What scores – those obtained offline or online – better reflect the person being tested? In our view – on the assumption that online testing takes place in a psychological environment that promotes self-focus, openness, and authenticity – the scores of tests filled out online that are aimed at assessing various personal qualifications reveal more valid reflections of the test-takers. Consequently, we argue that online testing is preferred; furthermore, it has to be encouraged, primarily because of its increased assessment validity, because the measurement covers traits being assessed in a fuller way, beyond mere convenience for the test-taker (and other advantages, listed earlier). This argument still needs to be supported empirically, or refuted; however, at least for a part of test-takers, it seems to be that the virtual environment induces a more valid reflection of their personality. An interesting question thus emerges: Is there anything typical of these particular test-takers? Are there test-takers for whom taking tests online causes the assessment to be more valid, whereas for others it makes no difference?

Recent examples of the very high level of equivalence between paper-and-pencil and online versions of the same tests have been reported in clinical tests used to diagnose psychiatric conditions (Collins & Jones, 2004; Kozma-Wiebe et al., 2006; Medalia et al., 2005), assess stress and depression (Herrero & Meneses, 2006), evaluate major personality traits (Chuah et al., 2006), appraise health behavior (Hewson & Charlton, 2005; Mangunkusumo et al., 2006), estimate cognitive abilities (Williams & McCord, 2006), and assess vocational variables (Bartram & Brown, 2004; Jones, Harbach, Coker, & Staples, 2002). However, findings of other studies, which identified particular differences between offline and online versions of the same test, raise the inevitable question: Which procedure better detects (that is, assesses more validly) test-takers' characteristics? For example, Andersson, Westöö, Johansson, and Carlbring (2006), in applying the Stroop Test (color naming of colorful color names), found that social phobic test-takers responded to the test items differently online from offline but inconsistently with offline differences found in their research and in previous studies. Buchanan et al. (2005) reported differences in factorial structure between paper-and-pencil and online versions of a memory test. Is there a certain psychologically driven cause for the difference between the online and offline versions that relates to certain characteristics of the test-takers (e.g., level of clinical disturbance)? Could it be, for example, that phobic people in cyberspace respond in a particular way that better reflects (and consequently leads to a more valid assessment of) their psychological condition?

On the basis of the present review and current ideas, still another question arises: Are we approaching a new, revolutionary way of human assessment

(Barak, 2006; Buchanan, 2001; Wilhelm & McKnight, 2002)? Does the Internet, in addition to its great practical and technical contribution to testing (Bartram, 2006), provide a whole new *psychological* platform for assessment and evaluation, one that will bring us closer to the desired goal of valid, ethical means of testing and assessment, thereby enhancing psychological diagnostics to previously unknown levels?

## Research and Applications

Much research has taken place in regard to online testing in recent years. New tests and types of tests have been adopted to be delivered online, and research has examined the similarity of the results, along with other important questions, to provide data to substantiate professional use. However, research that addresses the basic idea discussed here – that taking a test in a virtual environment might enhance test validity, at least for some types of tests and some type of test-takers – is still to be conducted.

Obviously, not all psychological tests can and should be converted into an online form and administered through the Internet. In some cases, this might prove totally erroneous because of the nature of the test, the trait measured, situational circumstances, or other possible factors (e.g., Buchanan, Ali, et al., 2005). In addition, questions regarding the feasibility and utility of online testing must still be investigated. Although online testing allows much convenience for many, as it saves having to appear at a certain physical location, it may introduce bias, whether related to the digital divide, computer or Internet anxiety, computer skills (including typing), or medical or physical factors impinging on computer accessibility (Bridgeman, Lennon, & Jackenthal, 2003). In addition, financial costs, for either test-takers or professionals, might be high and, therefore, undermine exploiting the advantages of online testing. Questions relating to continuous updates of test versions and standardization (test norms), copyrights, privacy protection, and so on (Barak, 2003, 2006) still have to be investigated, as well. Thus, we do not advocate eliminating offline testing procedures but rather allowing (and promoting) the adoption of the newer procedures.

Despite the lack of research on questions directly related to validity and the question we have raised in regard to the incremental validity of online tests, professional experience, in addition to existing empirical findings about various other issues relevant to online psychological testing, highly supports this means of testing and assessment (e.g., Buchanan, 2001, 2002; Buchanan, Johnson, & Goldberg, 2005), though some issues and problems need further development and research (Buchanan, 2007). Nor should test-takers' preferences for computer and Internet testing, found in studies in various domains, be underrated (e.g., Barak & Cohen, 2002; Lumsden, Sampson, Reardon, Lenz, & Peterson, 2004; Mangunkusumo et al., 2006), as the Internet has become a common ground for many. The argument advanced in this chapter, however, that cyberspace induces many people's authentic, natural behaviors, which are consequently reflected in responding to various stimuli, must still be empirically supported. If it is, then online psychological testing – even if perhaps conducted with some alterations and adjustments – might become not only technically possible and economically and socially feasible but actually a better way to assess and evaluate people's characteristics.

## Opportunities for Online Interviewing

The idea of conducting professional interviews online by using synchronous (i.e., chat or IM) or asynchronous (i.e., e-mail) communication modes was first raised in the late 1990s. It appeared that the computer could offer significant assistance for conducting interviews in that computerized conversations had the advantage of including subjects and questions that might sometimes be missed, as it was easy for the interviewer to glance over the interview transcript. It also was realized that this format could enhance objectivity in a personal interview, since irrelevant information (e.g., skin color, looks) was less intrusive and influential on interviewers (Zetin & Tasha, 1999). Hamilton and Bowers (2006), in the context of conducting e-mail interviews to collect data for their qualitative research, listed the major advantages of conducting interviews this way, among them: it was more convenient for both interviewer and interviewee, both had time to reflect on questions, there was no need for transcription and no loss of "raw" data, the audit trail was easily maintained, and there was increased reliability. However, they also noted some of the main disadvantages of online interviewing: the potential increased for loss of confidentiality, there was a lack of both spontaneity and important visual cues, and silence was missing as an interpretive moment (though this could have been accurately recorded). McCoyd and Schwaber Kerson (2006) reported unusual disclosures by women who were interviewed by e-mail in the context of a study on fetal anomaly; these disclosures perhaps would not have been made otherwise. Similarly, Beck (2005) used e-mails to interview women in the context of researching birth trauma. She pointed to the special experience that this method caused interviewees to go through, such as an enhanced feeling of being attended and listened to, a sense that someone cared, and a general experience of making a difference in their comments. Hunt and McHale (2007) provided a detailed example of e-mail interviewing of people who suffered from alopecia. They were able to collect information from participants who responded to invitation in online forums. Therefore, they apparently reached a broad sample, which provided relevant and important information for the psychologically-focused study. With their experience, these researchers developed guidelines for conducting e-mail interviews. These latter three examples may indicate that interviewees might feel more comfortable without having to make eye contact or a F2F encounter with interviewers, so they reveal more and are more accurate about themselves.

Online interviews have been noted not only for experiential but also for technical and practical advantages they afford. Yoshino et al. (2001) found online psychiatric interviews they conducted through televideo to be quite effective and reliable when using wideband (as most Internet communication is nowadays). Crichton and Kinash (2003) described three studies in which they successfully used online interviews. In addition to many other advantages, these authors especially emphasized the *engaging* factor of this type of interviewing, allowing dynamic, flowing, stimulating, and inviting conversations. In the context of research on AIDS, Davis, Bolding, Hart, Sherr, and Elford (2004) reported using synchronous communication software with some of the sample with whom they conducted online interviews. They emphasized the low cost, convenience, and readiness of unseen interviewees to open up. However, they also indicated difficulties associated with the ambiguity of the situation (i.e., unidentifiability and invisibility), that is, the textual interviews differed from F2F interviews in lacking traditional social components that are typical of personal interactions. Davies and Morgan (2005) reviewed the massive use of computerized, automated online-interviewing software used to identify distress (e.g., abuse) experienced by adolescents. They concluded that the use of this approach allowed better detection of sensitive issues that were typically not revealed in F2F situations. Mühlenfeld (2005) conducted a study in which students were interviewed online about behaviors usually unspoken about in public (e.g., shoplifting, masturbation). He compared two online methods – visible versus invisible interviewees. As expected, talking about issues was more prevalent than admitting them. No difference of these effects was found, however, between the two methods, and interviewees tended to expose themselves to a great degree in both types. Stieger and Göritz (2006) investigated the feasibility and credibility of interviewing people via IM software and found that most people were willing to be interviewed this way. They also found that information disclosed in these interviews was usually truthful, even though many of the interviewees were totally anonymous (that is, they could lie and deceive if they wanted to). The use of online interviews for a special population – people with disabilities – was shown to be very effective and perhaps more appropriate than F2F interviews (Bowker & Tuffin, 2002, 2003, 2004). With this particular population, the ability to communicate invisibly so that a visible handicap does not interfere with the interview and does not bias or (directly) affect the interviewer might be of crucial value in terms of the validity of interviewers' evaluations. At the same time, online, invisible interviews with people with visible handicap promote equal opportunities – a highly appreciated value in many societies. Egan, Chenoweth, and McAuliffe (2006), who used e-mail interviews with people with traumatic brain injury, emphasize the special value of time for reflection and insight for this type of handicap in using written, asynchronous communication channels. Another innovative development in implementing online interviewing was conducted by Paine, Reips, Stieger, Joinson, and Buchanan (2007), who used *automated* interviewing through ICQ to collect data concerning users' privacy concerns.

The researchers used this IM software with closed and open questions formats. Participants cooperated with the study and provided useful information.

These studies, representing pioneering attempts in this emerging approach, share, to the researchers' enthusiasm and amazement, what might be considered serendipitous findings. Actually, just like laypeople, uninformed professionals usually expect online interviews to provide erroneous, biased, manipulated, and, in many cases, faked content. This preconception is obviously related to the general view of the Internet as a trivial, casual, playground-like environment. It is a view, however, that misses the point that people actually express themselves in cyberspace quite openly, freely, and authentically. Research that has accumulated in recent years consistently shows that textual expressions in Internet writing are not casual and show strong foundations in the theory of individual behavior. For example, Barak and Miron (2005) found that suicidal people freely wrote in a distinct way in cyberspace that was different from other people, a characteristic that is consistent with the psychological theory of suicide and related offline research. In another context, Cohn, Mehl, and Pennebaker (2004) showed how people's free and casual writing on the Internet reflected real mood and social changes in relation to the events of September 11, 2001. Another study that illustrated how online writings authentically reflected thoughts and inner experiences was conducted by Stone and Pennebaker (2002), who showed how people candidly and naturally expressed themselves online after the death of Princess Diana. In a different sort of research, Marcus, Machilek, and Schütz (2006) found that owners of personal websites presented themselves in a way that was consistent with assessments made by a personality inventory. This evidence is in line with accumulating research showing that people's expressions online are less deceiving than assumed, contrary to popular belief (Caspi & Gorsky, 2006).

## Online Interviewing: Methods and Possibilities

Interviewing a person online entails more than just conducting a textual conversation through an online chat or e-mail software. Because of the factors mentioned, which make Internet communication unique, an online conversation frequently leads to a sort of intimate relationship in which an interviewee experiences relatively more release and opening up. They thus may respond to interviewers' questions at deeper and broader levels of self-disclosure than in F2F interviews, occasionally touching sensitive personal subjects or portraying emotionally laden behaviors toward interviewers. These special expressions could (and should) become an integral – and unique – part of the assessment and evaluation process so that an online interview is transformed into a "testing environment" rather than a mere exchange of information, enabling the dynamics of flow, presence, disinhibition, and "true self" to come into play to reveal significant characteristics of interviewees. Undoubtedly, such a special sort of interview requires specific training, and interviewers need to be skillful and prepared in handling online interviews, reacting professionally and ethically to a variety of circumstances, and producing valid assessments. The opportunities for online interviewing, however, are great and may significantly enhance the ability to assess people in a very different way from what has traditionally been done.

Online interviewing presents a very different approach to interviewing, regardless of its purpose, whether for education, employment, career choice, or clinical diagnostics. The basic assumption behind this approach is that meeting with a person at a certain place and a certain time and interacting with him or her F2F is not necessarily crucial in order to make a professional evaluation of that person. Without underestimating the value of nonverbal communication, personal appearance, and physical cues, this approach highlights the importance of two other key factors: verbal expressions, especially those made in writing, and invisibility, an advantage when interacting with another person.

For many people, writing provides a special opportunity to express themselves candidly and accurately, more so than through talking (Anthony, 2004; Suler, 2004b). There are several reasons for this phenomenon: First, when a person writes, she or he is more concentrated in expressing inner thoughts and feelings when responding to another person than she or he is when talking. A writer usually focuses on internal experiences rather than impressing another person, responding defensively while being physically exposed, and feeling examined and interrogated when talking to the other person. Writing often reflects inner-talk; that is, as though a person is talking to oneself. Second, even if an online interview is conducted in synchronous mode, let alone asynchronously, an interviewee has the opportunity to reflect and edit his or her responses to better reflect his or her thoughts and feelings. This is due to both a psychological factor, that of feeling less stressed by a visible, straight-looking interviewer, and a technical factor, being able to plan, correct, and rewrite text, in great contrast to personal expression using the spoken word. Third, the convenience component should not be undervalued. When both interviewee and interviewer meet at a time of choice (regularly independent of standard office hours), and each is located at a different place of choice and physical convenience, it is reasonable that the tension, stress, and anxiety typically caused by the situation – and that interferes with the very essence of the interview, impairing its validity – play a lesser role, allowing the interview to flow more smoothly and to touch more authentic issues. Fourth, the written interviews allow their future use for reanalysis and revaluation, supervision, and other uses (e.g., training, research) fully and accurately. The interviewer does not have to rely on his or her immediate impressions, which are sometimes too harsh and biased, but has the opportunity to read the interview transcript under better personal conditions to learn and to draw professional conclusions. Incidentally, the interviewee, too, can obtain a copy of the interview transcript for later reflection or even for making corrections or supplementing information if needed. Fifth, online interviews have the special advantage of neutralizing irrelevant influences on the interviewer (where these are indeed irrelevant), such as beauty and physical appearance, clothing, skin color, accent, and so on, which are known to affect interviewers' impressions (Shahani, Dipboye, & Gehrlein, 1993). The use of text, therefore, enables the interviewer to refer only to important and relevant issues. Obviously, if factors related to visible features are relevant for an assessment, an online interview might prove invalid or insufficient. Sixth, online interviews can be considered especially appropriate for initial or preliminary screening interviews, especially in the context of employee selection. They would save expense, and only applicants who passed the online interview stage would be invited for further application stages.

## Limitations and Need for Further Research

Online interviews have several limitations and drawbacks that sometimes make them problematic and may impair their validity as a professional source of psychological assessment. First, many people have difficulty, or are limited in, expressing themselves in writing. If this factor is not an integral part of the assessment itself, wrong impressions might emerge about these people. Second, many people do not feel comfortable conversing with another person without seeing and being visible to the interlocutor. This condition, too, might introduce an error ingredient into the assessment, especially if the interviewer is unaware of this personal factor. Third, many people type slowly or have technical limitations in operating the computer. These and other practical matters might negatively affect their impression in the interview. Fourth, physical appearance, nonverbal behavior, clothing, and other personal aspects, none of which can be identified in textual interviews, might be essential for the very evaluation in some cases. In other words, these factors may introduce a bias, on the one hand, but also may contribute to a more relevant, valid assessment, on the other. This means that the use of online interviews should be conducted on a *differential* basis, in reference to the specific purpose of the given interview.

## Opportunities for Online Situation Testing Through an Assessment Center

Given the approach presented in this chapter, the connection between an assessment center (AC) and cyberspace seems quite obvious. The Internet, with all its features, characteristics, and special advantages, could provide answers to some of the main problematic issues associated with the traditional AC. This section will first describe typical ACs and examine their common aspects. It will then glance at typical exercises used in an AC and clarify the main behavioral dimensions assessed through it. Finally, we will examine whether and how ACs can become more effective, and perhaps more valid, by applying them online.

Joiner (2000, p. 319) defines AC as "a process employing multiple techniques and multiple assessors to produce judgments regarding the extent to which a participant displays selected competencies." It consists of a standardized evaluation of behavior based on specifically developed job-related simulations, also referred to as *situation tests*. In addition to simulations, evaluations may also be based on interviews and psychological tests. Although there is no such thing as a typical AC (Spychalski, Quinones, Gaugler, & Pohley, 1997), professional guidelines, based on theory, research, and practice, have been laid down for an activity to be officially regarded as an AC. These guidelines require the inclusion of job analysis, behavioral classifications, multiple assessment methodology, multiple simulations, and multiple assessors for the effective implementation of an AC (Joiner, 2000).

Throughout an AC procedure, assessments are conducted on individuals in a standardized manner by trained assessors. Judgments about participants are made by multiple assessors and combined to form ratings for the competencies that the AC is designed to measure. The end product of an assessment center typically includes an overall assessment rating, as well as a written report that reflects both qualitative information describing a participant's performance and quantitative information representing specific ratings of competencies measured. Competencies refer to a cluster of observable behaviors (e.g., leadership). Common competencies that tend to be measured across ACs are communication, leadership, teamwork, drive, organizing and planning, problem solving, and tolerance for stress/uncertainty (Arthur, Day, McNelly, & Edens, 2003).

The exercises, or situation tests, used in AC are designed to resemble work situations that might actually occur. Simulations include in-basket exercises, group discussions, interviews with "subordinates" or "clients," fact-finding, decision-making problems, oral presentation, and written communication (Byham & Thornton, 1986). New and emerging exercises have been developed to fit developmental changes in organizations and jobs and to better simulate the current workplace. Other AC upgrades include the use of "a total simulation" (i.e., using common characters in developmental exercises) and the adoption of videotapes presenting an actual organizational environment and atmosphere. Typically, intelligence and ability tests are used in conjunction with ACs, as research shows that the combination of intelligence data and behavioral observations provides a markedly better means of evaluating people than does either factor alone (Thornton & Byham, 1982). Self-reports, supervisor's evaluations, and peer ratings are integrated into the data collected in many ACs.

Since its origin during World War II, the AC method has continued to increase in popularity for the purposes of selecting and developing employees. This increase has largely been fueled by research supporting the predictive validity of the AC method (Gaugler, Rosenthal, Thornton, & Bentson, 1987; Hunter & Hunter, 1984; Schmitt, Gooding, Noe, & Kirsch, 1984). Despite AC's popularity, however, some essential drawbacks have been noted. First, its cost is usually high. A traditional assessment center involves six to ten participants and two to four assessors, and lasts one to three days. Training of assessors, which is essential for the validity of ratings, consumes many hours, too, and adds to the high cost of the ongoing use of traditional ACs. In a typical AC, an assessor-manager leaves his or her job for two or three days to observe participants' performance in simulations and then spends an additional day or two in meetings with other observers to make final evaluations (Byham, 2006). In financial terms, the time of the assessors' simulations, observations, and meetings before, during, and after AC is also obviously extremely high, especially if overhead expenses (e.g., place, equipment, administration, refreshments) are added into the cost. Second, the need to organize a long meeting of many people at a certain time and place is exhausting and complicated and significantly interferes with their routine work and personal functioning.

## Online Assessment Center

Based on the theoretical considerations outlined earlier and the basic principles of AC, which are aimed at evaluating people's behavior for professional assessment, the Net can be exploited in an innovative way. For one thing, the training of assessors can be conducted online. This could include not only instruction and guidelines but also discussions among assessors, exercises in analyzing and evaluating multiple written cases, and discussions of ratings. The professionals (line managers and human resources people alike) do not have to leave their office and can "meet" at a certain online area. Moreover, if this training is conducted asynchronically (i.e., via a forum), time becomes flexible, too, to suit an individual's schedule. Furthermore, resources can effectively be used for numerous training workshops, thus saving much expendable costs. Once assessors are trained, they may be used in numerous ACs, regardless of their geographical location, enabling the use of human organizational resources to become more efficient, as well.

The main point of this proposal is that the execution of an AC may take place online. Participants – whether job applicants or an organization's employees being assessed for professional development – may take part in an AC team, regardless of their geographical location. Size limits may be adjustable according to task; several individuals or subgroups may meet in parallel, in either synchronous or asynchronous communication channels. For example, in executing an "in-basket" exercise, in which assignments are designed to create time pressure for participants, who are forced to determine priorities and make decisions on multiple tasks within a short time, a *synchronous* virtual room should be used. A participant receives assignments in real time and responses accordingly. The person's behaviors are fully and automatically documented and later assessed by distant assessors. This means of exploiting assessors is efficient not only in terms of time and location but also in having raw data (a participant's behaviors) logged for more reflective, less immediate evaluations. Other AC assignments – such as letter writing or writing comments on a document – may be executed *asynchronically*, with the participant electronically given the assignments and sending them for assessment at a later time.

Group simulations in cyberspace – either in an asynchronous or a synchronous channel – are easy to execute, monitor, observe, and maintain though an effective chat room should perhaps limit the number of participants. After basic introductions and preparation, participants may take part in a number of exercises generated by text communication from a distance. These simulations may include enrolling in role-play, such as supervisor-supervisee sessions, group discussions and decision making (e.g., NASA's Survival on the Moon), commercial negotiations, deliberation of moral issues, and other tasks that take place in ACs. In addition, if it seems relevant and desired, individual or group voice communication, integrated in advanced software that involve text, sound, and graphics, can be used to allow activities based on spoken deliberations.

It is important to note that the idea proposed here is not to invent a new AC but to convert its traditional form into an innovative format. Accumulating practical experience, along with exercises, assessment procedures, and research findings, is relevant to the proposed format, too, after necessary modifications have been made to adjust the AC activities into the online environment. However, despite the investment needed for this, we believe it will not only vastly improve convenience and meaningfully reduce costs, but first, it will lead to a significant enhancement in assessment validity. As stressed earlier, people usually behave more consistently with their personality and current emotional state when interacting in cyberspace, where factors of anonymity, invisibility, lack of eye contact, and textual-based communication are key features. Thus, the very purpose of AC becomes more realistic under these special virtual circumstances, and participants' assessment significantly more valid despite the lack of visual observation by assessors. As commonly takes place in online groups, the very virtual situation makes people in the group, and causes group processes, to be more blunt and saliently (textually) observable (McKenna, 2007; McKenna & Bargh, 1998; McKenna & Seidman, 2005a, 2005b). The dynamics of the online disinhibition effect directly affects people's behavior; hence, their overt behaviors might more validly reflect dispositions, mood, sensitivities, values, needs, and the like than in F2F situations. A "scenario bank," containing numerous activities suitable for various assessment purposes, can easily be developed to open up opportunities for the organization of an online AC dedicated to a particular purpose. Scenarios can be tagged digitally to signify an association with certain jobs, occupational requirements, and populations, thereby making collecting activities and constructing an online AC relatively simple.

It is also important to note that an AC conducted online, just like a traditional AC, should include interviews and testing, in addition to situation tests. In this way, online tests and online interviews could be integrated with other online activities to create a more comprehensive evaluation. An online AC might, then, be fully operated from a distance, be partly synchronous and partly asynchronous (depending on the specific design and requirements of the AC), and involve various individuals, dyads, and group activities; it would be assessed, at a later time, by a team of online-trained assessors. Such a structure may not only be convenient and less expensive than the traditional employment of AC, but it may even provide more valid evaluations, just as desired by the AC methodology (Byham, 2006).

Obviously, the current proposal needs to be thoroughly empirically examined. Several key questions need to be investigated: To what degree does the lack of nonverbal cues reduce the ability to assess people effectively and validly? Does the textual/verbal ability of participants contaminate participants' assessments, thus reducing validity? To what degree do participants' experience and proficiency with computers and Internet interact with their online behaviors and mask dimensions to be assessed? Given technological failures and limitations, to what degree does the procedure operate effectively? And given this limitation, is it feasible? How assessors should be trained best to conduct online evaluations? Do assessors feel sufficiently comfortable and reassured so that their evaluations are not affected by the online conditions? When (for what jobs, purposes, or people) might it be more worthwhile to use traditional F2F procedures than to go online? These important questions should accompany the development of online AC procedures.

## Problems in Online Assessment

Online assessment is not free of problems. Besides its many advantages and promises as an advanced approach that might add significant dimension to professional evaluations of people, there are specific limitations, characterized by the very online environment. The following sections identify the major problems. Undoubtedly, this area still needs research and development to become routine in professional practice.

### Authentication and Authorization

When interviewing or testing someone online, there is usually no definite way to verify the identity of the interviewee. Not that this problem is nonexistent offline, but it is easier to check and verify identity offline, especially through photo identification. Given that people are obviously motivated to make a good impression, especially in selection situations (in contrast to personal counseling or clinical diagnostics), a potential client might ask someone else to replace him or her as an interviewee or a test-taker. Anonymous and unprotected online tests provide the opportunity for manipulation (Johnson, 2005), though Bartram and Brown (2004) found little empirical evidence to support this claim even in a high-stakes testing situation. Although the use of a webcam might help to overcome (or lessen) this problem, inclusion of visibility might damage other important aspects of an online interview or of online testing; the camera cannot be a solution for asynchronous interviews. Several procedures related to online testing are available for authentication, such as supervised testing (Bartram, 2006); however, they do not provide an option in the case of online interviews. With those, the idea is that a person is interviewed in solitary and with his or her own facilities to promote a high degree of openness and disclosure.

## Technological Failures

Computers and communication networks rely heavily on software and hardware. Failure of a sole link in a long and complicated chain may cause the whole system to collapse. In using the Internet for the assessment purposes detailed here, this activity would not function properly if there were no perfect operation of the thousands of units that enable the system to operate effectively. For instance, the total reliance on electricity (on both ends of the communication dyad and at several mediation stations), without any backup or alternative, makes the whole activity very shaky. Although electrical power interruption is not a common or frequent experience for most people, the very dependence on uncontrolled resources – very different from traditional, F2F conduct – is scary and prevents many firms and professionals from adopting such innovative techniques (Schmidt, 2007).

Similarly, the use of online assessment depends on the smooth operation of complicated personal computers, servers, communication lines, electrical and electronic devices, and complex software. If we add to this list that software and hardware versions should usually be upgraded to fit Internet communication and that there should be a workable fit between the two parties communicating, then both should recognize that the system might not operate properly, and any such breakdown might cause frustration to either party.

## Differential Skills and Computer Anxiety

Basic skills and know-how in operating a personal computer and using online communication are mandatory for an online assessment. People differ, however, in their computer abilities and skills, from very basic to very advanced, which may significantly affect users' computer-related performance (Maki & Maki, 2002; Perry, Simpson, NicDomhnaill, & Siegel, 2003). These differences might be reflected in various types of behavior, from typing speed (relevant in an online chat conversation), to saving files or attaching files, to use of certain software. Obviously, differential skills might influence the way a person is perceived and evaluated, with prior judgments being made that are not necessarily related to the traits and characteristics being assessed. That is, this differential computer-skills factor might introduce an error variance into the quality of the evaluation.

In addition to, and perhaps related to, computer skills, another personal factor interferes with using a computer and the Internet: computer or Internet anxiety. This factor, too, which exists to different extents, causes differential computer functioning (Wood, Willoughby, Specht, Stern-Cavalcante, & Child, 2002), which might directly affect the way a user is perceived in online communication. Moreover, as has been documented, computer anxiety is related to gender: female computer users have been found to be more anxious than males (Broos, 2005), which might lead to an invalid, gender-biased assessment, even if there is no outright bias against women. It seems, however, that gender differences in this respect are gradually disappearing (Shaw & Gant, 2002; Whitaker, 2007) and may not at all constitute a factor in the future.

## The Digital Divide

Ownership, use, and familiarity with computers and Internet are related to socioeconomic class. This social differentiation creates what is known as "the digital gap/divide" (Dance, 2003; Wilson, Wallin, & Reiser, 2003). In using the Net for assessment and expecting people to own a computer, be connected to the Internet, and know how to use them, we may actually be treating people in an undesirable, biased manner. Taking computer ownership and knowledge for granted might not only be unfair toward certain social groups but may have the effect of introducing discrimination against certain people and giving others an advantage in obtaining psychological services, job applications, or acceptance to study programs. Although recent surveys show that the digital gap is decreasing (Judge, Puckett, & Bell, 2006; Korupp & Szydlik, 2005), at least within certain nations, it might still offer a significant factor for consideration in years to come (Pew Internet & American Life Project, 2005).

## Summary

In this chapter, we have attempted to review some of the major difficulties for which traditional methods of psychological assessment have been criticized and to propose a cyberspace transformation by developing innovative online alternatives to promote the professional mission of assessing people. It is our contention that because of unique psychological processes operating in cyberspace that affect people's behaviors, especially in causing them to open them up and so make their overt behaviors and expressions more authentic, the conducting of psychological testing, personal interviews, and situation tests online might offer a more valid source of psychological assessment. Regarding psychological testing, we described the well-documented problems characterizing the traditional paper-and-pencil approach and showed how and why online testing might become a more effective alternative. Concerning professional interviewing, we argued that online interviews – synchronous or asynchronous – not only could be performed but also some important aspects of which were actually preferred. Another common offline procedure for assessment that we proposed for conversion into cyberspace was an AC based on situation tests. We argued that in addition to improved convenience and reduced cost, the very validity of the psychological assessment might be enhanced by using online activities. Although we did note several problems and weaknesses related to applying these methods online, it seems to us that these are temporal in nature and that future technical and sociocultural developments will minimize them altogether. Research is needed to examine a number of issues related to our propositions. Nevertheless, cumulative knowledge seems to support the ideas delineated here.

## References

Aiken, L. R. (2003). *Psychological testing and assessment* (11th ed.). Boston, MA: Allyn & Bacon.

Alonzo, M., & Aiken, M. (2004). Flaming in electronic communication. *Decision Support Systems, 36*, 205–213.

Amichai-Hamburger, Y., Fine, A., & Goldstein, A. (2004). The impact of Internet interactivity and need for closure on consumer preference. *Computers in Human Behavior, 20*, 103–117.

Amichai-Hamburger, Y., Wainapel, G., & Fox, S. (2002). "On the Internet no one knows I'm an introvert": Extroversion, neuroticism, and Internet interaction. *CyberPsychology & Behavior, 5*, 125–128.

Anastasi, A., & Urbina, S. (1996). *Psychological testing* (7th ed.). Upper Saddle River, NJ: Prentice Hall.

Anderson, N. (2003). Applicant and recruiter reactions to new technology in selection: A critical review and agenda for future research. *International Journal of Selection and Assessment, 11*, 121–136.

Andersson, G., Carlbring, P., Kaldo, V., & Strom, L. (2004). Screening of psychiatric disorders via the Internet: A pilot study with tinnitus patients. *Nordic Journal of Psychiatry, 58*, 287–291.

Andersson, G., Westöö, J., Johansson, L., & Carlbring, P. (2006). Cognitive bias via the Internet: A comparison of Web-based and standard emotional stroop tasks in social phobia. *Cognitive Behaviour Therapy, 35*, 55–62.

Anthony, K. (2004). Therapy online – the therapeutic relationship in typed text. In G. Bolton, S. Howlett, C. Lago, & J. K. Wright (Eds.), *Writing cures: An introductory handbook of writing in counselling and psychotherapy* (pp. 133–141). Hove, East Sussex, UK: Brunner-Routledge.

Arthur, W., Jr., Day, E. A., McNelly, T. L., & Edens, P. S. (2003). A meta-analysis of the criterion-related validity of assessment center dimensions. *Personnel Psychology, 56*, 125–154.

Barak, A. (2003). Ethical and professional issues in career assessment on the Internet. *Journal of Career Assessment, 11*, 3–21.

Barak, A. (2006). Internet career assessment. In J. Greenhaus & G. Callanan (Eds.), *Encyclopedia of career development* (pp. 404–406). Thousand Oaks, CA: Sage.

Barak, A. (2007a). Emotional support and suicide prevention through the Internet: A field project report. *Computers in Human Behavior, 23*, 971–984.

Barak, A. (2007b). Phantom emotions: Psychological determinants of emotional experiences on the Internet. In A. Joinson, K. Y. A. McKenna, T. Postmes, & U. D. Reips (Eds.), *Oxford handbook of Internet psychology* (pp. 301–327). Oxford, UK: Oxford University Press.

Barak, A., & Bloch, N. (2006). Factors related to perceived helpfulness in supporting highly distressed individuals through an online support chat. *CyberPsychology & Behavior, 9*, 60–68.

Barak, A., & Buchanan, T. (2004). Internet-based psychological testing and assessment. In R. Kraus, J. Zack & G. Stricker (Eds.), *Online counseling: A handbook for mental health professionals* (pp. 217–239). San Diego, CA: Elsevier Academic Press.

Barak, A., & Cohen, L. (2002). Empirical examination of an online version of the self-directed search. *Journal of Career Assessment, 10*, 387–400.

Barak, A., & Dolev-Cohen, M. (2006). Does activity level in online support groups for distressed adolescents determine emotional relief. *Counselling and Psychotherapy Research, 6*, 186–190.

Barak, A., & English, N. (2002). Prospects and limitations of psychological testing on the Internet. *Journal of Technology in Human Services, 19*(2/3), 65–89.

Barak, A., & Miron, O. (2005). Writing characteristics of suicidal people on the Internet: A psychological investigation of emerging social environments. *Suicide & Life-Threatening Behavior, 35*, 507–524.

Bargh, J. A., Fitzsimons, G. M., & McKenna, K. Y. A. (2003). The self, online. In S. J. Spencer, S. Fein, M. P. Zanna, & J. M. Olson (Eds.), *Motivated social perception* (pp. 195–213). Mahwah, NJ: Erlbaum.

Bargh, J. A., & McKenna, K. Y. A. (2004). The Internet and social life. *Annual Review of Psychology, 55*, 573–590.

Bargh, J. A., McKenna, K. Y. A., & Fitzsimons, G. M. (2002). Can you see the real me? Activation and expression of the "true self" on the Internet. *Journal of Social Issues, 58*, 33–48.

Bartram, D. (2004). Assessment in organisations. *Applied Psychology: An International Review, 53*, 237–259.

Bartram, D. (2006). The internationalization of testing and new models of test delivery on the Internet. *International Journal of Testing, 6*, 121–131.

Bartram, D., & Brown, A. (2004). Online testing: Mode of administration and the stability of OPQ 32i scores. *International Journal of Selection & Assessment, 12*, 278–284.

Bauer, L., & McCaffrey, R. J. (2006). Coverage of the test of memory malingering, Victoria symptom validity test, and word memory test on the Internet: Is test security threatened? *Archives of Clinical Neuropsychology, 21*, 121–126.

Beck, C. T. (2005). Benefits of participating in Internet interviews: Women helping women. *Qualitative Health Research, 15*, 411–422.

Bischoff, R. J. (2004). Considerations in the use of telecommunications as a primary treatment medium: The application of behavioral telehealth to marriage and family therapy. *American Journal of Family Therapy, 32*, 173–187.

Bowker, N., & Tuffin, K. (2002). Disability discourses for online identities. *Disability & Society, 17*, 327–344.

Bowker, N., & Tuffin, K. (2003). Dicing with deception: People with disabilities' strategies for managing safety and identity online. *Journal of Computer-Mediated Communication, 8*(2). Retrieved October 20, 2006, from http://jcmc.indiana.edu/vol8/issue2/bowker.html.

Bowker, N., & Tuffin, K. (2004). Using the online medium for discursive research about people with disabilities. *Social Science Computer Review, 22*, 228–241.

Bridgeman, B., Lennon, M. L., & Jackenthal, A. (2003). Effects of screen size, screen resolution, and display rate on computer-based test performance. *Applied Measurement in Education, 16*, 191–205.

Broos, A. (2005). Gender and information and communication technologies (ICT) anxiety: Male self-assurance and female hesitation. *CyberPsychology & Behavior, 8*, 21–31.

Buchanan, T. (2001). Online personality assessment. In U. D. Reips & M. Bosnjak (Eds.), *Dimensions of Internet science* (pp. 57–74). Lengerich, Germany: Pabst Science Publishers.

Buchanan, T. (2002). Online assessment: Desirable or dangerous? *Professional Psychology: Research & Practice, 33*, 148–154.

Buchanan, T. (2007). Personality testing on the Internet: What we know, and what we do not. In A. Joinson, K. McKenna, T. Postmes & U. Reips (Eds.), *The Oxford handbook of Internet psychology* (pp. 447–460). Oxford, UK: Oxford University Press.

Buchanan, T., Ali, T., Heffernan, T. M., Ling, J., Parrott, A. C., Rodgers, J., & Scholey, A. B. (2005). Nonequivalence of on-line and paper-and-pencil psychological tests: The case of the prospective memory questionnaire. *Behavior Research Methods, 37*, 148–154.

Buchanan, T., Johnson, J. A., & Goldberg, L. R. (2005). Implementing a five-factor personality inventory for use on the Internet. *European Journal of Psychological Assessment, 21*, 115–127.

Byham, W. C. (2006, September). *What is an assessment center? The assessment center method, applications, and technologies.* Paper presented at the International Congress on Assessment Center Methods, London, UK. Retrieved November 20, 2006, from http://www.assessmentcenters.org/articles/whatisassess1.asp.

Byham, W. C., & Thornton, G. C., III. (1986). Assessment centers. In R. A. Berk (Ed.), *Performance assessment: Methods and applications* (pp. 143–166). Baltimore, MD: Johns Hopkins University Press.

Caplan, S. E. (2005). A social skill account of problematic Internet use. *Journal of Communication, 55*, 721–736.

Carlbring, P., Brunt, S., Bohman, S., Austin, D., Richards, J., Öst, L., & Andersson, G. (2007). Internet vs. paper and pencil administration of questionnaires commonly used in panic/agoraphobia research. *Computers in Human Behavior, 23*, 1421–1434.

Caspi, A., & Gorsky, P. (2006). Online deception: Prevalence, motivation, and emotion. *CyberPsychology & Behavior, 9*, 54–59.

Chaney, M. P., & Chang, C. Y. (2005). A trio of turmoil for Internet sexually addicted men who have sex with men: Boredom broneness, social connectedness, and dissociation. *Sexual Addiction & Compulsivity, 12*, 3–18.

Chuah, S. C., Drasgow, F., & Roberts, B. W. (2006). Personality assessment: Does the medium matter? No. *Journal of Research in Personality, 40*, 359–376.

Cohn, M. A., Mehl, M. R., & Pennebaker, J. W. (2004). Linguistic markers of psychological change surrounding September 11, 2001. *Psychological Science, 15*, 687–693.

Collins, F. E., & Jones, K. V. (2004). Investigating dissociation online: Validation of a web-based version of the Dissociative Experiences Scale. *Journal of Trauma & Dissociation, 5*, 133–147.

Cooper, A., Griffin-Shelley, E., Delmonico, D. L., & Mathy, R. M. (2001). Online sexual problems: Assessment and predictive variables. *Sexual Addiction & Compulsivity, 8*, 267–285.

Crichton, S., & Kinash, S. (2003). Virtual ethnography: Interactive interviewing online as method. *Canadian Journal of Learning and Technology, 29*(2). Retrieved January 22, 2007, from http://www.cjlt.ca/content/vol29.2/cjlt29-2_art-5.html.

Csikszentmihalyi, M. (1990). *Flow: The psychology of optimal experience*. New York: Harper and Row.

Dance, F. E. X. (2003). The digital divide. In L. Strate, R. L. Jacobson, & S. B. Gibson (Eds.), *Communication and cyberspace: Social interaction in an electronic environment* (2nd ed., pp. 171–182). Cresskill, NJ: Hampton Press.

Davies, M., & Morgan, A. (2005). Using computer-assisted self-interviewing (CASI) questionnaires to facilitate consultation and participation with vulnerable young people. *Child Abuse Review, 14*, 389–406.

Davis, M., Bolding, G., Hart, G., Sherr, L., & Elford, J. (2004). Reflecting on the experience of interviewing online: Perspectives from the Internet and HIV study in London. *AIDS Care, 16*, 944–952.

Eder, R. W., & Harris, M. M. (Eds.). (2005). *The employment interview handbook*. Thousand Oaks, CA: Sage.

Egan, J., Chenoweth, L., & McAuliffe, D. (2006). Email-facilitated qualitative interviews with traumatic brain injury survivors: A new and accessible method. *Brain Injury, 20*, 1283–1294.

Emmelkamp, P. M. G. (2005). Technological innovations in clinical assessment and psychotherapy. *Psychotherapy and Psychosomatics, 74*, 336–343.

Erlanger, D., Feldman, D., Kutner, K., Kaushik, T., Kroger, H., Festa, J., Barth, J., Freeman, J., Broshek, D. (2003). Development and validation of a Web-based neuropsychological test protocol for sports-related return-to-play decision-making. *Archives of Clinical Neuropsychology, 18*, 293–316.

Festinger, L., Pepitone, A., & Newcomb, T. (1952). Some consequences of deindividuation in a group. *Journal of Abnormal and Social Psychology, 47*, 382–389.

Fritsche, I., & Linneweber, V. (2006). Nonreactive methods in psychological research. In M. Eid & E. D. Diener (Eds.), *Handbook of multimethod measurement in psychology* (pp. 189–203). Washington, DC: American Psychological Association.

Gaugler, B. B., Rosenthal, D. B., Thornton, G. C., III, & Bentson, C. (1987). Meta-analysis of assessment center validity. *Journal of Applied Psychology, 72*, 493–511.

Hamilton, R. J., & Bowers, B. J. (2006). Internet recruitment and e-mail interviews in qualitative studies. *Qualitative Health Research, 16*, 821–835.

Hanna, R. C., Weinberg, B., Dant, R. P., & Berger, P. D. (2005). Do Internet-based surveys increase personal self-disclosure? *Database Marketing & Customer Strategy Management, 12*, 342–356.

Harman, J. P., Hansen, C. E., Cochran, M. E., & Lindsey, C. R. (2005). Liar, liar: Internet faking but not frequency of use affects social skills, self-esteem, social anxiety, and aggression. *CyberPsychology & Behavior, 8*, 1–6.

Haythornthwaite, C., & Hagar, C. (2004). The social worlds of the Web. *Annual Review of Information Science and Technology, 39*, 311–346.

Herrero, J., & Meneses, J. (2006). Short Web-based versions of the perceived stress (PSS) and Center for Epidemiological Studies-Depression (CESD) Scales: A comparison to pencil and paper responses among Internet users. *Computers in Human Behavior, 22*, 830–846.

Hewson, C., & Charlton, J. P. (2005). Measuring health beliefs on the Internet: A comparison of paper and Internet administrations of the multidimensional Health Locus of Control Scale. *Behavior Research Methods, 37*, 691–702.

Hsu, M., Yen, C., Chiu, C., & Chang, C. (2006). A longitudinal investigation of continued online shopping behavior: An extension of the theory of planned behavior. *International Journal of Human-Computer Studies, 64*, 889–904.

Hunt, N., & McHale, S. (2007). A practical guide to the e-mail interview. *Qualitative Health Research, 17*, 1415–1421.

Hunter, J. E., & Hunter, R. F. (1984). Validity and utility of alternative predictors of job performance. *Psychological Bulletin, 96*, 72–98.

Hyler, S. E., Gangure, D. P., & Batchelder, S. T. (2005). Can telepsychiatry replace in-person psychiatric assessments? A review and meta-analysis of comparison studies. *CNS Spectrums, 10*, 403–413.

International Test Commission. (2006). International guidelines of computer-based and Internet-delivered testing. *International Journal of Testing, 6*, 143–171.

Jacobson, D. (2001). Presence revisited: Imagination, competence, and activity in text-based virtual worlds. *CyberPsychology & Behavior, 4*, 653–673.

Johnson, J. A. (2005). Ascertaining the validity of individual protocols from Web-based personality inventories. *Journal of Research in Personality, 39*, 103–129.

Joiner, D. A. (2000). Guidelines and ethical considerations for assessment center operations: International task force on assessment center guidelines. *Public Personnel Management, 29*, 315–331.

Joinson, A. (1998). Causes and implication of disinhibited behavior on the Internet. In J. Gackenbach, (Ed.), *Psychology and the Internet, intrapersonal, interpersonal, and transpersonal implications* (pp. 43–60). San Diego, CA: Academic Press.

Joinson, A. (2003). *Understanding the psychology of Internet behaviour.* Basingstoke, UK: Palgrave Macmillan.

Joinson, A. N. (2001). Self-disclosure in computer-mediated communication: The role of self-awareness and visual anonymity. *European Journal of Social Psychology, 31*, 177–192.

Joinson, A. N., McKenna, K., Postmes, T., & Reips, U.-D. (Eds.). (2007). *Oxford handbook of Internet psychology.* Oxford, UK: Oxford University Press.

Joinson, A. N., & Paine, C. B. (2007). Self-disclosure, privacy, and the Internet. In A. N. Joinson, K. Y. A. McKenna, T. Postmes, & U.-D. Reips (Eds.), *Oxford handbook of Internet psychology* (pp. 235–250). Oxford, UK: Oxford University Press.

Jones, W. P. (2004). Testing and counseling: A marriage saved by the Internet? In J. W. Bloom & G. R. Walz (Eds.), *Cybercounseling & cyberlearning: An encore* (pp. 183–202). Alexandria, VA: American Counseling Association.

Jones, W. P., Harbach, R. L., Coker, J. K., & Staples, P. A. (2002). Web-assisted vocational test interpretation. *Journal of Employment Counseling, 39*, 127–137.

Judge, S., Puckett, K., & Bell, S. M. (2006). Closing the digital divide: Update from the early childhood longitudinal study. *Journal of Educational Research, 100*, 52–60.

Kiesler, S., Siegel, J., & McGuire, T. W. (1984). Social psychological aspects of computer-mediated communication. *American Psychologist, 39*, 1123–1134.

Kleiman, T., & Gati, I. (2004). Challenges of Internet-based assessment: Measuring career decision-making difficulties. *Measurement & Evaluation in Counseling & Development, 37*, 41–55.

Konradt, U., Hertel, G., & Joder, K. (2003). Web-based assessment of call center agents: Development and validation of a computerized instrument. *International Journal of Selection and Assessment, 11*, 184–193.

Korupp, S. E., & Szydlik, M. (2005). Causes and trends of the digital divide. *European Sociological Review, 21*, 409–422.

Kozma-Wiebe, P., Silverstein, S. M., Fehér, A., Kovács, I., Ulhaas, P., & Wilkniss, S. M. (2006). Development of a world-wide web based contour integration test. *Computers in Human Behavior, 22*, 971–980.

Lee, H. (2005). Behavioral strategies for dealing with flaming in an online forum. *Sociological Quarterly, 46*, 385–403.

LoBello, S. G., & Zachar, P. (2007). Psychological test sales and Internet auctions: Ethical considerations for dealing with obsolete or unwanted test materials. *Professional Psychology: Research and Practice, 38*, 68–70.

Luce, K. H., Winzelberg, A. J., Das, S., Osborne, M. I., Bryson, S. W., & Taylor, C. B. (2007). Reliability of self-report: Paper versus online administration. *Computers in Human Behavior, 23*, 1384–1389.

Lumsden, J. (2007). Online-questionnaire design guidelines. In R. A. Reynolds, R. Woods, & J. D. Baker (Eds.), *Handbook of research on electronic surveys and measurements* (pp. 44–64). Hershey, PA: Idea Group.

Lumsden, J. A., Sampson, J. P., Jr., Reardon, R. C., Lenz, J. G., & Peterson, G. W. (2004). A comparison study of the paper-and-pencil, personal computer, and Internet versions of Holland's self-directed search. *Measurement & Evaluation in Counseling & Development, 37*, 85–94.

Maki, W. S., & Maki, R. H. (2002). Multimedia comprehension skill predicts differential outcomes of Web-based and lecture courses. *Journal of Experimental Psychology: Applied, 8*, 85–98.

Malamuth, N., Linz, D., & Yao, M. (2005). The Internet and aggression: Motivation, disinhibitory, and opportunity aspects. In Y. Amichai-Hamburger (Ed.), *The social net: Human behavior in cyberspace* (pp. 163–190). New York: Oxford University Press.

Mandrusiak, M., Rudd, M. D., Joiner, T. E., Jr., Berman, A. L., Van Orden, K. A., & Witte, T. (2006). Warning signs for suicide on the Internet: A descriptive study. *Suicide and Life-Threatening Behavior, 36*, 263–271.

Mangunkusumo, R. T., Duisterhout, J. S., de Graaff, N., Maarsingh, E. J., de Koning, H. J., & Raat, H. (2006). Internet versus paper mode of health and health behavior questionnaires in elementary schools: Asthma and fruit as examples. *Journal of School Health, 76*, 80–86.

Marcus, B., Machilek, F., & Schütz, A. (2006). Personality in cyberspace: Personal Web sites as media for personality expressions and impressions. *Journal of Personality and Social Psychology, 90*, 1014–1031.

McCoyd, J. L. M., & Schwaber Kerson, T. (2006). Conducting intensive interviews using email: A serendipitous comparative opportunity. *Qualitative Social Work, 5*, 389–406.

McKenna, K. Y. A. (2007). Through the Internet looking glass: Expressing and validating the true self. In A. Joinson, K. McKenna, T. Postmes, & U.-D. Reips (Eds.), *Oxford handbook of Internet psychology* (pp. 203–220). Oxford, UK: Oxford University Press.

McKenna, K. Y. A., & Bargh, J. A. (1998). Coming out in the age of the Internet: Identity "demarginalization" through virtual group participation. *Journal of Personality and Social Psychology, 75*, 681–694.

McKenna, K. Y. A., & Bargh, J. A. (1999). Causes and consequences of social interaction on the Internet: A conceptual framework. *Media Psychology, 1*, 249–269.

McKenna, K. Y. A., & Bargh, J. A. (2000). Plan 9 from cyberspace: The implication of the Internet for personality and social psychology. *Personality and Social Psychology Review, 4*, 57–75.

McKenna, K. Y. A., & Green, A. S. (2002). Virtual group dynamics. *Group Dynamics, 6*, 116–127.

McKenna, K. Y. A., Green, A. S., & Gleason, M. E. J. (2002). Relationship formation on the Internet: What's the big attraction? *Journal of Social Issues, 58*, 9–31.

McKenna, K. Y. A., & Seidman, G. (2005a). Social identity and the self: Getting connected online. In W. R. Walker, & D. J. Herrmann (Eds.), *Cognitive technology* (pp. 89–110). Jefferson, NC: McFarland.

McKenna, K. Y. A., & Seidman, G. (2005b). You, me, and we: Interpersonal processes in electronic groups. In Y. Amichai-Hamburger (Ed.), *The social net: Human behavior in cyberspace* (pp. 191–217). New York: Oxford University Press.

McMillan, S. J., & Morrison, M. (2006). Coming of age with the Internet: A qualitative exploration of how the Internet has become an integral part of young people's lives. *New Media & Society, 8*, 73–95.

Medalia, A., Lim, R., & Erlanger, D. (2005). Psychometric properties of the Web-based work-readiness cognitive screen used as a neuropsychological assessment tool for schizophrenia. *Computer Methods and Programs in Biomedicine, 80*, 93–102.

Meier, A. (2004). Technology-mediated groups. In C. D. Garvin, L. M. Gutiérrez, & M. J. Galinsky (Eds.), *Handbook of social work with groups* (pp. 479–503). New York: Guilford.

Moral-Toranzo, F., Canto-Ortiz, J., & Gómez-Jacinto, L. (2007). Anonymity effects in computer-mediated communication in the case of minority influence. *Computers in Human Behavior, 23*, 1660–1674.

Mühlenfeld, H. U. (2005). Differences between "talking about" and "admitting" sensitive behaviour in anonymous and non-anonymous Web-based interviews. *Computers in Human Behavior, 21*, 993–1003.

Naglieri, J. A., Drasgow, F., Schmit, M., Handler, L., Prifitera, A., Margolis, A., & Velasquez, R. (2004). Psychological testing on the Internet: New problems, old issues. *American Psychologist, 59*, 150–162.

Nosek, B. A., Banaji, M., & Greenwald, A. G. (2002). Harvesting implicit group attitudes and beliefs from a demonstration web site. *Group Dynamics, 6*, 101–115.

Paine, C., Reips, U.-D., Stieger, S., Joinson, A., & Buchanan, T. (2007). Internet users' perceptions of "privacy concerns" and "privacy actions." *International Journal of Human-Computer Studies, 65*, 526–536.

Perry, E. L., Simpson, P. A., NicDomhnaill, O. L., & Siegel, D. M. (2003). Is there a technology age gap? Associations among age, skills, and employment outcomes. *International Journal of Selection and Assessment, 11*, 141–149.

Pew Internet & American Life Project (2005). *The future of the Internet*. Retrieved October 15, 2006, from http://www.pewinternet.org/pdfs/PIP_Future_of_Internet.pdf.

Prentice-Dunn, S., & Rogers, R. W. (1982). Effects of public and private self-awareness on deindividuation and aggression. *Journal of Personality ands Social Psychology, 43*, 503–513.

Quayle, E., Vaughan, M., & Taylor, M. (2006). Sex offenders, Internet child abuse images and emotional avoidance: The importance of values. *Aggression and Violent Behavior, 11*, 1–11.

Reid, D. J., & Reid, F. J. M. (2005). Online focus groups: An in-depth comparison of computer-mediated and conventional focus group discussions. *International Journal of Market Research, 47*, 131–162.

Reips, U.-D. (2002). Standards for Internet-based experimenting. *Experimental Psychology, 49*, 243–256.

Reips, U.-D. (2006). Web-based methods. In M. Eid & E. Diener (Eds.), *Handbook of multimethod measurement in psychology* (pp. 73–85). Washington, DC: American Psychological Association.

Sale, R. (2006). International guidelines on computer-based and Internet-delivered testing: A practitioner's perspective. *International Journal of Testing, 6*, 181–188.

Schatz, P., & Browndyke, J. (2002). Applications of computer-based neuropsychological assessment. *Journal of Head Trauma Rehabilitation, 17*, 395–410.

Schmidt, W. C. (2007). Technical considerations when implementing online research. In A. Joinson, K. McKenna, T. Postmes, and U.-D. Reips (Eds.), *Oxford handbook of Internet psychology* (pp. 459–470). Oxford, UK: Oxford University Press.

Schmitt, N., Gooding, R. Z., Noe, R., A., & Kirsch, M. (1984). Meta-analysis of validity studies published between 1964 and 1982 and the investigation of study characteristics. *Personnel Psychology, 37*, 407–422.

Selwyn, N., Gorard, S., & Furlong, J. (2005). Whose Internet is it anyway? Exploring adults' (non)use of the Internet in everyday life. *European Journal of Communication, 20*, 5–26.

Shahani, C., Dipboye, R. L., & Gehrlein, T. M. (1993). Attractiveness bias in the interview: Exploring the boundaries of an effect. *Basic & Applied Social Psychology, 14*, 317–328.

Shaw, L. H., & Gant, L. M. (2002). Users divided? Exploring the gender gap in Internet use. *CyberPsychology & Behavior, 5*, 517–527.

Sillence, E., & Briggs, P. (2007). Please advise: Using the Internet for health and financial advice. *Computers in Human Behavior, 23*, 727–748.

Sommers-Flanagan, J., & Sommers-Flanagan, R. (2002). *Clinical interviewing* (3rd ed.). New York: Wiley.

Spears, R., & Lea, M. (1992). Social influence and the influence of the "social" in computer-mediated communication. In M. Lea (Ed.), *Contexts of computer-mediated communication* (pp. 30–65). London, UK: Harvester Wheatsheaf.

Spears, R., & Lea, M. (1994). Panacea or Panopticon? The hidden power in computer-mediated communication. *Communication Research, 21*, 427–459.

Spychalski, A. C., Quinones, M. A., Gaugler, B. B., & Pohley, K. (1997). A survey of assessment center practices in organizations in the United States. *Personnel Psychology, 50*, 71–90.

Stieger, S., & Göritz, A. S. (2006). Using instant messaging for Internet-based interviews. *CyberPsychology & Behavior, 9*, 552–559.

Stone, L. D., & Pennebaker, J. W. (2002). Trauma in real time: Talking and avoiding online conversations about the death of Princess Diana. *Basic & Applied Social Psychology, 24*, 173–183.

Suler, J. R. (2002). Identity management in cyberspace. *Journal of Applied Psychoanalytic Studies, 4*, 455–460.

Suler, J. (2004a). The online disinhibition effect. *CyberPsychology & Behavior, 7*, 321–326.

Suler, J. (2004b). The psychology of text relationships. In R. Kraus, J. Zack, & G. Stricker (Eds.), *Online counseling: A handbook for mental health professionals* (pp. 19–50). San Diego, CA: Elsevier Academic Press.

Suler, J. R., & Phillips, W. L. (1998). The bad boys of cyberspace: Deviant behavior in a multimedia chat community. *CyberPsychology & Behavior, 1*, 275–294.

Thompson, P. A. (2003). What's fueling the flames in cyberspace? A social influence model. In L. Strate, R. L. Jacobson, & S. B. Gibson (Eds.), *Communication and cyberspace: Social interaction in an electronic environment* (2nd ed., pp. 329–347). Cresskill, NJ: Hampton Press.

Thornton, G. C., III, & Byham, W. C. (1982). *Assessment centers and managerial performance*. New York: Academic Press.

Thornton, G. C., III, & Rupp, D. E. (2005). *Assessment centers in human resource management: Strategies for prediction, diagnosis, and development*. Mahwah, NJ: Erlbaum.

Tichon, J. G., & Shapiro, M. (2003). The process of sharing social support in cyberspace. *CyberPsychology & Behavior, 6*, 161–170.

Tippins, N. T., Beaty, J., Drasgow, F., Gibson, W. M., Pearlman, K., Segall, D. O., & Shepherd, W. (2006). Unproctored Internet testing in employment settings. *Personnel Psychology, 59*, 189–225.

Turkle, S. (2004). *Whither psychoanalysis in computer culture? Psychoanalytic Psychology, 21*, 16–30.

Walther, J. B. (1996). Computer-mediated communication: Impersonal, interpersonal, and hyperpersonal interaction. *Communication Research, 23*, 3–43.

Whitaker, B. G. (2007). Internet-based attitude assessment: Does gender affect measurement equivalence? *Computers in Human Behavior, 23*, 1183–1194.

Wilhelm, O., & McKnight, P. E. (2002). Ability and achievement testing on the World Wide Web. In B. Batinic, U.-D. Reips, & M. Bosnjak (Eds.), *Online social sciences* (pp. 151–180). Seattle, WA: Hogrefe & Huber.

Williams, J. E., & McCord, D. M. (2006). Equivalence of standard and computerized versions of the Raven Progressive Matrices Test. *Computers in Human Behavior, 22*, 791–800.

Wilson, K. R., Wallin, J. S., & Reiser, C. (2003). Social stratification and the digital divide. *Social Science Computer Review, 21*, 133–143.

Wood, E., Willoughby, T., Specht, J., Stern-Cavalcante, W., & Child, C. (2002). Developing a computer workshop to facilitate computer skills and minimize anxiety for early childhood educators. *Journal of Educational Psychology, 94*, 164–170.

Wu, S. Y., & He, Z. (2004). A dynamic Web educational assessment system. In K. Morgan, C. A. Brebbia, J. Sanchez, & A. Voiskounsky (Eds.), *Human perspectives in the Internet society: Culture, psychology and gender* (pp. 449–457). Southampton, UK: WIT Press.

Yao, M. Z., & Flanagin, A. J. (2006). A self-awareness approach to computer-mediated communication. *Computers in Human Behavior, 22*, 518–544.

Yoshino, A., Shigemura, J., Kobayashi, Y., Nomura, S., Shishikura, K., Den, R., Wakisaka, H., Kamata, S., & Ashida, H. (2001). Telepsychiatry: Assessment of televideo psychiatric interview reliability with present- and next-generation Internet infrastructures. *Acta Psychiatrica Scandinavica, 104*, 223–226.

Zetin, M., & Tasha, G. (1999). Development of a computerized psychiatric diagnostic interview for use by mental health and primary care clinicians. *CyberPsychology & Behavior, 2*, 223–229.

# 7 Down the Rabbit Hole: The Role of Place in the Initiation and Development of Online Relationships

*Andrea J. Baker*

When Lewis Carroll's Alice falls down the hole into Wonderland, she encounters a variety of situations in various places: a garden, a forest, a pool, a kitchen, a castle, and a courtroom, among others. The characters she meets who become her acquaintances, friends, and enemies differ depending on her location in her travels, and, of course, her size. She follows the White Rabbit who is terrified of her larger-than-human height in the hallway. She learns to adjust her size to match the places, objects, animals, and people who cross her pathways. People have likened "cyberspace" to the world found through the mirror, the virtual reality on the other side contrasted to the everyday physical world.

As the experience of people online accumulated, researchers differentiated modes of relating within cyberspace such as the use of the asynchronous and the synchronous or real-time media. They have begun to illuminate differences in the types of spaces, places, or settings online (see Baker, 2002, 2005; Baker & Whitty, 2008; McKenna, 2007; Whitty & Carr, 2006). A current line of inquiry attempts to explicate interactions that originate but do not remain in cyberspace, or relationships that span online and offline places. Researchers of online relationships recognize that people online often "felt as though they have gotten to know each other quite well" (Walther & Parks, 2002, p. 549) before meeting offline (Baker, 1998), entering "mixed mode relationships" (Walther & Parks, 2002, p. 542). People develop strong feelings for each other in cyberspace, and forge relationships, from casual acquaintance to close friendships, and intimate partnerships sometimes leading to marriage (see, for example, Baker, 1998, 2005; Ben Ze'ev, 2004; Cooper & Sportolari, 1997; Joinson, 2003; McKenna & Bargh, 2000; McKenna, Green, & Gleason, 2002; Merkle & Richardson, 2000; Wallace, 1999; Whitty & Gavin, 2001). These connections first take place in a virtual world, without the two factors of physical attraction and spatial propinquity, dimensions previously thought essential for interpersonal bonding.

Taking off from the Alice's adventures in new places, this chapter addresses two questions. First, and with primary emphasis, (1) how does the particular online place or space in which a romantic pair meets influence the course of the relationship, especially in the early stages? Then, (2) how does timing, the pacing of the relationship by members of the couple, interact with space to affect the development of a potential couple pairing? Examining primary data and looking at the relevant literature on online dating, the chapter begins the exploratory analysis of how place relates to initial attraction and further commitment in romantic relationships in cyberspace.

## Introduction to Place and Online Relationships

People meet at various places online. The kind of meeting place indicates the kinds of people who gather there, the commonalities they share, their first impressions, and the nature of their initial contact (see Baker, 1998, 2005). McKenna and Bargh (2000) described how sites in cyberspace contain different "gating" properties than physical space and have fewer barriers to interaction. Baker and Whitty (2008) and McKenna (2007) have recently noted that features of various types of online places produce multiple patterns in online relating. The kind of site or online meeting place provides different types of knowledge about the other and points to specific media for first person-to-person contact, for example. "Place" here refers to the space where two people first encounter each other online, and then later on, if they choose to connect in physical space, the kind of place or location of their meeting offline.

An "online relationship" is defined as one where the two in the dyad first met online and are looking to each other for a romantic involvement. In beginning their relationships, the two may have consciously searched for intimate partners, or met online as friends or acquaintances and later developed romantic intentions. The data and literature come mainly from researchers studying intimate pairs and individuals who are dating (or considering it), living together or married. Although personal relationships such as friendships can begin online, and even family relationships can occur mainly online, these are categories of dyads that deserve separate study and, thus, are mentioned only as they relate to the findings on intimate online relationships.

This chapter discusses first, the issues of place or space online and then the intersection of place and time in the formation and development of online relationships. Examining that combination, in particular, may open up new areas for research of relationships in cyberspace. In addition to citations from relevant studies, this chapter draws on the data from research on online couples by the author (see Baker, 2005) and later data collection with quotations taken from interviews conducted through phone and e-mail and from questionnaires provided by pairs who met online. Individuals received pseudonyms upon entry into the research.

## The "Where": Place in Online Relationships

In the discussion of "place," this section first examines (a) the distinction between online and offline places – the parameters of "cyberspace" (Gibson, 1984) versus "real life" places or locations. Included here is the concept of proximity or propinquity's role in interpersonal attraction and how people approximate propinquity in cyberspace.

Moving into (b) the types of places where people interact online, this chapter addresses the goals and dynamics of dating sites in contrast to virtual communities, including discussion boards, games, social networking sites, and chat rooms. Finally, geographical distance (c) between potential partners who meet online is examined, and how that distance affects the process of developing relationships online.

## Place Online and Offline: Attraction in Cyberspace Versus "in Real Life"

Cyberspace and offline reality share properties, and they also differ in kinds of interaction within the two spheres. In the early days of Internet research, researchers treated cyberspace as a pale reflection of "real life," where people related through low bandwidth. Areas comparing interactions in cyberspace to the offline world, or in real life, are first, physical attraction and propinquity, and then, common interests and their relation to the initiation of relationships in cyberspace.

### Physical Attraction and Propinquity Online

In cyberspace, the role of physical attraction is lesser than in physical space, depending on the place. In the theories of attraction before widespread computer-mediated communication, appearance is, in many cases, the prime factor, if not the only one in how people become romantically intertwined (Berscheid & Walster, 1978; Hatfield & Sprecher, 1986), along with closeness in physical space or propinquity. Statistical studies of married couples affirm relative homogamy of age (see Fraboni, 2004; Wheeler & Gunter, 1987) and other demographic characteristics, and earlier research points to factors of attitude similarity and attractiveness in initiation of relationships (see Byrne et al., 1968). In contrast with the primacy of appearance, even in dating sites where photos are common and where people sort through personal profiles partly on the basis of physical appearance, other factors such as place of residence, interests, and style of writing can offset appearance. Older theories of attraction include propinquity or physical presence along with physical attraction. Propinquity or proximity online can mean closeness or co-location in cyberspace without nearness in physical space. If two people meet regularly at a discussion board, even if they post at different times, they grow to know each other, and expect their regular appearances, similar to offline neighbors or co-workers in contiguous offices.

Physical attraction and spatial proximity seem much less important in forming intimate relationships online, given the web (www) and e-mail, which link people from locations worldwide through the media of written communication (see Baker, 1998, 2005; Cooper & Sportolari, 1997; Fiore & Donath, 2004; McKenna & Bargh, 2000; Merkle & Richardson, 2000). Some people in relationships communicate by video or webcams, although almost no one from the author's primary database did so, and none used video more than rarely. Even when presenting photographs or avatars, the process of becoming acquainted with someone begins in a virtual or nonphysical plane, online, leaving the choice of whether to meet in person until later, after assessing what is known already through information provided online.

Although Al Cooper coined the "Triple A" model of accessibility, affordability, and anonymity (Cooper, 1999) to address the popularity of sex in cyberspace, these three attributes help reveal the appeal of meeting people online for all kinds of intimate relationships. Without so much emphasis on physical appearance, cyberspace bonds often begin with mutual self-disclosure and rapport based on similarity of the individuals (see, e.g., Byrne, London, & Reeves, 1968; Duck & Craig, 1975; Pilkington & Lydon, 1997). The connections "stem from emotional intimacy rather than lustful attraction" (Cooper, McLoughlin, & Campbell, 2000, p. 523). This is not to say that the dimension of physical attraction is unimportant. In its absence, the couple will usually not continue the relationship. As one person in the research on couples (Baker, 2005) who met online described the process:

> So, while I don't doubt that I fell in love before the meeting, I think the meeting validated that. Let me use a really bad analogy: Online shopping. I can fill my shopping cart and submit my credit card number. But if something goes wrong after I hit "send," or I somehow forget to hit send, it's all pretty pointless. I've purchased nothing.     (Rosa, interview through e-mail)

Rosa had seen a picture of her future spouse, a head shot that she found unflattering, in comparison to the actual man. She spoke of how both she and her partner liked what they saw upon meeting in person.

On the Internet, people can first get to know others, and then later decide whether to meet, rather than the other way around as in physical space (Rheingold, 1993, p. 26). Attraction begins online, often through the written word or a combination of pictorial and textual representation instead of simply a physical presence. The "click" of felt compatibility comes through connecting in a place online and then communicating through text and frequently by voice before meeting face-to-face (F2F).

## Common Interests and Similarity in Cyberspace

Propinquity or proximity online means that two people have come to find themselves in the same area online, whether playing a game, discussing a television show, or sorting through profiles on a dating site. They have signaled a similar goal, whether to socialize, to gather information, or to seek entertainment.

Depending on the type of site, they have often announced their availability for relationships, whether directly in a dating site ad, or more indirectly with references to spouses or significant others in a profile, or in conversation with people sharing the virtual place.

If two people meet (offline) at a tractor pull, for example, they can assume a certain interest in common. This also applies online, for example, people in an age sixty-and-over group, who discuss movies they've just seen. In a dating site, the availability is announced, a willingness to find at least some kind of relationship, from serious to casual. The difference with places online is that they are often easier to access, using a browser and a search engine or through e-mailing people in the know.

Wright (2004) contrasted cyberspace and real-life space when he looked at exclusively Internet-based relationships (EIBs) in comparison to primarily Internet-based relationships (PIBs). The EIBs take place only on the Internet, while the PIBs contain people interacting both online and offline. Within the PIBs, Wright did not separate those who met online first, the "mixed mode" relationships (Walther & Parks, 2002) that move offline from an online start. He states along with researchers such as Barnes (2003) and Baker (2005) that shared interests replace proximity online. Similarity of interests comes across perhaps more obviously online, says Wright, because the online communication through text in e-mail or chat mutes other variables such as age and appearance.

Downplaying age came up for one online couple when they met at an online dating site. Each chose age limits that excluded the other because their age difference exceeded fifteen years. Elliot saw a profile that attracted his interest in a list of the 100 most recent people to sign up for the site on its home page. He noticed a nickname, "Jordan," that he thought stood for Jordan Baker in the Fitzgerald novel *The Great Gatsby*. Actually, his partner chose a relative's name; however, the couple had much in common, nonetheless:

> I wrote her first, based on both her handle . . . and the text of her ad which indicated a sense of humor (albeit a trifle warped – something I like) and a continuing interest in Theatre and Literature, two thing which are as essential as oxygen to my life.
>
> She replied with a brief "what you wrote was really interesting; I'm busy now but will write more later" note; and she did; and, during the first few exchanges, we discovered an astonishing confluence of unusual and idiosyncratic commonalities, including the fact that about two weeks before we began writing, she had visited a friend in Chicago who lived three blocks from me and had, literally, walked past my apartment several times.
>
> (Elliot, questionnaire)

This couple had posted no photographs, although they exchanged them after beginning their e-mail correspondence. They soon discovered a common fondness for the musical *Pippin* and for the poet Mary Oliver, and all the writings of J. D. Salinger. The two married a little over a year after meeting online.

## Place Online: Dating Sites Versus Online Communities

Two major types of online places for people forming relationships include the online dating sites, and other places, such as discussion forums, chat rooms, e-mail listservs, social networking sites, and games and virtual worlds. These kinds of sites other than the dating services are grouped together here and called online communities, or virtual communities (VCs). People visiting online dating sites have different goals, at least at first, than those at other sites. The sites also differ in how many people tend to establish offline relationships with each other. Finally, the dynamics of forming relationships in the two types of sites are discussed.

### Goals of Online Places and Participants

Members of any particular online place enter with similar goals. People with common interests frequent the same types of online places or spaces, or URLs, the website addresses, in a more technical sense. Within discussion groups, games, chat rooms, and dating services, the individual purposes or motives of participating members may vary, although each type of place has a manifest goal related to the type of activity or conversation found there. Thus, similar kinds of online places created for particular purposes, contain people with similar goals or reasons for being there.

The process of developing an online relationship, including the timing, moves in various directions with different starting and end points related to what the parties desire from the relationship. What the two people want will vary, on the whole, by the kind of site they visit.

Goals of people seeking intimacy online can range from desire for a casual encounter of either brief acquaintanceship or sexual contact (see, for example, Whitty & Fisher, Chapter 8, this volume; Wysocki & Thalken, 2007), to a commitment as deep as marriage or lifelong partnership. Researchers examining members of a large dating site have identified other goals in-between casual and serious intimate relationships, such as meeting a larger quantity of dating partners, becoming more experienced at dating, and finding friends online (Gibbs, Ellison, & Heino, 2006). They found that most people in their study of Match.com sought someone for a dating relationship of some kind. None of the partners' initial goals precluded building a long-lasting, committed relationship.

In fact, some dating and married couples claim they were looking for friends or were actually friends first either in the course of interaction in a VC or in the overt search for compatible others explored through online dating (Baker, 1998, 2005). A public television broadcast about "love" presented a woman about to marry her online partner telling the story of how they first met at a dating site: "Monica found Mark on-line by seeking friends and connections in her new area code. They met and liked each other immediately. They had a lot in common including their work as musicians" (Konner, 2006). The bride said that she and Mark had built a good friendship on the phone so that when she moved to Austin, she agreed to meet him for dinner. When he suggested they date, however, she hesitated, thinking that dating was a step in another direction from their current relationship. She had entered the site with the thought of finding friends rather than a romantic bond.

Another woman, a member of an online community, told how she married an online friend. Her partner was "strictly a friend online," but they became romantically involved offline over a three-year period (Lethsa, quoted in Carter, 2005). Friendship is probably more commonly the goal at online communities than dating sites because people are driven to join because of an interest in discussing particular topics, playing games, or interacting with people they may enjoy. A participant in this author's research explains in an e-mail that meeting in a VC "worked" for her:

> ... mainly because we were not in that community to meet a mate. We were there because we were interested in the community first, to engage in stimulating conversation, to challenge our bases of knowledge, and share our opinions and experiences.    (Miranda, e-mail)

Presuming daters have a variety of goals or motives propelling them to sign up for dating services, two researchers suggest that one dating site alone may not fulfill all their goals (Fiore & Donath, 2004). Site designers would have trouble meeting all of their users' needs for different types of interactions. Even within the diversity of goals, most participants in a recent study of the Match.com dating site wanted to find a person for some kind of dating relationship (Gibbs et al., 2006), although with varying levels of commitment. An advantage of the dating site for couples is the explicitness of the goal of meeting a dating partner, whereas VCs do not generally filter out married people, those already in a relationship, or those who have no interest in becoming coupled.

Showing availability through marital status or presence or absence of other partners is a way of announcing goals in joining an online venue. Dating sites provide boxes where people can check off any or all options that people look for in signing up with a profile. They ask daters to select and mark their own marital status and the status of people they seek to encounter. Some sites explicitly limit their membership to single people who want committed relationships, while others permit different marital statuses and goals that are more casual. The mainstream sites often classify goals into categories as "long-term relationship" or "serious relationship," "short-term relationship," "friend," "activity partner," "casual dating," or "play." Newcomers can choose one or more goals. People who check off "discreet" or use the term in their profiles are understood to have other relationships, whether marriage or live-in partners.

The VCs let people reveal in public or more privately their availability for relationships with those present in the discussion, the game, or the chat room. Sometimes participants describe their spouses and children in their profiles, or they list who lives with them, including pets. People may post photos, depending on community norms. Any information revealed about their age, marital status, and place of residence is usually voluntary rather than fixed by categories provided at the site. VCs differ in how much they require real names rather than just a user ID, although many members know each other primarily by their nicknames. At some VCs, nicknames, or "nicks," relate to the subject matter of the group, such as fans of rock groups who name themselves after band members or particular songs. In others, like those on the dating sites, the nick either describes a personal interest or hobby or is a form of their real names.

## Types of Places and Frequency of Personal Relationships

In two seminal studies of relationships in cyberspace, Parks and his co-authors (Parks & Floyd, 1996; Parks & Roberts, 1998) determined that the majority of people in two types of online groups had formed at least one "personal relationship." The authors studied people in newsgroups, threaded discussion groups on topics of interest, and later, in MOOs, which are text-based virtual realities, and "object-oriented" MUDs, or Multiple User Domains, most commonly used for role-playing games. Of people in newsgroups (Parks & Floyd, 1996), 60.7 percent started relationships, while 93.6 percent in MOOs (Parks & Roberts, 1998) did so, most commonly building friendships (as opposed to more intimate relationships). The researchers found that most of those forming relationships progressed to another communication channel outside of the group, including phone and snail mail. About a third in both types of online communities had gone on to meet f2f. People in MOOs (1998) formed many more romantic partnerships than the members of newsgroups (1996), 26.3 percent to 7.9 percent.

The size of the groups and the goal of the groups made a difference in numbers of people starting online relationships with each other. The immediacy of the communication, in real time in MOOs, as opposed to asynchronous posts on a discussion board, may contribute to the number of relationships developed, along with the group size and goal. Within the newsgroup, the level of experience or length of time in the group and frequency of posting affected the likelihood of forming a relationship (Parks & Floyd, 1996).

In a study of MUDs, Utz (2000) found that more 76.6 percent of her respondents, members of three online adventure games, formed personal relationships. Her research highlighted the role of a player's goal in the degree of involvement in bonding between members. The people most likely to connect with others outside the game play were, first, those uninterested in either game playing or in role-playing but who were there for the interaction online. The role-players were slightly more interested than the game players, whereas those skeptical that friendships could occur online did not form them as much as the other three groups. Those players also used much less "paralanguage" or emoticons and "emotes," nonverbal expressions common in MUDs and MOOs. These include "smilies," such as ☺ and :-D, as well as phrases indicating nonverbal reaction to what others say, such as applause or blowing kisses. The average participant experience in the MUDs studied by Utz was nineteen months, similar to Parks and Floyd's typical newsgroup member of two years.

## The Process of Initiating Relationships in Dating Sites and VCs

The process that occurs in identifying and contacting potential partners online differs with those who meet in online dating sites (DSs) as opposed to those who meet in online communities (Baker, 2005) or VCs. In this chapter, the two terms *online community* and *virtual community* are used synonymously, to mean social groups of people interacting using the Internet. The term *virtual community* (Rheingold, 1993) became popularized early in the history of the World Wide Web, whereas *online community* arose later to emphasize how these groups were taken more seriously and had more "real" impact than the original term perhaps implied. Couples encounter potential partners differently, whether looking specifically for others who meet a formal or informal set of criteria at dating sites, or running into them while participating in more "naturalistic" (McKenna, 2007) settings, groups outside the dating sites.

Before the first meeting with the other person online at a DS, the online daters (1) see others in a setting delimited by their individual parameters set to include the kind of people they consider desirable. Then they can choose to click on any profiles that turn up within the search criteria. In this first online encounter of a potential partner, online daters see only the profile or online ad, and recently, on some sites, can access a voice-recorded message if someone has paid to put one up. The joiner of the VC sees all those who are online at the time he or she goes on. The VC person may talk/write in real time, synchronously, seeing what happens from the time of login. In a lag situation, the asynchronous, posters respond at their leisure to previously written comments, even though people may post within seconds of each other, mimicking real time interactions.

Selection of potential partners (2) can happen very fast in online dating sites. During each login, daters tend to select people quickly in one-shot explorations of profiles, whereas VC members get to know each other over time and have access to previous posts going back weeks, months, and years. In VCs, people see each other's names in each posting and thus become familiar with each other in that sense (McKenna & Bargh, 2000). However, knowledge of hobbies and characteristics not specified during written participation in the community may or may not appear in profiles of VC members. Photos typically do not show up in VC profiles, unless the community norms mandate them, whereas many on the dating sites post pictures of themselves contained in their ads or they exchange them by e-mail. Matching occurs (3) automatically in a dating site through the software, with profiles appearing that were set to match the criteria specified by the user. The online dater can change the criteria at any time, to increase or decrease the available pool of matches. In a VC, matching is completely under the control of the individual participant.

In the online DS, people usually express interest (4) by sending an e-mail, or "wink," to the person selected. The site conceals the private e-mail addresses to allow only communications through the site itself, until the participants decide to exchange personal e-mail addresses. In some cases, the daters may use instant message (IM) to indicate desire to connect, if the site has that option. In a VC, people use "backchanneling," or communication outside the public board, to indicate interest in developing further conversation. This usually happens through e-mail or a private message or IM at first. In a VC, people can post publicly too, expressing tastes or views that concur with the other person's before going to a private mode of communication. Ultimately, the mechanism of personal connection is similar, although the amount of knowledge may vary greatly at each type of site.

The online dater may have expounded at length about themselves, or not very much at all, depending on personal inclination and the structure of the dating site and its profiles. In the VC, the participants may see each other write, play, or chat for long periods and can often access archived writings. A woman talks about her searches on a discussion forum for information about Leon's history there:

> One of things that I did, Leon had been there for a year . . . I went back through every thread, searched out every single word, wanted to know if he was flirting with other women . . . I wouldn't had been interested in him if he had been . . .
> His interest was in the things that I was interested in. The environment. I liked the fact that he was an artist . . . His tone . . . His spirituality came through. When I started to realize how spiritual he was, I went back into all the things he wrote in Spirituality . . . I went back to every conference and read everything he wrote . . . for a lot of reasons. He used the same tone with other women . . . I am so monogamous, I had to make sure the person I was with was monogamous.        (Margo, phone interview)

Another person talks about what she liked better about VCs than meeting men elsewhere:

> I could see good things in the way Ferris responded to others' postings online, as well as with me. One thing that didn't work about past online relationships was that I could not observe the men interacting with others with any depth. It was always one-on-one contact. But the format of the community allowed for community, a wide range of conversational topics, a good deal of depth of conversation, and a great opportunity to observe other people interacting in a variety of styles.        (Miranda, e-mail)

VCs often have archives going back to their beginnings, allowing partici-pants to see prospective partners' posts about a variety of subjects and to see how they present themselves and respond to others. Of course, a dater may do a search to see whether information on the other person pops up online or may pay for services that identify current addresses and presence or absence of criminal records.

## Types of Places: Technical Features

Some sites require or encourage avatars, member-created visual self-representations that accompany an online name. Depending on the site, avatars may include cartoon figures or photos (see Suler, 1996–2007). Avatars are usually found in games, large and small, and also in places such as *The SIMS* and *Second Life*, virtual worlds, where people meet to interact in various types of conversations and activities and to buy virtual property and build virtual dwellings. Some of these sites require payment either to join or to attain privileges at higher levels and thus resemble the dating sites that usually ask members to pay if they want to contact others beyond a brief trial period. Most discussion boards online are free or based on voluntary contributions although the long-lived board The WELL (www.well.com) and the recent incarnation of Salon Table Talk (tabletalk.salon.com) charge members to join.

Technical features of sites influence outcomes of interaction, in that availability of photos, chat mechanisms, and more recently webcams and voice recordings may encourage authenticity. People intent on circumventing honesty, however, can concoct completely false identities, a practice much less common than popular news accounts portray (see Lenhart, Rainie, & Lew, 2001). On a dating site with age categories, people sometimes adjusted their ages slightly downward, reasoning that they would not appeal to those younger potential partners if they did not (Ellison, Heino, & Gibbs, 2006). They saw this as acceptable within the site parameters and often revealed their deception to others in the first e-mail or two. Places with interaction of avatars allow people to create likenesses of themselves or to create characters very different from themselves, such as fantasy creatures or animals. Norms of each place and available options influence the forms of the avatars. The site may offer individuals a variety of clothing, hairstyles, headgear, or other add-ons such as wings of different sizes and shapes. As a participant in online games, Taylor (2003) has written about how designers control images projected by the range of choices they offer to members of virtual worlds. In conversation with other avatars, people in games and virtual worlds share how much or how little they match their avatars, either on site or through the backchannels of private chat or e-mail.

## Places to Meet Online and Offline: Geographical Distance

Wherever people meet online, if they like each other, they may want to meet in person, or offline. Leaving out the "exclusively internet-based relationship" (Wright, 2004), online daters or friends wishing to deepen their connections often desire to encounter the person "in the flesh." Early computer aficionados contrasted the virtual world with physical space by calling the offline world "real life." People from online would arrange not for a meeting but a "meat" in "meatspace," still part of the hacker's dictionary (online jargon file, Raymond, 2003) to distinguish the earthy physical space from the ethereal cyberspace.

The following sections describe how the type of meeting place online relates to the geographical locations of participants. Although most people available for new relationships may desire potential partners who live within walking distance, where they set their outer limits of travel distance varies. Residents of remote or rural areas may realize that potential partners live faraway, whereas people in New York City perceive that many others of all ages and interests live within a small geographical area. Before the Internet, and also today, people ranked cities according to the number of singles there. Online, the type of place makes a difference in who tends to show up and from where. Members of dating sites and VCs may delimit their geographical boundaries differently. Deciding where to meet in person involves picking the particular kind of meeting place for the offline setting as well as choosing the geographical location for the first encounter.

## Meeting Place Online and Place of Residence of Partners

On the dating site, the importance of place outweighs many other factors, perhaps following only appearance and age for people who will not travel to meet others. At the site, partners can pre-limit the distance they search within. Meeting in a VC suggests that members come from many physical locations, if the VC does not emerge from a locally based offline group. A VC may have an international membership or one limited to a particular country, if the native language is required. The location of the originating group or the founder may influence the residency of a typical participant, at least at first. Theoretically, on the Internet, any space is open to those with access to it.

When people encounter those who live out of their geographical area, they either reject them, as on a dating site when their settings say someone must live within so many miles of their home, or they go ahead, nonetheless, with pursuing a relationship. The geographical distance between potential partners is a factor among people who wish to pursue relationships wherever they happen to meet online. Overcoming distance at various stages of the relationships may involve sticking with online communication modes and then moving to long-distance phone calls. With available cell or mobile phone plans and online long-distance services like Skype, the financial cost may have declined from the past. At some point, partners have to decide who is going to travel to the other when they meet offline. If the relationship continues, eventually the partners will choose where to live, in either of their current locations or somewhere

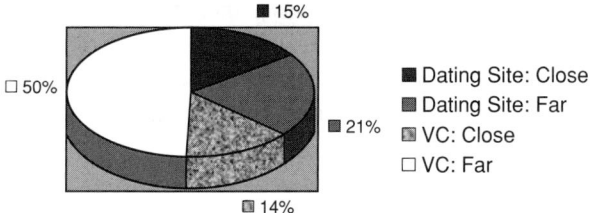

Figure 7.1. *Online meeting place and geographical distance of partners*
*(n = 92 couples).*

else. Sometimes they strike a deal whereby one offers to move, if the other
agrees to eventually move where they like.

As people hit if off in the naturalistic settings, they may tend toward openness
in how far they will go geographically to meet their partners. They are united
by common interests, and have likely already built a satisfactory bond before
they decide to proceed further. Comfortable with chatting or posting with those
they might never meet offline they can take the time to discover if they would
like to share more of their lives than they already do.

In the researcher's study of ninety-two Internet couples, eighty-nine from
Baker (2005) and three more gathered later on, a third met on dating sites
and another third met at real-time chat groups or online games. The final
third met through discussion boards, posting asynchronously. Combining the
people at chats, games, and discussion boards shows that nearly two-thirds
of the couples met at VCs (Figure 7.1.) These people who met outside of
dating sites tended to talk to those faraway from them in geographical distance more than those from the matchmaking sites. The classification of "far"
means that each member of the couple had to live outside the state of the
other for the United States, outside the province or country for Canada and
Europe, or farther away. Thirteen couples contained partners from two different continents, mainly Europe and North America, with two people from Asia
and two from Australia. "Close," conversely, means individuals who lived no
farther than within the state, province, or country of residence of their partners.

Observing online meeting place by geographical distance offline or comparative place of residence of the individuals within each couple, the pie chart
in Figure 7.1 illustrates that half the sampled couples in the study met at VCs
and the individuals in them resided far from each other. The other half was split
among the other three groups: dating site couples living farther away, dating
site couples who lived closer, and VC couples who resided relatively nearby.

These figures are not to suggest that most members of couples who meet
online come from places distant to each other, but to identify where the people
studied reside at first and later on in the development of their relationships.
Each research project about online dating or relationship formation likely has a
different mix of those geographical couplings, depending on the dating sites or

VCs studied, as well as how the sample was gathered. Differences in findings may relate partly to variations in online and offline places of study participants. Online research that traces movement from online to offline locations should take into account the geographical factor of both the online and offline meeting places.

## Meeting Offline: Choosing a Place

People exploring relationships usually come to a juncture where they want to meet in person, to see whether the connections they have explored will go further offline. They especially want to know whether they "click" in real life the way they have online. Aside from deciding which mode they prefer for communication, the pair chooses where to meet offline. They pick from a range of offline places, from coffee shops to restaurants and from hotels to their own homes, if they plan to stay overnight. Couples may decide before the actual meeting that they need a plan "B," an exit route if they would rather not spend the original amount of time planned. Conversely, some couples may extend their visits, finding their partners particularly interesting (Baker, 2005). If they stay overnight, they often have to decide whether to share sleeping quarters.

Here is where geographical distance as well as length of time of communication can influence people's choices. When people live in the same city, they can plan to meet briefly to validate each other's impressions. When they live far apart, the traveling partner, or both people, if meeting at a neutral location, has committed more time and money to the meeting. Ironically, people who met at their own private residences had more chance of success or probability of staying together (at the last time of contact by the researcher) than couples who met at hotels and other public places. These people generally communicated for longer periods of time, and may have felt quite comfortable with each other by the time they made the decision on where to meet offline.

Much more research is needed on how couples select their offline meeting place and how the place fits with the length of their communication and further development of their relationship or its decline. The quality of communication allows the couple to agree on the location of the beginning of their offline relationship, if the meeting carries the mutual attraction and friendship forward. The location can mark the relationship's ending if either or both do not like what they see, hear, or feel from the other person.

## The Intersection of Place and Timing: Two Dimensions of Online Relationships

Although timing could be the subject of another article, here it is discussed as it relates to the places people meet online and offline. Place and timing interact in a number of different ways to develop or retard the online relationship. In this chapter, "timing" means the sequence and length of events in the process of communication online and offline. The concept of timing encompasses decisions on when to move forward and when to escalate the bonding through various means of communication. Timing also refers to the method of communication and whether people interact in real time as if they were co-present in space, or delayed response mode.

Bringing in time or timing into the process of online relationships sets up the notion of relationship stages. Depending on place, the relationship has a certain beginning, either reading profiles and e-mailing or interacting in an online group. In either track, people may progress to another deeper stage of relating, if they decide they are compatible. People coordinate the speed at which they progress, reaching a balance of mutual desire to continue or, conversely, to end their interaction.

The topics here include mode of communication, whether in real time or not, and relation to place. Also discussed is the length of time before meeting and its dependence on place and, finally, an examination of the effects of place and time, moving toward an understanding of factors in the success of online relationships.

## Synchronous Versus Asynchronous Communication and Place Online

Some online spaces are chat rooms, allowing participants to write in real time. Game players also relate in real time in places called "virtual worlds." Virtual worlds are simulated environments where people interact using avatars. Someone new to the virtual world of *Second Life* comments on how the immediacy of synchronous communication affected her:

> I have been very active in SL and have formed several relationships. As a result, I experimented a bit with "textual intercourse" in SL and then in chat – got seduced actually – and I was really surprised at now much impact typing can have on you! But I am generally turned off by the more blatant sexual overtones, and just like RL, I prefer intimacy to raw sex."        (Cassie, online posting, used by permission in e-mail)

Some places contain only asynchronous options, such as posting in discussion boards, or sending e-mail. Other spaces, although mainly asynchronous, have chat or IM options built in for people who wish to use them whenever they like. Within those places, whether an online dating site or a VC, if communication is usually asynchronous, a feature showing when someone is in the chat room helps avoid the situation of waiting silently for another chatter to show up.

One feature of online relationships is deciding on communication mode after the couple meets. If two people meet through chat, they may typically continue that or switch to the phone. Joe Walther's early work (1992) has documented how even synchronous written communication proceeds more slowly, taking more time than verbal talk, causing some couples to proceed to the phone and

Table 7.1. *Time of meeting offline by place of meeting online and distance (n = 91 couples)*

| | Dating site | | VC | | |
| --- | --- | --- | --- | --- | --- |
| | Close | Far | Close | Far | Totals |
| Less than a month | 6 | 1 | 1 | | (8) |
| One to three months | 7 | 13 | 10 | 13 | (43) |
| Four to seven months | | 3 | 2 | 15 | (20) |
| Eight to 11 months | | 1 | | 4 | (5) |
| 12 months or over | 1 | 1 | | 13 | (15) |
| TOTAL | (14) | (19) | (13) | (45) | (91) |

use that as their main medium. If a couple meets by searching profiles and then e-mailing, or discussing issues at an online forum, they can decide to stay with e-mail, which allows for thought and revision, unlike the real-time media. Of crucial importance is that the two must agree on the best communication mode to use to develop their relationship.

## Time and Place: Delay Before Meeting Offline and Type of Online Meeting Site

The data gathered from the eighty-nine couples in *Double Click* (Baker, 2005) plus a few more couples joining the research later (*n* = 91 pairs, not counting the one couple not meeting offline) includes geographical distance of the partners, type of site or place they met online, and amount of time lapsed between their online and offline meeting. Table 7.1 shows a relationship between the place they met and the timing of the lag between their online and offline meeting.

Most of the members of couples who waited the longest times to meet, a year or more, were from geographically distant places. Most couples who met at VCs rather than dating sites took a longer time to meet. Two couples from VCs with geographically distant relationships even waited more than two years to meet. (Even with collapsed cells, some contain cells with *n*'s too small for statistical analysis.)

Collapsing the five categories into three lengths of time before meeting offline, less than a month, one to seven months, and more than seven months produces the bar graph in Figure 7.2. It shows people in DSs typically meet within a short rather than a long period whether they live close or far apart, whereas people from VCs usually engage in longer online correspondence or phone contact before meeting offline, especially when they live faraway. People in DS have presumably committed to meeting potential partners by joining the site, although some members browse profiles without seeking to

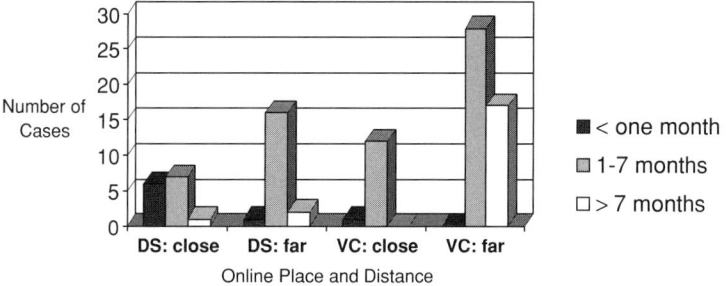

Figure 7.2. *Length of time before meeting F2F by type of online meeting place and geographical distance of partners (n = 91 couples).*

connect further. Converting the raw data from Table 7.1 and Figure 7.2 into percentages shows that 21 percent of those from dating sites met within a month or less, whereas only 2 percent of VC participants did. Conversely, 29 percent of people from VCs took seven months or longer to meet offline, while only, 9 percent of people from DSs waited that long, regardless of geographical distance. Although the sample was not random, an issue for researchers of online relationships is to specify both the distance between partners and the type of site of their study participants before drawing conclusions from their data about timing of offline meetings.

Almost all of the couples who waited a year or longer to meet offline met at virtual communities, not dating sites. They came to know each other in a more "naturalistic" way (see McKenna, 2007) rather than seeking out a dating partner or mate directly. Most of the people who met within a month's time came from dating sites. These daters wanted to interact F2F with potential partners quite quickly, which was easier to accomplish when they lived closer. No one from a VC in the couples studied met in less than a month after meeting first online.

## Place and Deception: The Online Presentation of Self

Although an in-depth treatment of the issue of online deception is beyond the scope of this chapter, a few points about place or settings, goals, and honesty can be made. (For comparisons of self-revelation and honesty online versus offline, see, for example, Cornwell & Lundgren, 2001; Hancock, Thom-Santelli, & Ritchie, 2004; Joinson, 2001; Tidwell & Walther, 2002). At DSs, no real names are used, unless a first name is combined with some numbers or another word. The process of revealing identity usually follows a path from on-site e-mail to personal e-mail to phone number before meeting in person. The two people control the flow of information. In VCs, anonymity ranges from none at all, with people using true or real first and last names to total protection of identity, with people hidden by avatars and names chosen from site-provided lists as in *Second Life*. In chat rooms, people regularly select nicknames related to the topic area and in some discussion boards, such as fan groups, people choose names derived from the celebrities or shows of interest.

When people wish to know each other more than casually, the issue of honesty rises in importance. Upon entering any site, a person can decide which level of honesty appeals to him or her within the technical parameters and norms of the site, coupled with a personal preference within those constraints. On a discussion board, members become known to each other by their histories there and in interactions elsewhere. One interesting feature bringing the two settings closer is that some dating sites (see http://www.plentyoffish.com) now have opportunities for daters to speak about each other on the site after they communicate in private, either affirming or disconfirming what is presented by a dater.

Goffman (1956) described how people present themselves in social situations, how they "manage impressions" of others by highlighting positive features and de-emphasizing or hiding negative ones. Rather than divide online participants into honest and deceiving, researchers may want to look at the slight deceptions prevalent at dating sites as commonly accepted attempts to present an appealing persona. People who want to develop relationships know that any major deceptions will emerge over time. Based on cases of couples that were available for analysis during the years of the data collection, Baker (2005, 2002) found that people meeting online who lied about crucial facts such as marital status had less success in maintaining their relationships than those who were honest.

## Place, Timing, and Outcome: A Concluding Note on the Success of Online Relationships

Building a framework from the data of couples that met online, this author (Baker, 2005) coined the acronym POST to discuss which couples seemed to have greater chances of success (Baker, 2005, 2002) or of creating marriages and other long-term intimate relationships. For the (P) factor, place of meeting affects which kinds of people are at a site, influencing degree of common interest and affecting mutuality of goals. Examining the type of place where people meet online and then also offline is crucial in understanding the dynamics of online relationships. People who meet in VCs and in their homes offline seem to have a better chance of success overall than others. Not discussed in this chapter, variations in handling the obstacles (O) a couple faces, and how each chooses to present himself or herself online, or self-presentation (S), fill out the model. Here analyzed mainly in conjunction with place, timing (T) includes responding to the person's initial contact to deciding when to move to another medium, how intimate to become online, and as outlined in this chapter, when to take the relationship offline.

Communication affects all four factors of the POST model, and of course, the four factors may affect the quantity and quality of communication as well. Communication skills and modes determine how the couple reacts after first encountering each other online in a particular type of place, and how the two people can overcome any obstacles such as distance, finances, and other relationships to decide on a place to meet offline. Decisions about how to present themselves to the other involve choices about each dater's honesty, with or without mild to extreme withholding of personal information or outright deception. Communication affects the timing or pacing of shared thoughts, feelings, and movement to the next level of commitment in continuing or stopping the relationship. The textual communication of the couple is the product of their online interaction. It constitutes the whole of the online relationship, unless audio or visual means of communication supplement the written word.

The details of types of online places examined here, along with the relations of aspects of time to place, can help future researchers specify patterns and problems in the development of online relationships. Whether at dating sites or virtual communities, the number of people forming intimate partnerships continues to grow worldwide (see Barak, 2007). Researchers can complement and inform each other's work by stating not only "who" they are studying but "where" people have found their partners online and how that place makes a difference to the relationship process.

## References

Baker, A. (1998). Cyberspace couples finding romance online then meeting for the first time in real life. *CMC Magazine*. Retrieved June 15, 2007, from http://www.december.com/cmc/mag/1998/jul/baker.html.

Baker, A. (2002). What makes an online relationship successful? Clues from couples who met in cyberspace. *CyberPsychology & Behavior, 5*, 363–375.

Baker, A. (2005). *Double click: Romance and commitment among online couples.* Cresskill, NJ: Hampton Press.

Baker, A., & Whitty, M. (2008). Researching romance and sexuality online: Issues for new and current researchers. In S. Holland (Ed.), *Remote relationships in a small world* (pp. 34–52). New York: Peter Lang.

Barak, A. (2007). Phantom emotions: Psychological determinants of emotional experiences on the internet, In A. Joinson, K. McKenna, T. Postmes, and U. Reips (Eds.), *The Oxford handbook of internet psychology* (pp. 303–329). Oxford: Oxford University Press.

Bargh, J., McKenna, K. Y. A., & Fitzsimons, G. M. (2002). Can you see the real me? Activation and expression of the "true self" on the internet. *Journal of Social Issues, 58*, 33–48.

Barnes, S. (2003). *Computer-mediated communication.* Boston, MA: Pearson Education.

Ben Ze'ev, A. (2004). *Love online.* Oxford, UK: Oxford University Press.

Berscheid, E., & Walster, E. (1978). *Interpersonal attraction*. Reading, MA: Addison-Wesley.

Byrne, D., London, O., & Reeves, K. (1968). The effects of physical attractiveness, sex, and attitude similarity on interpersonal attraction. *Journal of Personality, 36*, 259–271.

Carter, D. (2005). Living in virtual communities: An ethnography of human relationships in cyberspace. *Information, Communication & Society, 8*, 148–167.

Cooper, A. (1999). Sexuality and the Internet: Surfing into the new millennium. *CyberPsychology & Behavior, 1*, 181–187.

Cooper, A., McLoughlin, I., & Campbell, K. (2000). Sexuality in cyberspace: Update for the 21st century. *CyberPsychology & Behavior, 4*, 521–536.

Cooper, A., & Sportolari, L. (1997). Romance in cyberspace: Understanding online attraction. *Journal of Sex Education and Therapy, 22*, 7–14.

Cornwell, B., & Lundgren, D. (2001). Love on the Internet: Involvement and misrepresentation in romantic relationships in cyberspace vs. realspace. *Computers in Human Behavior, 17*, 197–211.

Duck, S., & Craig, G. (1975). Effects of type of information upon interpersonal attraction. *Social Behavior and Personality, 3*, 157–64.

Ellison, N., Heino, R., & Gibbs, J. (2006). Managing impressions online: Self-presentation processes in the online dating environment. *Journal of Computer-Mediated Communication, 11*(2). Retrieved June 15, 2007, from http://jcmc.indiana.edu/vol11/issue2/ellison.html.

Fiore, A. T., & Donath, J. (2004). *Online personals: An overview*. Paper presented at the Conference on Human Factors in Computing Systems, Vienna, Austria. Retrieved June 15, 2007, from http://smg.media.mit.edu/papers/atf/chi2004_personals_short.pdf.

Fraboni, R. (2004). *Marriage market and homogamy in Italy: An event history approach*. National Statistical Office. Retrieved February 1, 2007, from http://paa2004.princeton.edu/download.asp?submissionId=41515.

Gibbs, J., Ellison, N., & Heino, R. (2006). Self-presentation in online personals: The role of anticipated future interaction, self-disclosure, and perceived success in Internet dating. *Communication Research, 33*(2), 1–26.

Gibson, W. (1984). *Neuromancer*. New York: Ace Books.

Goffman, E. (1956). *The presentation of self in everyday life*. New York: Doubleday.

Hancock J., Thom-Santelli, J., & Ritchie, T. (2004). *Deception and design: The impact of communication technology on lying behavior*. Proceedings of the SIGCHI Conference on Human Factors in Computing Systems (pp. 129–134), Vienna, Austria.

Hatfield, E., & Sprecher, S. (1986). *Mirror, mirror: The importance of looks in everyday life*. Albany, NY: SUNY Press.

Joinson, A. (2001). Self-disclosure in computer-mediated communication: The role of self-awareness and visual anonymity. *European Journal of Social Psychology, 31*, 177–192.

Joinson, A. (2003). *Understanding the psychology of Internet behaviour: Virtual worlds, real lives*. Basingstoke, UK: Palgrave Macmillan.

Konner, J. (2006). *The mystery of love* (PBS). Retrieved June 15, 2007, from http://www.themysteryoflove.org.

Lenhart, A., Rainie, L., & Lewis, O. (2001). *Teenage life online: The rise of the instant-message generation and the Internet's impact on friendships and family relationships*. Washington, DC: Pew Internet & American Life Project.

McKenna, K. Y. A. (2007). A progressive affair: Online dating to real world mating. In M. Whitty, A. Baker, & J. Inman (Eds.), *Online matchmaking* (pp. 112–124). Basingstoke, UK: Palgrave MacMillan.

McKenna, K. Y. A., & Bargh, J. (2000). Plan 9 from cyberspace. *Personality and Social Psychology Review, 4*, 57–75.

McKenna, K. Y., Green, A., & Gleason, M. (2002). Relationship formation on the internet: What's the big attraction? *Journal of Social Issues, 58*, 9–31.

Merkle, E., & Richardson, R. (2000). Digital dating and virtual relating: Conceptualizing computer mediated romantic relationships. *Family Relations. 49*, 187–192.

Parks, M., & Floyd, K. (1996). Making friends in cyberspace. *Journal of Computer-Mediated Communication, 1*(4). Retrieved June 15, 2007, from http://www.usc.edu/dept/annenberg/vol1/issue4/parks.html.

Parks, M., & Roberts, L. (1998). "Making moosic": The development of personal relationships on line and a comparison to their off-line counterparts. *Journal of Social and Personal Relationships, 15*, 517–537.

Pilkington, N., & Lydon, J. (1997). The relative effect of attitude similarity and attitude dissimilarity on interpersonal attraction. *Personality and Social Psychology Bulletin, 23*, 107–122.

Raymond, E. (2003). *The on-line hacker jargon file* (version 4.4.7). Retrieved June 15, 2007, from http://catb.org/jargon/html/M/meatspace.html.

Rheingold, H. (1993). *The virtual community: Homesteading on the electronic frontier*. Reading, MA: Addison-Wesley.

Suler, J. (1996–2007). *The psychology of cyberspace*. Retrieved June 15, 2007, from http://www.rider.edu/~suler/psycyber/psycyber.html.

Taylor, T. L. (2003). Intentional bodies: Virtual environments and the designers who shape them. *International Journal of Engineering Education, 19*, 25–34.

Tidwell, L. & Walther, J. (2002). Computer-mediated communication effects on disclosure, impressions, and interpersonal evaluations: Getting to know one another a bit at a time. *Human Communication Research, 28*, 317–348.

Utz, S. (2000). Social information processing in MUDs: The development of friendships in virtual worlds. *Journal of Online Behavior, 1*(1). Retrieved June 15, 2007, from http://www.behavior.net/JOB/v1n1/utz.html.

Wallace, P. (1999). *The psychology of the Internet*. Cambridge, UK: Cambridge University Press.

Walther, J. (1992). Interpersonal effects in computer-mediated interaction: A relational perspective. *Communication Research, 19*, 52–90.

Walther, J., & Parks, M. (2002). Cues filtered out, cues filtered in: Computer-mediated communication and relationships. In M. Knapp & J. Daly (Eds.), *Handbook of interpersonal communication* (pp. 529–563). Thousand Oaks, CA: Sage.

Wheeler, R., & Gunter, B. (1987). Change in spouse age difference at marriage: A challenge to traditional family and sex roles? *Sociological Quarterly, 28*, 411–421.

Whitty, M. & Carr, A. (2006). *Cyberspace Romance: The psychology of online relationships*. Basingstoke, UK: Palgrave MacMillan.

Whitty, M., & Gavin, J. (2001). Age/sex/location: Uncovering the social cues in the development of online relationships. *CyberPsychology & Behavior, 4*, 623–630.

Wright, K. (2004). On-line relational maintenance strategies and perceptions of partners within exclusively Internet-based and primarily Internet-based relationships. *Communication Studies, 55*, 418–432.

Wysocki, D., & Thalken, J. (2007). Whips and chains? Fact or fiction? Content analysis of sadomasochism in Internet personal advertisements. In M. Whitty, A. Baker, & J. Inman (Eds.), *Online matchmaking*. Basingstoke: Palgrave MacMillan.

# 8 The Sexy Side of the Internet: an Examination of Sexual Activities and Materials in Cyberspace

*Monica T. Whitty and William A. Fisher*

"Every technological innovation creates deviant as well as respectable possibilities" (Edgley & Kiser, 1981, p. 59). Edgley and Kiser (1981) were referring to "Polaroid sex," that is, instant photography methods used to create homemade pornography. A quarter of a century later, this statement may equally be applied to the Internet. Ever since the beginnings of the World Wide Web, people have engaged in online sexual activities. These activities include, but are not limited to, cybersex, hot chatting, locating others to have sex with offline, seeking information or advice about sexual health, romance and relationships, downloading pornography, and purchasing erotic materials.

In this chapter, we explore the many types of available online sexual activities and the types of people who engage in these activities. We also examine the pros and cons of the sexy side of the Internet. On the one hand, we argue that the Internet can be used to explore one's sexuality, but on the other, some people become too obsessed with engaging in online sexual activities. Importantly, the Internet can also be used to educate both adolescents and adults about sexual issues. Finally, this chapter turns to examine the future of online sexual activities.

## The Beginnings of Internet Sex

People have been engaging in Internet sexual activities since its inception. Although at first individuals were limited to textual exchanges, many found no difficulties with talking "dirty" online and reconstructing the body online. This is nicely illustrated in Carol Parker's (1997) book, *The Joy of Cybersex*:

| | |
|---|---|
| Gersh | I press against you ... |
| geekgirl | and I rub my belly to slick my hand with oil |
| Gersh | pushing against you ... hot ... Can't take my eyes off you ... Watching you arch ... |
| geekgirl | stroking lightly up your thigh with one hand ... stroking my breast with the other as my nipples harden under your gaze ... sigh |
| Gersh | my hand dips down and strokes between your legs ... just a touch ... |

geekgirl    my legs part a little . . . hips moving slowly
Gersh       Deeper this time . . . I can feel you . . . wet . . . warm . . . mmmmhhhh

Definitions have been given to the varying levels of sexual activities online. For instance, hot chat is "when two or more individuals engage in discourses which move beyond light-hearted flirting" (Whitty & Carr, 2006, p. 21). In contrast, cybersex is "generally understood to be synchronous communication in cyberspace where two or more individuals engage in discourses about sexual fantasies" while typically masturbating at the same time (Whitty & Carr, 2006, p. 21).

Bulletin board systems (BBs) were an especially popular space in the early days of the Internet and many of these bulletin board systems were sexual in nature. BBs were a precursor to the World Wide Web; however, they look very different from spaces currently available on the Internet. BBs were typically single-line systems, which meant that only one user could be online at a time. Individuals could only communicate using text. Even in the early days, BBs were social spaces where people met, had discussions, published articles, downloaded software, and even managed to play games. Some of these were moderated by a systems operator who would sometimes censor messages. Users could leave both public and private messages.

Some BBs were especially designed for people to meet others who share their sexual interests and to live out their sexual desires online or offline. Social scientists have examined the sites and the people who use them (e.g., Wysocki, 1998; Wysocki & Thalken, 2007). Wysocki (1998) was for instance interested in seeing whether online sex was a replacement for face-to-face relationships or whether instead it enhanced them. She interviewed participants using a BB called the "Pleasure Pit." In this study, she identified five main reasons for using sexually explicitly BBs, including anonymity, time constraints in one's personal life, the ability to share sexual fantasies with other people, the desire to participate in online sexual activity, and to find people with similar sexual interests to meet face-to-face. Wysocki also found that many of the people she interviewed did not reveal to their offline partners exactly how they were using the Internet as a sexual outlet.

## The Internet: a Potent Medium for Sexual Activity

From the early days of the Internet, researchers across disciplines have been interested in whether engaging in online sexual activities can be harmful or therapeutic. Turkle (1995) was one of the early theorists who advocated that online sex could be emotionally and physically powerful. Whitty (2003a, 2004) has argued that engaging in cyberflirting can be very therapeutic for some individuals, especially shy people, and Cooper and his colleagues have considered online sex to be threatening for some and healthy for others (e.g., Cooper, Scherer, & Marcus, 2002). Cooper (1998) proposed that the Internet is a potent medium for sexual activity because it is accessible, affordable, and anonymous. This he referred to as the Triple A Engine.

Others also maintain that the Internet can have a seductive appeal – so much so that some people are believed to have cybersex addictions. These individuals are compulsively involved in engaging in online sexual activities, such as cybersex, or downloading pornography, such that Internet sexual activity interferes with personal and social adjustment. Cooper, Delmonico, and Burg (2000) found a small proportion of individuals whose online sexual behavior is clearly compulsive. They also found that both women and gay men were more highly represented in the group of individuals they identified to be cybersex compulsives. Daneback, Ross, and Månsson (2006) found that online sexual compulsives were more likely to be men who are in a relationship, are bisexual, and have a sexually transmitted infection (STI). Schneider (2000) has argued that cybersex addiction is a major contributing factor to separation and divorce. Moreover, Schneider's (2000) study found that about half (52%) of cybersex users had lost interest in relational sex.

Another problematic online sexual activity is Internet infidelity. Internet infidelity can of course be both emotional and sexual forms of infidelity (see Whitty, 2003b, 2005, 2007; Whitty & Carr, 2005, 2006). However, in this chapter, we are more concerned with the sexual component of Internet infidelity. Whitty (2003b, 2005) has found that sexual activities online, such as cybersex and hot chatting, are perceived by many to be a relationship transgression and that people can be just as upset by these transgressions as they might be from offline penetrative sex. She also found that cybersex posed a greater threat to the relationship than downloading pornography. As further support, Parker and Wampler (2003) have found that interacting in adult chat rooms, having cybersex, having telephone sex, becoming a member of an adult website, and engaging in cybersex various times were viewed as acts of infidelity.

In addition to identifying different types of online behaviors that might be perceived to be relationship transgressions, researchers have theorized about why these acts might be upsetting to couples. Whitty and her colleague (Whitty, 2003b, 2005; Whitty & Carr, 2005, 2006) have suggested that desiring another and the time dedicated to another upset individuals. Moreover, the act of keeping one's online sexual activities secret ought to be deemed as unfaithful.

Of course, one's Internet infidelities might initiate online and progress offline. Moreover, there are webpages that have been set up to hook up people looking for an offline affair. For example, Philanderers.com (http://www. philanderers.com) is an online service to introduce people seeking an extramarital offline relationship. They write on their site that:

> Why you are here is our main concern. Helping you sort out your thoughts, provide some direction for your extramarital affair, and a safe, secure outlet for your extramarital desires is our mission.
>
> We are not a sex or personals site that provides empty promises. Our clientele are well educated and informed before they become members. We

are not "the biggest," "the best" or the "most popular" – we don't want to be. We are honest, forthright and caring. Three things that we value in our extramarital web-relations.

Come in and explore. Learn why you may want to pursue an extramarital affair and what you can do about it. Find out the reasons why this may be just the right place for you. Find out how you can fulfill your extramarital desires.    (Anonymous, Philanderers.com)

Interestingly, some software designers have been cashing in on individuals' fears that their partners might be cybercheating. Such software can track not only every webpage one's spouse visits but also every keystroke they make. For example, Spector (n.d.) advertises that its software enables one to "see exactly what your spouse, kids and employees have been doing online and offline."

## Pedophiles on the Internet

The numbers of pedophiles who use the Internet to prey on children has been of growing concern over the years. Offenders often inhabit online areas such as chat rooms and MySpace and use seduction techniques to lure in their victims. For instance, they will listen and pretend to empathize with children. They might initially build up a friendship with a child to gain his or her trust and then move onto sexually exploiting children. This exploitation might happen online via sexual talk or requesting naked pictures of children or could move offline. Sometimes a pedophile will try to groom minors by sending them erotic pictures and website addresses in an attempt to lure the minor into believing that sexual acts between youth and adults is common and enjoyable. The Internet is arguably an attractive arena for pedophiles as they can be anonymous and hence believe they are more likely to get away with their crimes. Nonetheless, police across the world are putting their energies into locating and arresting these criminals (Fulda, 2002).

## Internet Pornography

Pornography, unsurprisingly, permeates the Internet. During the past decade, explosive growth in the availability of sexually explicit text, visual, and audio materials on the Internet has provided anonymous, cost-free, and unfettered access to an essentially unlimited amount and variety of sexual imagery (Fisher & Barak, 2001; Freeman-Longo, 2000). Adult men and women – as well as boys and girls – can acquire sexually explicit materials on the Internet effortlessly and privately, with essentially no cost, no age limitations, and no impediments, reflecting their self-directed expression and gratification and sexual interests and inclinations. The sexually explicit materials that are consumed may in turn affect, not at all or profoundly, the sexual interests and dispositions that guided the individual to seek out Internet sexually explicit materials in the first place.

The type of pornography available online is quite varied. There is obviously the professional commercial pornography that individuals can purchase online. However, amateur pornography is equally popular (Jacobs, 2004) and often sold online. Some individuals are happy to make their homemade videos freely available. Others enjoy swapping erotic pictures via chat rooms and newsgroups (Griffiths, 2004). One type of pornography that has been a source of consternation for lovers and scholars of Japanese popular culture is manga and anime pornography (Dahlquist & Vigilant, 2004). Some of this form of pornography presents human fantasies in interesting ways – performing acts that are not humanly possibly. Fans of this type of pornography are often drawn in because they believe it is better than real sex (Dahlquist & Vigilant, 2004). However, it has been argued that some hentai (adult-oriented material that presents extreme graphics of sexual imagery) goes too far. For example, Dahlquist and Vigilant (2004) state:

> The experience of hentai is morally distancing. Tentacle hentai offers the telegenetic signs of the most perverse and debased sexualities. It opens for fantastic examination a sexuality that transgresses all "simulated" moralities of the "real" world., where tentacle sex between nubile girl-women and cloned boy-men monsters are the order of the day – a monstrous sex-feast of the most abnormal acts: pedophilic bestiality, sex with machines, sex with cyborgs, sex with dangerous protruding tentacles, and, of course, an endless stream of the most debasing, brutal, and humiliating rape images.        (pp. 99–100)

Psychological theory has been employed to conceptualize potential effects of exposure to Internet sexually explicit materials (see Fisher & Barak, 2001). On the basis of relevant theory and research (e.g., Bogaert, 1993, 2001; Eysenck, 1978; Malamuth, 1989a, 1989b; Malamuth, Addison, & Koss, 2001; Mosher, 1980, 1988; Snyder & Ickes, 1985), it can be hypothesized that antisocial personality characteristics will encourage a limited number of individuals to exploit the Internet to seek out antisocial sexually explicit materials (e.g., rape, degradation) that gratify and reinforce their antisocial inclinations. The "goodness of fit" (Mosher, 1980, 1988) of the individual's antisocial personality with antisocial sexual content easily selected and accessed via the Internet may be theorized to promote considerable depth of involvement with antisocial sexual materials, loss of awareness of the actual constraints on action found in reality regarding enactment of antisocial sexual behavior, and uniquely strong negative effects of the availability of Internet pornography on individual enactment of antisocial sexual behaviors, such as, for example, sexual aggression or coercion enacted by men against women.

A complementary point of view, also based on relevant theory and research (e.g., Barak & Fisher, 1997; Barak, Fisher, Belfry, & Lashambe, 1999; Bogaert, 1993, 2001; Fisher & Barak, 1991, 2001; Malamuth et al., 2001; Mosher, 1980, 1988; Snyder & Ickes, 1985), asserts that most individuals – those in the normal range – will be inclined to exploit the Internet to seek out sexually explicit materials that are more or less consistent with their lifetime learning histories concerning acceptable versus unacceptable sexual behavior. Such materials would be likely to gratify and encourage acceptable, normal range sexual fantasy or sexual behavior that is already within the individual's repertoire (see, for example, Fisher & Byrne, 1978; Mann, Sidman, & Starr, 1973). In fact, the "poorness of fit" of normal range personality characteristics with antisocial sexual content available on the Internet is assumed to provoke avoidance and rejection of such material and termination of contact with antisocial sexually explicit content if encountered accidentally. According to the foregoing "confluence" analysis (see Fisher & Barak, 2001; Malamuth et al., 2001), individuals with highly antisocial personality characteristics will he highly susceptible to antisocial sexual content on the Internet – or anywhere else (including the evening news and any number of Biblical passages), while individuals with a lifetime learning history and expectations about acceptable and unacceptable sexual or other behavior will be unlikely to access or act on antisocial sexual content on the Internet.

Despite widespread public concern about the proliferation of sexually explicit imagery on the Internet (see, for example, the *Time* cover story, as early as 1995 [Elmer-Dewitt, 1995] as well as Cooper, Scherer, Boise, & Gordon, 1999; Rimm, 1995; Sprenger, 1999; and the U.S. Communications Decency Act of 1996, subsequently declared unconstitutional), there is surprisingly little systematic research concerning the prevalence of specific sexually explicit content – antisocial, neutral, or otherwise – on the Internet. Experimental research concerning effects of exposure to Internet sexually explicit materials is almost as sparse. Barak and Fisher (1997) report an investigation in which male university students interacted with sexually explicit software on personal computers that permitted them to either view geometric forms passively, nude females passively, nude females with control over browsing speed and direction, or nude females with control over browsing speed, direction, zoom focus on favored body parts, and manipulation of the nude female's coloring. Compared with exposure to geometric forms, no effects of exposure to even the most high-level manipulation and control over female sexually explicit pictures were seen on any outcome variable, including attitudes toward women, likelihood of sexual harassment, or verbal aggression against a female confederate. Similarly, Barak, Fisher, Belfry, and Lashambe (1999) had male undergraduates browse Internet bookmark lists that contained 0 percent, 10 percent, 50 percent, or 80 percent sexually explicit websites, and found no effects of exposure to increasing levels of Internet sexually explicit content on outcome measures that included attitudes toward women, likelihood of rape, and willingness to work under the supervision of a female manager.

In correlational research, Emmers-Sommer and Burns (2005) report that users of pornography that depicts sexual coercion more strongly endorse rape myths than do nonusers of such materials. In contrast, Fisher and Barak (2001) report that since the spectacular growth of availability in Internet sexually

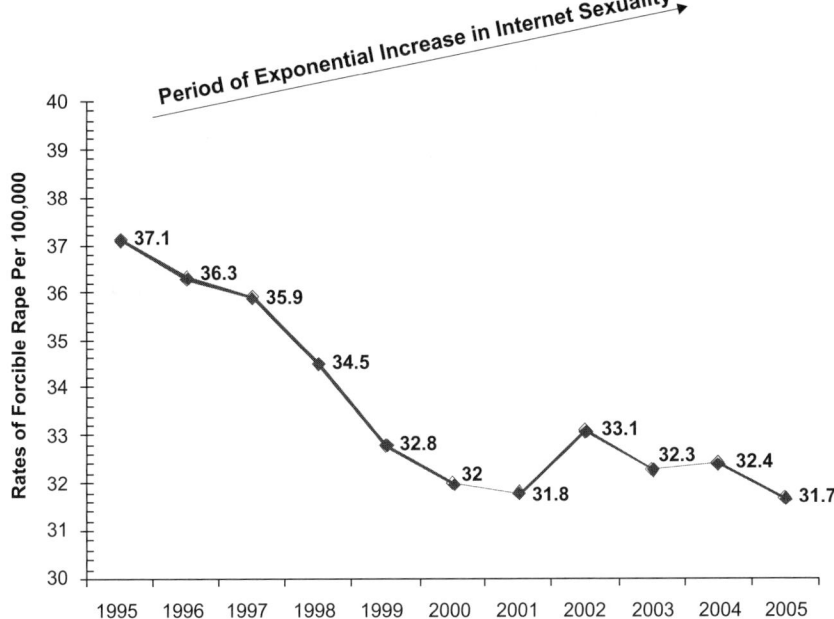

Figure 8.1. *Rates of reported sexual assault, 1995–2005, during a time of exponential increase in availability of Internet pornography. Adapted from Fisher, W. A., & Barak, A. (2001). Internet pornography: A social psychological perspective on Internet sexuality.* Journal of Sex Research, *38, 1–11.*

explicit material began in the mid-1990s, rates of reported forcible sexual assault in the United States have declined by some 15 percent from a rate of 37.1/100,000 in 1995 to a rate of 31.7/100,000 in 2005 (see Figure 8.1). Similarly, D'Amato (2006) has reported that the four U.S. states with the *lowest* rates of Internet access have *increased* rates of forcible rape by 53 percent from 1980 to 2000, while the four U.S. states with the *highest* rates of Internet access have *decreased* rates of rape by 27 percent during this period. Evidence for a confluence model of intense effects of sexually explicit materials on those with antisocial personality dispositions is also lacking in relation to findings for sex offenders' reported use of pornography, which generally either does not differ from or is lesser than that of controls (see, for example, Abel, Becker, & Mittleman, 1985; Becker & Stein, 1991; Goldstein & Kant, 1973; Langevin et al., 1988; Malamuth et al., 2001; for an exception see Marshall, 1988).

At least one highly interactive, software-based antipornography intervention, *Peggy's Porn Guide* (Isaacs, 2003) has been developed and tested, with a view toward Internet deployment as an educational immunization against pornographic messages that link sexuality and sexual violence. Research by Isaacs and Fisher (in press) involved exposing men to (among other stimuli) violent and degrading pornographic videos taken from the Internet, accompanied by interactions with Peggy, a buxom antipornography educator, and results suggest that such interventions may assist men to recognize and reject

a

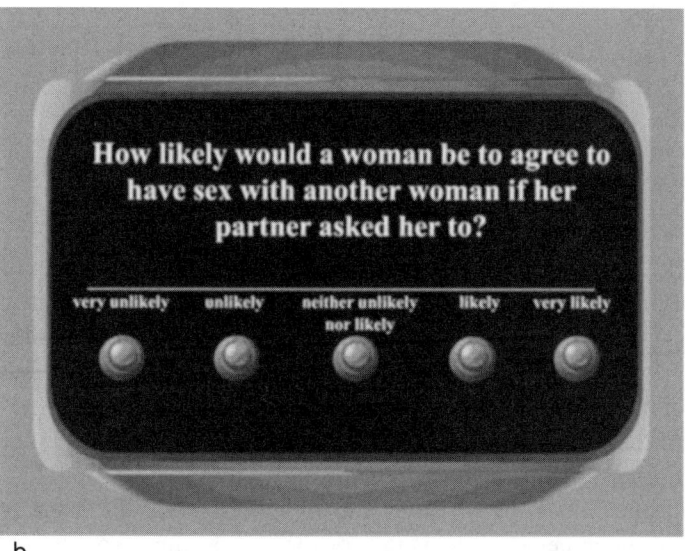

b

Figure 8.2. *Screen shots illustrating the* Peggy's Porn Guide *antipornography intervention (Isaacs, 2003).*

themes of sexual violence portrayed in Internet sexually explicit materials. Screenshots illustrating the *Peggy's Porn Guide* intervention are presented in Figure 8.2.

Given public concern about Internet sexually explicit materials and the paucity of research on prevalence and effects of Internet pornography, research beyond extant work (e.g., Barak et al., 1999; Fisher & Barak, 2001; Isaacs, 2003) is clearly needed.

## Internet sex Education

An additional and potentially positive aspect of the Internet is the way it has been used to educate people about sex. Sexual and reproductive health challenges as abiding and diverse as sexual dysfunction (Basson et al., 2000, 2004; Fisher, Boroditsky, & Morris, 2004b; Laumann & Rosen, 1999; Zilbergeld, 1992), contraceptive method choice (Black, Francouer, & Rowe, 2004a, 2004b, 2004c; Fisher et al., 2004a, 2004b), adolescent sexual activity (Byrne, Kelly, & Fisher, 1993; Fisher & Boroditsky, 2000), sexually transmitted infection (Acker, Goldwater, & Dyson, 1992; Fisher & Fisher, 1992; Centers for Disease Control and Prevention, see at: http://www.cdc.gov./std/default.htm), and the experience of menopause (Fisher, Sand, Lewis, & Boroditsky, 2000; Writing Group for the Women's Health Initiative Investigators, 2002) confront individuals worldwide who need accessible, expert, and personally relevant information. Sexuality and reproductive health education efforts – aimed at providing individuals with information, motivation, and behavioral skills that will enable them to avoid sexual and reproductive health problems and achieve well-being in this area (Barak & Fisher, 2001, 2003; J. Fisher & Fisher, 1992; W. Fisher & Fisher, 1993, 1999) – are increasingly exploiting the Internet to deliver sexual and reproductive health promotion content.

### Exploiting Unique Characteristics of the Internet for Sexual and Reproductive Health Education

It has been asserted that the Internet's core characteristics are uniquely and optimally suited to the communication of sexual and reproductive health education (Barak & Fisher, 2001, 2002, 2003). The Internet is *affordable* to audiences who seek or require sexual and reproductive health content; it is *accessible* at any time of day or night and at an enormous number of locations worldwide; it is *acceptable* and regarded as a credible and legitimate communication channel; and it is *anonymous* or at least perceived as such by users, who can access this sexual and reproductive health information channel while *alone*, unobserved, and unmonitored (Barak & Fisher, 2001, 2002, 2003; Cooper, 1998; Cooper et al., 2000). Moreover, individuals using the Internet to access sexuality and reproductive health education material can do so with little or no fear of censure or stigma owing to their level of sexual knowledge or sexual ignorance, their age or physical appearance, or the nature of their specific sexual interests, inclinations, or questions. From the point of view of the creation of sexual and reproductive health education initiatives, the Internet can be an exceedingly efficient and cost-effective channel for collecting and communicating the most expert and up-to-date information to the widest possible audience, and it is capable of providing rich, interactive, and individually tailored audio, visual, and text information to sexuality and reproductive health education consumers. For these reasons, Internet-assisted sexual and reproductive health websites have proliferated (for example, http://www.sexualhealth.com; http://www.iwannaknow.org; http://www.goaskalice.columbia.edu; http://www.teensource.org; http://www. teenwire.com), and at least one widely used website (http://www.sexual ityandu.ca) has been explicitly based on a sophisticated and well-validated behavioral science model of sexual and reproductive health promotion (e.g., Byrne et al., 1993; J. Fisher & Fisher, 1992; W. Fisher & Fisher, 1992, 1999).

### Comprehensive, Theoretically Grounded, Internet-Based Sexual and Reproductive Health Education: Sexualityandu.ca – masexualite.ca

The sexualityandu.ca website provides an illustration of a comprehensive, theoretically grounded, Internet-based approach to sexual and reproductive health education. Responding to sexual and reproductive health challenges facing Canadians, the Society of Obstetricians and Gynaecologists of Canada, together with other interested organizations, initiated a sexual and reproductive health promotion project which – while initially focused on traditional media (e.g., books, brochures, and the like) quickly changed course and decided to invest resources in an Internet-driven comprehensive sexual and reproductive health platform (Barak & Fisher, 2003). Recognizing that the accessible, affordable, and anonymous nature of the Internet provided optimum conditions for seeking and assimilating sexual and reproductive health content, and the tremendous efficiencies of an Internet-based approach for collecting and conveying comprehensive, expert, and up-to-date materials in this domain, sexualityandu.ca – masexualite.ca was created as a bilingual English-French website. Sexualityandu.ca – masexualite.ca contains sexual and reproductive health promotion content dedicated and directed separately to teens, parents, adults, teachers, and health care professionals. This content is created by a panel of experts, and it is continuously updated and conveyed with rich, interactive, audio, visual, and text materials. Website content and approach is grounded in the Information-Motivation-Behavioral Skills (IMB) model (J. Fisher & Fisher, 1992; W. Fisher & Fisher, 1993, 1999), which has been adopted by Health Canada (2003) as a well-validated model for sexual and reproductive health promotion intervention. The IMB model (J. Fisher & Fisher, 1991; W. Fisher & Fisher, 1993, 1999) is based on an integration of social and health psychology theory and research and holds that individuals who are well-informed and possess easy-to-apply sexual and reproductive health knowledge, who have attitudes and norms that motivate them to enact sexual and reproductive health practices, and who possess the behavioral skills necessary to act effectively, are likely to engage in sexual and reproductive health promotion behavior. Conversely, the poorly informed, the poorly motivated, and those who lack relevant behavioral skills are likely to engage in sexual and reproductive health risk behaviors (see J. Fisher & Fisher, 2000, for a review of empirical support for the IMB model). Accordingly, sexualityandu.ca – masexualite.ca's educational approach exploits the Internet to communicate comprehensive sexual and reproductive health information, motivation, and behavioral skills content to diverse audiences.

The teen section of sexualityandu.ca – masexualite.ca contains information concerning traditionally focal issues (e.g., puberty, contraception, sexually transmitted infections), emerging issues (e.g., drug-assisted sexual assault), conveys scriptlike and easy-to-apply information for addressing sexual and reproductive health problems, and a set of engaging audiovisual games and virtual scenarios (e.g., "It's Party Time," "War of the Condoms") that permit an adolescent to try out sexual choices and address the consequences of these choices in virtual space. The parent section of the website discusses the parental role in sexual and reproductive health promotion; provides information, motivation, and behavioral skills content concerning puberty, adolescence, and living with teenagers, and approaches to talking with teens about sexual and reproductive health issues; and links to essential resources. The adult section of sexualityandu.ca – masexualite.ca includes relevant material concerning sexual function and dysfunction, contraception, and scriptlike tips for talking with partners about sexuality, among other topics; and the teacher's section of the website is provides detailed information concerning approaches, strategies, lesson plans, and directly applicable materials for delivering sexual and reproductive health education in the classroom. The health care professionals section of the website conveys information about clinician-patient communication about sexual and reproductive health; male and female sexual function; contraception, disability, and illness, menopause; and domestic violence.

The creators of sexualityandu.ca – masexualite.ca have devoted considerable resources to creating and updating content and presenting it in rich, interactive fashion to convey easy to act on information, motivation to act, and behavioral skills for acting effectively in promoting sexual and reproductive health, as the IMB model stipulates. Moreover, considerable resources have been devoted to design issues (the sexualityandu.ca – masexualite.ca logo, seen in Figure 8.3, is a Canadian underground classic) and to public service and paid advertising, including bus shelter and subway ads, radio spots, and widespread distribution of sexualityandu.ca – masexualite.ca mouse pads and rulers in high schools, physicians offices, and other consumer contact settings. The net result of this activity is that sexualityandu.ca – masexualite.ca is visited by some 280,000 unique visitors each month, for an average of approximately ten minutes per visit (see Figure 8.4), illustrating the efficiency and reach of Internet-driven sexuality education and the access and comfort level of its users.

## A Specialized, Theoretically Grounded, Internet Compatible Approach to Health Promotion for HIV-Positive Persons: Lifewindows

Highly active antiretroviral therapy (HAART) represents the single most important achievement in the treatment of HIV since the beginning of the HIV/AIDS epidemic (Dybul, Fauci, Bartlett, Kaplan, & Pau, 2002). Within the decade since its introduction, HAART has dramatically reduced the morbidity

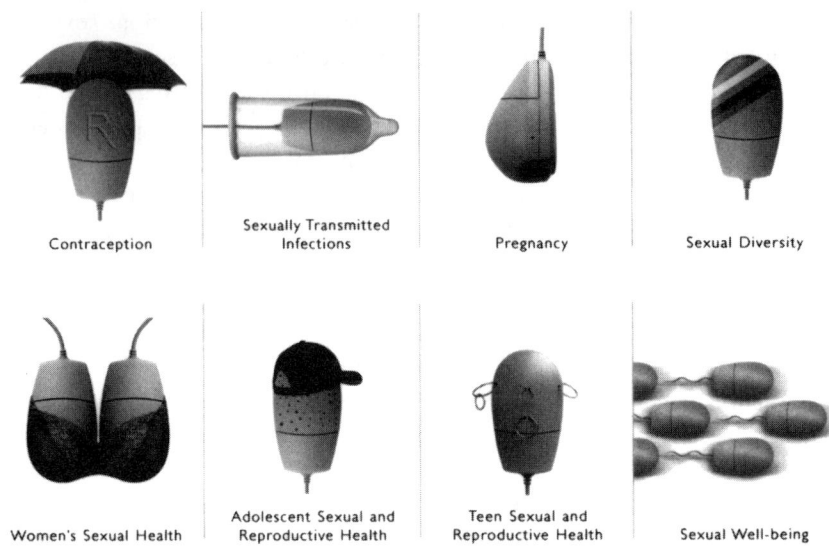

Figure 8.3. *Sexualityandu.ca website logo.*

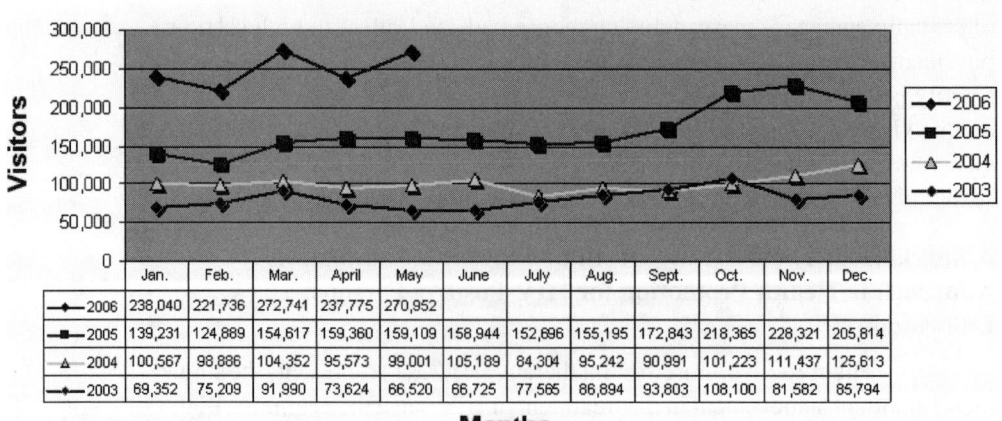

Figure 8.4. *Sexualityandu.ca – masexualite.ca unique website visitors, 2003–2006.*

and morality of HIV infection, and, where available, HAART has changed HIV from an always fatal disease into a chronic infection. Despite these dramatic benefits, however, HAART regimens are often complex, side-effect laden, toxic, and extremely unforgiving of suboptimal adherence (Altice, Mostashari, & Friedland, 2001; Holzmer, Henry, Portillo, & Miramontes, 2000; Fisher, Fisher, Harman, & Amico, 2006). Unless an HIV-positive individual is 90 percent adherent to his or her HAART regimen, viral resistance may develop and the HIV-positive individual's health may be severely compromised (Paterson et al., 2000). At present, some 57–77 percent of HIV-positive patients are unable to adhere to HAART at necessary levels (Montessori et al., 2000; Rigsby et al., 2000).

*Lifewindows* (Lifewindows Working Group, Center for Health, Intervention, and Prevention, University of Connecticut) is a specialized, IMB model–based approach to promotion of adherence to HAART among HIV-positive persons that employs sophisticated, completely interactive, and highly attractive software. *Lifewindows* is currently being tested in clinical settings, with some 500 HIV-positive men and women, with a view toward future widespread dissemination of an empirically validated educational intervention via computer kiosks in clinical settings and on the Internet. *Lifewindows* participants – HIV-positive patients on antiretroviral therapy – are greeted by Marcus (see Figure 8.5), a friendly and supportive "guide" who works with patients, taking them through a richly illustrated medication adherence assessment routine, and a comprehensive review of patient information, motivation, and behavioral skills barriers to adherence to HAART. Based on adherence levels and identified information, motivation, and behavioral skills barriers to adherence, HIV-positive participants are encouraged to choose from among twenty relevant intervention activities. Adherence promotion intervention activities range from richly illustrated simulations in which participants position icons indicating their daily activities (which are converted into naturally occurring cues for taking medication), to "Positive Voices," in which a panel of articulate HIV-positive persons discuss their own strategies for managing adherence, to "Doc Talk," in which highly expert and patient-friendly HIV care physicians take the time to answer common patient questions about HAART adherence and toxicity. Other adherence promotion interventions that are interactively offered on the basis of individual patient needs include "Bill the Pill," a humorous cartoon that describes ways to make taking medication easier, "Bloodstream Animation," a cartoon to teach exactly how HAART works, why adherence is critical, and how nonadherence damages the immune system and health, and "Side Effects" prescribes scriptlike approaches to dealing with side effects of HAART that work against adherence. *Lifewindows* assists HIV-positive patients to set goals for adherence, "remembers" patient adherence goals and concerns, and "checks in" with patients periodically. Once again, the *Lifewindows* approach, like the sexualityandu.ca approach, is based on validated behavior change theory, and it explicitly exploits the anonymity,

Figure 8.5. *Lifewindows introduction screen and adherence promotion intervention screen examples.*

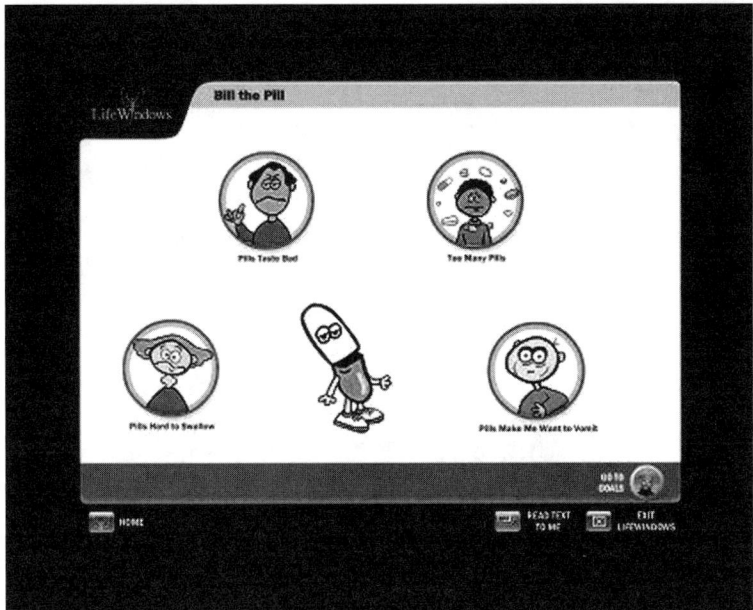

(c)

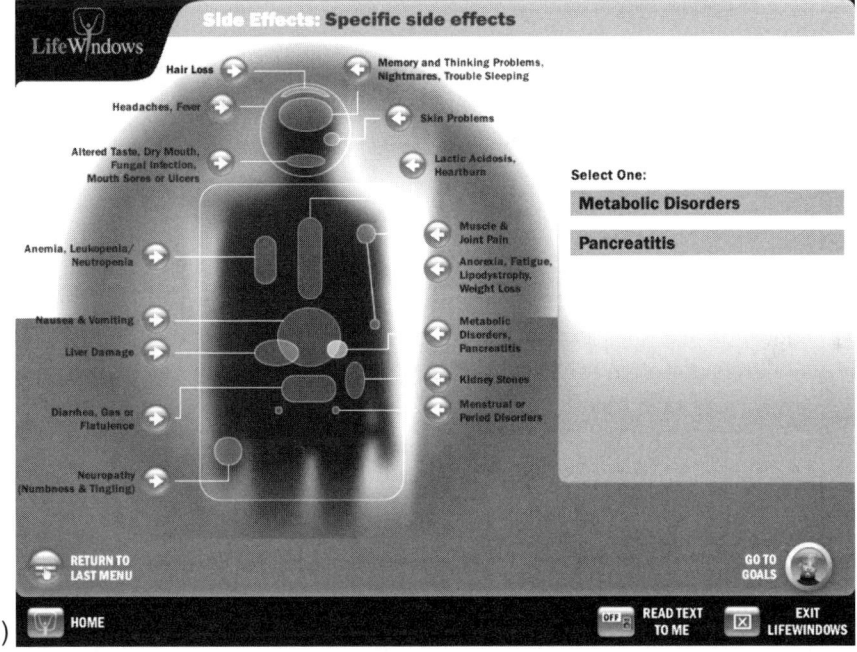

(d)

Figure 8.5 *(continued)*

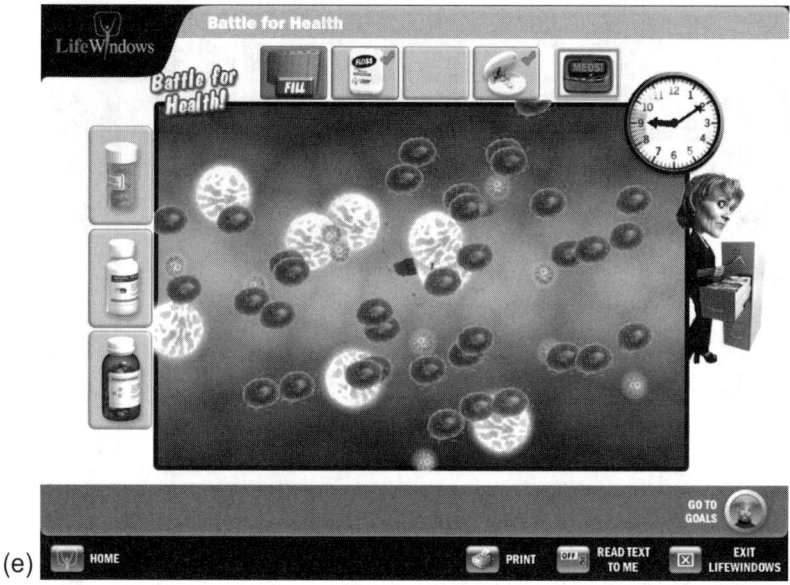

Figure 8.5 *(continued)*

accessibility, affordability, and aloneness characteristics of patient-computer interaction on Internet, which facilitate nonjudgmental and personally relevant and applicable health promotion intervention, in this instance specialized and targeted toward lifesaving adherence to HAART.

## Internet-Based Sexuality Education: Second Thoughts

Despite the promise of Internet-based sexuality education as an efficient and effective channel for sexual health promotion, we note that health education websites in general are quite variable in accuracy and that website users are often not sensitive to or discerning of such differences in website quality (see Morahan-Martin, Chapter 3; see Smith, Gertz, Alvarez, and Lurie's [2000] discussion of variable sex education website quality). Moreover, research focused on sexual health education websites shows that use of search engines with terms such as sexual health and sex education may identify a preponderance of pornographic sites and a small minority of useful and legitimate sex education sites (Smith, Gertz, Alvarez, & Lurie, 2000). Use of search engines to locate specific sexual health information (e.g., condom use instructions, sexually transmitted disease symptoms) however, was much more efficient and produced usable results very rapidly (Smith, Gertz, Alvarez, & Lurie, 2000). In addition, Bay-Cheng's (2001) content analysis of sex education websites found that – mirroring classroom-based sex education – web-based sex education had a heavy emphasis on sexual problems and a frequent moralizing focus. At the same time, experimental research has demonstrated that Internet-based sex education has positive effects on reproductive health knowledge in populations as diverse as disabled North American women

(Pendergrass, Nosek, & Holcomb, 2001) and mainland Chinese high school and college students (Lou, Zhao, Gao, & Shah, 2006). Further research and application of Internet technology to provide accessible, anonymous, and high-quality sexual and reproductive health education efficiently and effectively is clearly a future objective.

## The Rainbow Web? Gays, Lesbians, and the Internet

There is a strong basis for assuming, once again, that the core characteristics of the Internet – accessibility, affordability, acceptability, anonymity, and aloneness – might make it an extremely good medium for communication with and among members of sexual minorities who experience, in addition to numerical minority, enduring stigma. As it happens, the Internet *has* proven to be an extremely widely exploited channel for communication among gay, lesbian, bisexual, and transgendered (GLBT) individuals worldwide. A special issue of the *International Journal of Sexuality and Gender Studies* (see, for example, Alexander, 2002; Heinz, Gu, Inuzuka, & Zender, 2002) has been devoted to GLBT individuals' use, presence, and identity on the Internet, and the interested reader may peruse any number of GLBT-focused and friendly websites (e.g., Gay.com, http://www.gay.com; PlanetOut, http://www.planetout.com).

Perhaps inevitably, the Internet has had both positive and negative effects on the GLBT community. The Internet can be employed as a venue for coming out and for learning about and exploring gay identity and gay community in the safety, anonymity, and user-controlled environment of the web (see, for example, Munt, Bassett, & O'Riordan, 2002), and it can be employed as an anonymous and effective means for conducting research with GLBT individuals who would not otherwise be available for research participation (see, for example, Chiasson et al., 2006; Pequegnat et al., 2007).

The Internet can be a potentially safer space for GLBT individuals to explore their sexuality. Mathy (2007) found in her large sample of 7,037 participants that heterosexuals are significantly less likely than others of the same sex to use the Internet to explore their sexuality. Moreover, she found that bisexual men were more likely than heterosexuals to use the Internet to engage in offline risky sexual behaviors (e.g., anonymous sex with strangers). Interestingly, Mathy found that a larger proportion of male bisexuals compared with gays had stated that they used the Internet to explore their sexual fantasies. In contrast, a larger percentage of gays compared with male bisexuals claimed they engaged in online sexual activities as a way of coping with stress, to meet dates, and to meet for pure sex.

The Internet provides an ideal context for meeting – and having unsafe sex with – other members of sexual minorities, and research has repeatedly found that use of the Internet to find sexual partners may be very common among men who have sex with men, and that men who find male sexual partners on the Internet are at considerably greater risk of sexually transmitted infection, including HIV, than men who do not (see Benotsch, Kalichman, & Cage,

2004; McFarlane, Bull, & Rietmeijer, 2000; Liau, Millett, & Marks, 2006). At the same time, however, the Internet may also prove to be an exceptionally suitable means for reaching sexual minority communities with prevention messages. For example, the World Health Organization (2000) reports on the use of Internet users' screen names, obtained from chat rooms, to convey prevention information during a syphilis epidemic among homosexual men in San Francisco, which resulted in a substantial increase in men seeking screening and care for this infection. Others (Grove, 2006) report on Internet-based interventions to address barebacking (unprotected anal intercourse among men who have sex with men), and Internet-based research on suicidality among gay and bisexual men and women on five continents, that could provide critical guidance for Internet-based prevention interventions. Although space limitations preclude further discussion, this brief introduction to the subject of the Internet and the GLBT community suggests that core characteristics of the Internet make this a highly appropriate channel for communication with and among sexual minorities and that the effect of the Internet in this community may be immense, health relevant, and in need of research and prosocial exploitation.

## The Future of Online Sex

Online sexual activities no longer are restricted to text, pictures, videos, webcams, and audio. Nowadays, while still in its infancy, we have *teledildonics*. Teledildonics is essentially a virtual reality application that allows individuals to have sex interactively with people miles away. At present, mobile phones can call up and activate internally worn vibrators. Futurists have dreamed up many other potential ways that technology can be used to pleasure people. In the future, we expect that full body suits will exist that will be able to stimulate all five senses (Whitty & Carr, 2006).

## Conclusions

This is obviously not the final story about online sexual activities. We expect that people will continue to harness the Internet to live out their sexual fantasies – and as a substitute for living out their sexual fantasies. We also expect that more problems will emerge for couples as the Internet becomes a more common and accessible part of individuals' lives – and that couples sexual relationships may be enriched by what they may learn on the Internet. Given the amount of research that has found that individuals can benefit from exploring their sexuality online, therapists ought to consider also new ways to assist their clients. Moreover, educators and health workers need to find new ways to use the Internet to provide credible information to those seeking out help and information about sexuality and sexual health issues. The Internet, and its potential positive and negative effect on sexuality, is clearly only in its early stages of development, with a future yet to unfold.

## References

Abel, G. G., Becker, J. V., & Mittleman, M. S. (1985). *Sex offenders*. Paper presented at the 11th annual meeting of the International Academy of Sex Research, Seattle, WA.

Acker, L. E., Goldwater, B. C., & Dyson, W. H. (1992). *AIDS proofing your kids: A step-by-step guide*. Pickering, Ontario: Mattacchione.

Alexander, J. (2002). Homo-pages and queer sites: Studying the construction and representation of queer identities on the World-Wide Web. *International Journal of Sexuality and Gender Studies, 7*, 85–106.

Altice, F. L., Mostashari, F., & Friedland, G. H. (2001). Trust and the acceptance of and adherence to antiretroviral therapy. *Journal of Acquired Immune Deficiency Syndromes, 28*, 47–58.

Barak, A., & Fisher, W. A. (1997). Effects of interactive computer erotica on men's attitudes and behavior toward women: An experimental study. *Computers in Human Behavior, 13*, 353–369.

Barak, A., & Fisher, W. A. (2001). Towards an Internet-based, theoretically driven, innovative approach to sexuality education. *Journal of Sex Research, 38*, 324–332.

Barak, A., & Fisher, W. A. (2002). The future of Internet sexuality. In A. Cooper (Ed.), *Sex and the Internet: A guide for clinicians* (pp. 263–280). New York: Bruner-Routledge.

Barak, A., & Fisher, W. A. (2003). Experience with an Internet-based, theoretically grounded educational resource for the promotion of sexual and reproductive health. *Sexual and Relationship Therapy, 18*, 293–308.

Barak, A., Fisher, W. A., Belfry, S., & Lashambe, D. R. (1999). Sex, guys, and cyberspace. Effects of Internet pornography and individual differences on men's attitudes toward women. *Journal of Psychology and Human Sexuality, 11*, 63–91.

Basson, R., Berman, J., Burnett, A, Derogatis, L., Ferguson, D., Fourcroy, J., et al. (2000). Report of the international consensus development conference on female sexual dysfunction: Definitions and classifications. *Journal of Urology, 163*, 888–893.

Basson, R., Leiblum, S., Brotto, L., Derogatis, L., Fourcroy, J., Fugl-Meyer, K., et al. (2004). Revised definitions of women's sexual dysfunction. *Journal of Sexual Medicine, 1*, 40–48.

Bay-Cheng, L. Y. (2001). SexEd.Com: Values and norms in Web-based sexuality education. *Journal of Sex Research, 38*, 241–251.

Becker, J., & Stein, R. M. (1991). Is sexual erotica associated with sexual deviance in adolescent males? *International Journal of Law and Psychiatry, 14*, 85–96.

Benotsch, E. G., Kalichman, S., & Cage, M. (2004). Men who have met sex partners via the Internet: Prevalence, predictors, and implications for HIV prevention. *Archives of Sexual Behavior, 31*, 173–188.

Black, A., Francoeur, D., & Rowe, T. (2004a). Canadian contraception consensus: Part 1. *Journal of Obstetrics and Gynaecology Canada, 143*, 143–156.

Black, A., Francoeur, D., & Rowe, T. (2004b). Canadian contraception consensus: Part 2. *Journal of Obstetrics and Gynaecology Canada, 43*, 219–236.

Black, A., Francoeur, D., & Rowe, T. (2004c). Canadian contraception consensus: Part 3. *Journal of Obstetrics and Gynaecology Canada, 143*, 347–387.

Bogaert, A. F. (1993). *The sexual media: The role of individual differences*. Unpublished doctoral dissertation, Department of Psychology, University of Western Ontario, London, Ontario, Canada.

Bogaert, A. F. (2001). Personality, individual differences, and preferences for the sexual media. *Archives of Sexual Behavior, 30*, 29–53.

Byrne, D., Kelley, K., & Fisher, W. A. (1993). Unwanted teenage pregnancies: Incidence, interpretation, intervention. *Applied and Preventive Psychology, 2*, 101–113.

Chiasson, M. A., Parsons, J. T., Tesoriero, J. M., Carballo-Dieguez, A., Hirshfield, S., & Remien, R. H. (2006). HIV behavioral research online. *Journal of Urban Health, 83*, 73–85.

Cooper, A. (1998). Sexuality and the Internet surfing into the new millennium. *CyberPsychology & Behavior, 1*, 187–193.

Cooper, A. (2000). Cybersex and sexual compulsivity: The dark side of the force. *Sexual Addiction and Compulsivity, 7*, 1–3.

Cooper, A., Delmonico, D. L., & Burg, R. (2000). Cybersex users, abusers, and compulsives: New findings and implications. *Sexual Addiction & Compulsivity, 7*, 5–29.

Cooper, A., Scherer, C. R., Bois, S. C., & Gordon, B. I. (1999). Sexuality on the Internet: From sexual exploration to pathological expression. *Professional Psychology: Research and Practice, 30*, 154–164.

Cooper, A., Scherer, C., & Marcus, I. D. (2002). Harnessing the power of the Internet to improve sexual relationships. In A. Cooper (Ed.), *Sex & the Internet: A guidebook for clinicians* (pp. 209–230). New York: Brunner-Routledge.

Dahlquist, J. P., & Vigilant, L. G. (2004). Way better than real: Manga sex to tentacle hentai. In D. D. Waskul (Ed.), *Net.sex: Readings on sex, pornography, and the Internet* (pp. 91–103). New York: Peter Lang.

D'Amato, A. (2006). *Porn up, rape down*. Northwestern Public Law Research Paper No. 913013. Retrieved June 15, 2007, from http://ssrn.com/abstract=913013.

Daneback, K., Ross, M. K., & Månsson, S.-A. (2006). Characteristics and behaviors of sexual compulsives who use the Internet for sexual purposes. *Sexual Addiction & Compulsivity: The Journal of Treatment and Prevention, 13*, 53–67.

Dybul, M., Fauci, A. S., Bartlett, J. G., Kaplan, J. E., & Pau, A. K. (2002). Guidelines for using antiretroviral agents among HIV-infected adults and adolescents. *Annals of Internal Medicine, 137*, 381–433.

Edgley, C., & Kiser, K. (1981). Polaroid sex: Deviant possibilities in a technological age. *Journal of American Culture, 5*, 59–64.

Elmer-Dewitt, P. (1995). On a screen near you: Cyberporn. *Time, 146*, 1.

Emmers-Sommer, T. M., & Burns, R. J. (2005). The relationship between exposure to Internet pornography and sexual attitudes toward women. *Journal of*

*Online Behavior*, *1*(4). Retrieved March 1, 2007, from http://www.behavior.net/JOB/v1n4/emmers-sommer.html.

Eysenck, H. J. (1978). *Sex and personality*. London: Sphere.

Fisher, J. D., & Fisher, W. A. (1992). Changing AIDS risk behavior. *Psychological Bulletin, 111*, 455–474.

Fisher, J. D., & Fisher, W. A. (2000). Theoretical approaches to individual level change in HIV risk behavior. In J. Peteson, & R. DiClemente (Eds.), *Handbook of HIV prevention* (pp. 3–55). New York: Plenum.

Fisher, J. D., Fisher W. A., Amico, K. R., & Harman, J. J. (2006). An information-motivation-behavioral skills model of adherence to antiretroviral therapy. *Health Psychology, 25*, 462–473.

Fisher, W. A., & Barak, A. (1991). Pornography, erotica, and behaviour: More questions than answers. *International Journal of Law and Psychiatry, 14*, 65–84.

Fisher, W. A., & Barak, A. (2001). Internet pornography: A social psychological perspective on Internet sexuality. *Journal of Sex Research, 38*, 1–11.

Fisher, W. A., & Boroditsky, R. (2000). Sexual activity, contraceptive choice, and reproductive health risk among single Canadian women aged 15–19: additional findings from the Canadian contraceptive study. *Canadian Journal of Human Sexuality, 9*(2), 79–93.

Fisher, W. A., Boroditsky, R. B., & Morris, B. (2004a). Canadian contraception study 2002: Part II. *Journal of Obstetrics and Gynaecology Canada, 26*, 646–656.

Fisher, W. A., Boroditsky, R. B., & Morris, B. (2004b). The 2002 Canadian contraception study: Part I. *Journal of Obstetrics and Gynaecology Canada, 26*, 580–590.

Fisher, W. A., & Byrne, D. (1978). Individual differences in affective, evaluative, and behavioral responses to an erotic film. *Journal of Applied Social Psychology, 8*, 355–365.

Fisher, W. A., & Fisher, J. D. (1993). A general social psychological model for changing AIDS risk behavior. In J. Pryor & G. Reeder (Eds.), *The social psychology of HIV infection* (pp. 127–153). Hillsdale, NJ: Erlbaum.

Fisher, W. A., & Fisher, J. D. (1999). Understanding and promoting sexual and reproductive health behavior. In R. Rosen, C. Davis, & H. Ruppel (Eds.), *Annual review of sex research* (Vol. 9, pp. 39–76). Mason City, IA: Society for the Scientific Study of Sex.

Fisher, W. A., Sand, M., Lewis, W., & Boroditsky, R. (2000). Canadian Menopause Study: I. Understanding women's intentions to utilize hormone replacement therapy. *Maturitas, 37*, 1–14.

Freeman-Longo, R. E. (2000). Children, teens, and sex on the Internet. *Sexual Addiction and Compulsivity, 7*, 75–90.

Fulda, J. S. (2002). Do Internet stings directed at pedophiles capture offenders or create offenders? And allied questions. *Sexuality & Culture, 6*, 73–100.

Goldstein, M. J., & Kant, H. S. (1973). *Pornography and sexual deviance*. Berkeley, CA: University of California Press.

Griffiths, M. (2004). Sex addiction on the Internet. *Janus Head, 7*(1). Retrieved February 27, 2007, from http://www.janushead.org/7–1/Griffiths.pdf.

Grove, C. (2006). Barebacking websites: Electronic environments for reducing or inducing HIV risk. *AIDS Care, 18*, 990–997.

Health Canada. (2003). *Canadian guidelines for sexual health education*. Ottawa: Minister of Public Works and Government Services.

Heinz, B., Gu, L., Inuzuka, A., & Zender, R. (2002). Under the rainbow flag: Webnetting global gay identities. *International Journal of Sexuality and Gender Studies, 7*, 107–124.

Holzmer, W. L., Henry, S. B., Portillo, C. J., & Miramontes, H. (2000). The client adherence profiling intervention tailoring (CAP-IT) intervention for enhancing adherence to HIV/AIDS medications: A pilot study. *Journal of the Association of Nurses in AIDS Care, 11*, 36–44.

Isaacs, C. R., & Fisher, W. A. (in press). A computer-based educational intervention to address potential negative effects of Internet pornography. *Communication Studies, 59(1)*.

Jacobs, K. (2004). Pornography in small places and other spaces. *Cultural Studies, 18*, 67–83.

Langevin, R., Lang, R. A., Wright, P., Handy, L., Frenzel, R. R., & Black, E. L. (1988). Pornography and sexual offences. *Sexual Abuse: A Journal of Research & Treatment, 1*, 335–362.

Laumann, E. O., Paik, A., & Rosen R. C. (1999). Sexual dysfunction in the United States: Prevalence and predictors. *Journal of the American Medical Association, 281*, 537–544.

Liau, A., Millett, G., & Marks, G. (2006). Meta-analytic examination of online sex-seeking and sexual risk behavior among men who have sex with men. *Sexually Transmitted Diseases, 33*, 576–584.

Lou, C., Zhao, Q., Gao, E., & Shah, I. H. (2006). Can the Internet be used effectively to provide sex education to young people in China? *Journal of Adolescent Health, 39*, 720–728.

Malamuth, N. M. (1989a). The Attraction to Sexual Aggression Scale: Part 1. *Journal of Sex Research, 26*, 26–49.

Malamuth, N. M. (1989b). The Attraction to Sexual Aggression Scale: Part 2. *Journal of Sex Research, 26*, 324–354.

Malamuth, N. M., Addison, T., & Koss, M. (2001). Pornography and sexual aggression: Are there reliable effects and can we understand them? *Annual review of sex research*. Vol. 11. Mason City, IA: Society for the Scientific Study of Sexuality.

Mann, J., Sidman, J., & Starr, S. (1973). Evaluating social consequences of erotic films: An experimental approach. *Journal of Social Issues, 29*, 113–131.

Marshall, W. L. (1988). The use of sexually explicit stimuli by rapists, child molesters, and nonoffenders. *Journal of Sex Research, 25*, 267–288.

Mathy, R. M. (2007). Sexual orientation moderates online sexual activities. In M. T. Whitty, A. J. Baker, J. A. Inman (Eds.), *Online matchmaking* (pp. 159–177). Basingstoke: Palgrave Macmillan.

McFarlane, M., Bull, S. S., & Rietmeijer, C. A. (2000). The Internet as a newly emerging risk environment for sexually transmitted diseases. *Journal of the American Medical Association, 284*, 443–446.

Montessori, V., Heath, K. V., Yipp, B., Hogg, R. S., O'Shaughnessy, M. V., & Montaner, S. G. (2000, February). *Predictors of adherence with triple combination antiretroviral therapy*. Paper presented at the 7th Conference on Retroviruses and Opportunistic Infections, San Francisco.

Mosher, D. L. (1980). Three dimensions of depth of involvement in human sexual response. *Journal of Sex Research, 16*, 1–42.

Mosher, D. L. (1988). Pornography defined: Sexual involvement theory, narrative context, "goodness of fit." *Journal of Psychology and Human Sexuality, 1*, 67–85.

Munt, S. R., Bassett, E. H., & O'Riordan, K. (2002). Virtually belonging: Risk, connectivity, and coming out on-line. *International Journal of Sexuality and Gender Studies, 7*, 127–137.

Parker, C. (1997). *The joy of cybersex: Confessions of an internet addict*. Kew, Australia: Reed Books.

Parker, T. S., & Wampler, K. S. (2003). How bad is it? Perceptions of the relationship impact of different types of Internet sexual activities. *Contemporary Family Therapy, 25*, 415–429.

Paterson, D. L., Swindells, S., Mohr, J., Brester, M., Vergis, E. N., Squier, C., Wagener, M. M., & Singh, N. (2000). Adherence to protease inhibitor therapy and outcomes in patients with HIV infection. *Annals of Internal Medicine, 133*, 21–30.

Pendergrass, S., Nosek, M. A., & Holcomb, J. D. (2001). Design and evaluation of an Internet site to educate women with disabilities on reproductive health care. *Sexuality & Disability, 19*, 71–83.

Pequegnat, W., Simon Rosser, B. R., Bowen, A. M., Bull, S. S., DiClemente, R. J., Bockting, W. O., Elford, J., Fishbein, M., Gurak, L., Horvath, K., Konstan, J., Noar, S. M., Ross, M. W., Sherr, L., Spiegel, D., & Zimmerman, R. (2007). Conducting Internet-based HIV/STD prevention survey research: Considerations in design and evaluation. *AIDS and Behavior, 11*, 505–521.

Rigsby, M. O., Rosen, M. I., Beauvais, J. E., Cramer, J. A., Rainey, P. M., O'Malley, S. S., Dieckhaus, K. D., & Rounsaville, B. J. (2000). Cue-dose training with monetary reinforcement: Pilot study of an antiretroviral adherence intervention. *Journal of General Internal Medicine, 15*, 841–847.

Rimm, M. (1995). Marketing pornography on the information superhighway: A survey of 917,410 images, descriptions, short stories, and animations downloaded 8.5 million times by consumers in over 2000 cities in forty countries, provinces, and territories. *Georgetown Law Review, 83*, 1849–1934.

Schneider, J. P. (2000). Effects of cybersex addiction on the family: Results of a survey. *Sexual Addiction & Compulsivity, 7*, 31–58.

Smith, M., Gertz, E., Alvarez, S., & Lurie, P. (2000). The content and accessibility of sex education information on the Internet. *Health Education & Behavior, 27*, 684–694.

Snyder, M., & Ickes, W. (1985). Personality and social psychology. In G. Lindsey and E. Aronson (Eds.), *Handbook of social psychology* (Vol. II, 3rd ed., pp. 883–943), New York: Random House.

Spector Soft, Inc. (n.d.). *Stop infidelity with Spector*. Retrieved March 1, 2007, from http://www.spywaredirectory.com/spector_win.asp.

Sprenger, P. (1999, September 30). The porn pioneers. *The Guardian* [Online]. Retrieved June 15, 2007, from http://technology.guardian.co.uk/online/story/0,,255578,00.html.

Turkle, S. (1995). *Life on the screen: Identity in the age of the Internet*. London: Weidenfeld & Nicolson.

Whitty, M. T. (2003a). Cyber-flirting: Playing at love on the internet. *Theory and Psychology, 13*, 339–357.

Whitty, M. T. (2003b). Pushing the wrong buttons: Men's and women's attitudes towards online and offline infidelity. *CyberPsychology & Behavior, 6*, 569–579.

Whitty, M. T. (2004). Cyber-flirting: An examination of men's and women's flirting behaviour both offline and on the Internet. *Behaviour Change, 21*, 115–126.

Whitty, M. T. (2005). The "realness" of cyber-cheating: Men and women's representations of unfaithful Internet relationships. *Social Science Computer Review, 23*, 57–67.

Whitty, M. T. (2007). Manipulation of self in cyberspace. In B. H. Spitzberg, & W. R. Cupach. *The dark side of interpersonal communication* (2nd ed., pp. 93–120). Mahwah, NJ: Erlbaum.

Whitty, M. T., & Carr, A. N. (2005). Taking the good with the bad: Applying Klein's work to further our understandings of cyber-cheating. *Journal of Couple and Relationship Therapy, 4*(2/3), 103–115.

Whitty, M. T., & Carr, A. N. (2006). *Cyberspace romance: The psychology of online relationships*. Basingstoke: Palgrave Macmillan.

World Health Organization. (2000). *Use of the Internet as a public health intervention tool for an outbreak of syphilis.* Retrieved June 15, 2007, from http://www.scielosp.org/scielo.php?pid=S0042-96862000001000016&script=sci_arttext.

Writing Group for the Women's Health Initiative Investigators. (2002). Risks and benefits of estrogen plus progestin in healthy postmenopausal women: principal results from the Women's Health Initiative randomized controlled trial. *Journal of the American Medical Association, 288*, 321–333.

Wysocki, D. K. (1998). Let your fingers to do the talking: Sex on an adult chat-line. *Sexualities, 1*, 425–452.

Wysocki, D. K., & Thalken, J. (2007). Whips and chains? Fact or fiction? Content analysis of sadomasochism in Internet personal advertisements. In M. T. Whitty, A. J. Baker, & J. A. Inman. (Eds.), *Online matchmaking* (pp. 178–196). Basingstoke: Palgrave Macmillan.

Zilbergeld, B. (1992). *The new male sexuality*. Bantam: New York.

# 9 The Contact Hypothesis Reconsidered: Interacting Via Internet: Theoretical and Practical Aspects

*Yair Amichai-Hamburger*

Intergroup conflict is sadly part of our existence. Such conflicts exist around the globe originating through differences, for example, in beliefs, religion, race, and culture. The degree of conflict between rival groups varies from mild hostility to all-out war, leading to the loss of thousands of lives every year. The field of intergroup conflict has attracted the attention of many social psychologists who have attempted to understand the phenomenon and to provide solutions to end it.

These scholars concentrated their research on the structure of such conflicts that they perceived as comprising three major aspects: cognitive, affective, and behavioral. The cognitive aspect is demonstrated by the stereotype held by one group toward the other; the affective aspect by the prejudice held regarding the other group, and the behavioral aspect by discrimination against this group.

The fundamental component found in intergroup conflict is the stereotype – the negative perception of the other group. Stereotypes may include negative perceptions of a variety of characteristics such as traits, physical characteristics, and expected behaviors. People generally believe that their group (the ingroup) is a heterogeneous group, whereas members of the other group (the outgroup) are all similar to one another. This perception, known as the homogeneity effect, is one of the bases for our tendency to stereotype the members of the outgroup and claim that they are *all*, for example, hostile, liars, and lazy (Linville, Fischer, & Salovey, 1989; Linville & Jones, 1980). This process is compounded by the perception of a total lack of similarity between our ingroup and the outgroup; thus, the outgroup members are perceived *as being totally* different from us (Pettigrew, 1997). This total "us versus them" serves to enhance the stereotypical perception.

People have a strong tendency to search for, and pay more attention to information that confirms their existing perceptions and, at the same time, ignore information that conflicts with these perceptions (Fiske & Neuberg, 1990; Snyder & Swann, 1978; Trope & Thompson, 1997). This confirmation bias reduces the likelihood of people changing their stereotypes. This difficulty is compounded because when the rival groups do interact, the phenomenon of the "self-fulfilling prophecy" is likely to play a part. In other words, when we have a negative stereotype against an outgroup member, we are likely to behave toward the outgroup in line with our preconceived perceptions of it, without regard to the way in which the group actually behaves. Our negative approach is likely to lead the outgroup members to respond in accordance with our expectations, thus giving us, the ingroup, evidence that our initial negative stereotypes were correct. These behaviors are likely to create a closed cycle of negative conduct out from which it is hard to break.

People tend to activate their stereotypes on others without being aware that they doing so (Devine, 1989; Gilbert & Hixon, 1991). Since those responsible for these attitudes and behaviors are unaware of them, it makes them particularly difficult to combat. Awareness of prejudices is a necessary prerequisite for the solution of intergroup conflict.

The contact hypothesis came to prominence in 1954, following the decision of the U.S. Supreme Court to end the segregation of black and white students in the education system. It was widely believed that once the two groups had contact with one another, there would be an end to ethnic prejudice and discrimination. An appendix attached to this Supreme Court ruling records the support given to it by thirty-two leading anthropologists, psychiatrists, psychologists, and sociologists (Cook, 1984).

Allport (1954) believed that the expectations of the Supreme Court judges and their supporters were unrealistic and that placing different ethnic groups together would not be sufficient to eliminate the negative stereotypes they held. He argued that what would be created would be a situation in which schoolchildren from different ethnic backgrounds had only casual contact with one another. Rather than alleviating tensions, this was likely to create anxiety and lead to the reinforcement of the negative stereotypes they already held. In other words, contact per se was unlikely to be an effective tool for overcoming prejudice. Allport's prediction has been borne out by a study carried out by Stephan (1986) in which he reported that the cessation of racial segregation in the American educational system had not led to the end of prejudice. Stephan analyzed studies that had examined this issue and found that only 13 percent of the studies reported an improvement in the way black people are perceived by whites, 34 percent of the studies found no change, and 53 percent found an increase in negative perception.

In what became the Contact Hypothesis, Allport (1954) suggested that in order for a contact to create a positive effect, a set of conditions must be met. The four most important criteria are the following:

1. *Equal status*: To counteract the stereotype, the higher status group must hold a contact with a member of the outgroup who is of equal status. If this is not the case, the contact is likely to lead to a confirmation of fixed stereotypes.

2. *Cooperation*: Cooperation between the rival groups toward a superordinate goal is likely to reduce the stereotypes.

3. *Intimate contact*: The contact has to create a context in which the participants can really learn to know the other side. If the contact is restricted to an artificial level, stereotypes are likely to remain unchanged.

4. *Institutional support and willingness to participate*: Having the support of the authorities is likely to create positive expectations from the contact and build positive social norms enhancing positive contact. The participants must be contributing to the contact of their own volition and not because they have been compelled to do so (Allport, 1954; Amir, 1969, 1976).

Many scholars have used the Contact Hypothesis and made adjustments to the preconditions in accordance with their empirical results (Brown, 2000). However, an extended list of required conditions is also likely to make the intergroup contact less practicable. In a recent article, Amichai-Hamburger and McKenna (2006) suggested that the traditional face-to-face (F2F) contact suffers from three main obstacles: (1) practicality, (2) anxiety, and (3) generalization.

## Practicality

If it is to be carried out according to Allport's (1954) conditions, the contact confronts logistical stipulations that in many cases are difficult to achieve. For example, organizing a meeting among members of opposing groups raises both financial and practical issues. Bringing together groups that are geographically distant from one another may prove very costly, and bringing together those that live in segregated areas may prove logistically challenging.

Another issue is that of equal status. Equal status between the group representatives may be actually hard to achieve, since within-group interactions people tend to be highly sensitive in discerning subtle cues that may be indicative of status (e.g., Hogg, 1993).

## Anxiety in Contact

Intergroup anxiety is the result of the anticipation of negative reactions during the intergroup encounter (Stephan & Cookie, 2001; Stephan & Stephan, 1996). Intergroup interactions are often more anxiety provoking than interpersonal ones, and such anxiety may not be conducive to harmonious social relations (Islam & Hewstone, 1993; Stephan & Stephan, 1985; Wilder, 1993). When an individual is anxious, he or she is more likely to use heuristics. Thus, if an intergroup contact produces significant levels of anxiety in the individual or individuals involved, he or she is more likely to apply stereotypes to the outgroup (Bodenhausen, 1990; Bodenhausen & Wyer, 1985). Wilder (1993) pointed out that when they are in a state of anxiety, group members are likely to ignore any disconfirming information supplied in the contact context. Under such conditions, when a member of the outgroup behaves in a positive manner that contradicts the expectations of the other side, members of the ingroup do not alter their opinions and only recall the outgroup as behaving in a manner consistent with their negative perception. In such a case, the contact between these members is unlikely to bring about any change in the group stereotype (Wilder & Shapiro, 1989).

## Generalization From Contact

One of the greatest challenges to the contact hypothesis is whether the results of a positive contact with a member of the outgroup will be generalized further. Group saliency during the interaction appears to be critically important to a successful generalization. There is much debate among researchers about the optimum level of salience. For example, Brewer and Miller (1984) suggested that for a contact to succeed, group saliency should be low. However, Hewstone and Brown (1986) suggested that, for a positive contact to have a wider group-level impact, individual participants need to be seen as representatives of their group so that the outgroup identity is highly salient. Hamburger (1994) suggested that what seems to be a lack of generalization is in many cases a result of overly rigid measures of stereotype change (see Garcia-Marques & Mackie, 1999; Hewstone & Hamberger, 2000; Paolini, Hewstone, Rubin, & Pay, 2004).

### Contact Over the Internet: The Contact Hypothesis Online

The Internet may be the key to overcoming many of the difficulties mentioned above.

*Equal status*: Many of the cues individuals typically rely on to gauge the internal and external status of others are not in evidence on line.

*Cooperation toward superordinate goals*: Virtual workgroups have proved an effective tool worldwide; in fact, Galegher and Kraut (1994) found that the final product produced by virtual workgroups was similar in overall quality to that produced by F2F group members. This is especially likely to be the case when technology used provides the capability for information-rich communication (Bell & Kozlowski, 2002).

*Institutional support and willingness to participate*: This might well be easier to achieve online because institutions may feel that participating in an Internet contact may be seen as taking less of a risk than a F2F contact (Bargh & McKenna, 2004). This, too, may make it easier for group members to volunteer to participate and for leaders to support such a meeting.

*Intimacy*: Cook (1962) suggested that as the contact process progresses and participants begin to form closer relationships, the groups were likely to display a more favorable attitude toward one another. He stressed the importance of the "acquaintance potential," or the opportunity provided by the situation for the contact participants to get to know one another. Recent research into the importance of personalized interaction (e.g., Miller, 2002) and intergroup friendships (e.g., Pettigrew, 1997, 1998) has reawakened interest in this aspect of the contact. It also has a particular relevance to this discussion on contact through the Internet. One of the major advantages of Internet interactions over face-to-face interactions is the general tendency for individuals to engage in greater self-disclosure and more intimate exchanges there. Interactions online tend to become "more than skin deep" and to do so quite quickly (e.g., McKenna, Green, & Gleason, 2002; Walther, 1996).

*Anxiety*: Many of the situational factors that can foster feelings of anxiety in social situations (e.g., having to respond on the spot, feeling under visual scrutiny) are absent in online interactions. Online participants have more control over how they present themselves and their views (e.g., being able to edit one's comments before presenting them). People may feel better able to express themselves and feel more at ease with their online partners than they would if they were interacting in person.

*Generalization from the contact*: One of the advantages of online communication is that one can quite easily manipulate the degree of individual versus group saliency in a given contact situation to achieve a desired outcome. Following Leah Thompson's procedure (see Thompson & Nadler, 2002), each member briefly introduces him or herself at the beginning of the interaction and adds a statement stressing his or her typicality as a member. As the online interaction progresses, group norms will quickly begin to emerge (Spears, Postmes, Lea, & Wolbert, 2002). These norms will be distinct from those that operate when the members of each group are alone together, and they will also be distinct from those of the other group; rather, these norms will emerge from the combined membership of the two groups in the online setting. The norms created will lead to heightened feelings of attachment and camaraderie among the participants. Thus, the necessary balance of a sense of both "us and them" will be evoked, allowing for acceptance and generalization.

The online environment may be said to heighten the perception of the individual members as representative of their disparate groups, while simultaneously fostering feelings of kinship and attachment to the "new group" composed of all members taking part in the exercise. There are a number of means by which the first can be achieved. For instance, all members may be given pseudonyms that are evocative of the group they represent.

## The Net Intergroup Contact Platform: a New Innovation

The Net Intergroup Contact (NIC) platform is a new website, at the time of writing, in its final stages of development. It is dedicated to improving the relationships between rival groups around the world. The basis for the

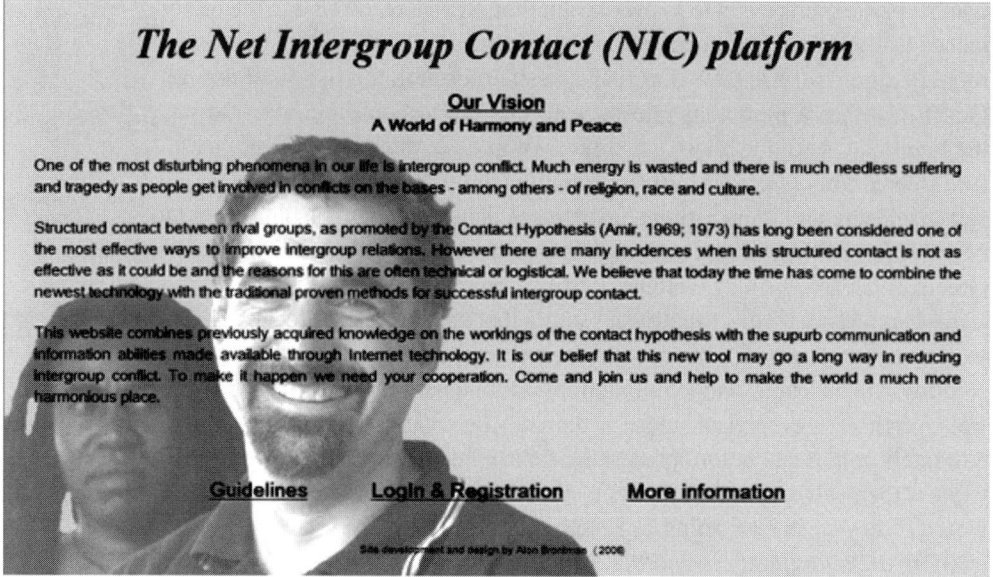

Figure 9.1. *Home page of the Net Intergroup Contact (NIC) platform.*

NIC platform is the Contact Hypothesis and the psychology of the Internet. The group behind the website includes social-organizational psychologists and webmasters. The front page of the platform (Figure 9.1) includes a call for people to join the vision of finding solutions to intergroup conflicts worldwide. The platform demonstrates a sequence of stages involved in forming an intergroup contact that surfers who wish to be involved in this project may employ.

The NIC platform focuses on intergroup contact through the Internet, which starts online and only moves to a F2F contact after certain conditions have been met. However, this platform could equally be used for other types of intergroup contact, for example, to support an ongoing F2F contact, or as a service for a F2F contact that in essence has finished its work but has a need to hold occasional follow-up meetings. This could be especially important since there is a danger that even the results of a successful contact may not be sustained because the positive contact dynamic has not been maintained. It is also the case that sometimes F2F contact sessions are held very infrequently because of the busy schedules of participants or their physical distance from one another. In such cases, the NIC platform, when used in-between F2F sessions, may prove a useful tool in maintaining the continuity of the contact.

*Breaking the dissimilarity perception*: The NIC platform aims to provide information about the other side. This knowledge leads participants away from a position of seeing the other side as homogeneous toward a heterogeneity perception of the outgroup. This new information should also lead to the discovery of cross-cutting categories (CCC) between the rival groups. These are important because, once the different groups learn what they share in common, goodwill is created, which makes it easier to deal with the more painful issues when they arise. This CCC perception is believed to encourage cooperation toward superordinate goals. Making people dependent on each other forces them to learn more about one another and enhances the salience of CCC (Cook, 1984).

## The Human Factor

*Leaders*: The home page of the website contains a request for group leaders. These leaders will be required to: (1) organize a group of participants from their ingroup; (2) organize a data bank on their group; and (3) facilitate the group during the contact.

Organizing the group will involve bringing together group representatives who are willing to participate in a net contact with the outgroup. The leader may recruit the participants from people in his or her own circle of acquaintances or he or she may use the website as a platform for recruitment (or a combination of the two). The leader is also responsible for building the data bank on the ingroup. The data bank will include information group members believe is important for the outgroup to know about them.

The leader's role is to facilitate his or her group during the contact. He or she should attempt to inspire the group with the vision of solving the intergroup conflict. In addition, he or she will explain the code of behavior expected from participants. The leader has to be aware of the needs and feelings of the group and to discuss with members their feelings and fears with regard to the contact and to support their difficulties. The leader must be respected by the group members so that the messages can be transferred effectively.

*Platform supervisor*: The contact will be supervised by a social psychologist who is an expert with the field of intergroup conflict in general and the contact hypothesis in particular. The supervisor will also be familiar with the group dynamic. Before the supervision of any contact, the leader will learn about the conflict, including (1) the histories of the different sides to the conflict; (2) the main issues of conflict; and (3) past attempts to improve intergroup relations, both successes and failures. In addition, the supervisor will be expected to learn the cultural norms and etiquette of both sides.

The supervisor will guide the leaders from both groups. She or he will not participate in the contact sessions themselves, but will closely observe the dynamic. Following each session, the supervisor will hold discussions over the Internet with the group leaders. Should the supervisor feel the need to intervene during a session, he or she may do so by sending a message that may be read only by the leader and will not be accessible in the public arena. The supervisor is the website representative for the group leaders and will review any complaints regarding the platform. The group leaders are responsible for the behavior of the participants. If a participant behaves in a way that contravenes the rules or the ethos of contact, by for example behaving aggressively toward the outgroup, the group leader should take appropriate action, either with a warning or by excluding the individual from the participating group.

Each group will comprise five to seven participants. Their participation is completely voluntary. They will either be familiar with the leader before the project or will have been recruited through the website. Those who are selected will be individuals who are willing to learn about the outgroup and are open-minded enough to listen to its members.

## Pre-Contact Process

To enhance the likelihood that the contact will be successful, a number of phases have to be carried out before the groups actually meet. This pre-contact stage might take from a few weeks to a number of months, but it is crucial to prepare for the contact properly.

The following steps should be followed:

1. *Initiating the contact*: Group leaders together with the NIC management will set up the contact project. A specific social psychologist is nominated as supervisor for the contact. It is likely that the NIC will have been approached by a leader of a group involved in a conflict. In such a case, the NIC management will attempt to find a group leader from the rival group who is willing to lead his or her group in the contact.

2. *Call for participants*: The leader takes responsibility for recruiting the group members. This includes advertising where necessary.

3. *Setting up the data bank*: Leaders are in charge of creating the interactive data bank.

4. *Behavioral code*: Group members sign an agreement explaining the behavior code expected from them. The agreement will also contain clauses pertaining to the degree of commitment expected from participants.

5. *Internet ingroup meeting*: Group members become familiar with other participants from their group.

6. *Questionnaire*: Group members fill out an online questionnaire dealing with their interests and hobbies.

7. *Learning about the outgroup*: Group members participate in an interactive introduction to the contact; this involves learning about the outgroup as a preparation for the contact.

8. *CCC*: Group members receive information on the outgroup members, including their interests and pastimes. Ingroup members will then find that they have hobbies and interests in common, and this will create CCC between the participants from both groups.

9. *Vision meeting*: Group members will hold a last session separately before contact. This session is supervised by the leader and the supervisor. The

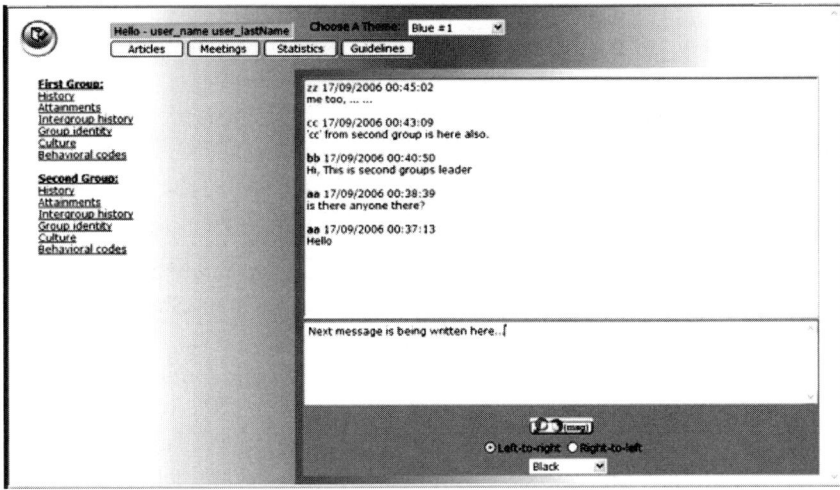

Figure 9.2. *Details from the data bank available for participants.*

supervisor will review the vision and values of the NIC and work to motivate the members before their first meeting.

At this stage, the groups are ready for the first contact.

## The Data Bank

The data bank on each group will contain information arranged
according to the following criteria: (1) information given by the group leaders;
(2) information designated by the the supervisor as crucial information on the
group; (3) feedback from users: participants from both groups will be asked frequently to evaluate the information given: what is redundant, what is missing,
and what should be extended.

The data bank will enable an interactive learning process to take place
before the actual contact so that people will become familiar with the outgroup (see Figure 9.2). It will also be available in real time during the contact. In this way, a participant who is unsure about whether a certain code
of behavior is suitable will be able to find out by using the interactive data
bank.

The data will be divided into several main sections:

1. The historical background of the group.
2. Successful milestones in the group's history.
3. Major principles on which the group is based.
4. Cultural characteristics.
5. Behavioral codes.
6. Major issues of conflict between the groups.

## The Contact Process

The contact process described here is recommended, but should be adapted to suit the individual contact because overly rigid guidelines might interfere with the dynamics of the specific contact process. The initial process we suggest is built on the following stages:

1.      The supervisor will meet with each group separately and learn their expectations and anxieties before the sessions start. She or he will be able to answer any questions participants may have.
2.      *Initial intergroup contact*: Five sessions to build familiarity between group members.
3.      *Intergroup cooperation*: cooperating on a superordinate goal project.
4.      *Areas of disagreement*: Five contact sessions will be held dealing with the major issues of the dispute.

*The initial five contact sessions* should set a positive tone for the whole process. At the start of the first session, the supervisor will be presented as the professional authority supervising the contact. Participants will then introduce themselves, giving their name, background, and their expectations for the contact. The supervisor will go on to explain the process in general and will attempt to create an understanding between the participants about the aims of the contact. Several group simulations will be used to encourage people to get to know one another. Participants will have received information on CCC with regard to themselves and the outgroup members. During the final two of the initial five introductory contact sessions, the participants together with their group leaders and the psychologist will choose the superordinate goal toward which the groups will cooperate. During these early stages, the issues over which there are disputes will be avoided, to be dealt with at a later stage.

*Cooperation toward the superordinate goal stage* aims to create interdependence between the participants. Before the contact, group leaders together with the supervisor will assess options for possible superordinate goals. Their assessment will take into account both their understanding of the psychological profile of the group members and the suitability of these projects in terms of practical considerations, including the time available for completion. The members of both groups will together choose one of the options. This will be the task that all members commit themselves to carry out. The task has to be broad and significant to create a deep involvement among members of both groups. The group leader will monitor the involvement and commitment of each participant. Many websites offer projects that fit the profile we seek to provide; see, for example, the online volunteering websites http://www.onlinevolunteering.org or http://www.volunteermatch.org.

These websites offer many possibilities for significant social projects that can serve as the context for cooperation between all group members toward the achievement of a superordinate goal.

After the completion of the project, the groups will move on to the third stage, dealing with the real issues in the conflict. By this stage, it is hoped that participants will feel comfortable with one another and will be more prepared to understand the other group's point of view on the issues in conflict, even if they do not necessarily accept them. The principles of conflict management will be invoked here to encourage participants to listen to the other side.

This is the most fragile stage of the process. It is here that the group leaders and the supervisor will have to consult one another frequently. The pace at which the two sides move toward a solution will depend on many factors, including the needs and abilities of the participants, their negotiating style, and the complexity of the dispute. The number of sessions taken or the stage reached at the end of each session is of far less importance than the sustaining of the momentum in a positive atmosphere.

*Obstacles to progress*: Two major obstacles that could potentially seriously impede or even destroy a contact are (1) misusing the platform for flaming against the outgroup and (2) lack of commitment to the process.

*Flaming*: Anonymity can serve as a double-edged sword. On one hand, it allows people to express themselves more openly and honestly than they would if they knew they could be identified. On the other hand, this anonymity may be exploited and lead participants to become abusive, for example, by sending aggressive messages (Joinson, 2003). This has been found to be more common in Internet groups as compared with F2F groups (Orengo Castellá, Zornoza Abad, Prieto Alonso, & Peiro Silla, 2000), which, in turn may lead to an escalation of the intergroup conflict (Branscomb, 1995; McKenna & Green, 2002). To prevent this from occurring, a number of preconditions must be met before a candidate is accepted to participate in a contact. All candidates have to sign a contract that states they accept the rules of the website and will not use abusive language under any circumstances. The contact is supervised and group leaders are instructed to cool tempers should the debate become too heated. In cases of a blatant hostility, leaders are instructed to forbid the offender from staying in the group; the offender will be asked to leave immediately. In such a case, there is no place for lenience since flaming is likely to escalate extremely quickly (Douglas & McGarty, 2001) and place the project at risk. In case of mild hostility, a warning will be given to the offender, together with a caution that any repetition of this type of behavior will lead to his or her expulsion from the contact.

*Lack of commitment*: The fact that participants may be surfing from their homes and may not have met their group leaders or the other members of their group F2F may lead to lack of commitment to the process. This could lead to participants being absent from virtual meetings or leaving the process before it is completed. Participants who are not fully obligated to the contact will create an atmosphere of lack of commitment and cause others not to see the contact as a serious enterprise. To counter this possible tendency, the commitment of candidates will be assessed carefully before they are permitted to take part in the contact. This increases the match between participants' needs and group goals, which enhances commitment. To discourage passivity among group members, group leaders will encourage their members to increase the communication within the group using all possible channels. This was found by Kim (2000) to increase the level of commitment of an individual to the community. In addition, throughout the encounter, the leader will emphasize the benefits to members (based on the match between their needs and the group goal). During the pre-contact meetings and during the contact, it is vital to encourage members to express themselves (Rheingold, 1993) and to give them positive feedback for their contribution and endeavors (Shore & Tetrick, 1991).

Despite these concerns, we believe that the mechanisms in place on the Internet that allow for supervision of discussions, together with a proper understanding of joint expectations and a careful selection of both group leaders and members, should prevent these obstacles from occurring. Moreover, efforts will be made throughout the contact to make the participants feel part of a project and so increase their commitment. For example, the system allows those in charge of the contact to be in touch with group members individually (and vice versa). Participants will also be asked for their feedback at several stages throughout the process. In this way, we hope to enhance their feeling of belonging and of being significant members. Should a group member fail to attend a session without prior notice, the leader will contact him or her and find out the reason. In this way, we hope to increase involvement and prevent unaddressed resentments from building up.

## Future Software Development

The NIC website as described here is a prototype. Below we describe some future possibilities that, we believe, would enhance this platform.

*Constant improvement of the NIC platform*: One of the great advantages of Internet contact is that every detail is automatically recorded and so data are automatically available for analysis. This analysis will highlight mistakes and also show organizers how to build on successes.

The feedback questionnaires that participants will be required to fill out at different stages in the contact will also give organizers an opportunity to learn from the responses and perceptions of the participants. The insights of group leaders and the supervisor, together with records of their discussions during the contact, will constitute another valuable source of information. In this way, the NIC platform may be constantly improved and brought up to the highest levels of performance. We hope to be able to learn more about important components of the contact; for example: (1) those problems that are likely to arise during the contact; (2) the dynamic that occurs before a group member leaves the contact; (3) the profiles of successful and unsuccessful contacts. This and other feedback mechanisms create a system dedicated to constant improvement.

*Bridging the language barrier*: One issue that arises when coordinating meetings among groups with different native tongues is that of communication. Usually participants will be selected who can communicate through a common language – often one that is not native to either group; or translators will be provided. However, happily, software is currently being developed that will allow individuals interacting through a text-based environment to receive messages in their own language, even though those messages were originally written in another tongue. There are already a number of text translation tools currently available for use on the Internet. None has yet reached the point of refinement and accuracy needed for a successful exchange of ideas with all nuances included, but the translation programs are improving at a rapid pace (e.g., Climent et al., 2003; Coughlin, 2001). This will mean that potentially excellent participants who, because of a language barrier, are currently unable to represent their people as part of an intergroup contact, will be able to do so. Moreover, when each party is able to "speak" in his or her native language, feelings of similarity and kinship are generally enhanced.

*Moving From NIC to F2F Contact:* When participants feel ready to move from the NIC platform to F2F contact, this will be carried out using a graded approach. This step-by-step approach ensures a greater chance of success than an immediate transfer from online discussions to face-to-face discussions (Amichai-Hamburger & Furnham, 2006; Amichai-Hamburger & McKenna, 2006). Using this model, organizers can use a gradual process to help both the individual participants and the group become comfortable with the contact situation at each level of intimacy before moving to the next level and eventually meeting in person. The main steps in this graded contact are as follows:

1. *Communicating by text only*: This text-only interaction is the most common form of communication over the Internet. This stage will continue until the participant feels secure in this form of contact and his or her anxiety levels are negligible.

2. *Text and image*: Participants will continue to use the text method with which they feel secure, but will simultaneously view a live video image of the person with whom they are interacting. When low-level social anxiety has been established, participants will transfer to the next stage.

3. *Communicating by video and audio*: At this stage, people will still interact from their secure environment and still without physical proximity to their conversation partner. However, use of text messages by the participant will be reduced; instead he or she will communicate orally. In addition, a live image of the participant will be transferred to the other participant. Again, when a satisfactory level of comfort has been achieved, participants may progress to the next stage.

4. *F2F interaction*: This is the stage of regular F2F interaction. It is the last stage in the process that is predicted to bridge the gap successfully between text-only Internet contact and total exposure through a F2F encounter and do so in a way that continually preserves low levels of anxiety among participants. This approach has received strong backing from the research of McKenna and her colleagues (Bargh, McKenna, & Fitzimmons, 2002; McKenna et al., 2002). They found that when interactions initially start over the Internet and then move to a F2F environment, participants not only like one another more than they would were they to have initially begun their interaction in person, but when the F2F meeting does take place, it serves to heighten already strong feelings of liking and kinship.

*Emotions and contact*: Prejudice against different groups may be based on different types of negative affect; that is, different types of emotion, for example, anger, fear, guilt, envy, or disgust (Glick, 2002; Mackie & Smith, 2002). These different types of affects yield different kinds of discrimination against the outgroup: Prejudice based on fear is likely to cause a defensive reaction in order to defend the ingroup status (Neuberg & Cottrell, 2002), whereas prejudice based on guilt resulting from distress caused in the presence of the outgroup is likely to lead to avoidance (Glick, 2002). Any attempt to reduce prejudice must tackle the relevant affect. If efforts are concentrated on an irrelevant affect, for example, the diminution of outgroup fears, when the relevant affect is guilt, it is unlikely to prove effective.

When the Internet is used as a platform for contact between rival groups, it is possible to create the contact around a context that tackles the specific affect that is the basis for prejudice. If, for example, the dominant affect is disgust, the supervisor together with the teams may analyze its sources and ensure that the data bank addresses them explicitly. In addition, the supervisor and the group leader can work with the group to ensure that they transfer information to the other side, which will counteract this process.

*Building a community*: Our aim is to use the NIC platform to increase the number of Internet intergroup contacts throughout the world. The participants to these contacts will gradually become a virtual community. We plan to use our past successes to encourage our current intergroup contacts and, in a similar way, our successful graduate participants may act as role models or even mentors to our current group members. The increasing number of groups participating through the NIC will lead to a corresponding growth in the database, so that this, too, will become an important source of information. The database will also serve as a major resource for research into intergroup conflict and may open significant opportunities for creating social change in different parts of the world.

## Last Word

One of the most disturbing and harmful phenomena worldwide is that of intergroup conflict. Much needless suffering of innocent people is caught up in these disputes, and many resources and much energy are invested by those trying to either prevent these conflicts or fan them. The Contact Hypothesis was developed as a way to try to solve some of these disputes by bringing the warring factions together in an optimal environment. Despite these efforts, many difficulties have remained. We believe that the Internet will prove to be a vital tool in the effort to alleviate intergroup conflict. The Internet environment not only creates opportunities to alter perceptions, but also overcomes many of the practical difficulties involved in holding intergroup contacts. This chapter describes an innovative approach to finding solutions to intergroup conflicts through the Net Intergroup Contact platform, a website that is, at the time of writing, just ready to launch itself into this thorn-filled arena. The site was created to allow effective interaction between different groups with differing views and beliefs. The site calls on participants to follow one basic rule, to show respect for the other side through choosing their words carefully and considering the sensitivities of others. The NIC is in its early stages, and there is no doubt that it will face significant challenges in the future and will need to adapt accordingly. Our aim is to employ the NIC platform in real conflicts around the world. We see it as having a potentially important role in helping to find solutions for, for example, the Protestant–Catholic conflict in Ireland and the Israeli-Palestinian conflict in the Middle East. Working together with experts in specific areas of conflict will help us to adapt the NIC platform, where necessary, to accommodate the needs of different groups. The fact that the system and the different encounters are fully documented will lead to efficiency and success in understanding the changes that need to be made to the platform and implementing them.

The Internet has created new possibilities for interaction between people and sophisticated ways to manage information. It is now our challenge to use these abilities to seek effective solutions to the intergroup conflicts around the world.

## References

Allport, G. W. (1954). *The nature of prejudice*. Cambridge, MA: Addison-Wesley.

Amichai-Hamburger, Y., & Furnham, A. (2006). The positive net. *Computers in Human Behavior, 23*, 1033–1045.

Amichai-Hamburger, Y., & McKenna, K. Y. A. (2006). The contact hypothesis reconsidered: Interacting via the Internet. *Journal of Computer-Mediated Communication, 11*, 825–843.

Amir, Y. (1969). Contact hypothesis in ethnic relations. *Psychological Bulletin, 71*, 319–342.

Amir, Y. (1976). The role of intergroup contact in change of prejudice and ethnic relations. In P. A. Katz (Ed.), *Towards the elimination of racism* (pp. 73–123). New York: Plenum Press.

Bargh, J. A., & McKenna, K. Y. A. (2004). The Internet and social life. *Annual Review of Psychology, 55*, 573–590.

Bargh, J. A., McKenna, K. Y. A., & Fitzimmons, G. M. (2002). Can you see the real me? Activation and expression of the "true self" on the Internet. *Journal of Social Issues, 58*, 33–48.

Bell, B., & Kozlowski, S. W. (2002). A typology of virtual teams, implications for effective leadership. *Group & Organization Management, 27*, 14–49.

Bodenhausen, G. V. (1990). Stereotypes as judgmental heuristics: Evidence of circadian variations in discrimination. *Psychological Science, 1*, 319–322.

Bodenhausen, G. V., & Wyer, R. S. (1985). Effects of stereotypes on decision-making and information-processing strategies. *Journal of Personality and Social Psychology, 48*, 267–282.

Branscomb, A. W. (1995). Anonymity, autonomy, and accountability: Challenges to the First Amendment in cyberspaces. 104 *Yale L.J.* 1639–1679.

Brewer, M. B., & Miller, N. (1984). Beyond the contact hypothesis: Theoretical perspectives on desegregation. In M. Hewstone & R. J. Brown (Eds.), *Contact and conflict in intergroup encounters* (pp. 281–302). Oxford: Blackwell.

Brown, R. J. (2000). *Group processes: Dynamics within and between groups* (2nd ed.). Oxford: Blackwell.

Climent, S., Moré, J., Oliver, A., Salvatierra, M., Taulé, M., Sanchez, I., & Vallmanya, L. (2003). Bilingual newsgroups in Catalonia: A challenge for machine translation. *Journal of Computer-Mediated Communication, 9*(1). Retrieved April 28, 2006, from http://jcmc.indiana.edu/vol9/issue1/climent.html.

Cook, S. W. (1962). The systematic analysis of socially significant events: A strategy for social research. *Journal of Social Issues, 18*, 66–84.

Cook, S. W. (1984). Cooperative interaction in multiethnic contexts. In M. Brewer (Ed.), *Groups in contact: The psychology of desegregation* (pp. 155–185). Orlando, FL: Academic Press.

Coughlin, D. (2001). Correlating automated and human assessments of machine translation quality. In *Proceedings of MT Summit IX* (pp. 63–70) New Orleans, LA.

Devine, P. G. (1989). Stereotypes and prejudice: Their automatic and controlled components. *Journal of Personality and Social Psychology, 56*, 5–18.

Douglas, K. M., & McGarty, C. (2001). Identifiability and self-presentation: Computer-mediated communication and intergroup interaction. *British Journal of Social Psychology, 40*, 399–416.

Fiske, S. T., & Neuberg, S. L. (1990). A continuum of impression formation, from category-based to individuating processes: Influences of information and motivation on attention and interpretation. In M. P. Zanna (Ed.), *Advances in experimental social psychology* (Vol. 23, pp. 1–74). San Diego, CA: Academic Press.

Galegher, J., & Kraut, R. E. (1994). Computer-mediated communication for intellectual teamwork: An experiment in group writing. *Information Systems Research, 5,* 110–138.

Garcia-Marques, L., & Mackie, D. M. (1999). The impact of stereotype incongruent information on perceived group variability and stereotype change. *Journal of Personality and Social Psychology, 77,* 979–990.

Gilbert, D. T., & Hixon, J. G. (1991). The trouble of thinking: Activation and application of stereotypic beliefs. *Journal of Personality and Social Psychology, 60,* 509–517.

Glick, P. (2002). Sacrificial lambs dressed in wolves' clothing: Envious prejudice, ideology, and the scapegoating of Jews. In L. S. Newman & R. Erber (Eds.), *Understanding genocide: The social psychology of the Holocaust* (pp. 113–142). London: Oxford University Press.

Hamburger, Y. (1994). The contact hypothesis reconsidered: Effects of the atypical outgroup member on the outgroup stereotype. *Basic Applied Social Psychology, 15,* 339–358.

Hewstone, M., & Brown, R. J. (1986). Contact is not enough: An intergroup perspective on the Contact Hypothesis. In M. Hewstone & R. J. Brown (Eds.), *Contact and conflict in intergroup encounters* (pp. 1–44). Oxford: Blackwell.

Hewstone, M., & Hamberger, J. (2000). Perceived variability and stereotype change. *Journal of Experimental Social Psychology, 36,* 103–124.

Hogg, M. A. (1993). Group cohesiveness: A critical review and some new directions. *European Review of Social Psychology, 4,* 85–111.

Islam, M. R., & Hewstone, M. (1993). Dimensions of contact as predictors of intergroup anxiety, perceived out-group variability, and out-group attitude: An integrative model. *Personality and Social Psychology Bulletin, 19,* 700–710.

Joinson, A. N. (2003). *Understanding the psychology of Internet behaviour: Virtual worlds, real lives.* New York: Palgrave Macmillan.

Kim, J. A. (2000). *Community building on the Web: Secret strategies for successful online communities.* Berkeley, CA: Peachpit Press.

Linville, P. W., Fischer, G. W., & Salovey, P. (1989). Perceived distributions of the characteristics of ingroup and outgroup members. *Journal of Personality and Social Psychology,* 57, 165–188.

Linville, P. W., & Jones, E. E. (1980). Polarized appraisals of out-group member. *Journal of Personality and Social Psychology, 38,* 689–703.

Mackie, D. M., & Smith, E. R. (Eds.). (2002). *From prejudice to intergroup emotions: Differentiated reactions to social groups.* Philadelphia: Psychology Press.

McKenna, K. Y. A., & Green, A. S. (2002). Virtual group dynamics. *Group Dynamics: Theory, Research and Practice, 6,* 116–127.

McKenna, K. Y. A., Green, A. S., & Gleason, M. (2002). Relationship formation on the Internet: What's the big attraction? *Journal of Social Issues, 58,* 9–31.

Miller, N. (2002). Personalization and the promise of contact theory. *Journal of Social Issues, 58,* 387–410.

Neuberg, S. L., & Cottrell, C. A. (2002). Intergroup emotions: A biocultural approach. In D. M. Mackie & E. R. Smith (Eds.), *From prejudice to intergroup relations: Differentiated reactions to social groups* (pp. 265–283). New York: Psychology Press.

Orengo Castellá, V., Zornoza Abad, A. M., Prieto Alonso, F., & Peiro Silla, J. M. (2000). The influence of familiarity among group members, group atmosphere and assertiveness on uninhibited behavior through three different communication media. *Computers in Human Behavior, 16*, 141–159.

Paolini, S., Hewstone, M., Rubin, M., & Pay, H. (2004). Increased group dispersion after exposure to one deviant group member: Testing Hamburger's model of member-to-group generalization. *Journal of Experimental Social Psychology, 40*, 569–585.

Pettigrew, T. F. (1997). The affective component of prejudice: Empirical support for the new view. In S. A. Tuch & J. K. Martin (Eds.), *Racial attitudes in the 1990s: Continuity and change* (pp. 76–90). Westport, CT: Praeger.

Pettigrew, T. F. (1998). Intergroup contact theory. *Annual Review of Psychology, 49*, 65–85.

Rheingold, H. (1993). *The virtual community*. Reading, MA: Addison Wesley.

Shore, L. M. & Tetrick, L. E. (1991). A construct validity study of the survey of perceived organizational support. *Journal of Applied Psychology, 76*, 637–643.

Snyder, M., & Swann, W. B. (1978). Hypothesis testing processes in social interaction. *Journal of Personality and Social Psychology, 36*, 1202–1212.

Spears, R., Postmes, T., Lea, M., & Wolbert, A. (2002). When are net effects gross products? The power of influence and the influence of power in computer-mediated communication. *Journal of Social Issues, 58*, 91–107.

Stephan, W. G. (1986). The effects of school desegregation: An evaluation 30 years after Brown. In M. J. Saks & L. Saxe (Eds.), *Advances in Applied Social Psychology* (Vol. 3, pp. 181–206). New York: Erlbaum.

Stephan, W. G., & Cookie, W. (2001). *Improving intergroup relations*. Newbury, CA: Sage.

Stephan, W. G., & Stephan, C. W. (1985). Intergroup anxiety. *Journal of Social Issues, 41*, 157–175.

Stephan, W. G., & Stephan, C. W. (1996). Cognition and affect in stereotyping: Parallel interactive networks. In D. W. Mackie & D. L. Hamilton (Eds.), *Affect cognition and stereotyping: Interactive processes in group perception* (pp. 111–136). Orlando, FL: Academic Press.

Thompson, L., & Nadler, J. (2002). Negotiating via information technology: Theory and application. *Journal of Social Issues, 58*, 109–124.

Trope, Y., & Thompson, E. (1997). Looking for the truth in all the wrong places? Asymmetric search of individuating information about stereotyped group members. *Journal of Personality and Social Psychology, 73*, 229–241.

Walther, J. B. (1996). Computer-mediated communication: Impersonal, interpersonal, and hyperpersonal interaction. *Communication Research, 23*, 13–43.

Wilder, D. A. (1993). The role of anxiety in facilitating stereotypic judgments of out-group behavior. In D. M. Mackie & D. L. Hamilton (Eds.), *Affect, cognition, and stereotyping: Interactive processes in group perception* (pp. 87–109). San Diego, CA: Academic Press.

Wilder, D. A., & Shapiro, P. (1989). Role of competition-induced anxiety in limiting the beneficial impact of positive behavior by an out-group member. *Journal of Personality and Social Psychology, 56*, 60–69.

# 10 Influences on the Nature and Functioning of Online Groups

*Katelyn Y. A. McKenna (Yael Kaynan)*

Groups within the electronic realm share many characteristics in common with groups that meet and function in shared physical spaces. Groups in both domains can be quite diverse in terms of the composition and personality characteristics of members, the purpose and goals of the group, and the contextual setting in which the group functions. A variety of factors likely affect and influence the structure and functioning of any given group. Many, if not most, of these factors can potentially influence the group, regardless of the domain (electronic or face-to-face) and produce similar outcomes. There are qualities of electronic communication settings and qualities of physical settings that can uniquely influence the dynamics of a group in those respective settings (see McKenna & Green, 2002; McKenna & Seidman, 2005 for reviews).

This chapter delves into the workings of online groups and examines potentially influential factors for group functioning. The chapter is divided into three sections, which examine (1) the role of the motivations and personality characteristics of individual members within the group, (2) the way in which different categories or kinds of online groups distinctly function (including support groups), and (3) aspects of the internal dynamics of online groups, such as cohesiveness, status and stereotypes, and performance.

## Individuals and Groups

### Individual motivations of members

Classical motivation theory indicates that all behavior is motivated in some way and that an individual will engage in particular behaviors to further a desired end (e.g., Atkinson & Birch, 1970; Lewin, 1951). Motivations are not fleeting but rather are enduring and pan-situational. The motivations that lie behind an individual's behavior find expression through situationally appropriate goals. The goals and motivations of group members, along with the behaviors prompted by those goals, can, of course, have a strong effect on nearly all aspects of the group. It is not always a simple task to tease apart the links between motivation, behavior, and outcome, however. Highlighted next are two arenas in which difficulty can arise when attempting to understand the workings of a group.

*Different goals, same behavior, different outcomes.* Different motives and goals held by different individuals may underlie the same surface behavior. For instance, someone may join and participate in an illness support group with the goal of gathering more information about the illness. Another individual might participate in the same group to gain social support. Still another may take part to demonstrate support for family member or a friend who suffers from the illness and who may or may not be part of the group. Participation in the group may lead to quite different social and psychological consequences for these individuals, even though they are engaging in the same kinds of activities online (see McKenna & Bargh, 1999; McKenna, Green, & Smith, 2001).

*Different motivational processes, same consequences.* To further muddy the waters, similar outcomes may result from different underlying motivational processes. For instance, we know that when anonymous group interaction is coupled with high group salience, the result tends to be increased adherence to the group norms (Spears, Postmes, Lea, & Wolbert, 2002). On the flip side, greater conformity to group norms can also be the result of identifiability if certain self-presentational motivations (e.g., to make a positive impression) are in operation (e.g., Barreto & Ellemers, 2000; Douglas & McGarty, 2001).

How an individual uses the available resources and interacts with others online will depend to a large extent on that person's motivations and goals. It is not only the individual for whom a particular motivation is operating that is affected, however, but the group as an entity itself. The goals of individual group members can interact not only with the Internet communication situation to produce social and psychological effects for that individual but also inevitably affect the processes and functioning of the group as a whole.

## Personality Differences Among Members

Personality characteristics of members can strongly influence the functioning of the online group just as they can influence the functioning of an offline group. There are two personality characteristics in particular that have been found to play out differently in online group interactions than they do in traditional face-to-face interactions. Should a group be composed of a member (or members) possessing these personality traits, then the internal group dynamics are likely to be quite different if the interaction takes place online than if the group meets in person. Not only are the dynamics likely to be different but also the structure and performance of the group in question are likely to be influenced. These characteristics and their influence on the group are discussed next.

*The socially anxious member*: In traditional face-to-face group interactions, individuals who experience social anxiety generally take a less active role than do their outgoing counterparts (Leary, 1983). They tend to respond more slowly and less consistently in group interactions (Cervin, 1956) than do nonanxious members. Kogan and Wallach (1967) among others have found that shy group members are more likely to exhibit indecisiveness and to engage more readily in opinion shifts. Further, in a task-oriented group, the socially anxious members tend to be better satisfied with the group performance even when that performance is substandard (Zander & Wulf, 1966). Finally, socially anxious members tend to be liked less well than nonanxious members in the group.

In online groups, however, the behavior and the standing of socially anxious members are quite different (McKenna & Seidman, 2005). Because many of the situational factors that can trigger and exacerbate feelings of social anxiety (e.g., having to respond on the spot, talking to someone face-to-face) are absent in online interactions, introverted individuals are able to engage in the group interaction on equal footing. As the study discussed below demonstrates, the online environment allows them to interact more comfortably and with less reticence than they would in a face-to-face situation.

McKenna and colleagues conducted a laboratory study examining the effects of communication modality and social anxiety on small-group interaction (McKenna, Seidman, Buffardi, & Green, 2007). Consistent with their responses on the Interaction Anxiousness Scale, socially anxious individuals in the face-to-face condition reported feeling anxiety, shyness, and discomfort during the group interaction, while the opposite was true for nonanxious participants. In marked contrast, interacting online produced significantly different results. Participants reported feeling significantly less anxious, shy, and uncomfortable, and more accepted by their fellow group members than did those who interacted face-to-face, but these effects were qualified by differences in levels of social anxiety. That is, the extroverted participants felt equally comfortable, outgoing, and accepted interacting online and in person. For those experiencing high levels of social anxiety, however, the mode of communication proved pivotal to their feelings of comfort, shyness, and acceptance. Moreover, the reports of the socially anxious participants in the online condition on these measures were virtually identical to those of nonanxious participants in the face-to-face condition.

Those experiencing anxiety in social situations have also been found to take more active leadership roles in online groups. McKenna and colleagues conducted a second study in which participants were again preselected based on their interaction anxiety scores. The subjects were randomly assigned to interact in groups of four, each group comprising an equal number of anxious and nonanxious members, either online or face-to-face. They then engaged in a decision-making task, following which they rated each of their interaction peers on measures of leadership, degree of participation in the discussion as compared with the other members, extroversion, and how much they liked the person based on their interaction. Peer ratings showed that socially anxious participants were as likely as their nonanxious counterparts to be perceived as leaders within the respective groups and to participate as actively when the interaction took place online. In the face-to-face condition, nonanxious participants more often received the leadership votes and were the more active participants.

*The aggressive member*: Another personality characteristic that may have a stronger influence within online groups is aggressiveness. Many of the social constraints that generally serve to moderate an aggressive or dominating personality within face-to-face groups are absent within online group interaction (Sproull & Kiesler, 1985). The de-individuating conditions under which many online interactions take place can decrease a member's sense of personal accountability (Spears et al., 2002) and thus increase his or her willingness to engage in obnoxious or antisocial behavior within the group. Friction between members can be exacerbated within the online environment as a result. Much has been made of the "flame wars" that can erupt within, and sometimes splinter apart, large online groups. Groups with open membership online often find that they have attracted the attention of a "troll" – someone who joins the group with the goal of undermining and embroiling the larger group in conflict. Depending on the norms and structure of the group, such aggressive members may or may not meet with success (McKenna & Seidman, 2005).

Aggressiveness need not take an antisocial and obnoxious form, however. Just as in face-to-face interactions, members who, acting within social bounds, are more persistent in pushing their agendas while simultaneously taking an active and strong role in the group will exert a strong influence on the group. In an environment stripped of cues beyond the text, it is quite possible that the "mere exposure" effect (Zajonc, 1965) would result in the persistent member exercising greater influence over the group than would occur in other settings.

## Different Groups, Different Dynamics

Not all electronic groups are the same. Groups with certain characteristics and purpose will produce different effects on members than those effects that will result from groups having quite different characteristics and purpose. In other words, the various features of communication will interact with the character and purpose of the group; the interpersonal effects of electronic interaction will vary as a function of the social context. Five distinct kinds of groups are discussed, with attention focused on the particular characteristics of the group that are likely to lead to divergent outcomes.

### Organizational Groups

Organizational groups, whether functioning in an online or face-to-face environment, differ in many ways from groups that have a largely social purpose. Within social settings online, features of electronic communications (such as anonymity, the lack of physical presence, and the ability to exercise greater control over one's side of the exchange) can lead to greater self-disclosure and feelings of closeness (see Joinson & Paine, 2007). Within an organizational setting, however, these same features can lead to the opposite result: research has shown them to produce greater distrust between parties when it comes to issues such as negotiations.

Thompson and colleagues (see Thompson & Nadler, 2002, for a review) have led the field in the study of electronic negotiations. They identified a major problem that arises in "e-gotiation": Negotiating partners often make implicit assumptions about time delays that occur in receiving responses from their opponents. Negotiation partners attribute quite different motivations to such delays than do partners who are interacting in a purely social framework. For instance, in a negotiation situation, people tend to assume that the other party will receive and read an e-mail as soon as they have sent it. They therefore expect an immediate response. If delays in receiving the response occur, they assume the delay is due to stalling, power plays, or disrespect by the other party (rather than assuming that the person has not yet read their message or is unable to respond instantaneously for any number of wholly non-Machiavellian reasons). As a result, exchanges between negotiating partners can become acrimonious, and they are less likely to reach a satisfactory agreement.

## The Garden-Variety Social Group

The least researched kind of group, both online and off, is perhaps also the most common kind of group. The majority of group-related research has focused on business or organizational groups, political, civic, or community-at-large groups, highly specialized groups, or support groups (discussed below). Garden-variety groups such as the coffee klatch and the chess club have rarely been the sole focus of research.

One line of research that does specifically focus on such mainstream groups examines them in terms of a distinction between common bond and common identity groups. In common bond groups (such as among a group of friends), attachment to the group is based on the bonds that exist between the group members; in common identity groups (such as a sports team), attachment to the group is based on identification with the group as a whole (i.e., its purpose and goals) rather than on bonds between individual members (see Prentice, Miller, & Lightdale, 1994). Prentice and her colleagues examined traditional groups that fell into these two categories, and Sassenberg (2002) has examined equivalent groups on the Internet. In both communication venues, the research indicates that in common identity groups, as compared with common bond groups, there is greater adherence to group norms. Common identity groups and the norms that develop within them thus have been found to have a greater effect on individual members' behavior. Thus, the kind of group to which one belongs (whether online or offline) matters. As is discussed next, even further distinctions can be made when the common identity is a stigmatized one.

## Stigmatized Groups

For those with socially stigmatized aspects of identity, participation in an electronic group devoted to that identity aspect can prove to be particularly beneficial for the individual. Identifying others who share an embarrassing or socially sanctioned aspect of identity in one's everyday life can be quite difficult and the social risks that accompany such attempts can be large. Within the online environment, however, the situation is different. By interacting under a protective mantle of anonymity, people can seek out others who share these aspects of self online with far fewer costs and risks to their everyday social life. Because there is often no equivalent "offline" group, membership and participation in a relevant virtual group can become an important part of one's social life and can have powerful effects on one's sense of self and identity.

Extending the findings of Prentice et al. (1994) and Sassenberg (2002), McKenna and Bargh (1998, study 1) found that people with stigmatized and concealable social identities (see Frable, 1993; Jones et al., 1984), such as homosexuality or fringe ideological beliefs, are more responsive to the feedback they received from other group members than are individuals taking part in nonmarginalized groups. In other words, the norms of such groups exert a stronger than usual influence over members' behavior. These members are motivated to behave in such a way as to gain acceptance and positive evaluation from their fellow group members. Thus, compared to the mainstream Internet groups, within the stigmatized identity groups, participation significantly increased when there was positive feedback from the other group members and decreased following negative feedback.

According to Deaux's (1996) model of social identity, active participation in a stigmatized-identity group should lead to the incorporation of the virtual group membership into the self. Individuals then tend to be motivated to make this important and new aspect of self into a social reality (e.g., Gollwitzer, 1986) by sharing it with important others. In line with this, McKenna and Bargh (1998, studies 2 and 3) found that many participants taking part in such online groups had, as a result of their Internet group participation, come out to their family and friends about this stigmatized aspect of themselves for the first time in their lives. Through their participation, they benefited from increased self-acceptance and felt less socially isolated and different. Clearly, membership and participation in Internet groups can have powerful effects on one's self and identity.

## Support Groups

The role of active participation as an important mediator becomes clear when examining whether positive benefits will accrue for an individual who participates in an online support group. Barak and Dolev-Cohen (2006) conducted a longitudinal study with emotionally distressed adolescents who were taking part in Sahar, a free online support network for those experiencing emotional distress in Israel. While the researchers found that, on average, the emotional distress of the participants did not lessen because of membership in the group, the degree of active participation in the group did significantly affect emotional distress. Those who engaged in more active participation in the first month of the study experienced significantly less emotional distress by the third month of the study as compared with those who participated less. The emotional distress of those who did not participate as actively remained at the same (high) level recorded at the beginning of the study. In line with these findings, greater participation in community support websites for the elderly, such as SeniorNet, is associated with lower perceived life stress (Wright, 2000).

For those who lack adequate support from members of their established social networks, online support groups may prove to be an important additional emotional resource to be used. For instance, a study of diabetics (Barrera, Glasgow, McKay, Boles, & Feil, 2002) found that those assigned to participate in online diabetes support groups felt that they had received more support, in general, than did those asked to use the Internet only to gather information about their illness (and to thus rely only on their offline social network for support). Participation in an online support group for the hearing impaired was also found to be particularly beneficial for participants with little "real-world" support (Cummings, Sproull, & Kiesler, 2002). Online support groups may be particularly crucial for those who feel actively barred from turning to family, friends, and physically based support groups. Davison, Pennebaker, and Dickerson (2000) found that people are particularly likely to turn to Internet support groups if they are suffering from an embarrassing, stigmatized illness, such as AIDS, alcoholism, or prostate cancer, because of the relative anonymity of the online community. These patients feel anxiety and uncertainty and are thus highly motivated by social comparison needs to seek out others with the same illness.

Yet again, however, differences between kinds of support groups can lead to quite different outcomes and to different group dynamics. For instance, Blank and Adams-Blodnieks (2007) found strong differences in the communicators in breast cancer support groups compared with those taking part in prostate cancer support groups online. Groups related to the female-oriented disease were composed largely of survivors themselves (87%), with spouses of the survivors making up only 3 percent of the group membership. In contrast, both spouses (29%) and family and friends of survivors (17%) were active members in the groups related to the male-oriented malady, with the survivors themselves making up just slightly more than half (54%) of the group. These differences in membership composition translated into differences in the kinds of support sought (emotional versus treatment-related) as well as the topics addressed in the two kinds of groups.

Galegher, Sproull, and Kiesler (1998) have found that, within online support groups, the process by which members establish legitimacy (and acceptance) unfolds somewhat differently than occurs in the garden-variety common bond group. Members in support groups tend to signal their legitimacy as bona-fide members of the group in their postings more so than do those who interact in groups devoted to hobbies, such as cooking groups. They do so by indicating within their post how long they have been participating in the group (either by posting or by reading) or by making references to the groups shared history.

Moreover, providing such legitimacy claims seems to be an important component to actually attaining legitimacy and inclusion within online support groups. When Galegher et al. (1998) examined posts that received feedback versus those that received none, they found that members were significantly more likely to respond to the poster if an "I'm a legitimate member" claim was made than if it was not. Indeed, of the posts that received no response from other members of the support group, almost all of them lacked a clear membership claim. In other words, those posts that did not explicitly acknowledge the common bond of the group were ignored by the other members. It is thus perhaps not surprising that 80 percent of the posts that asked for information or advice included a claim to group membership even if such queries were asked by frequent participants (and thus readily identifiable members) in the group. Clearly, the explicit establishment –and continual reestablishment – of legitimacy has become a norm particular to online support groups and, as is discussed in greater detail in the next section, an important component of group cohesion and influence within these groups.

## Internal Dynamics of Groups

### Cohesion and Influence

Many factors affect the cohesiveness of a group, the degree to which members of a group will exert influence on one another, and the extent to which they will be affected by the norms of the group. Certainly, in online groups, the anonymity versus identifiability of group members is particularly important in promoting or hindering cohesion and influence.

Spears et al. (2002) have argued that anonymous communication within groups leads to a sense of depersonalization by the group members. That is, when members feel an absence of personal accountability and personal identity then the group-level identity becomes more important. When the group-level identity is thus heightened, Spears et al. (2002) have shown that group norms can have an even stronger effect than occurs in face-to-face interactions. The degree to which the group identity is salient, however, plays an important role in determining what the effects of anonymity will be on the development and influence of group norms.

For instance, Spears, Lea, and Lee (1990) found that when members of online groups interacted under anonymous conditions and group salience was high, normative behavior increased in those groups as compared with electronic groups in which members were anonymous but the salience of the group was low. An intermediate level of conformity to group norms was evinced whether group salience was high or low for those participants who interacted under individuating conditions.

The interaction between anonymity and identity salience is most clearly delineated in a set of studies examining the effects of primed behavior in electronic groups. Postmes, Spears, Sakhel, and De Groot (2001) primed participants with either task-oriented or socioemotional behavior before taking part in electronic groups under either anonymous or identifying conditions. Members in the anonymous groups displayed behavior consistent with the respective prime they received, considerably more so than did their counterparts who interacted under identifiable conditions within their groups. Normative behavior strengthened over time in the anonymous groups, with the members conforming even more strongly to the primed behavior. In contrast, when members were identifiable to other group members, their behavior ran counter to the norms and became even more prime-inconsistent over time.

## Status and Power

According to McClendon (1974), equal status increases the likelihood for perceived similarities both within and between groups and so enhances the likelihood for improvement in their relationship. This is particularly the case when it comes to groups containing minority members, and in the reduction of stereotypes when there is ingroup and outgroup interaction (Pettigrew, 1971). In face-to-face encounters, even very subtle differences in manner of dress, body language, use of personal space, and the seating positions taken in the room can belie real (or perceived) status differences. As Hogg (1992) has shown, within group interactions people tend to be highly sensitive in discerning subtle cues that may be indicative of status.

Online interactions have somewhat of advantage here because many, although not all, of the cues that individuals typically rely on to gauge the internal and external status of others are not typically in evidence. Yet status differences can and do manifest themselves in online groups as well. As Sassenberg, Boos, and Klapproth (2001) have shown, those perceived as experts in terms of task-related knowledge are generally regarded as more useful resources for information as well as given more room in interactive discussions to express their points of view. When such differences do become evident and they are *specifically* relevant within the context of the discussion or the task, they can have an even more pronounced influence than occurs in a comparable face-to-face interaction (see Postmes et al., 2002).

In other situations, even when status differences are known, electronic interaction tends to ameliorate some of the effects of status differentials. For instance, when bringing together members of two established groups, the members are likely to be well aware of the internal pecking order within their own group even if they do not have knowledge of the established hierarchy among the other group's members. In face-to-face interactions, such distinctions within the groups often quickly become apparent to all, as those who stand lower tend to speak up less often and, in ways both obvious and subtle, give deference to those with higher status within their group.

Such is not the case in electronic interactions. One aspect of electronic communications that has long been decried (e.g., Sproull & Kiesler, 1985) is the tendency, within organizational settings, for there to be a reduction in the usual inhibitions that typically operate when interacting with one's superiors. In other words, existing internal status does not carry as much weight and does not affect the behavior of the group members to such an extent. Underlings are more likely to speak up, to speak "out of turn," and to speak their mind. Thus, electronic interaction makes power less of an issue during discussion that leads group members, regardless of status, to contribute more to the discussion (Spears et al., 2002).

There are distinct advantages to having participants engage in a "group contact" from the privacy of their respective homes. Participants are likely to feel more comfortable and less anxious in their familiar surroundings. Further, research has shown that public, as opposed to private, settings can exacerbate the activation and use of stereotypes, especially when it comes to those tied to racial prejudice (e.g., Lambert et al., 2003). As Zajonc (1965) has shown, an individual's habitual or dominant response is more likely to emerge in public settings, whereas the individual is likely to be more open and receptive to altering the habitual response when in a private sphere. Research has shown that even when participants interact in quite "public" electronic venues – but do so from the privacy of their homes – they tend to feel that it is a private affair (e.g., McKenna & Bargh, 2000; McKenna, Green, & Gleason, 2002). Thus, interacting electronically from home should serve to inhibit the activation of stereotypes as compared with a more public and face-to-face setting in a new environment.

## The Emergence of Group Leaders

In online groups and in face-to-face groups, as group membership becomes increasingly salient, members tend to become highly sensitive to prototypical characteristics of the group, that is, to the characteristics that distinguish that group from other groups. They also become sensitive to how they and other members compare with that prototype. As the social identity theory of leadership (e.g., Hogg & Reid, 2001) suggests, when there is a high degree of overlap between an individual's characteristics (e.g., goals, values, and attitude) and the group prototype, that individual is likely to emerge as a group leader.

Research by Hogg (1992) and others has shown that people have a heightened awareness for even subtle differences in prototypicality among their fellow group members. They are able to delineate which members most closely conform to the prototype (the leaders) and which fit the mold to a lesser degree (the followers). Group leaders are thus those individuals who seem to best embody the behaviors and norms to which the other group members are attempting to adhere.

We tend to think of leaders as not only embodying the group prototype but also as individuals who actively influence the behaviors of the other group members. In the case of established groups, that is certainly the case. Such is not the case when it comes to newly formed groups, however. In new groups, individuals who best fit the prototype do emerge as leaders but not because they are actually exerting any influence over the group. Rather, they are perceived (by the other group members) to be exerting an influence over the less prototypical members. In reality, however, it is not the individual who is exercising the influence but the prototype that the leader happens to most closely fit (e.g., Hogg & Reid, 2001).

We would expect that the social identity theory of leadership would apply even more strongly in electronic groups than in face-to-face groups for a number of reasons. Factors that have been shown to be influential in determining who will be seen as best fitting the group prototype, such as physical appearance and interpersonal dominance, are not generally in operation in online interactions. In face-to-face groups, the individual who most closely fits the goals, values, and ideals of the group might nonetheless be dismissed as a potential leader by other members because biasing factors such as the prospective leader's age, physical attractiveness, and race may play a role in their assessment. Age and race are often counter-prototypical features and people are often not aware that such factors are negatively affecting their judgments about someone (see Bargh, 1989; Brewer, 1988). Because such factors are not generally in evidence in online groups, they would not play an influential role and thus would not hinder the most prototypical individual's rise to leadership. As discussed earlier, this has been shown to be the case for individuals who, in face-to-face group interactions, are reticent, shy, and relegated to follower roles but in online interactions prove to be outgoing, active members who can attain leadership roles (McKenna et al., 2007).

## Group Performance

Today many organizations have working teams whose members are dispersed all around the world and who frequently communicate, cooperate, and complete tasks through the Internet. Successful outcomes routinely occur even though, in many cases, the team members have never met one another and are unlikely to do so. This phenomenon is known as a *virtual team*. The development and utilization of virtual teams is becoming increasingly common within organizations, particularly as the benefits of including virtual teams have become more evident (Cascio, 2000). For instance, employers find that telecommuting increases worker productivity and improves attendance (Abreu, 2000).

The evidence accumulated thus far seems to indicate that tasks performed by virtual teams are done equally well as those conducted by face-to-face work teams. Dennis (1996) along with his colleague Kinney (Dennis & Kinney, 1998) have conducted a number of studies examining the functioning of face-to-face and virtual work teams and discovered differing trends that nonetheless lead to the same unexceptional result for both. For instance, they found that members of verbally interacting work groups tend to share less vital information than do members of electronic work groups and hence make poor decisions. Yet, members of the electronic groups also tend to make poor group decisions, despite exchanging 50 percent more of the vital information needed to make an optimal decision. Galegher and Kraut (1994) also found that for virtual work groups the final product was similar in overall quality to that produced by face-to-face group members.

As Brandon and Hollingshead (2007) note, technology "intertwines" with the specific tasks being performed to influence group outcomes. In particular, some tasks are better suited and better results will be achieved through text-based interaction, while others require higher levels of media richness (e.g., Hollingshead & Contractor, 2002).

## Conclusion

Many elements can contribute to and shape the nature and functioning of online groups. Some factors are equally influential for groups that operate in the traditional face-to-face sphere. Some factors, while having been found to exert an influence on traditional groups, play a greater or a lesser role within online groups. Yet other factors appear uniquely to influence the dynamics of online groups.

Different categories or kinds of groups online operate differently. The organizational group will function differently than will the recreational group or the support group. Groups within those larger categories will differ from one another as well, as they are influenced by the composition of their individual members. The various goals and the personality characteristics of the members will, for instance, uniquely affect the group in question.

Issues such as the degree of anonymity of the members and the salience of the group identity, to name a few, will uniquely interact with the situational context in which the group is functioning, the personality characteristics of the members, and so forth to shape the behavior of the members and the overall group dynamic and structure. All of these factors make the dynamics of online groups dynamic indeed.

## References

Abreu, S. (2000). *How to manage telecommuters.* Retrieved April 27, 2006, from http:// cnnstudentnews.cnn.com/2000/TECH/computing/06/19/telecommuting.idg.

Atkinson, J. W., & Birch, D. (1970). *The dynamics of action.* New York: Wiley.

Barak, A., & Dolev-Cohen, M. (2006). Does activity level in online support groups for distressed adolescents determine emotional relief? *Counselling and Psychotherapy Research, 6,* 186–190.

Bargh, J. A. (1989). Conditional automaticity: Varieties of automatic influence in social perception and cognition. In J. S.Uleman & J. A. Bargh (Eds.), *Unintended thought* (pp. 3–51). New York: Guilford Press.

Barrera, M., Jr., Glasgow, R. E., McKay, H. G., Boles, S. M., & Feil, E. G. (2002). Do Internet-based support interventions change perceptions of social support? An experimental trial of approaches for supporting diabetes self-management. *American Journal of Community Psychology, 30,* 637–654.

Barreto, M., & Ellemers, N. (2000). You can't always do what you want: Social identity and self-presentational determinants of the choice to work for a low-status group. *Personality and Social Psychology Bulletin, 26,* 891–906.

Blank, T. O., & Adams-Blodnieks, M. (2007). The who and the what of usage of two cancer online communities. *Computers in Human Behavior, 23,* 1249–1257.

Brandon, D. P., & Hollingshead, A. B. (2007). Categorizing on-line groups. In A. Joinson, K. Y. A. McKenna, U. Reips, & T. Postmes (Eds.), *The Oxford handbook of Internet psychology* (pp. 105–120). Oxford: Oxford University Press.

Brewer, M. B. (1988). A dual process model of impression formation. In T. K. Srull & R. S. Wyer, Jr. (Eds.), *A dual process model of impression formation. Advances in social cognition* (Vol. 1, pp. 1–36). Hillsdale, NJ: Lawrence Erlbaum.

Cascio, W. E. (2000). Managing virtual workplace. *Academy of Management Executive, 14*(3), 81–90.

Cervin, V. (1956). Individual behavior in social situations: Its relation to anxiety, neuroticism, and group solidarity. *Journal of Experimental Psychology, 51,* 161–168.

Cummings, J., Sproull, L., & Kiesler, S. (2002). Beyond hearing: Where real world and Online support meet. *Group Dynamics: Theory, Research, and Practice, 6,* 78–88.

Davison, K. P., Pennebaker, J. W., & Dickerson, S. S. (2000). Who talks? The social psychology of illness support groups. *American Psychologist, 55,* 205–217.

Deaux, K. (1996). Social identification. In E. T. Higgins & A. W. Kruglanski (Eds.), *Social psychology: Handbook of basic principles* (pp. 777–798). New York: Guilford Press.

Dennis, A. R. (1996). Information exchange and use in group decision making: You can lead a group to information but you can't make it think. *MIS Quarterly, 20,* 433–455.

Dennis, A. R., & Kinney, S. T. (1998). Testing media richness theory in the new media: The effects of cues, feedback, and task equivocality. *Information Systems Research, 9,* 256–274.

Douglas, K. M., & McGarty, C. (2001). Identifiability and self-presentation: Computer-mediated communication and intergroup interaction. *British Journal of Social Psychology, 40*, 399–416.

Frable, D. E. S. (1993). Being and feeling unique: statistical deviance and psychological marginality. *Journal of Personality, 61*, 85–110.

Galegher, J., & Kraut, R. E. (1994). Computer-mediated communication for intellectual teamwork: An experiment in group writing. *Information Systems Research, 5*, 110–138.

Galegher, J., Sproull, L., & Kiesler, K. (1998). Legitimacy, authority, and community in electronic support groups. *Written Communication, 15*, 493–530.

Gollwitzer, P. M. (1986). Striving for specific identities: The social reality of self-symbolizing. In R. Baumeister (Ed.), *Public self and private self* (pp. 143–159). New York: Springer.

Hogg, M. A. (1992). *The social psychology of group cohesiveness*. London: Harvester, Wheatsheaf.

Hogg, M. A., & Reid, R. A. (2001). Social identity, leadership, and power. In A. Y. Lee-Chai & J. A. Bargh (Eds.), *The use and abuse of power: Multiple perspectives on the causes of corruption* (pp. 159–180). Philadelphia: Psychology Press.

Joinson, A. N., & Paine, C. B. (2007). Self-disclosure, privacy, and the Internet. In A. N. Joinson, K. Y. A. McKenna, U. Reips, & T. Postmes (Eds.), *The Oxford handbook of Internet psychology* (pp. 237–252). Oxford: Oxford University Press.

Jones, E. E., Farina, A., Hastorf, A. H., Markus, H., Miller, D. T., & Scott, R. A. (1984). *Social stigma: The psychology of marked relationships*. San Francisco: W. H. Freeman.

Kogan, N., & Wallach, M. A. (1967). Group risk taking as a function of members' anxiety and defensiveness. *Journal of Personality, 35*, 50–63.

Lambert, A. J., Payne, B. K., Shaffer, L. M., Jacoby, L. L., Chasteen, A., & Khan, S. (2003). Stereotypes as dominant responses: On the "social facilitation" of prejudice in anticipated public contexts. *Journal of Personality and Social Psychology, 84*, 277–295.

Leary, M. R. (1983). Social anxiousness: The construct and its measurement. *Journal of Personality Assessment, 47*, 66–75.

Lewin, K. (1951). *Field theory in social science*. Chicago: University of Chicago Press.

McClendon, M. J. (1974). Interracial contact and the reduction of prejudice. *Sociological Focus, 7*(4), 47–65.

McKenna, K. Y. A., & Bargh, J. A. (1998). Coming out in the age of the Internet: Identity demarginalization through virtual group participation. *Journal of Personality and Social Psychology, 75*, 681–694.

McKenna, K. Y. A., & Bargh, J. A. (1999). Causes and consequences of social interaction on the Internet: A conceptual framework. *Media Psychology, 1*, 249–269.

McKenna, K. Y. A., & Bargh, J. A. (2000). Plan 9 from cyberspace: The implication of the Internet for personality and social psychology. *Personality and Social Psychology Review, 4*, 57–75.

McKenna, K. Y. A., & Green, A. S. (2002). Virtual group dynamics. *Group Dynamics: Theory, Research and Practice, 6*, 116–127.

McKenna, K. Y. A., Green, A. S., & Gleason, M. E. J. (2002). Relationship formation on the Internet: What's the big attraction? *Journal of Social Issues, 58,* 9–31.

McKenna, K. Y., Green, A. S., & Smith, P. K. (2001). Demarginalizing the sexual self. *Journal of Sex Research, 38,* 302–311.

McKenna, K. Y. A., & Seidman, G. (2005). You, me, and we: Interpersonal processes in online groups. In Y. A. Hamburger (Ed.), *The social net: The social psychology of the Internet* (pp. 191–217). New York: Oxford University Press.

McKenna, K. Y. A., Seidman, G., Buffardi, A. & Green, A. S. (2007). *Ameliorating social anxiety through online interaction. Manuscript under review.* Ben-Gurion University.

Pettigrew, T. F. (1971). *Racially separate or together?* New York: McGraw-Hill.

Postmes, T., Spears, R., Sakhel, K., & DeGroot, D. (2001). Social influence in computer-mediated communication: The effect of anonymity on group behavior. *Personality and Social Psychology Bulletin, 27,* 1243–1254.

Prentice, D. A., Miller, D. T., & Lightdale, J. R. (1994). Asymmetrics in attachments to groups and their members: Distinguishing between common-identity and common-bond groups. *Personality and Social Psychology Bulletin, 20,* 484–493.

Sassenberg, K. (2002). Common bond and common identity groups on the Internet: Attachment and normative behavior in on-topic and off-topic chats. *Group Dynamics: Theory, Research, and Practice, 6,* 27–37.

Sassenberg, K., Boos, M., & Klapproth, F. (2001). Wissen und problemlösekompetenz: Der einfluss von expertise auf den informationsaustausch in computervermittelter kommunikation [Knowledge and problem solving competence: The influence of expertise on information exchange in computer-mediated communication]. *Zeitschrift für Sozialpsychologie, 32,* 45–56.

Spears, R., Lea, M., & Lee, S. (1990). De-individuation and group polarization in computer-mediated communication. *British Journal of Social Psychology, 29,* 121–134.

Spears, R., Postmes, T., Lea, M., & Wolbert, A. (2002). When are net effects gross products? The power of influence and the influence of power in computer-mediated communication. *Journal of Social Issues, 58,* 91–107.

Sproull, L., & Kiesler, S. (1985). Reducing social context cues: Electronic mail in organizational communication. *Management Science, 11,* 1492–1512.

Thompson, L., & Nadler, J. (2002). Negotiating via information technology: Theory and application. *Journal of Social Issues, 58,* 109–124.

Wright, K. (2000). Computer-mediated social support, older adults, and coping. *Journal of Communication, 50,* 100–18.

Zajonc, R. B. (1965). Social facilitation. *Science, 149,* 269–274.

Zander, A., & Wulf, D. (1966). Members' test anxiety and competence: Determinants of a group's aspirations. *Journal of Personality, 34,* 55–70.

# 11   Online Motivational Factors: Incentives for Participation and Contribution in Wikipedia

*Sheizaf Rafaeli and Yaron Ariel*

Cyberspace has introduced new and intriguing means for knowledge sharing as well as new structures of mediated knowledge-building communities. Considering the various forms of online communities, it should be difficult to overstate the significance of Wikipedia as a landmark in building communal knowledge repositories.

Wikipedia is an online collaboratively written encyclopedia. It has unique aspects of users' involvement in the production of content and its function as a community. In less than five years of existence, Wikipedia has acquired both avid advocates and ardent adversaries. Although there have been some public and academic debates about the quality of its content, as the rapid growth of its articles and numbers of active users (Wikipedians) continues, most people agree that at least the English version of Wikipedia is approaching critical mass where substantial content disasters should become rare. Wikipedia's existence and success rely on users' inputs. Our chapter focuses on Wikipedians' incentives for contributing to Wikipedia. The popular observation is that Wikipedia only works in practice. In theory, it can never work. How does Wikipedia mobilize the levels of participation that make it "work in practice"?

Wikipedia's growth, from the time of its foundation in 2001, has been impressive in all conceivable dimensions. Expansion metrics have accelerated in terms of volume, numbers of articles, visitors, and percentage of contributors. There are, by the time of this writing, 250 language editions of Wikipedia. The English-language version is the largest. It contains more than two million articles. The German-language version has more than half a million articles and the French, Polish, Japanese, Dutch, Italian, Portuguese, Swedish, Spanish, Russian, and Chinese versions each boast over 100,000 articles.

According to Alexa.com traffic rankings, Wikipedia is among the top fifteen most visited sites. Google "top searches" of 2006 report that "Wikipedia" and "wiki" are tied for the tenth position in the list of most searched words. Furthermore, Wikipedia content is widely replicated on other websites (e.g., Answer.com).

In trying to understand contribution dynamics, we focus on the individuals who write Wikipedia, the so-called Wikipedians. The number of Wikipedians continues to rapidly grow. The English Wikipedia alone has exceeded 3 million registered users. Though these numbers might be biased in many ways (multiple registrations), Wikipedia statistics indicate (Figure 11.1) that currently

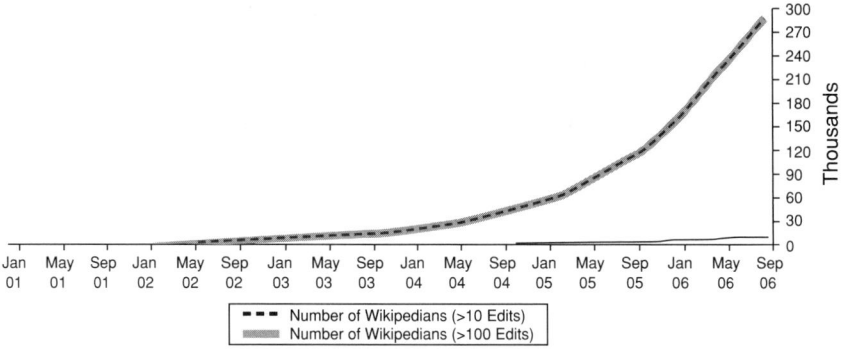

Figure 11.1. *Numbers of Wikipedian. Based on http://stats.wikimedia.org.*

there are more than 300,000 users in the various Wikipedia editions who have contributed at least ten edits, and the numbers grow exponentially by 5–10 percent a month.

## What is Wikipedia?

Wikis are online, web-based collaborative writing environments. Wikipedia is probably the most famous implementation of wiki-based platforms. There are currently numerous experiments in wiki-based environments. The experiments include knowledge management solutions, academic textbooks, Wiktionaries, WikiBooks, WikiQuotes, and more (for an updated list see mediawiki.org, which distribute free wiki-based software originally written for Wikipedia). Wikis in general and, specifically, Wikipedia embody and experiment with the utopian notions associated with Internet group behavior. Not surprisingly, both the resulting quality of the content of wikis and the equity in contribution efforts are controversial.

Wikis are group-editing tools that allow the formation and maintenance of online linked webpages, created by a group of users. The term *wiki* originated from the Hawaiian languages wherein "wiki-wiki" means fast and refers to the content as well as the software used to manage these pages. In a wiki, all users are potential authors and editors. To modify a page, a user simply clicks on an "edit page" link, changes the text in a text area, and submits the changes. Wiki platforms allow anyone (registered or anonymous) to add, change, or delete content on any of the pages (Leuf & Cunningham, 2001).

At the core of this chapter stands Wikipedia, an online wiki-based encyclopedia. Contrary to encyclopedias published in other formats, professional editors do not review Wikipedia content before material is published; instead, visitors to the online site monitor its content. Furthermore, individuals who have interest in the specific topic may purposefully follow recent changes and traffic (history pages) or engage in a conversation with other users on the subject (discussion pages).

Wikis support hyperlinks and have a simple text syntax for creating new content and internal crosslinks. Wiki is unusual among group communication mechanisms in that it allows the organization of contributions to be edited in addition to the content itself. Like many simple concepts, "open editing" has some profound and subtle effects on Wiki usage. Allowing everyday users to create and edit any page in a website is an exciting notion because it encourages democratic use of the web and promotes content composition by nontechnical users (Emigh & Herring, 2005).

## Studying Wikipedia

Wikipedia has captured the attention of researches across a variety of disciplines. There are several dynamic collections of wiki-research-related bibliographies available online. At least two yearly international conferences focus on Wikipedia (Wikimania: proceeding available at http://wikimania. wikimedia.org; and Wikisym: proceeding available at http://www.wikisym. org) that provide a variety of rich studies of the content, the process, and the behavior of users and creators. Much of the research attention is devoted to the technical aspects of the wiki database and interaction features. Table 11.1 summarizes some of the major fields of interest in Wikipedia research and provides pointers to relevant sources. Wikipedia is self-aware to an extent and documents studies about itself and its users on a webpage titled "Wiki Research Bibliography" (http://meta.wikimedia.org/wiki/Wiki_Research_Bibliography). This page contains many other links (Wikipedia's pages and external links) to webpages that continually update wiki-related research. The material in Table 11.1 goes beyond sources mentioned in the Wikipedia self-reference at the time of this writing. Table 11.1 focuses mostly on the social aspects of Wikipedia creation and use.

As indicated by Table 11.1, research has focused on Wikipedia (content quality and authority) and its technological structure and users (Wikipedians motivations, community aspects, and learning process). Ciffolilli (2003) describes Wikipedia as a community. He discussed early views on the processes of reputation within it and searched for reasons of its success. Lih (2004) analyzed citation of Wikipedia content in the press. Emigh and Herring (2005) have studied Wikipedia's functionality as an online encyclopedia. We will elaborate on some of these and other studies later in this chapter. Surveying Wikipedia-related studies, we find only a limited scope of studies that mention incentives for contributing content and other participatory elements. Why do people make the effort?

Wikipedia is probably one of the most salient examples of user-generated content. The notion of peer-produced content, in a "Wisdom of Crowds" (Surowiecki, 2004) setting, has captured both the imagination and headlines in recent scholarly and popular discourse of online behavior. Some

Table 11.1. *Fields of interest in research on Wikipedia*

| Field of study | References |
| --- | --- |
| Editorial and authorship consideration | Emigh & Herring, 2005; Miller, 2005 |
| Content quality | Chesney, 2006; Lih, 2004; Stvilia, Twidale, Gasser, & Smith, 2005; |
| Sharing and collaborative Knowledge building | Lih, 2004; Subramani & Peddibhotla, 2003 |
| Learning | Bruns & Humphreys, 2005; Forte & Bruckman, 2006; Ravid, 2006 |
| Motivation to contribute | Forte & Bruckman, 2006; Nov, 2007; Rafaeli, Ariel, & Hayat, 2005; Schroer & Hertel, 2007 |
| Wikipedians typologies | Bryant, Forte, & Bruckman, 2005; Gaved, Heath, & Eisenstadt, 2006; Majchrzak, Wagner, & Yates 2006 |
| Wikipedia as a community | Benkler, 2006; Ciffolilli, 2003; Voss, 2005 |
| Aspects of wiki technological features | Gabrilovich & Markovitch, 2007; Holloway, Bozicevic, & Börner, 2005; Viégas, Wattenberg, & Dave, 2004 |

marketing-oriented literature even terms the phenomena one of "pro-sumerism," a confusion or amalgam of the provider and recipient along the value creation chain. Our understanding of sociological and psychological aspects of Wikipedia should, therefore, investigate motivations to participate.

## Wikipedia Contributors

Perhaps the single most important insight about contributors to Wikipedia is that, in spite of their popular image and in possible conflict with some of the "democratic" rhetoric, they are neither equal nor uniform. Contributors to Wikipedia call themselves Wikipedians. Wikipedians are not all made in the same mold. Some register formally on the site, while most seem to remain semianonymous, identified only by IP (Internet Protocol) number. Even IP-only users are stratified according to whether they visit Wikipedia from the same (repeated) IP or are completely sporadic and unknown. Among those who decide to register, there are fine gradations of status, role, and hierarchy. Some Wikipedians are known to the world and their colleagues through pseudonyms, while others disclose their identity completely, revealing their name. Some Wikipedians maintain a user page, and some provide links to personal pages offsite, outside of Wikipedia. In the interactions among Wikipedia, authors, and editors, the degree of self-disclosure of participants is an important determinant of intimacy, sense of belonging and camaraderie, and the nature of interaction, as will be discussed later. The content on individual users pages, and the commitment made by the more deeply involved Wikipedians to particular areas of content reflect heavily on the continuity of coverage and community action. Thereby, identification is likely highly tied to motivation.

Gaved, Heath, and Eisenstadt (2006) suggest a typology of wiki users by the nature of their activity or type of contribution. Their classification is based on a survey of users of a wiki-based guide. The categories of the typology include three types: placeholders, completers, and housekeepers. *Placeholders* are users who prefer making many sparse entries (ensuring some coverage on every entry). *Completers* prefer to make fewer but more complete entries. *Housekeepers* enlist in the service of ensuring the completeness of entries and crosslinks. Another categorization offered by Majchrzak, Wagner, and Yates (2006) surveyed corporate Wiki users. They found a significant difference between the factors that motivated "synthesizers" and "adders" in contributing a corporate wiki. Synthesizers were concerned more with their own reputation and their effect on the wiki-related process, wiki users, and the whole organization. In contrast, Adders were more utilitarian and interested in completing immediate work responsibilities and less concerned with their own reputation.

In a much-cited blog on the topic, Bosworth (2006) suggests that despite Wikipedia's claims to egalitarianism the motivations to contribute in a wiki community constitute a two-stage reward system dividing between "new" (regular) users that gain small but satisfying rewards for basic participation and "fanatics" (administrators) who get the larger rewards through competition for special status. Bosworth claims that this reward system works in every Wikipedia page:

> Wikipedia self-selects for people who are obsessive about various subjects or just editing in general, as in every case the person or set of people willing to hammer their edits obsessively will win power over the page, and thus the reward of participation.

Virtual communities experience serious problems in sustaining the community due to lack of contributions. Although there is a lot of enthusiasm over online communities, many, or even most, fail. The virtual environment is overloaded with empty communities or communities where many of the participants are "lurkers" or "free riders" (Adar & Huberman, 2000). Furthermore, even when virtual communities do persist, it is usually only a small ratio of the more vigorous contributors that keep the community active. Many studies find that cyberspace phenomena distribute following power laws, such as Pareto distribution and Zipf's law of participation in online community (e.g., Lada & Bernardo, 2002).

Power law distributions have been observed in diverse phenomena (Axtell, 2001; Comellas & Gago, 2005; Gabaix, Gopikrishanan, Pelrou, & Stanley, 2004). In relation to online communities, Adar and Huberman (2000) found that on Gnutella (a peer-to-peer service) 10 percent of users supply 87 percent of all content. Similarly, Lakhani and Hippel (2003) found that only 4 percent of the members of open-source development communities provide 50 percent of answers on a user-to-user help site. Peddibhotla and Subramani (2007) refer to the notion of "critical mass," indicating the disproportionate contributions of the minority of contributors to public document repositories.

The distribution of activity on Wikipedia is in line with that reported for other virtual communities. The founder of Wikipedia reported that 2.5 percent of the users contribute 80 percent of all the content. Furthermore, 50 percent of the content is generated by only 1 percent of the contributors (cited in Tapscott & Williams, 2007). Benkler (2006) looking at the growth in Wikipedias' contributors writes:

> The shift in strategy toward an open, peer-produced model proved enormously successful. The site saw tremendous growth both in the number of contributors, including the number of active and very active contributors, and in the number of articles included in the encyclopedia.    (p. 71)

Thus, the numbers reported by Benkler also indicate a power law distribution; for example, in June 2005, there were 48,721 Wikipedians who contributed on at least ten occasions, 16,945 "active contributors" who contributed at least 5 times a month, and only 3,016 "very active" Wikipedians who contributed more than 100 times during last month. The ratios of these numbers remain fairly stable over the years. The vast audience of users is even larger. Any examination of motivations needs to stay aware of the overarching power law reality: the whole universe of contributors forms only a small percentage of those who use the system.

We propose that Wikipedians' participation should be examined from several distinct perspectives:

1.    Professional versus nonprofessional participation
2.    Constructive, confrontational, and vandalistic participation
3.    Continuous versus one-time participation
4.    Anonymous versus identifiable participation
5.    Content contribution, community involvement, and (silent) participation in the form of lurking.

Some of this work has already been done in other cyberspace-related studies. For example, Joyce and Kraut (2006) on predicting users' continued participation in newsgroups; Kalman, Ravid, Raban, and Rafaeli, 2006 on silence in computer-mediated communication; Soroka and Rafaeli (2006) on online lurking behavior. As we will detail, early examinations of Wikipedians' motivations have taken aim at the psychological, sociological, community-oriented, economical, gratificational, and interactional aspects of potential sources for motivation. In the following, we will review the work in each of these areas to date.

## Motivational Factors Research

The study of human motivations has a long tradition in behavioral sciences. Cofer and Appley (1964) surveyed the interest in motivational phenomena as a research field and suggest it can be dated, as a modern construct, to Darwin and Freud. Maslow's (1970) widely cited work proposes five levels of needs that drive human activities, ranging from physiological needs to the need for self-actualization. Is participation in Wikipedia solely self-actualization?

Deci (1975) underlines a distinction between "intrinsic motivation" and "external rewards." Although the first are psychological factors that include the desire for competence and self-determination, the second includes factors such as direct or indirect monetary compensation and other's recognition. Based on these observations, Hars and Ou (2001) also propose a distinction between motivations that are rooted in the psychology of the individual (internal factors) and external factors (rewards) that originate from the environment, which will be used as a basis for identifying potential factors that lead programmers to participate in open-source development. Thompson, Meriac, and Cope (2002) indicate that extrinsic rewards might actually decrease intrinsic motivations. Thus, users who were never offered extrinsic rewards were more self-motivated.

Theories and models from diverse disciplines address active and passive participation in virtual communities. This chapter will highlight approaches that might explain motivations to contribute on the part of Wikipedians.

Several theories rely on psychological explanations, such as the humanistic perspectives, to define what causes our intrinsic needs or motivations to operate. Various social psychology explanations such as group dynamics also try to explore the effect of motivations on online community (Ling et al., 2005). Sociological explanations and especially social network analysis models are another way to capture the reasons for contribution and participation in a community. Media studies have a long tradition of uses and gratifications perspectives that can be easily applied to online community (Sangwan, 2005). Finally, searching the incentives that users have in participating in and contributing to a community gives rise to some economic explanations (Kollock, 1999; Raban, Ravid, & Rafaeli, 2005).

## Psychological Explanations for Contributing to an Online Community

From a psychological perspective, Joyce and Kraut (2006) found that users who contribute more content to an online community were more likely to repeat their participation in that community. They suggest that some users are self-motivated to write more in general, while some users who invest time or effort in the community continue to participate in it to maintain their self-presentation and to avoid cognitive dissonance about their reasons for investing their time in that community. Joyce and Kraut suggest it is likely that newcomers' interaction with a group (initial postings followed by others' responses) will be a first step in their commitment to the group. Ling et al. (2005) report that users will contribute more to the community if they believe that their contributions are important to the group's performance, if they believe that their contributions will be identifiable, and if they like the group they are working with.

According to a functionalist perspective in psychology, individuals perform certain activities because they serve one or more functions. Snyder and Cantor (1998) suggest four clusters of functions:

1.  Value-expressive: a way of expressing one's values about altruistic concern for others.
2.  Utilitarian: rewards from the person's external environment; a person might contribute to a repository to receive monetary or other rewards.
3.  Social adjustive: doing a certain thing may lead an individual to better fit in with the peer group.
4.  Knowledge: by engaging in particular task, an individual might have a new learning experience and be able to exercise one's knowledge, skills, and other abilities.

Is it possible that Wikipedia contributions are explained simply through pure altruism? From a sociological perspective, Kollock (1999) is unequivocal: "literal altruism" is a rare phenomenon. In replacement for the negated literal altruism, Kollock suggests several possible motivations for contribution to online communities among them: anticipated reciprocity, sense of efficacy, and attachment or commitment. *Anticipated reciprocity* refers to person's motivation to contribute in the expectation that one will receive useful help and information in return. A related factor to anticipated reciprocity is users' identity persistence when record of past actions and contributions is kept and attributed to the contributor. Another related factor to anticipated reciprocity is well-defined group boundaries. Both identity persistence and group boundaries are factors of the anticipated reciprocity as the online community eventually balances itself. Community members avoid those who never give or conversely make an effort to help those who have contributed in the past. A *sense of efficacy* refers to a person who contributes valuable information to an online community because influencing this community may support her own self-image as an efficacious person. *Attachment or commitment* to online community refers to a person who contributes to the group when individual and collective outcomes are merged or somewhat balanced.

Ciffolilli (2003) distinguishes between personal and social motivations of Wikipedians. Self-motivations involve satisfaction, efficacy, and intrinsic drive to acquire knowledge. Social motivations involve a desire to take part in the production of a collective good, a need for belonging, and a need to support a specific community. Motivations may also be ethical or they may be related to reputation, which may become a source of authority. Following Rheingold (1993), Kollock also suggests that users contribute to get prestige in the community. Building community prestige is a key motivation of individuals' contributions to the group. The first stage in building one's reputation is quite simple in Wikipedia. The "history" function allows exploration of previous versions of each article. Through history one can and many do trace the authors. Ciffolilli (2003) argue that Wikipedians' reputation correlates with the number of their contributions. Erickson and Herring (2005) defined the notion of "persistence conversation" to describe a human-to-human interaction carried out over computer networks and which, unlike face-to-face conversation, leaves traces. As will be discussed later, we suggest these conversations should be examined as Wikipedia's enabled interactivity.

## Substitutes for Economic Payback?

Contributing content or other acts of participating in Wikipedia are not directly remunerated. Rewards, if any, are rarely tangible. Thus, most theories and expectations rooted in a traditional economic perspective have less of a direct relation to the examination of motivations to contribute to knowledge repositories such as Wikipedia. In more directly and monetarily rewarded contexts, such as the Google Answers site, for example, Rafaeli, Raban, and Ravid (2005, 2007) found that higher-priced and better-tipped responders were more likely to participate. However, even in the presence of specific and salient monetary rewards, the economic incentive was strongly moderated by social variables. Higher participation was documented to be a function of an interaction between money and social reference. Wiertz and Ruyter (2007) investigated why customers are willing to contribute to firm-hosted technical support online communities. They, too, found that knowledge contribution to these communities is strongly influenced by a customer's tendency for online interaction, feeling of commitment to the community, and the perceived informational value. These three incentives are mentioned throughout this chapter.

Subramani and Peddibhotla (2003) describe the content contributed to a repository as a public good since once it is given to a person it is cheap or free to provide to everyone else and supposedly

> a rational person will contribute to a repository only if he gets incentives to compensate for his effort. More importantly, such incentives will work only when the person is recruited for the task. In public knowledge repositories, however, there is no active recruiting. Moreover, because of the large number of participants, it is not possible for a central authority to monitor each individual and provide tailor-made incentives to induce contribution.

The intervening and moderating force of social variables above the obvious role of private interest appears here too.

Tapscott and Williams (2007) claim that the transition from the industrial to the information-based economy changed more than the way we produce and circulate. Social relations around the co-production of content and the relational structure surrounding it evolve into "wikinomics." Peer production is the key element of such economic environment, and people contribute without any direct payment for diverse motivations. Tapscott and Williams also suggest three conditions for this kind of peer work to perform well:

1. *Cost for the contributors is low.* With Wikipedia, for example, production of information and knowledge building is central. There are widely circulated critiques of Wikipedia's user interface. These critiques suggest that learning the editing procedures (and their continuing developments) of Wikipedia is becoming a complicated task for the average users (see http://www.wikitruth.info for multiple criticisms). If these critiques prove correct or gain momentum, it will mean that the cost for contribution is raised, thus expected participation may decline.

2. *Tasks are "chunked out into bite-size pieces"* (Tapscott & Williams, 2007, p. 70). In other words, minor editing is available and boosts participation because the threshold for initial participation is low.

3. *Low cost of integration and quality control.* Indeed, wiki technology is based on volunteer administrators and requires relatively little overhead.

Because contributing to Wikipedia is not explained by immediate economic reward, we should search Wikipedians' incentives through the subjective value of information. Contrary to other goods or services, once information is produced, its replication is almost costless, and it cannot be consumed or spent (Bates, 1989; Raban & Rafaeli, 2007; Shapiro & Varian, 1999). Bates (1989) argues that the value of information has a paradoxical nature. The value of information lies in its content and structure; one cannot evaluate information without using it, so to evaluate it, one should be exposed to it. However, after being exposed to it, your evaluation may change. Similarly, Shapiro and Varian (1999) argue that information is an "experience good," and therefore, its value is revealed only after consumption. Nevertheless, there are some similarities between information and other resources, as in the case of the principle of the diamond-water paradox that highlights the nature of subjective evaluation, where water is available, people value diamonds highly, and while in an arid desert, people would value water more highly than diamonds.

Ahituv and Neuman (1986) divide studies of the value of information into three approaches: the normative value approach, realistic value approach, and subjective value approach. The *normative value approach* proposes that individuals (always) have some preliminary knowledge about the occurrence of events that are relevant to a specific decision. In that sense, an individual assigns objective or subjective probabilities to the information because of his or her prior knowledge. In a synthetic environment with given parameters, this knowledge should help the individual make perfect evaluations of information. However, the Wikipedia environment does not offer its contributors this kind of stability. The *realistic value approach* usually includes the implementation of an experimental research, before and after design. This approach examines the revealed value of information by measuring the effect of new information on the outcomes. Using this approach, one must assume the measurability of all associated variables. In Wikipedia, evaluating information relying on this approach is suitable only in the case of organized participation, such as students contributing to Wikipedia as a required assignment. We find the third approach to be more promising when studying Wikipedia. The *subjective value approach* asserts that the value of information is a reflection of the individuals' impression of information (e.g., Raban & Rafaeli, 2007; Rafaeli & Raban, 2003).

The behavior of individuals who contribute to open-source programs might shed a light on the economical perspective, which is relevant also to Wikipedians. Although the most open-source programmers are not compensated for their contributions directly, they may receive indirect rewards by increasing their marketability and skill base or selling related products and services. This might be the case for some Wikipedians who contribute to receive external rewards. Hars and Ou (2001) suggest, based on a survey of programmers, that those who work on open-source products and follow open-source and GNU software rules may view their participation as an investment from which they expect future returns:

1. Revenues from related products and services: Open-source software provide many opportunities for selling related products and services.
2. Human capital: Open-source programmers may also participate in open-source projects to expand their skill base.
3. Self-marketing: Programmers may also regard working for open-source software as an effective way to demonstrate their capability and skillfulness in programming.
4. Peer recognition: Many open-source programs desire fame and esteem, which is associated with future returns.
5. Personal needs: Many open-source projects were initiated because a programmer had a personal need for specific software.

## Wikipedians' Gratifications

Another productive approach for examining Wikipedians' motivations is located in the results of their actual activities. What are the gratifications they seek or obtain? Relying on psychological humanistic approach (such as the work of Maslow and Rogers), media scholars have been developing an extensive literature about a user-centered approach and theoretical tradition named "uses and gratifications" (Katz, Blumler & Gurevitch, 1973; Ruggiero, 2000). Combined with a sociological perspective and later with critical studies, the original definitions of the uses and gratifications theory suggested that

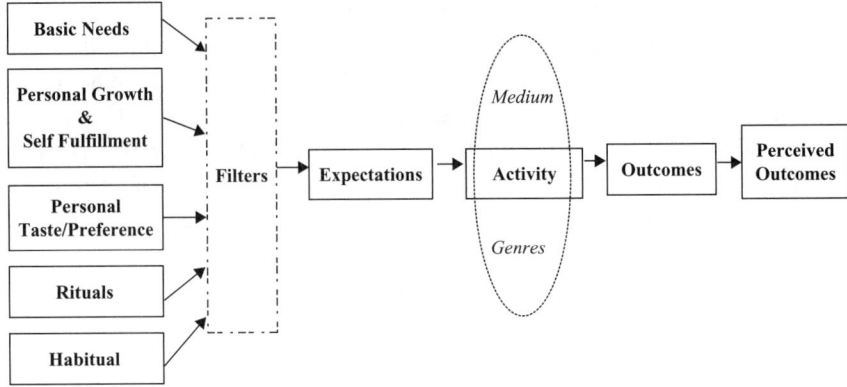

Figure 11.2. *Uses and gratifications comprehensive model.* Source: *Ariel, 2005.*

members of the media audience are not passive in their relations with the media. On the contrary, audience members seek specific media and content in active ways to obtain specific gratifications (Katz et al., 1973). The new platforms offered by cyberspace emphasize the relevance of this approach for examining users motivations in virtual environments (e.g., Grace-Farfaglia, Dekkers, Sundararajan, Peters, & Park, 2006; Jung, Youn, & McClung, 2007; Lin, 2002; Sangwan, 2005; Stafford, Stafford, & Schkade, 2004).

Traditional studies of uses and gratifications used five generic clusters of needs that media could fulfill: cognitive, affective, personal integrative, social integrative, and diversion needs (Rubin, 1986). Let us elaborate each of these clusters:

1.   Cognitive needs represent the intrinsic desire for information acquisition, knowledge, and understanding.
2.   Affective needs related to emotional experiences and intrinsic desire for pleasure, entertainment, and aesthetics.
3.   Personal integrative needs that derive from individuals' desire to appear credible, be perceived as confident, and have high self-esteem.
4.   Social integrative needs are affiliation needs where the individual wants to be part of a group to have a sense of belonging.
5.   Diversion needs, which relate to the need for escape and diversion from problems and routines.

Although these motivation clusters serve as basic guidelines for the uses and gratifications study of any medium, surveying the literature reveals a more complex model which is illustrated in Figure 11.2.

Obviously, a medium such as the Internet and a context such as Wikipedia have more two-way flows and more complex types of use, motivations, and gratifications. Let us describe how the research of Wikipedians' motivational factors for contributing content to Wikipedia can be examined according to the model presented in Figure 11.2. Motivations to contribute to Wikipedia might originate from five factors:

1. Basic needs: In rare cases, overly committed and involved Wikipedians might need their activity in Wikipedia as it maintains their own notions of self. These cases should be considered pathological or unhealthy and are probably not the norm. Contribution to Wikipedia might be very attractive but is probably only rarely a response to a basic need.

2. Personal growth and self-fulfillment: Fulfillment of Wikipedians' gratifications such as the need to belong to a community. This gratification is probably fairly widespread. Does Wikipedia provide self-actualization? Does it do so even in anonymous settings?

3. Personal taste or preference: Wikipedians who contribute because they enjoy performing activities in Wikipedia (editing, discussing, or voting on subjects). The degree to which active behavior on Wikipedia is intrinsically rewarding should be of great interest for further research. It is here that the most promising and long-lasting innovation may reside.

4. Rituals: Wikipedians who perform activities in Wikipedia as part of ceremonies and rhythms of their personal life. To what extent is the contribution to public knowledge repositories woven into day-to-day practice for some people, as, for instance, reading newspapers, participating in online chat and forums, or calling up the local talk radio show might be for others. Initial survey evidence suggests that this is the case, at least, for early Wikipedians (Rafaeli, Ariel, Hayat, 2005).

5. Habitual: Wikipedians who contribute as a routine, without thinking or acting because of a specific explicit incentive.

As can be seen in Figure 11.2, these five factors are transformed into Wikipedians' expectations toward the outcomes of their performance in Wikipedia. "Filters" are external and internal effects on the formation of expectancy, such as community norms or time limitation, which can strengthen or weaken ones' motivation. The actual contribution activity is placed within medium and genres conventions. Thus, active Wikipedians might become administrators and a novice Wikipedian might perform nonnormative actions in editing an article. The outcomes of Wikipedians' contribution in Wikipedia are for the most part very visible to all. Anyone can examine name and date of edit, user statistics, and the like. Nevertheless, the outcomes perceived by Wikipedians themselves are situated in a feedback loop and thus serve as the real generators of the motivational process.

## Wikipedia as a Knowledge-Building Community

An important factor of incentives for participating and contributing content to Wikipedia is related to its affordance through the collaborative process of knowledge sharing and knowledge building. Similar to open-source projects and other document repositories, being an active user in Wikipedia means taking part in a mutual learning process.

Zhang and Feng (2006) examined Wikipedia as a case study of motivations for contributing open-source software. They suggest that open-source software developers might have an intrinsic motivation rooted in the fun of programming and learning. Based on textual analysis, their results indicate that the collaboration in the Wikipedia process enhances incentive to contribute.

Peddibhotla and Subramani (2006) propose that knowledge sharing by contributing to a document repository (e.g., Wikipedia) is a form of prosocial behavior (Batson, 1998) because individual contributions lead to benefits for others whether there are any benefits for the contributor himself. Subramani and Peddibhotla (2003) examine users' personal written profiles in a public repository of product reviews as a source of data to glean their motivations. They propose four motivations for users' contribution to document repositories: (1) altruism versus (2) utilitarian motives, (3) reciprocity, and (4) knowledge motive. Expression of altruism refers to users who share their experience with a product, recommending or criticizing products with the goal of saving other readers' time or helping them with a purchase decision. Subramani and Peddibhotla consider in contrast the utilitarian motives. These involve obtaining a material benefit in return for contributing. Benefits could be tangible (such as free products or money) or reputational (which might lead eventually to tangible benefits). Similar to Kollock (1999) they found reciprocity as a motive for contributing document repositories. Reciprocity refers to individuals who wrote reviews as a form of reciprocation for the benefit they had received from other reviewers in the past. The fourth motive is knowledge in which the activity of contributing serves as a self-cognitive incentive such as improving writing skills, organization, and clarification of thoughts.

In a later article, Peddibhotla and Subramani (2007) suggest differentiating "other-oriented" and "self-oriented" motives. Whereas the other-oriented motives refer to social affiliation, altruism, and reciprocity, the self-oriented motives refer to self-expression, personal development, utilitarian motives, and enjoyment. Thus, should we consider contributing to Wikipedia (as a form of knowledge repository) to be a self- or other-oriented motive?

Rafaeli, Ariel & Hayat (2007) discuss Wikipedia as a virtual knowledge-building community:

> Wikipedia is a constant work-in-progress, a method for creating and sustaining collaborative knowledge building, and a metaphor for growing and accumulating knowledge in a social sphere.

Thus, Wikipedia encompasses more than just plain information as its tool set contains meta-data and meta-information. Furthermore, users' ability to generate diverse discussions (not just encyclopedia related content) and contextualized pages with their archives (history page) position Wikipedia as an interactive, collaborative authoring tool.

## Wikipedians' Sense of Community as a Motivator

One of the strongest motivations to participate and contribute to a community is users' sense of community. Echoes of this insight were already mentioned earlier and in work by Kollock (1999) and Majchrzak et al. (2006). McMillan and Chavis (1986, p. 9) define "sense of community" as

> a feeling that members have of belonging, a feeling that members matter to one another and to the group, and a shared faith that members' needs will be met through their commitment to be together.

Wikipedia defined itself as a community, and special spaces in Wikipedia are dedicated for communal activities. The rhetoric of community is to be found everywhere. Do the readers pick up this rhetoric as a call for action? Rafaeli, Ariel and Hayat (2005) found some confirmative evidence of users' sense of community in Wikipedia in their survey of a selected sample of highly active Wikipedians. The data for this study were collected using an online web questionnaire, which was posted in the "community portal" of the several Wikipedias (English, German, Italian, Arabic, and Hebrew). Results revealed various aspects of communal perceptions (e.g., teamwork) and activities (multiple relations inside and outside Wikipedia boundaries).

Using terminology reminiscent of the notion of sense of community, Ren, Kraut, and Kiesler (2007) suggest the Common Identity Theory and Common Bond Theory as a way for examining users' attachment to the online group, as a whole or as individuals. They suggest that

> despite their conceptual distinction, identity-based attachment may evolve into bond-based attachment and vice versa. This result would be predicted from the fact that both types of engagement lead people to participate in the community. This participation, in turn, should create opportunities and conditions under which people develop the other type of attachment. Thus, those who begin interacting in an online sports community because of their interest in a local team might later make friends in the community. Conversely, people who join to be with friends might later become attached to the team and the community surrounding it.     (p. 401)

We propose Wikipedians' attachment to other Wikipedians or to the whole Wikipedia community is fostered by the multiple opportunities of its enabled interactivity.

Let us review now, in further detail, the various elements composing a persons' sense of community (Chavis & Pretty, 1999; McMillan & Chavis, 1986). Community is sensed through membership, influence, integration, and fulfillment of needs, and shared emotional connection. Although fulfillment of members' personal and communal needs is similar to the gratifications previously discussed, the additional three elements proposed will be discussed with its relevance to studying Wikipedians' sense of community.

Users' membership in a community is accounted for by various attributes: foremost are the community boundaries that indicate who belongs and who does not. Another important factor is identification and sense of belonging to the community. The element of membership as part of users' sense of community is even more significant in Wikipedia since being a member in Wikipedia is self-selected and self-commitment process.

The power to influence is yet another element of users' sense of community. Influence in a community is bidirectional: members of a group feel empowered to have influence over what a group does (otherwise, they would not be motivated to participate), and group cohesiveness depends on the group's having some influence over its members. In Wikipedia, contributors can have immediate influence on article content and can take part in many editorial and community life decisions. Participation is the direct and unmediated vehicle for achieving such influence. Thus, in Wikipedia, a community contribution is as direct a component of community life as it might be anywhere.

Shared emotional connection is primarily an attribution of the community-shared history. Many features contribute to the shared emotional connection, including the quality of interactions as well as its intensity and the amount of time they are willing to spend performing these interactions. In earlier studies of online communities, the tendency to use first-person plural in reference to the collection of participants was noted to be an indirect indicator of emotional involvement. When "users" refer to each other as "we" or "us," they are likely to be more emotionally involved (Sudweeks, Mclaughlin, & Rafaeli, 1998). Wikipedians are known to use the same sort of plural, first-person approach. Wikipedians interactions as another possible explanation of motivation to contribute will be discussed next.

## Wikipedia-Enabled Interactivity

A more generic examination of users' participation in other, similar cyberspace environments might shed light on Wikipedians incentives for contributing content or for participating in other ways in Wikipedia. For example, consider the cases of participation in open source projects (Hars & Ou, 2001) and peer-to-peer sharing (Adar & Huberman, 2000) mentioned earlier.

In the case of online games, Bartle (1996) identified and described four types of Multiple User Domain (MUDs) players: achievers, explorers, socializers, and killers. Alongside the scale between acting and interacting, Bartle describes *achievers* as the players who give themselves game-related goals (usually some form of points gathering), thus acting within the MUDs world. *Explorers* aspire to discover as much as they can about the MUDs, thus interacting with the virtual world defined by it. *Socializers* use MUDs communicative facilities for interacting with other players and apply role-taking opportunities for social purposes. *Killers* are different. They use various MUDs tools to act on other players, causing them distress or, in rare cases, to help them.

Joyce and Kraut (2006) examine what causes a person who posts once to an online group to repeat and contribute to it again. They suggest three possible explanations in which group interactions might increase newcomers' commitment to the community: (1) Repeated actions lead to positive reinforcements, thus users are more likely to continue their participation in a community if they receive a response. Receiving a response, a positive response, and a response that brings about some of the users explicit needs are all considered as reinforcing events. (2) Reciprocal exchange within the community can set up an unspoken obligation to the group. This would hold true even in the case of unequal exchanges. (3) Personal bonds with group members because of interactions foster commitment to the community.

In a sense, Joyce and Krauts's explanations speak to the importance of interactivity in online communities. In a study of online helping in Internet groups, Wasko and Faraj (2000) suggest that altruism, generalized reciprocity, and community interest created by ongoing interaction of the members of the online groups are important motivations. Thus, a possible role in user incentives and continued participation in Wikipedia is played by enabled interactivity.

On Wikipedia, there are ample opportunities to "interact," even in the strictest sense of interactivity. In addition to editing actions performed on the blank page and on text entered by others earlier, there are discussion pages for each article; conversations in users' personal pages, and one-time special projects devoted to creating categories or ramping up levels of internal linking. There are discussions of fund-raising drives and modification of editing rules. There are votes held and campaigns conducted. Wikipedia is rife with opportunities for participants to weave into the social structure. We propose that this weaving, conducted through acts of dyadic interactivity as well as larger-scale, community-based interaction, plays a central role in motivating the more active of the participants. We expect these opportunities to play a major part in motivating the base rate of participation and in explaining Wikipedia's long-run success. Of course, these energized motivations are of interest for other Wiki-driven environments as well. As Wiki processes multiply, and the wiki tool set spreads out from the narrow world of encyclopedias into broader applications in knowledge management, the interactive arrangements and the manner they feed into motivations become even more important.

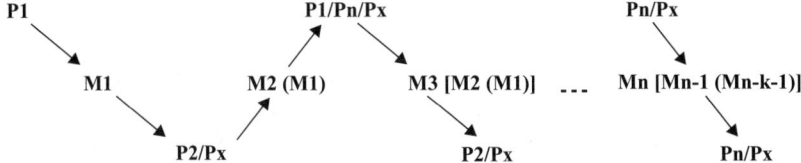

Figure 11.3. *Interactivity as a process-related variable – revisited model. P: Player (Wikipedian) – P1...n – a community member (target player). Px – an unknown community member. M: Message (Information) – M1...n – numbered by temporal sequence. Adapted from: Rafaeli & Ariel, 2007.*

Interactivity has been defined in many different ways over the years. An examination of the possible effects of interactivity in Wikipedia supports a definition of interactivity as a process-related variable (Cho & Leckenby, 1999; Macias, 2003; Rafaeli, 1988; Rafaeli & Sudweeks, 1997). Rafaeli (1988) defined interactivity as

> a variable characteristic of communication settings ... an expression of the extent that in a given series of communication exchanges, any third (or later) transmission (or message) is related to the degree to which previous exchanges referred to even earlier transmissions.     (p. 111)

In this definition, interactivity is predicated on the relatedness of sequential messages. Rafaeli and Sudweeks (1997) emphasize that these exchanges are simultaneous, continuous, and carry a social-binding force. Thus, we suggest Wikipedias' interactivity could be examined along the guidelines of the model proposed in Figure 11.3.

To study Wikipedias' interactivity, we should examine various indicators of information transmissions (or messages) within the community. The proposed model (Figure 11.3) for examining interactivity is similar to Rafaeli (1988) and Rafaeli and Sudweeks' (1997) models of interactivity. Although the original model examined direct interactivity between two persons (in each sequence), this model includes consideration of the indirect interactivity between community members (known or unknown), such as Wikipedia.

As mentioned earlier, a variety of scholars found evidence for correlation between interactivity and motivation in online communities (e.g., Joyce & Kraut, 2006; Kollock 1999; Rafaeli & Ariel, 2007; Subramani & Peddibhotla, 2003). Wikipedia enables interactivity through various community-based interactions. These interactions, described in Figure 11.3, stimulate user-generated content and knowledge building procedures. Thus, searching for the possible motivations for active participation in this process is essential for understanding how interactivity works in a virtual community, such as Wikipedia.

## Early Empirical Findings and Conclusions

The theory of Wikipedia needs to catch up with its practice. Wikipedia has been growing at impressive rates. Most if not all of this growth is grass-roots and bottom up. This growth is not explained by traditional vectors of funding, fiat, or momentum. Instead, the multidimensional, sociological, and psychological motivations of individual contributors take center stage.

Based on Clary et al.'s (1998) six motivational categories for volunteering, Nov (2007) surveyed possible Wikipedians motivations for contributing to Wikipedia: (1) express values of altruism by sharing their knowledge with others; (2) social engagement via the collaborative dynamics of Wikipedia; (3) exercising various knowledge, skills, and abilities; (4) promoting their current or future professional career; (5) protecting one's (Wikipedian) ego by sharing knowledge with those who do not have this knowledg; (6) enhancing one's ego through the public exhibition of their knowledge. Nov suggests two more categories addressing Wikipedians' motivations: (7) fun (echoes of Ludenic theory; see Rafaeli, 1986) and (8) ideology for contributing to Wikipedia as a variant of open-source application (based on Hars & Ou, 2001). Results of a survey of 151 respondents who are heavy Wikipedia contributors, indicates fun and ideology ranked the highest, whereas promoting one's career and social engagement ranked the lowest. Rafaeli, Ariel and Hayat's (2005) survey reveals that the strongest motivators are cognitive (e.g., "learning new things" and "intellectual challenge"), affective (e.g., "pleasure"), and, contrary to Nov's (2007) results, integrative (e.g., "sharing my knowledge with other Wikipedians" and "contributing to other people"). Similarly, Schroer and Hertel (2007) surveyed German Wikipedians, searching for potential predictors of Wikipedians engagement and satisfaction from contributing to Wikipedia and their perceived task characteristics. Their results reveal that satisfaction was determined by perceived benefits, identification with the Wikipedia community, and task characteristics.

As indicated at the opening of this chapter, we believe that Wikipedia is less than egalitarian. It might even be worth stating that the rumors of widespread, even anarchic democracy on Wikipedia were both premature and wrong. The collaboration on Wikipedia is enabled more by differentiating variables and processes than by equalizing rules and norms. The motivations of contributors are therefore both variable and of great interest. The accomplishments of Wikipedia and the large and growing social and cultural effect brought about by it, as well as the widespread adoption of wiki tools and Wiki culture warrant investigation of the structure and beliefs that serve as fuel for users to generate user-generated content. Much-needed future work on these issues can be directed at the contrasts between the various strands of explanation: psychological, sociological, community-oriented, economical, gratificational, and interactional aspects as potential sources for motivation.

To summarize, it appears that the search for Wikipedians participation and contributions should not be limited to one perspective or one-dimensional scale for measuring motivations. We propose that the continuing examination of Wikipedians' participation should involve contrasting (1) professional versus nonprofessional participation; (2) constructive, confrontational, and vandalistic participation; (3) continuous versus one-time participation; (4) anonymous versus identifiable participation; (5) content contribution, community involvement, and (silent) participation in the form of lurking. Wikipedia's continued growth and the implementation of wiki methods in other content and action domains offer ample opportunities for examining these dimensions. The challenge for further research is in an assessment of the relative strengths and the interactions between these dimensions.

## References

Adar, E., & Huberma, B. A. (2000). Free riding on Gnutella. *First Monday, 5*(10). Retrieved on October 24, 2007, from http://firstmonday.org/issues/issue5_10/adar/index.html.

Ahituv, N., & Neuman, S. (1986). Decision making and the value of information. In R. Galliers (Ed.), *Information analysis: Selected readings* (pp. 19–43). Reading, MA: Addison-Wesley.

Ariel, Y. (2005, March). *Web user's gratifications expectations.* Presented at the Seventh International Conference General Online Research – GOR05, University of Zurich, Switzerland.

Axtell, R. L. (2001). Zipf distribution of U.S. firm sizes. *Science, 293*(5536), 1818–1820.

Bartle, R. (1996). Hearts, clubs, diamonds, spades: Players who suit MUDS. *Journal of MUD Research, 1*(1). Retrieved on October 24, 2007, from http://www.mud.co.uk/richard/hcds.htm.

Bates, B. J. (1989). Information as an economic good: A re-evaluation of theoretical approaches. In B. D. Ruben & L. A. Lievrouw (Eds.), *Mediation, Information, and Communication: Information and Behavior* (Vol. 3). New Brunswick, NJ: Transaction.

Batson, C. D. (1998). Altruism and prosocial behavior. In D. T. Gilbert, S. Fiske, and G. Lindzey (Eds.), *The handbook of social psychology* (4th ed., pp. 282–316). New York: McGraw-Hill.

Benkler, Y. (2006). *The wealth of networks: How social production transforms markets and freedom.* London: Yale Press.

Bosworth, A. (2006). Why Wikipedia works. *Alex Bosworth's Weblog.* Retrieved January 2006 from http://sourcelabs.com/cgi-bin/mt/mt-tb.cgi/72.

Bruns, A., & Humphreys, S. (2005). Wikis in teaching and assessment – the M/Cyclopedia project. *Proceedings of the 2005International Symposium on Wikis*, San Diego, CA, pp. 25–32.

Bryant, S., Forte, A., & Bruckman, A. (2005). Becoming Wikipedian: Transformation of participation in a collaborative online encyclopedia. *Proceedings of GROUP International Conference on Supporting Group Work*, Sanibel Island, FL, pp. 1–10.

Chavis, D. M., & Pretty, G. (1999). Sense of community: Advances in measurement and application. *Journal of Community Psychology, 27*, 635–642.

Chesney, T. (2006). An empirical examination of Wikipedia's credibility. *First Monday. 11*(11). Retrieved on October 25, 2007, from http://firstmonday.org/issues/issue11_11/chesney/index.html.

Cho, C.-H., & Leckenby, J. D. (1999). Interactivity as a measure of advertising effectiveness. In M. S. Roberts (Ed.), *Proceedings of the American Academy of Advertising* (pp. 162–179). Gainesville: University of Florida.

Ciffolilli, A. (2003). Phantom authority, self-selective recruitment and retention of members in virtual communities: The case of Wikipedia. *First Monday, 8*(12). Retrieved on October 25, 2007, from http://firstmonday.org/issues/issue8_12/ciffolilli/index.html.

Clary, E. G., Snyder, M., Ridge, R. D., Copeland, J., Stukas, A. A., Haugen, J., et al. (1998). Understanding and assessing the motivations of volunteers: A functional approach. *Journal of Personality and Social Psychology, 74*, 1516–1530.

Cofer, C. N., & Appley, M. H. (1964). *Motivation: Theory and research.* New York: John Wiley & Sons, Inc.

Comellas, F., & Gago, S. (2005). A star-based model for the eigenvalue power law of Internet graphs. *Physica A – Statistical Mechanics and Its Applications, 351*(2–4), 680–686.

Deci, E. (1975). *Intrinsic motivation.* New York: Plenum Press.

Emigh, W., & Herring, C. S. (2005, January). Collaborative authoring on the Web: A genre analysis of online encyclopedias. *Proceedings of the 38th Annual Hawaii International Conference on System Sciences (HICSS'05)*, p. 99a.

Erickson, T., & Herring, S. C. (2005). *Persistent conversation: A dialog between research and design.* Paper presented at The Thirty-Eighth Hawaii International Conference on System Sciences, Los Alamitos, CA.

Forte, A., & Bruckman, A. (2006). From Wikipedia to the classroom: Exploring online publication and learning. *Proceedings of the International Conference of the Learning Sciences* (Vol. 1, pp. 182–188), Bloomington, Indiana.

Gabaix, X., Gopikrishanan, P., Pelrou, V., & Stanley, H. E. (2004). A theory of power law distributions in financial market fluctuations. *Nature, 423*, 267–270.

Gabrilovich, E., & Markovitch, S. (2007, January). *Computing semantic relatedness using Wikipedia-based explicit semantic analysis.* Proceedings of the 20th International Joint Conference on Artificial Intelligence (IJCAI), Hyderabad, India.

Gaved, M., Heath, T., & Eisenstadt, M. (2006). *Wikis of locality: Insights from the open guides.* Proceedings of the 2006 International Symposium on Wikis, Odense, Denmark.

Grace-Farfaglia, P., Dekkers, A. Sundararajan, B., Peters, L., & Park, S.-H. (2006). Multinational Web uses and gratifications: Measuring the social impact of online participation across national boundaries. *Electronic Commerce Research, 6,* 71–96.

Hars, A., & Ou, S. (2001, January). Working for free? Motivations of participating in open source projects. *Proceedings of the 34th Annual Hawaii International Conference on System Sciences (HICSS-34).* Vol. 7, p. 7014.

Holloway, T., Bozicevic, M. & Börner, K. (2005). *Analyzing and visualizing the semantic coverage of Wikipedia and its authors.* Unpublished manuscript. Retrieved on October 25, 2007, from http://arxiv.org/abs/cs.IR/0512085.

Joyce, E., & Kraut, R. E. (2006). Predicting continued participation in newsgroups. *Journal of Computer-Mediated Communication, 11,* 723–747.

Jung, T., Youn, H., & McClung, S. (2007). Motivations and self-presentation strategies on Korean based "Cyworld" Weblog format personal home pages. *CyberPsychology & Behavior, 10,* 24–31.

Kalman, Y. M., Ravid G., Raban, D. R., & Rafaeli S. (2006). Pauses and response latencies: A chronemic analysis of asynchronous CMC. *Journal of Computer Mediated Communication 12,* 1–23.

Katz, E., Blumler, J. G., & Gurevitch, M. (1973). Uses and gratifications research. *Public Opinion Quarterly, 37,* 509–523.

Kollock, P. (1999). The economies of online cooperation: Gifts and public goods in cyberspace. In M. Smith & P. Kollock (Eds.), *Communities in cyberspace.* London: Routledge.

Lada, A. A., & Bernardo, A. H. (2002). Zipf's law and the Internet. *Glottometrics, 3,* 143–150.

Lakhani, K. R., & Hippel, E. V. (2003). How open source software works: "Free" user-to-user assistance. *Research Policy, 32,* 923–943.

Leuf, B., & Cunningham, W. (2001). *The Wiki way: Quick collaboration on the Web.* Reading, MA: Addison-Wesley.

Lih, A. (2004). *Wikipedia as participatory journalism: Reliable sources? Metrics for evaluating collaborative media as a news resource.* Paper presented at The Fifth International Symposium on Online Journalism, Austin, Texas.

Lin, A. C. (2002). Perceived gratifications of online media service use among potential users. *Telematics and Informatics, 19,* 3–19.

Ling, K., Beenen, G., Ludford, P. J., Wang, X., Chang, K., Li, X., Cosley, D. Frankowski, D., Terveen, L., Rashid, A., Resnick, P., & Kraut, R. (2005). Using social psychology to motivate contributions to online communities. *Journal of Computer Mediated Communication, 10*(4). Retrieved on October 25, 2007, from http://jcmc.indiana.edu/vol10/issue4/ling.html.

Macias, W. (2003). A preliminary structural equation model of comprehension and persuasion of interactive advertising brand web sites. *Journal of Interactive Advertising, 3*(2). Retrieved October 25, 2007, from http://www.jiad.org/vol3/no2/macias/index.htm.

Majchrzak, A., Wagner, C., & Yates, D. (2006). *Corporate wiki users: Results of a survey.* Proceedings of the 2006 International Symposium on Wikis, Odense.

Maslow, A. H. (1970). *Motivation and personality* (2nd ed.) New York: Harper & Row.

McMillan, D. W., & Chavis, D. M. (1986). Sense of community: A definition and theory. *Journal of Community Psychology, 14,* 6–23.

Miller, N. (2005). Wikipedia and the disappearing "author." *ETC: A Review of General Semantics, 62*, 37–40.

Nov, O. (2007). What motivates Wikipedians, or how to increase user-generated content contribution. *Communications of the ACM, 50*, 60–64.

Peddibhotla, N. B., & Subramani, M. R. (2006, August). *Understanding the motivations of contributors to public document repositories: An empirical study.* Academy of Management Annual Meeting, Atlanta, Georgia.

Peddibhotla, N. B., & Subramani, M. R. (2007). Contributing to public document repositories: A critical mass theory perspective. *Organization Studies, 28*, 327–346.

Raban, D. R., & Rafaeli, S. (2007). Investigating ownership and the willingness to share information online. *Computers in Human Behavior, 23*, 2367–2382.

Raban, D. R., Ravid, G., & Rafaeli, S. (2005). *Paying for answers: An empirical report on the Google Answers information market.* Paper presented at the AoIR: Internet Research 6.0: Internet Generations, Chicago, Illinois.

Rafaeli, S. (1986). The electronic bulletin board: A computer-driven mass medium. *Computers and the Social Sciences, 20*, 123–136.

Rafaeli, S. (1988). Interactivity: From new media to communication. In R. P. Hawkins, J. M. Wiemann, & S. Pingree (Eds.), *Advancing communication science: Merging mass and interpersonal process* (pp. 110–134). Newbury Park, CA: Sage.

Rafaeli, S., & Ariel, Y. (2007). Assessing interactivity in CMC research. In A. N. Joinson, K. Y. M. McKenna, T. Postmes, & U.-D. Reips (Eds.), *The Oxford handbook of Internet psychology* (pp. 71–88). Oxford: Oxford University Press.

Rafaeli, S., Ariel, Y., & Hayat, T. (2005, August). *Wikipedia community: Users' motivations and knowledge building.* Presented at Cyberculture 3rd Global Conference, Prague, Czech Republic.

Rafaeli, S. Ariel, Y., & Hayat, T. (2007). Virtual knowledge-building communities. In G. D. Putnik & M. M. Cunha (Eds.), *Encyclopedia of networked and virtual organizations.* Hershey, Pal: Idea Group.

Rafaeli, S., & Raban, R. D. (2003). Experimental investigation of the subjective value of information in trading. *Journal of the Association for Information Systems, 4*, 119–139.

Rafaeli, S., Raban, R. D., & Ravid, G. (2005, November). *Social and economic incentives in Google Answers.* ACM Group 2005 Conference, Sanibel Island, Florida.

Rafaeli, S., Raban, D. R., & Ravid, G. (2007). How social motivation enhances economic activity and incentives in the Google Answers knowledge sharing market. *International Journal of Knowledge and Learning, 3*, 1–11.

Rafaeli, S., & Sudweeks, F. (1997). Networked interactivity. *Journal of Computer-Mediated Communication, 2*(4). Retrieved on October 25, 2007, from http://jcmc.indiana.edu/vol2/issue4/rafaeli.sudweeks.html.

Ravid, G. (2006, December). Wikibook uses in higher education courses. *Organizations and Society in Information Systems (OASIS).* Workshop (IFIP Working Group 8.2 Research Workshop) in ICIS, Milwaukee.

Ren, Y., Kraut, R. E., & Kiesler, S. (2007). Applying common identity and bond theory to the design of online communities. *Organizational Studies, 28*, 377–408.

Rheingold, H. (1993). *The virtual community*. Reading, MA: Addison-Wesley.

Rubin, A. M. (1986). Uses, gratifications, and media effects research. In J. Bryant & D. Zillmann (Eds.), *Perspective on media effects*. Mahwah, NJ: Lawrence Erlbaum.

Ruggiero, E. T. (2000). Uses and Gratification Theory in the 21st century. *Mass Communication & Society, 3*, 3–37.

Sangwan, S. (2005, January). *Virtual community success: A users and gratifications perspective*. Proceedings of the 38th HICSS Conference, Honolulu, Hawaii.

Schroer, J., & Hertel, G. (2007). *Voluntary engagement in an open web-based encyclopedia: Wikipedians, and why they do it*. Virtual Collaboration Network. Retrieved [month day year], from http://www.abo.psychologie.uni-wuerzburg.de/virtualcollaboration.

Shapiro, C., & Varian, H. R. (1999). *Information rules: A strategic guide to the network economy*. Boston: Harvard Business School Press.

Snyder, M., & Cantor, N. (1998). Understanding personality and social behavior: A functionalist strategy. In D. T. Gilbert, S. T. Fiske, & G. Lindzey (Eds.), *The handbook of social psychology* (Vol. 1, pp. 635–679). Boston: McGraw-Hill.

Soroka, V., & Rafaeli, S. (2006, May). *Invisible participants: How cultural capital relates to lurking behavior*. Paper presented at the WWW 2006, Edinburgh, Scotland.

Stafford, T., Stafford, M., & Schkade, L. (2004). Determining uses and gratifications for the Internet. *Decision Sciences, 35*, 259–288.

Stvilia, B., Twidale, M. B., Smith, L. C., & Gasser, L. (2005). Assessing information quality of a community-based encyclopedia. In *Proceedings of the International Conference on Information Quality – ICIQ 2005*. Cambridge, MA, pp. 442–454.

Subramani, M. R., & Peddibhotla, N. (2003). *Contributing to document repositories – An examination of prosocial behavior*. Information and Decision Sciences Department, University of Minnesota, Minneapolis.

Sudweeks, F., McLaughlin, F., & Rafaeli, S. (1998). *Network and NetPlay: Virtual groups on the Internet*. Cambridge, MA: AAAI Press/MIT Press.

Surowiecki, J. (2004). *The wisdom of crowds: Why the many are smarter than the few and how collective wisdom shapes business, economies, societies, and nations*. New York: Doubleday.

Tapscott, D., & Williams, A. D. (2007). *Wikinomics: How mass collaboration changes everything*. New York: Portfolio.

Thompson, L. F., Meriac, J. P., & Cope, J. G. (2002). Motivating online performance: The influences of goal setting and Internet self-efficacy. *Social Science Computer Review, 20*, 149–160.

Viégas, F. B., Wattenberg, M., & Kushal, D. (2004, April). Studying cooperation and conflict between authors with history flow visualizations. *CHI 2004* (Preliminary report).

Voss, J. (2005). Measuring Wikipedia. In *Proceedings International Conference of the International Society for Scientometrics and Informetrics*: 10th. Stockholm, Sweden.

Wasko, M. M., & Faraj, S. (2000). It is what one does: Why people participate and help others in electronic communities of practice. *Journal of Strategic Information Systems, 9*, 155–173.

Wiertz, C., & Ruyter, K. (2007). Beyond the call of duty: Why customers participate in firm-hosted online communities. *Organization Studies. 28*, 349–378.

Zhang, M., & Feng Z. (2006, December). *Intrinsic motivation of open content contributions: The case of Wikipedia.* Workshop on Information Systems and Economics (WISE), Chicago, Illinois.

# 12 How Internet-Mediated Research Changes Science

*Ulf-Dietrich Reips*

## Introduction

Science and the Internet: Its most appealing, usable, and integrating component, the World Wide Web, came from its laboratories. Fifteen years after the invention of the web, it has become such an integral part of the infrastructure of modern societies that young people cannot imagine a world without it. It has become even easier to imagine a world without roads and cars than a world without the World Wide Web.

Time to ask in what ways the Internet had and is having an impact on science. How is what once came from the laboratory influencing that laboratory's structure and the researchers working in it? In particular, how is it influencing the way research is conducted? Tim Berners-Lee, who invented the World Wide Web at CERN in Geneva, wrote in 1998:

> The dream behind the Web is of a common information space in which we communicate by sharing information. Its universality is essential: the fact that a hypertext link can point to anything, be it personal, local or global, be it draft or highly polished. There was a second part of the dream, too, dependent on the Web being so generally used that it became a realistic mirror (or in fact the primary embodiment) of the ways in which we work and play and socialize. That was that once the state of our interactions was on line, we could then use computers to help us analyse it, make sense of what we are doing, where we individually fit in, and how we can better work together.

This quote describes two important issues that are crucial for the topic of this chapter, universality and transparency. *Universality* is a principle underlying both science (Merton, 1942) and the web. Neither works well, if the principle is violated. From the similarity of science and the web, it can be predicted that e-commerce business models only work if they do not violate this principle. Also, it can be predicted that science and the web work well together – possibly not so surprising, because the web was developed at a scientific institution. The second important issue mentioned by Berners-Lee is the notion that the web allows us to analyze interactions of its users and thus gain insight into our lives – the very idea of using the Internet for social and behavioral science: Internet science.

In 1997 I wrote a piece titled "Science in the Year 2007" (Reips, 1998), describing a day in the life of a scientist in 2007 that nowadays doesn't sound surprising at all, even though it contained many technologies and uses of technologies that were not common then. The scientist would wake up in the morning and take a look at the LCD screen hanging at the wall next to her bed, checking reports from remote servers that run her Internet-based research studies, that is, data mining projects, online surveys, and web experiments. She publishes in online journals and bases her text on automatically generated reports with integrated three-dimensional figures. She collaborates via screen sharing and by decentralized work with others on modules of the same project, and communicates in encryptable forum discussions with colleagues she found via a search engine search. Furthermore, she uses living documents that change depending on previously defined factors and uses a web browser that adapts to her language and preferred style of appearance. We are there now.

Finally, in 2003, a report of the American National Science Foundation on initiating the development of "cyberinfrastrucure" suggested that "a new age has dawned in scientific and engineering research" (Atkins et al., 2003). The report continues:

> The amounts of calculation and the quantities of information that can be stored, transmitted, and used are exploding at a stunning, almost disruptive rate. Vast improvements in raw computing power, storage capacity, algorithms, and networking capabilities have led to fundamental scientific discoveries inspired by a new generation of computational models . . . Powerful 'data mining' techniques operating across huge sets of multi-dimensional data open new approaches to discovery. Global networks can link all these together and support more interactivity and broader collaboration.

This chapter attempts to provide this new Internet-mediated approach to scientific endeavour with some firm grounding and offers examples of its possible application. First, typical activities by scientists are described and how they have changed under the influence of the Internet. Then, the areas of data mining, data collection, and publishing activities are explored in-depth. Examples show how more interactivity and broader collaboration has manifested itself in the scientific community and beyond.

## Dimensions of Scientific Activity

Science and the daily life of scientists have changed in multiple ways because of the Internet. The changes have affected all dimensions of scientific activity: Communication, information gathering, data collection, publication, teaching, and grant acquisition. The Internet supports and integrates scientific activities, resulting in faster research cycles (Figure 12.1).

*Communication* with colleagues around the world has proliferated in speed and quality since e-mail became available to many universities as one of the early Internet services (e.g., on VAX mainframes), long preceding the WWW (e.g., Freeman, 1984). Because of the small bandwidth needed and its (mostly) text-only nature, e-mail is the most used of all Internet services. Nie and Erbring

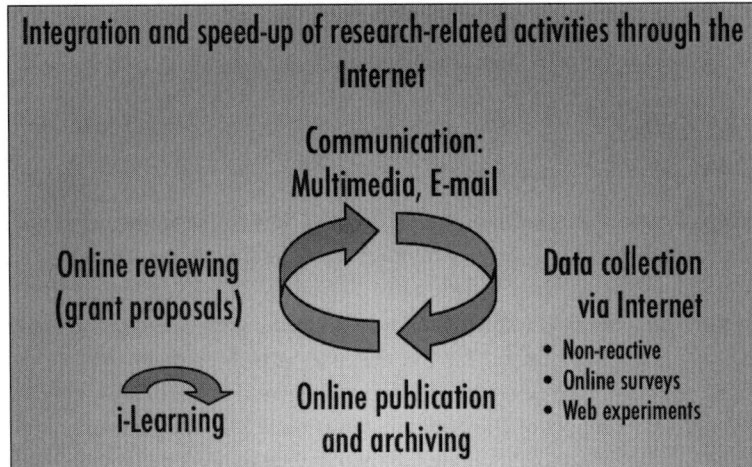

Figure 12.1. *A circle of scientific activities that is influenced and progressively integrated by the Internet.*

(2002) found that "email is by far the most common Internet activity, with 90% of all Internet users claiming to be emailers" (p. 277). However, new developments such as social networking technologies and the ever-increasing improvements in connection speed for a growing audience may change the proportions of user activities on the Internet. Currently, the proliferation of high bandwidth, the peer-to-peer principle, and "killer apps" like Skype (skype.com) is leading to a state of affairs where virtual meetings take place with fewer technical difficulties than ever before. Matzat (2002) reviews the implications of Internet discussion groups for informal academic communication. He concludes that there is no convincing evidence for unified effects of Internet-based communication, such as better transfer of information, production of new knowledge, or intensification of existing contacts. Neither the hypotheses of a growing global village nor the balkanization of academic communication (Van Alstyne & Brynjolfsson, 1996) are trends generalizable across all scientific disciplines and networks.

The core scientific activity, *data collection*, undergoes an unprecedented historical change in scale and number of opportunities in the social and behavioral sciences (Reips, 1997, 2000). Reips (2006) published data from a web service for scientists for the recruitment of online participants, the web experiment list at http://genpsylab-wexlist.unizh.ch/, showing an exponential increase in data collection activities on the Internet. Figure 12.2 depicts an updated chart of this increase, showing that the exponential increase may now turn into a steep linear trend.

*Online publication*, at least in the form of self-archiving and for per article download fees by journals, is rapidly changing the publication landscape. The activities around the key concept of open access show even aspects of a revolutionary movement (Harnad, 1995, 2001). Closely tied to publication issues is *citation analysis* and related forms of evaluation, which is nowadays

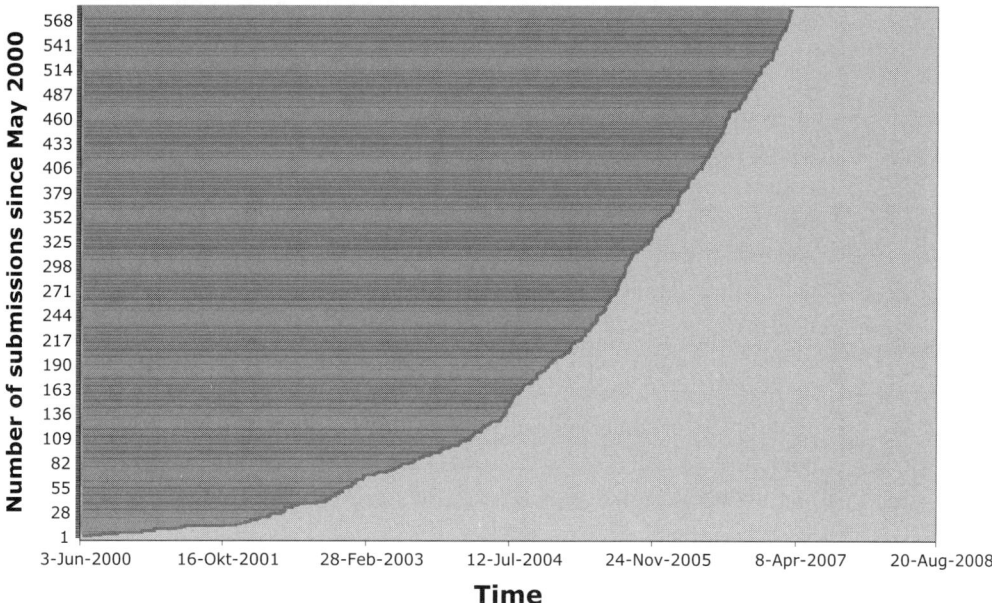

Figure 12.2. *Number of studies registered to the web experiment list and web survey list since May 2000 (earlier studies were entered en bloc and therefore are not included here).*

automatically conducted via large networked publishing databases. Citation analysis, online publication, and Internet-based data collection will be discussed more in detail later in this chapter.

*Teaching* and *grant acquisition* procedures have also been affected by the Internet. E-learning and i-teaching are proliferating, these activities are beginning to integrate with research activities, particularly in the social and behavioral sciences (Reips & Matzat, 2006). Funding agencies deliver guidelines and forms via their websites, funding proposals, and also proposal reviews can often be submitted via online forms or via e-mail.

And, of course, *information gathering* is supported generally by search engines, specialist websites, and aggregation engines (e.g., folksonomies like Flickr, 43things.com, or YouTube), and specifically by scientific data-mining services (e.g., Google Scholar and Web of Science in bibliometrics).

Internet-based research affects science in multiple ways during the research cycle. I will now take a closer look at one of the core activities in science: data collection and its methods, and how and when it was affected by the Internet.

## History and Types of Internet-Based Research Methods

When the interactive WWW became available with the implementation of forms in HTML standard 2.0, the first few pioneers of

Internet-based research discovered that this technology can be used in social and behavioral research. The first HTML-based psychological questionnaires appeared on the Internet in 1994. Krantz, Ballard, and Scher (1997) and Reips (1997) conducted the first Internet-based experiments in 1995. In September, 1995, I opened the first web-based laboratory for experimental studies, the Web Experimental Psychology Lab (http://www.psychologie. unizh.ch/sowi/Ulf/Lab/WebExpPsyLab.html[1]). Early web-based assessments appeared around the same time (Buchanan, 2001; also see review by Barak & Buchanan, 2004). The number of studies conducted via the World Wide Web has grown ever since, the growth curve was empirically shown to follow an exponential path (Reips, 2006), which may now turn into a steep linear trend (see Figure 12.2).

Examples for social and behavioral studies currently in progress can best be found on designated websites, the reader may visit studies linked at the Web Experimental Psychology Lab or at the following Web sites:

- Web experiment list (Reips & Lengler, 2005): http://genpsylab-wexlist.unizh.ch/
- Web survey list: http://genpsylab-wexlist.unizh.ch/browse.cfm? action = browse&modus = survey
- Psychological Research on the Net by Krantz: http://psych. hanover.edu/research/exponnet.html
- International Personality Item Pool by Goldberg: http://ipip.ori.org/ipip/
- Online Social Psychology Studies by Plous: http://www. socialpsychology.org/expts.htm
- Decision Research Center by Birnbaum: http://psych.fullerton.edu/mbirnbaum/decisions/thanks.htm

Tools to create Internet-based studies or response items for web questionnaires, to recruit participants, to include an Internet-based Big Five personality test with one's own study, to analyze log files, and to learn about Internet-based research can be found at the iScience Server at http://www.iscience.eu/ (Figure 12.3).

## Types of Internet-Based Research Methods

Internet-based studies can be categorized as *nonreactive Internet-based methods, web surveys*, *web-based tests*, and *web experiments*.

---

[1] Because Web addresses (URLs) may change, the reader is advised to use a search engine like Google (http://www.google.com/) to access the Web pages mentioned in this chapter. For example, type "Web Experimental Psychology Lab" into the search field and it will return the link to the laboratory as the first result listed. The Web Experimental Psychology Lab can also be accessed using the short URL http://tinyurl.com/dwcpx.

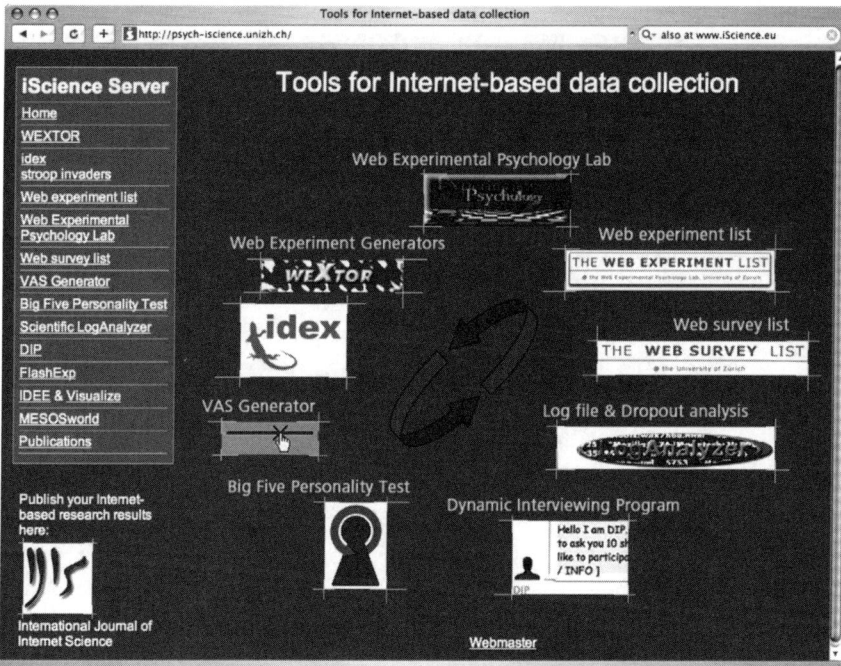

Figure 12.3. *The iScience Server at http://www.iscience.eu/.*

*Nonreactive Internet-based methods* refer to the use and analysis of existing databases and text collections on the Internet (e.g., server log files or contributions to mailing lists). The Internet provides an ocean of opportunities for non-reactive data collection and data mining. The sheer size of Internet corpora multiplies the specific strengths of this class of methods: Nonmanipulable events can be studied *in natura*, facilitating the examination of rare behavioral patterns (e.g., Fritsche & Linneweber, 2006). For example, Cohn, Mehl, and Pennebaker (2004) studied the online diaries of U.S. users of livejournal.com, a publicly accessible online diary site, for linguistic markers of psychological change surrounding September 11, 2001. With unprecedented precision, they were able to describe pronounced psychological processes in coping with the event. Barak and Miron (2005) examined the writing characteristics of suicidal people on the Internet by analyzing randomly selected freely written forum entries. Compared with other groups (e.g., highly distressed nonsuicidal persons or persons writing in a forum on watching television) suicidal persons had significantly more stable and global attributions, were distinctively more self-focused, and reported more unbearable psychological pain and cognitive constriction.

Recently, a new analytical level was reached with the development of publicly available real-time visualization devices as backends of large data collection services. For example, Akamai, a company that claims to monitor 20 percent of the world's Internet traffic, provides visitors at http://www.akamai.com/html/technology/visualizing_akamai.html with visualization of aggregated

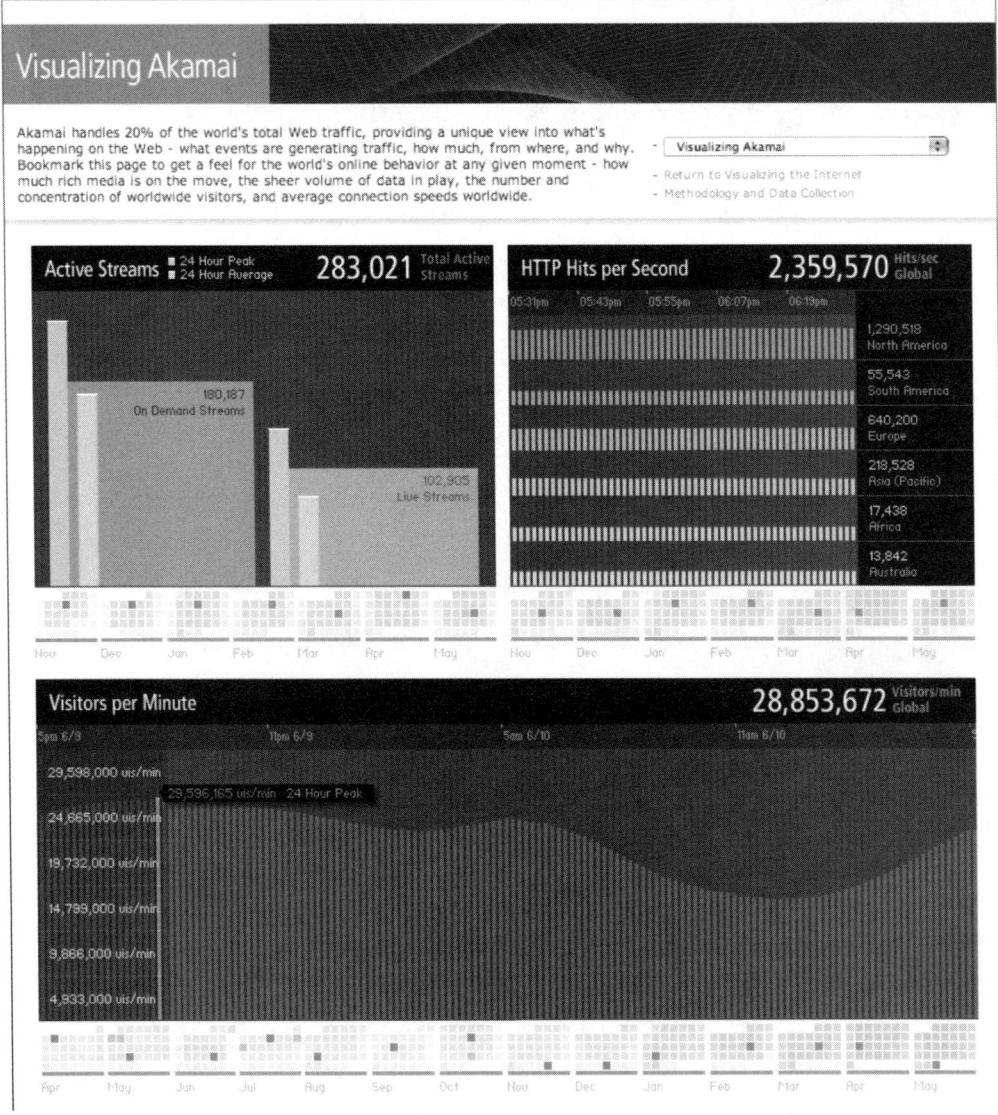

Figure 12.4. *The general Akamai Net Usage Index. Akamai claims to monitor 20 percent of the world's total web traffic.*

nonreactive behavior, including general net traffic by world region (Figure 12.4) and usage statistics for retail, music, and news consumption (Figure 12.5). Peaks in online media consumption, for instance, can be viewed by region and can be linked to compelling news events.

Many other websites, particularly many user forums, news sites, and music sites, begin to display statistics on certain user behaviors ("This story has been read 268 times") or even dynamically adjust their layout by reserving certain attractive spots for frequently viewed, commented, downloaded, or linked

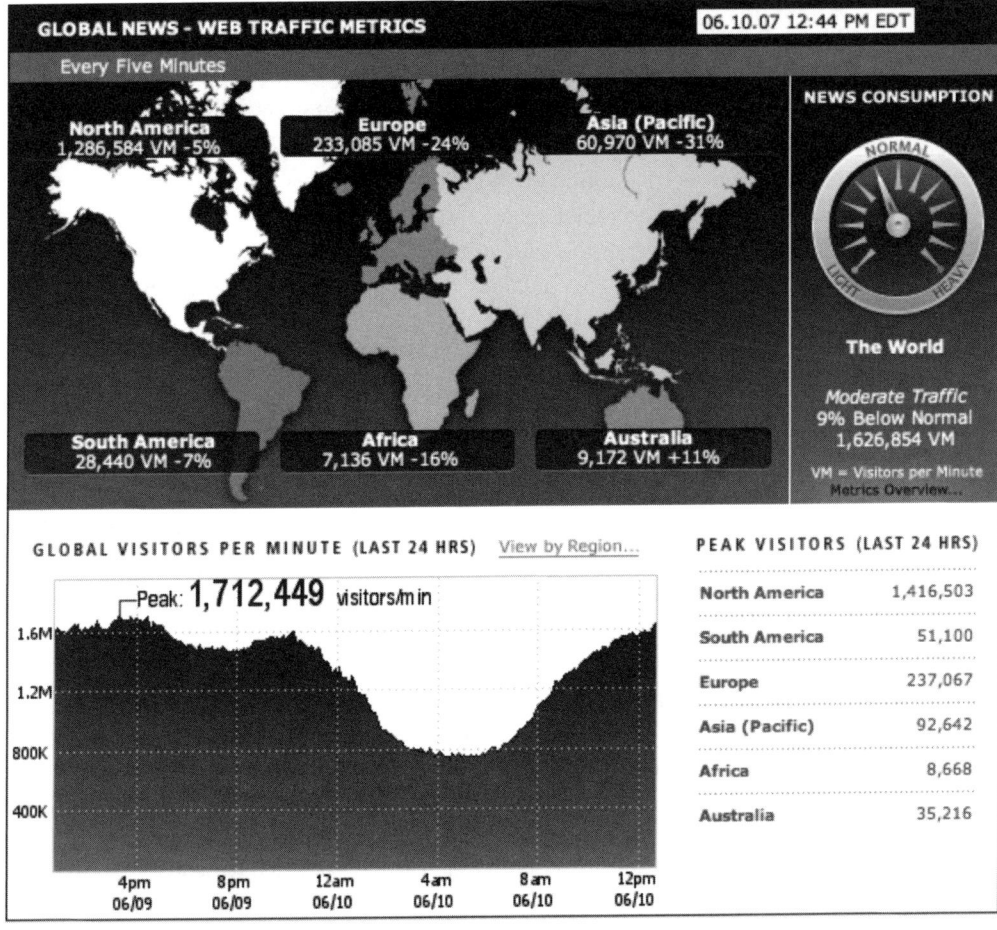

Figure 12.5. *The Akamai Net Usage Index for News. It enables users to monitor sociological and geographic trends of online media news consumption in real time around the clock. The index also features a list of events that may have had an impact on online media consumption.*

items. Depending on the content and on the type of site, self-promoting tendencies may result from the frequency feedback and further limit the questionable value of the resulting statistics.

An early, and more fine-grained example of the use of nonreactive data is the study of communicative behavior among members of several mailing lists, conducted in 1996 and 1997 (at a time when SPAM was a rare phenomenon) by Stegbauer and Rausch (2002). These authors were interested in the so-called lurking behavior (i.e., passive membership in mailing lists, newsgroups, and other forums). By analyzing the number and time of postings and the interaction frequencies pertaining to e-mail headers in contributions, Stegbauer and Rausch empirically clarified several questions regarding the lurking phenomenon. For instance, about 70 percent of subscribers to mailing lists could be classified as lurkers, and "among the majority of users, lurking is not a transitional phenomenon but a fixed behavior pattern [within the same social space]" (p. 267). However, the analysis of individuals' contributions to different mailing lists showed a sizeable proportion of people may lurk in one forum but are active in another. With this result, Stegbauer and Rausch empirically supported the notion of so-called weak ties as a basis for the transfer of knowledge between social spaces.

An (important) example of a nonreactive web-based method is log file analysis. Log files are the raw data that are written each time some information is requested from the Internet. An array of tools is available for log file analysis from web servers. Most of these tools are geared toward web masters of business websites, for example, the public domain analysis tool *FunnelWeb*, available from http://www.quest.com/funnel-web-analyzer/, and the commercial Web log analyzer *Summary*, available from http://www.summary.net/. Data from Internet-based research studies, in particular web experiments, can be analyzed with Scientific LogAnalyzer (Reips & Stieger, 2004). Scientific Log-Analyzer (http://genpsylab-logcrunsh.unizh.ch) reorganizes the log file data to a statistical software friendly one line per participant format and also performs dropout analyses.

*Web surveys*: The most commonly used web-based assessment method is the web survey. Examples can be viewed at the web survey list (http://genpsylab-wexlist.unizh.ch/browse.cfm?action=browse&modus=survey). The frequent use of surveys on the Internet can be explained by the apparent ease with which web surveys can be constructed, conducted, and evaluated. However, this impression of ease is somewhat fallacious. Work by Dillman and his group (Dillman & Bowker, 2001; Dillman, Tortora, & Bowker, 1998; Smyth, Dillman, & Christian, 2007; Smyth, Dillman, Christian, & Stern, 2006) has shown that many web surveys are plagued by problems of usability, display, sampling, or technology. Joinson and Reips (2007) have shown in experiments that the degree of personalization and the power attributable to the sender of an invitation to participate in the survey can affect survey response rates. Data quality can be influenced by degree of anonymity, and this factor as well as information about incentives also influence the frequency of dropout (Frick, Bächtiger, & Reips, 2001; O'Neil & Penrod, 2001). Design factors like the decision whether a "one screen, one question" procedure is applied may trigger context effects that turn results upside down (Reips, 2002a, 2007). Despite these findings, converging evidence shows that web-based survey methods result in qualitatively comparable results to traditional surveys (e.g., Cole, Bedesian, & Field, 2006; Deutskens, de Ruyter, & Wetzels, 2006; Krantz & Dalal, 2000; Luce et al., 2007; Smither, Walker, & Yap, 2004; but see Buchanan, Johnson et al., 2005), even in longitudinal studies (Hiskey & Troop, 2002).

Where differences between results from online and offline methods are found, there is often an obvious explanation in format (see previous paragraph), sampling, or expertise in using the input device. Established recruitment practices from undergraduate student populations versus visitors of particular websites, for instance, may easily result in sampling differences in background knowledge (Reips, 2000). In a web survey from landscape architecture and environmental planning, Roth (2006) asked Internet participants to rate aspects of landscapes (e.g., visual variety, beauty, visual naturalness, and overall scenic quality) from many different areas in Germany. Reliability of the web-based survey was established via both the test-retest-method and the split-half-method. Validity was shown by comparing the records gathered on the web with data collected (much more costly) during an on-site survey and with a traditional color print–based questionnaire. Results indicate that scenic quality (visual variety, beauty, visual naturalness, and overall scenic quality) can be validly recorded on the Internet, while missing background knowledge on the landscapes presented interfered with the assessment of a landscape's typicality. However, it was also established that demographic differences between groups of raters accounted only for very small portions of variance. Consequently, the results from the web survey have a high generalizability.

*Web-based psychological testing* can be considered one specific subtype of web surveying. Buchanan and Smith (1999), Buchanan (2001), Preckel and Thiemann (2003), Wilhelm and McKnight (2002), and Wilhelm, Witthöft, McKnight, and Größler (1999), among others, showed early on that web-based testing is possible if the particularities of the Internet situation are considered (e.g., computer anxiety may keep certain people from responding to a web-based questionnaire).

Barak and Hen (2007, Chapter 6) provide an excellent overview of the variety of the areas and purposes, where psychological assessment has been conducted through online instruments and procedures in recent years. Among them they list:

- clinical diagnostics of a variety of problems and concerns
- neuropsychological and rehabilitation assessment needed to enhance a therapeutic technique
- educational assessment needed to evaluate learning
- school-related adjustment
- the selection of candidates for specific study programs
- vocational, organizational, and career-related assessments needed for job selection
- work-related assessment among applicants or employees
- career counseling assessment for identifying personal abilities, interests, values, and personality characteristics relevant for choosing and developing specific career paths
- group and social assessment in order to identify and detect specific factors at work in the group, focus group, community, or organization.

But even though Internet-based assessments are widely used – how is their quality and can the assessments be justified? Buchanan and Smith found that an Internet-based self-monitoring test not only showed similar psychometric properties to its conventional equivalent but also compared favorably as a measure of self-monitoring. Their results support the notion that web-based personality assessment is possible. Similarly, Buchanan, Johnson, and Goldberg (2005) showed that a modified International Personality Item Pool (IPIP) inventory they evaluated appears to have satisfactory psychometric properties as a brief online measure of the domain constructs of the Five-Factor Model. Across two studies using different recruiting techniques, they observed acceptable levels of internal reliability and significant correlations with relevant criterion variables. However, the issue of psychometric equivalence of paper-and-pencil versions of questionnaires with their web-based counterparts remains one that depends on other factors. For instance, Buchanan, Johnson et al. (2005) could only recover two of four factor-analytically derived subscales of the Prospective Memory Questionnaire with a sample of $N = 763$ tested via the Internet. Buchanan and Reips (2001) showed that technical aspects of how the web-based test is implemented may interact with demography or personality and, consequently, introduce a sampling bias. In their study, they showed that the average education level was higher in web-based assessment if no JavaScript was used, and that Mac users scored significantly higher on Openness than PC users (the "Apple effect").

*Web-based experimenting* has become a widely used method of experimental research in the social and the behavioral sciences. A number of methods and techniques have been proposed (Reips, 2000, 2002b, 2002c) that promise to be useful to researchers and supportive to the method's quality. Although some of these techniques have empirically been shown to work (e.g., password techniques, the seriousness check, the warm-up technique [Reips, Morger, & Meier, 2001], the multiple site entry technique [Hiskey & Troop, 2002]), others have not been investigated beyond a theoretical exploration.

A recent trend in web experimenting has been research on effects of procedures and conditions of Internet-based research, such as the influence of social desirability (Joinson & Reips, 2007), information about incentives (Frick, Bächtiger, & Reips, 2001; Göritz, 2006; Heerwegh, 2006), personalization (Joinson & Reips, 2007; Joinson, Woodley, & Reips, 2007; Heerwegh & Loosveldt, 2006), voluntariness and anonymity (Reips & Franek, 2004), progress indicators (Bandilla, Bosnjak, Kaczmirek, & Neubarth, 2004; Heerwegh & Loosveldt, 2006), use of JavaScript (Buchanan & Reips, 2001; Schwarz & Reips, 2001), visual stimuli (Krantz, 2001), visual analogue scales (Reips & Funke, in press), visual grouping (Smyth, Dillman, Christian, & Stern, 2006), animation methods (Schmidt, 2001), types of nonresponse (Bosnjak, 2001), forced response (Stieger, Reips, & Voracek, 2007), survey length statements and survey sponsor logos (Heerwegh & Loosveldt, 2006), or gathering of personal information on drop-out in web-based studies (Frick, Bächtiger, & Reips, 2001; O'Neil & Penrod, 2001). Such effects triggered the development of guidelines in Internet-based research (Reips, 2002c). Another piece of the frame has been the development and evaluation of several web experimental techniques, such as the *multiple site entry technique*, the *warm-up technique*, the *high hurdle technique*, *experimental design for dropout analysis* (Reips, 1997, 2000, 2002b, 2002c), and custom *randomized response techniques* (Musch, Bröder, & Klauer, 2001).

Although web experiments seem to produce valid results if conducted properly (e.g., Krantz & Dalal, 2000), there is an alarming potential for "configuration errors" (Reips, 2002b). Just as these errors on part of the experimenter can be shown to bias experimental results, there may be biases caused by interactions between psychological processes in Internet use and the widely varying technical context (Reips, 2000; Schmidt, 2007).

## Online Publication

Publishing has probably been influenced by the Internet and the new media in general like no other area of profession. The rapid changes in technology, workflow, automatization, and integration of publishing processes reflected in terms such as *cross media*, *blogging*, and *digital preservation* have also captured scientific publishing. The relationship between scientists and publishers that had remained mostly unchanged for hundreds of years is in turmoil. From the viewpoint of scientists, the new developments offer the opportunity to get rid of a burdensome necessity that often procrastinated or even suppressed the free flow of ideas and communication.

### Open Access Publishing

Scientists and their institutions are moving fast toward the adoption of open access publishing and institutional or individual self-archiving. In some sciences, like physics, this process began early and is almost completed – thanks to a strong community-based working attitude and efforts by individuals like Paul Ginsparg, who created the famous e-print server arXiv (Brown, 2006). Open access publishing and self-archiving has long been advocated by Stevan Harnad (e.g., Harnad, 1995, 2001). In his analysis of "Zeno's paradoxon" (Harnad, 2001), he writes:

> Researchers, librarians, publishers and university administrators have so far been held back from self-archiving by certain prima facie worries, all of which are easily shown to be groundless. These worries are rather like "Zeno's Paradox": "I cannot walk across this room, because before I can walk across it, I must first walk half- way across it, and that takes time; but before I can walk half-way across it, I must walk half-half-way across it, and that too takes time; and so on; so how can I ever even get started?" This condition might better be called "Zeno's Paralysis."

It seems time to state the end of Zeno's paralysis in scientific publishing. From a few pioneering open access journals like Harnad's *Psycholoquy*, their number has now grown to more than 2,200 (*Directory of Open Access*

*Journals*, 2006). Examples include journals published exclusively online, such as *Sociological Research Online* (founded in 1996), the *Journal of Computer-Mediated Communication*, the *International Journal of Internet Science*, or, recently, the *Journal of Medical Internet Research*. Some journals, for example, *Atmospheric Chemistry and Physics* and other journals by the European Geosciences Union, combine open access with collaborative public peer review. Submitted manuscripts pass a quick check by the editor(s) and then are published as "discussion papers" in the journal's discussion forum, which is ISSN registered, so all contributions to the discussion can be officially cited and are guaranteed to stay permanently archived.

Self-archiving of peer-reviewed publications is popular: 95 percent of authors will comply with institutional self-archiving mandates, as reported in an international author survey (Swan, 2005), and 93 percent of journals already officially endorse author self-archiving, according to a registry of over 9,000 journal policies (University of Nottingham, 2006). Articles that are available online are cited more often (Lawrence, 2001), probably because they are simply more accessible (Hitchcock, Brody, Gutteridge, Carr, & Harnad, 2003).

## Citation Analysis

At the late end of the publication timeline are citations and their analysis. Services like Thomson Scientific Web of Science and Google Scholar aggregate millions of references that can be analyzed and put to use in manifold ways. For example, citation links between articles can be tracked backward and forward, similar articles can be found by overlap of reference lists. Evolving trends can be spotted by monitoring publications with quickly increasing citations rates. The Thomson Scientific Hot Papers Database (http://www.in-cites.com/a-prod/sw-hp.html) uses these and other data in defining and monitoring emerging fields.

The emergence of *social web software* turned out to be a hotbed for the development of new community-supported open access citation services. For example, CiteULike (http://www.citeulike.org/) (Figure 12.6). CiteULike was written by Richard Cameron in November 2004, and he is running it privately since then. In telling his thoughts behind the development of CiteULike he delightfully describes the stepwise collaborative and community-building processes behind social software:

> So, the obvious idea was that if I use a web browser to read articles, the most convenient way of storing them is by using a web browser too. This becomes even more interesting when you consider the process of jointly authoring a paper. There is a point where all the authors need to get together and get all the articles they wish to cite into the one place. If you do this process collaboratively on a web site, then it's easier.
>
> The next obvious leap is that if all the references are available via a web interface on a central server, it would be really nice to see what your colleagues

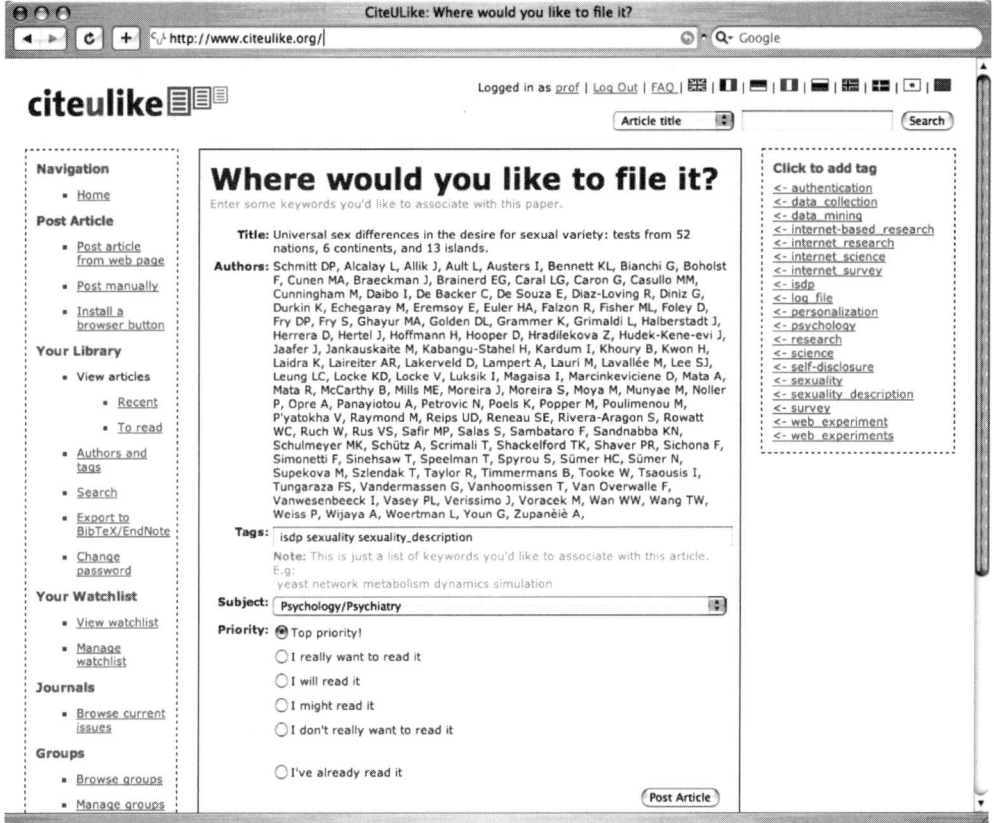

Figure 12.6. *The CiteULike citation service for easy bibliography building by click of a button in archives like CiteSeer or PubMed and many associated Web sites. CiteULike contains tagging features, reminder functions (watchlists), search and filtering, and export options, among others.*

are reading and be able to show them what you're reading. It cuts down on the number of emails saying 'have you seen this article?'

In fact, if enough users register on the system, you'll probably find people reading the same articles as you. That provides a great way of keeping on top of the literature – you simply share it with people who have common interests.

If we have a model of everyone's library being completely open, then our reference manager has suddenly transformed itself into a piece of social software. That's what CiteULike aims to be.

Another citation service is Zotero (http://www.zotero.org/). It is a plug-in module for web browsers (not a web service like CiteULike) and integrates particularly well with the Firefox web browser. It can sense when users are viewing a book, article, or other bibliography item on the web. On many research and library sites, Zotero will find and automatically save the full reference information. Since it lives on one's personal computer, it can communicate with word processing software, where reference information is needed most.

### Integration of Internet-Based Research and Online Publishing

The open access *International Journal of Internet Science* (http://ijis.net) requires authors to include links to the reported Internet-based studies in published articles, so readers can experience what study participants went through. In reference to the high prevalence of nonresponse in Internet-based studies (Musch & Reips, 2000; Reips, 2000, 2002b) authors are asked to report response rates, dropout curves (or dropout rates at least), and item nonresponse rates. It welcomes submission of studies that were planned to analyze types of nonresponse as dependent variables.

Because some scientists begin asking why peer-reviewed articles should be published in commercial publishers' journals at all, if hosting, archiving, and the peer-review process can be organized independently (e.g., via open peer commentary), we are likely to see further rapid development in the publishing market. Particularly, in those areas of the behavioral and social sciences where Internet-based research methods are feasible, an integration of the research with the reports they are published in (demonstrations of the experimental materials within the article or even "live articles" that adapt to changing results, in particular with nonreactive research and data mining) seems only a matter of time.

## How Internet-Based Research Methods Change Science

Just as laboratory research was revolutionized by the introduction of computers in the 1970s (e.g., Connes, 1972; Hoggatt, 1977), we are now experiencing a revolution through Internet-based research (Musch & Reips, 2000). And just as computerized research allowed for advances in research methodology such as accurate measurements of response times, item-branching capabilities, and reduction of the tendency to respond in a socially desirable way (e.g., Booth-Kewley, Edwards, & Rosenfeld, 1992), the Internet offers new advantages to the researcher. Of course, because Internet-based research methods are rooted in computer-based assessments, all of the computer-related advantages and disadvantages apply. However, the Internet offers further possibilities. Reips (2000, 2002c) lists and describes about twenty advantages (see Table 12.1), for example, control of motivational confounding, better access to a large number of demographically and culturally diverse participants as well as to rare and specific participant populations, and avoidance of experimenter biases and demand characteristics (Reips, 2000).

Many of the scientifically most valuable advantages of Internet-based science become visible on second view only: ease of access to many participants is one of the first reasons many who contemplate conducting Internet-based studies (Musch & Reips, 2000) cite. But sheer numbers are often not necessary or even corruptive beyond an optimal point (the optimal number of research participants can be determined by a power analysis).

Table 12.1. *Web experiments: advantages, disadvantages, and solutions (adapted from Reips, 2002c)*

| Advantages of web experiments | Disadvantages with solutions |
| --- | --- |
| (1) Ease of access to a large number of demographically and culturally diverse participants (e.g., a study conducted in three languages with 440 women from more than nine countries; Bohner, Danner, Siebler, & Samson, 2002); | (1) Possible multiple submissions – can be avoided or controlled by collecting personal identification items, by checking internal consistency as well as date and time consistency of answers, and by using techniques such as *subsampling, participant pools,* or handing out *passwords* (Reips, 2000). There is evidence that multiple submissions are rare in Web experiments (Reips, 1997). |
| (2) ... as well as to rare and specific participant populations (Mangan & Reips, 2007; Schmidt, 1997). | |
| (3) Better generalizability of findings to the general population. | Generally, (2) experimental control may be an issue in some experimental designs, but is less of an issue when using between-subjects designs with random distribution of participants to experimental conditions. |
| (4) Generalizability of findings to more settings and situations (because of high external validity). | |
| (5) Avoidance of time constraints. | |
| (6) Avoidance of organizational problems, such as scheduling difficulties, as thousands of participants may participate simultaneously. | (3) Self-selection can be controlled by using the *multiple site entry technique.* |
| | (4) Dropout is always an issue in web experiments. However, dropout can be turned into a detection device for motivational confounding. Also, dropout can be reduced by implementing a number of measures, such as promising immediate feedback, giving financial incentives, and by personalization (Frick, Bächtiger, & Reips, 2001). |
| (7) Highly voluntary participation. | |
| (8) Ease of acquisition of just the optimal number of participants for achieving high statistical power while being able to draw meaningful conclusions from the experiment. | |
| (9) Detectability of motivational confounding. | |
| (10) Reduction of experimenter effects. | (5) The reduced or absent interaction with participants during a web experiment creates problems, if instructions are misunderstood. Possible solutions are pretests of the materials and providing the participants with the opportunity for giving feedback. |
| (11) Reduction of demand characteristics. | |
| (12) Cost savings of lab space, person hours, equipment, administration. | |
| (13) Greater openness of the research process. | (6) The comparative basis for the web experiment method is relatively low. This continues to change. |
| (14) Ease of access to the number of people who see the invitation but do not participate. | (7) External validity of web experiments may be limited by their dependence on computers and networks. Also, many studies cannot be done by web. However, where comparable, results from Web and lab studies are often identical (Krantz & Dalal, 2000). |
| (15) Ease of comparing results with results from a locally tested sample. | |
| (16) Greater external validity through greater technical variance. | |
| (17) Ease of access for participants (bringing the study to the participant instead of the opposite). | |
| (18) Public control of ethical standards. | |

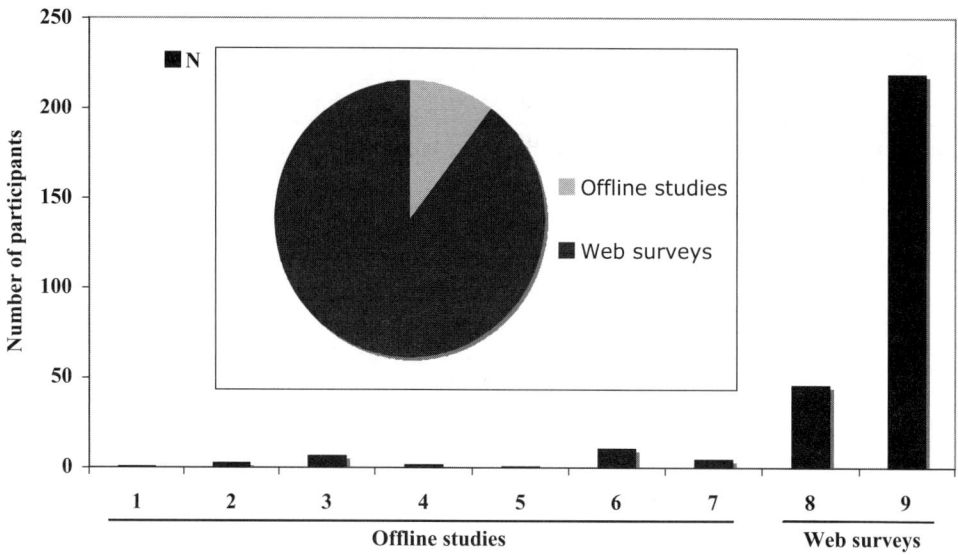

Figure 12.7. *Findings on all nine studies conducted in twenty years of research on the rare condition sexsomnia from Mangan and Reips (2007), highlighting crucial improvements in scientific endeavor regarding rare and sensible conditions made possible by Internet-based research. With two web surveys it was possible to gather data from five times as many people in the target population as in all other (offline) studies combined.*

And the greater variance in sample demographics that in some studies and on a macroscopic level may be seen as an advantage of Internet-based research (Reips, 1997, 2000, 2002b) may also be detrimental in other studies, where a homogeneous sample is sought (Brenner, 2002). Access to rare and specific participant populations, however, is a case particularly suited to advance science via Internet-based research. The following study serves as an example how this advantage nicely combines with the anonymity that can be achieved on the Internet.

Mangan and Reips (2007) conducted web-based research with people suffering from sexsomnia, a newly identified rare medical condition whose sufferers engage in sexual behavior during their sleep. Problematic cases have forensic implications and often are highly distressing. Sexsomnia may frequently go unreported because of shame and embarrassment. Thus, little is known about this condition's demographics and clinical features. Because of the anonymity of the survey situation, the Internet is particularly suited for surveys on sensitive topics, and thus is presented by Mangan and Reips as the method of choice for their research on sexsomnia. With two web surveys it was possible to gather data from five times as many people in the target population as in all seven other (offline) studies combined that cover twenty years of research on sexsomnia (Figure 12.7).

While not exactly a rare population overall, but sometimes so on the Internet, Birnbaum reports that one of his students was able to gather responses from more than 4,000 seniors within seven days. The student recruited her participants via genealogy newsletters (Birnbaum & Reips, 2005). Reported in 2001, Birnbaum sampled members of the Society for Judgment and Decision Making and compared their decision strategies in solving a series of decision gambles with those by students and with those predicted by the society member's own favorite decision theories!

## The Wider Picture

The networking characteristic of the Internet is driving a number of revolutionary developments that are likely to profoundly change some areas in the basic and applied sciences. For example, over the past few years it has become possible to combine low-cost *digital health monitoring* devices with a networked database and intelligent software that renders crucial information in a graphical format that is meaningful to someone monitoring the patient or user (Obrenovic, Starcevic, Jovanov, & Radivojevic, 2002) and sends out alarms if necessary. Such i-health systems are able to measure temperature, heart rate, body fat, blood pressure, blood sugar, length of movements, and number of steps taken, among other parameters.

Data sets and interactive visualization of data have become available to a wide audience via the Internet and serve as resources for science, education, and business. A website that turns statistics available from the United Nations and other organizations into *interactive maps* is Globalis. "Globalis is an interactive world atlas . . . that aims to create an understanding for similarities and differences in human societies, as well as how we influence life on the planet." (http://globalis.gvu.unu.edu/). The site can be used to show seats in parliament held by women depending on country or compare the state of the world now with its prognosed state in 2050. Figure 12.8 shows a map of intact forests in North America, that is, larger blocks of forest areas that have seen little impact from human activity.

Pipeline Diversity Analysis (http://pda.uab.es/), is a web service in bioinformatics that can automate the process of searching for and analyzing genetic data via Internet. Biologists can search for small variations in the genomes of different individuals and different species using the data stored in large public genome databases, such as the Drosophila Polymorphism DataBase, which contains all the polymorphic sequences in the *Drosophila* genus. Biological Internet-based research methods of this kind are of immense help to the scientific community in dealing with the large amounts of molecular data that are generated worldwide.

One of the earliest websites for community building on the Internet by taking care of a real physical entity via remote control is the *Telegarden* at the University of Southern California (http://www.usc.edu/dept/garden/). It went

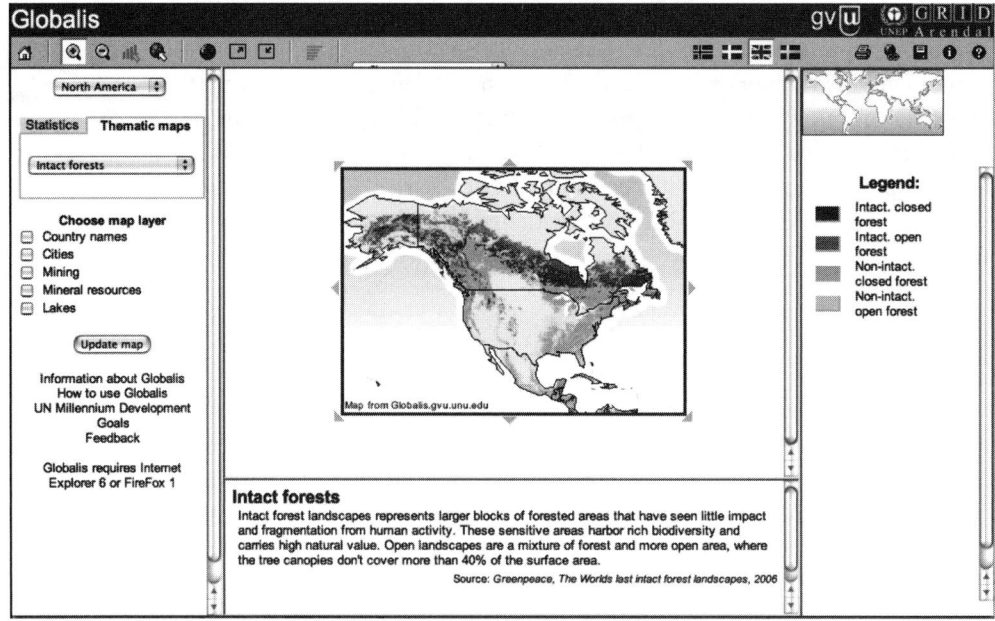

Figure 12.8. *Globalis interactive world maps, generated from statistics by the United Nations and other organizations. The figure shows intact forests, that is, larger blocks of forest areas that have seen little impact from human activity.*

online in June 1995 and later moved to the Ars Electronica Center in Austria (http://www.aec.at/). A robot was installed in the center of a circular garden and fitted with a plant growing light that slowly revolved around the garden (Figure 12.9). The robot could be controlled via Internet by guests or members of the Telegarden, with members having more privileges. Figure 12.10, from the Telegarden demonstration site shows how a user could try his gardening skills via remote mouse control. A forum and the website served as communication devices in community building – and so did the garden itself (McLaughlin, Osborne, & Ellison, 1997). As Randall Packer from the San Jose Museum of Art put it: "The Telegarden creates a physical garden as an environment to stage social interaction and community in virtual space. The Telegarden is a metaphor for the care and feeding of the delicate social ecology of the net." (http://queue.ieor.berkeley.edu/~goldberg/garden/Ars/). Eventually, the garden was retired in August 2004, but its memory lives on in the Telegarden archive at http://www.telegarden.org/tg/.

## Summary

In this chapter, I have made an attempt to review some of the major influences Internet-based research methods and the Internet have had and continue to have on science. Dimensions of scientific activities were analyzed in respect to changes and innovations coming from the web. Communication,

Figure 12.9. *Telegarden with robot.*

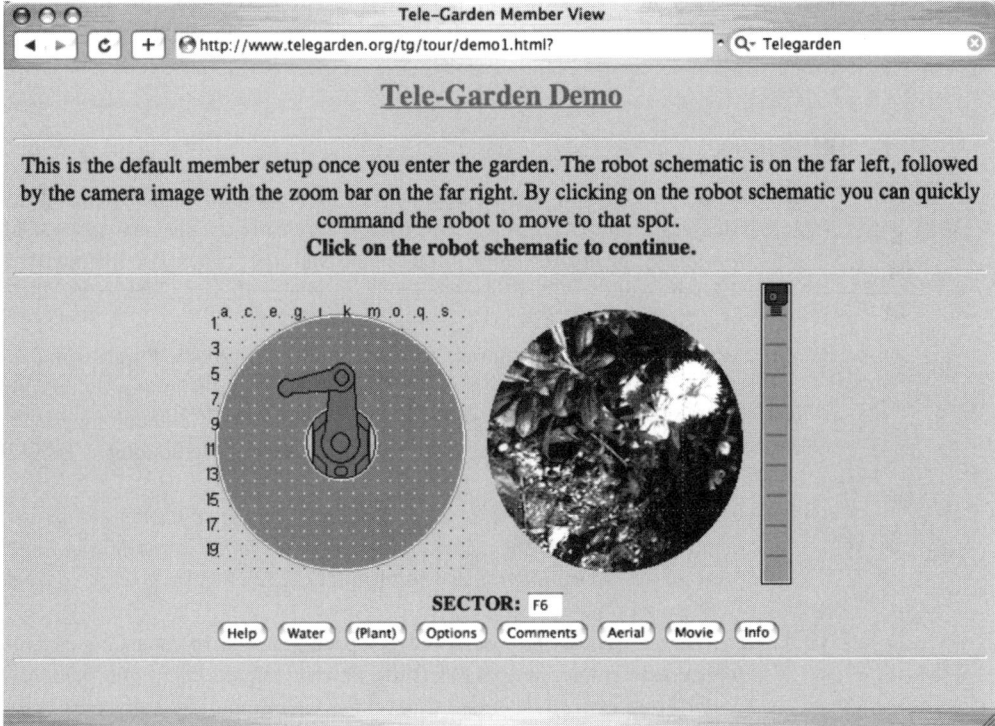

Figure 12.10. *Web-based Telegarden navigation device in demonstration mode.*

information gathering, data collection, publication, teaching, and grant acquisition are all affected, and they integrate progressively well. New technologies are developed that find their way into the laboratories and enable the true enactment of fundamental principles of scientific work: universality, transparency, internationality, and open access.

Internet-related influences on core scientific activities of data collection and publication were presented in detail. The history and types of Internet-based research methods, *nonreactive methods, web surveys, web-based tests*, and *web experiments* was explained. Many examples of Internet-based research were drawn from the behavioral and social sciences because they are more profoundly and in some respects uniquely (e.g., data collection opportunities) influenced by the Internet revolution. Disciplines like psychology, sociology, communication, economics, linguistics, and education experience a surge in Internet-related research. The natural sciences have been leading the path in other Internet-related activities. In particular, physics was at the forefront of adopting open access publishing, and of course, the World Wide Web was developed as a means of communication among physicists. The life sciences, arm in arm with computer sciences, are unsurpassed in developing large collaborative computation sites for analyzing molecular structures. No science seems unaffected, as was shown with examples from medicine, forestry, biology, and landscape architecture, among others.

Science is in the middle of a period of exciting developments that seem to affect the daily activities of scientists more profoundly than anything since the invention of the printing press. Thanks to the Internet, thanks to visionary minds.

## References

Atkins, D. E., Droegemeier, K. K., Feldman, S. I., Garcia-Molina, H., Klein, M. L., Messerschmitt, D. G., et al. (2003). *Revolutionizing science and engineering through cyberinfrastructure*. Report of the National Science Foundation Blue-Ribbon Advisory Panel on Cyberinfrastructure. Retrieved June 20, 2007, from http://www.nsf.gov/od/oci/reports/atkins.pdf.

Bandilla, W., Bosnjak, M., Kaczmirek, L., & Neubarth, W. (2004). *Progress indicators in filter based surveys: Computing methods and their impact on drop out*. Sixth International Conference on Social Science Methodology: Recent Developments and Applications in Social Research Methodology, Amsterdam, The Netherlands.

Barak, A., & Buchanan, T. (2004). Internet-based psychological testing and assessment. In R. Kraus, J. Zack, & G. Stricker (Eds.), *Online counseling: A handbook for mental health professionals* (pp. 217–239). San Diego, CA: Elsevier Academic Press.

Barak, A., & Hen, L. (2007). Exposure in cyberspace as means of enhancing psychological assessment. In A. Barak (Ed.), *Psychological aspects of cyberspace: Theory, research, applications*. Cambridge, UK: Cambridge University Press.

Barak, A., & Miron, O. (2005). Writing characteristics of suicidal people on the Internet: A psychological investigation of emerging social environments. *Suicide and Life-Threatening Behaviour, 35*, 507–524.

Berners-Lee, T. (1998). The World Wide Web: A very short personal history. Retrieved June 14, 2007, from http://www.w3.org/People/Berners-Lee/ShortHistory.html.

Birnbaum, M. H. (2001). A web-based program of research on decision making. In U.-D. Reips & M. Bosnjak (Eds.), *Dimensions of Internet science* (pp. 23–55). Lengerich, Germany: Pabst.

Birnbaum, M. H., & Reips, U.-D. (2005). Behavioral research and data collection via the Internet. In R. W. Proctor & K.-P. L. Vu (Eds.), *The handbook of human factors in Web design* (pp. 471–492). Mahwah, NJ: Erlbaum.

Bohner, G., Danner, U. N., Siebler, F., & Samson, G. B. (2002). Rape myth acceptance and judgments of vulnerability to sexual assault: An Internet experiment. *Experimental Psychology, 49*, 257–269.

Booth-Kewley, S., Edwards, J., & Rosenfeld, P. (1992). Impression management, social desirability, and computer administration of attitude questionnaires: Does the computer make a difference? *Journal of Applied Psychology, 77*, 562–566.

Bosnjak, M. (2001). Participation in non-restricted web surveys: A typology and explanatory model for item non-response. In U.-D. Reips & M. Bosnjak (Eds.), *Dimensions of Internet Science* (pp. 193–208). Lengerich: Pabst.

Brenner, V. (2002). Generalizability issues in Internet-based survey research: Implications for the Internet addiction controversy. In B. Batinic, U. D. Reips, & M. Bosnjak (Eds.), *Online social sciences* (pp. 93–113). Seattle, WA: Hogrefe & Huber.

Brown, D. (2006). *Scientific communication and the dematerialization of scholarship.* ProQuest Discovery Guides. Retrieved March 6, 2007, from http://www.csa.com/discoveryguides/scholarship/review.pdf.

Buchanan, T. (2001). Online personality assessment. In U. D. Reips & M. Bosnjak (Eds.), *Dimensions of Internet Science* (pp. 57–74). Lengerich, Germany: Pabst Science Publishers.

Buchanan, T., Ali, T., Heffernan, T. M., Ling, J., Parrott, A. C., Rodgers, J., et al. (2005). Nonequivalence of on-line and paper-and-pencil psychological tests: The case of the prospective memory questionnaire. *Behavior Research Methods, 37*, 148–154.

Buchanan, T., Johnson, J. A., & Goldberg, L. R. (2005). Implementing a five-factor personality inventory for use on the Internet. *Europe an Journal of Psychological Assessment, 21*, 115–127.

Buchanan, T., & Reips, U.-D. (2001). *Platform-dependent biases in online research: Do Mac users really think different?* Paper presented at German Online Research conference, Göttingen, Germany.

Buchanan, T., & Smith, J. L. (1999). Using the Internet for psychological research: Personality testing on the World Wide Web. *British Journal of Psychology, 90*, 125–144.

Cameron, R. (2004, November). *Citeulike: Frequently Asked Questions.* Retrieved March 6, 2007, from http://www.citeulike.org/faq/all.adp.

Cohn, M. A., Mehl, M. R., & Pennebaker, J. W. (2004). Linguistic markers of psycho-logical change surrounding September 11, 2001. *Psychological Science, 15*, 687–693.

Cole, M. S., Bedesian, A. G., & Feild, H. S. (2006). The measurement equivalence of web-based and paper-and-pencil measures of transformational leadership. *Organizational Research Methods, 9*, 339–363.

Connes, B. (1972). The use of electronic desk computers in psychological experiments. *Journal of Structural Learning, 3*, 51–72.

Deutskens, E., de Ruyter, K., & Wetzels, M. (2006). An assessment of equivalence between online and mail surveys in service research. *Journal of Service Research, 8*, 346–355.

Dillman, D. A., & Bowker, D. K. (2001). The Web questionnaire challenge to survey methodologists. In U.-D. Reips & M. Bosnjak (Eds.), *Dimensions of Internet science* (pp. 159–178). Lengerich, Germany: Pabst.

Dillman, D. A., Tortora, R. D., & Bowker, D. (1998). Principles for constructing Web surveys. *SESRC Technical Report 98-50*. Pullman, WA.

*Directory of Open Access Journals*. (2006). Retrieved October 23, 2007, from http://www.doaj.org/.

Freeman, L. C. (1984). The impact of computer based communication on the social structure of an emergent scientific specialty. *Social Networks, 6*, 201–221.

Frick, A., Bächtiger, M. T., & Reips, U.-D. (2001). Financial incentives, personal information and drop-out in online studies. In U.-D. Reips & M. Bosnjak (Eds.), *Dimensions of Internet Science* (pp. 209–219). Lengerich: Pabst.

Fritsche, I., & Linneweber, V. (2006). Non-reactive methods in psychological research. In M. Eid & E. Diener (Eds.), *Handbook of multimethod measurement in psychology* (pp. 189–203). Washington, DC: American Psychological Association.

Göritz, A. S. (2006). Incentives in Web studies: Methodological issues and a review. *International Journal of Internet Science, 1*, 58–70.

Harnad, S. (1995). A subversive proposal. In A. Okerson & J. O'Donnell (Eds.), *Scholarly journals at the crossroads: A subversive proposal for electronic publishing*. Washington, DC: Association of Research Libraries. Retrieved June 16, 2007, from http://www.arl.org/scomm/subversive/toc.html.

Harnad, S. (2001). For whom the gate tolls? How and why to free the refereed research literature online through author/institution self-archiving, now. Retrieved March 6, 2007, from http://www.cogsci.soton.ac.uk/~harnad/Tp/resolution.htm.

Heerwegh, D. (2006). An investigation of the effect of lotteries on web survey response rates. *Field Methods, 18*, 205–220.

Heerwegh, D., & Loosveldt G. (2006). An experimental study on the effects of personalization, survey length statements, progress indicators, and survey sponsor logos in web surveys. *Journal of Official Statistics, 22*, 191–210.

Hiskey, S., & Troop, N. A. (2002). Online longitudinal survey research: Viability and participation. *Social Science Computer Review, 20*, 250–259.

Hitchcock, S., Brody, T., Gutteridge, C., Carr, L., & Harnad, S. (2003). The impact of OAI-based search on access to research journal papers. *Serials, 16*(3).

Retrieved March 6, 2007, from http://opcit.eprints.org/serials-short/serials11.html.

Hoggatt, A. C. (1977). On the uses of computers for experimental control and data acquisition. *American Behavioral Scientist, 20*, 347–365.

Joinson, A. N., & Reips, U.-D. (2007). Personalized salutation, power of sender and response rates to Web-based surveys. *Computers in Human Behavior, 23*, 1372–1383.

Joinson, A. N., Woodley, A., & Reips, U.-D. (2007). Personalization, authentication and self-disclosure in self-administered Internet surveys. *Computers in Human Behavior, 23*, 275–285.

Krantz, J. H. (2001). Stimulus delivery on the Web: What can be presented when calibration isn't possible. In U.-D. Reips & M. Bosnjak (Eds.), *Dimensions of Internet Science* (pp. 113–130). Lengerich, Germany: Pabst.

Krantz, J. H., Ballard, J., & Scher, J. (1997). Comparing the results of laboratory and World-Wide Web samples on the determinants of female attractiveness. *Behavior Research Methods, Instruments, & Computers, 29*, 264–269.

Krantz, J. H., & Dalal, R. (2000). Validity of Web-based psychological research. In M. H. Birnbaum (Ed.), *Psychological Experiments on the Internet* (pp. 35–60). New York: Academic Press.

Lawrence, S. (2001). Free online availability substantially increases a paper's impact. *Nature, 411* (6837), 521. Retrieved June 14, 2007, from http://www.neci.nec.com/~lawrence/papers/online-nature01/.

Luce, K. H., Winzelberg, A. J., Das, S., Osborne, M. I., Bryson, S. W., & Taylor, C. B. (2007). Reliability of self-report: Paper versus online administration. *Computers in Human Behavior, 23*, 1384–1389.

Mangan, M., & Reips, U.-D. (2007). Sleep, sex, and the Web: Surveying the difficult-to-reach clinical population suffering from sexsomnia. *Behavior Research Methods, 39*, 233–236.

Matzat, U. (2002). Academic communication and Internet discussion groups: What kinds of benefits for whom? In B. Batinic, U.-D. Reips, & M. Bosnjak (Eds.), *Online Social Sciences* (pp. 383–402). Seattle, WA: Hogrefe & Huber.

McLaughlin, M., Osborne, K. K., & Ellison, N. B. (1997). Virtual community in a Telepresence environment. In S. Jones (Ed.), *Virtual culture* (pp. 146–168). London: Sage.

Merton, R. K. (1942). The normative structure of science. In R. K. Merton (Ed.), *The sociology of science: Theoretical and empirical investigations*. Chicago: University of Chicago Press [Reprint 1973].

Musch, J., Bröder, A., & Klauer, K. C. (2001). Improving survey research on the World-Wide Web using the randomized response technique. In U.-D. Reips & M. Bosnjak (Eds.), *Dimensions of Internet science* (pp. 179–192). Lengerich: Pabst.

Musch, J., & Reips, U.-D. (2000). A brief history of Web experimenting. In M. H. Birnbaum (Ed.), *Psychological experiments on the Internet* (pp. 61–88). San Diego, CA: Academic Press.

Nie, N. H., & Erbring, L. (2002). Internet and society: A preliminary report. *IT & Society, 1*, 275–283.

Obrenovic, Z., Starcevic, D., Jovanov, E., & Radivojevic, V. (2002). *An agent based framework for virtual medical devices.* Proceedings of the First International Joint Conference on Autonomous Agents and Multiagent Systems, pp. 659–660, Bologna, Italy.

O'Neil, K. M., & Penrod, S. D. (2001). Methodological variables in Web-based research that may affect results: sample type, monetary incentives, and personal information. *Behavior Research Methods, Instruments, and Computers, 33,* 226–233.

Preckel, F., & Thiemann, H. (2003). Online versus paper-pencil version of a high potential intelligence test. *Swiss Journal of Psychology, 62,* 131–138.

Reips, U.-D. (1997). Forschen im Jahr 2007: Integration von Web-Experimentieren, Online-Publizieren und Multimedia-Kommunikation [Science in the year 2007: Integration of web experimenting, online publishing, and multimedia communication]. In D. Janetzko, B. Batinic, D. Schoder, M. Mattingley-Scott, & G. Strube (Eds.), *CAW-97. Beiträge zum Workshop "Cognition & Web"* (pp. 141–148). Freiburg: IIG-Berichte 1/97.

Reips, U.-D. (1998). Forschung in der Zukunft [Future Science]. In T. Krüger & J. Funke (Eds.), *Psychologie im Internet: Ein Wegweiser für psychologisch interessierte User* (pp. 115–123). Weinheim: Beltz.

Reips, U.-D. (2000). The web experiment method: Advantages, disadvantages and solutions. In M. H. Birnbaum (Ed.), *Psychological experiments on the Internet* (pp. 89–114). San Diego, CA: Academic Press.

Reips, U.-D. (2002a). Context effects in Web surveys. In B. Batinic, U.-D. Reips, & M. Bosnjak (Eds.), *Online Social Sciences* (pp. 69–79). Göttingen, Germany: Hogrefe & Huber.

Reips, U.-D. (2002b). Internet-based psychological experimenting: Five dos and five don'ts. *Social Science Computer Review, 20,* 241–249.

Reips, U.-D. (2002c). Standards for Internet experimenting. *Experimental Psychology, 49,* 243–256.

Reips, U.-D. (2006). Internet-basierte Methoden [Internet-based methods]. In F. Petermann & M. Eid (Eds.), *Handbuch der Psychologischen Diagnostik* (pp. 218–225). Göttingen: Hogrefe.

Reips, U.-D. (2007). The methodology of Internet-based experiments. In A. Joinson, K. McKenna, T. Postmes, & U.-D. Reips (Eds.), *The Oxford handbook of Internet psychology* (pp. 373–390). Oxford, UK: Oxford University Press.

Reips, U.-D., & Franek, L. (2004). Mitarbeiterbefragungen per Internet oder Papier? Der Einfluss von Anonymität, Freiwilligkeit und Alter auf das Antwortverhalten [Employee surveys via Internet or paper? The influence of anonymity, voluntariness and age on answering behavior]. *Wirtschaftspsychologie, 6*(1), 67–83.

Reips, U.-D., & Funke, F. (in press). Interval level measurement with visual analogue scales in Internet-based research: VAS Generator. *Behavior Research Methods.*

Reips, U.-D., & Lengler, R. (2005). The web experiment list: A web service for the recruitment of participants and archiving of Internet-based experiments. *Behavior Research Methods, 37,* 287–292.

Reips, U.-D., & Matzat, U. (2006). Internet science and open access: First day of a honeymoon. *International Journal of Internet Science, 1*, 1–3.

Reips, U.-D., Morger, V., & Meier, B. (2001). "Fünfe gerade sein lassen": Listenkontexteffekte beim Kategorisieren ["Letting five be equal": List context effects in categorization]. Unpublished manuscript, retrieved October 23, 2007, from http://www.psychologie.unizh.ch/sowi/reips/papers/re_mo_me2001.pdf.

Reips, U.-D., & Stieger, S. (2004). Scientific LogAnalyzer: A Web-based tool for analyses of server log files in psychological research. *Behavior Research Methods, Instruments, & Computers, 36*, 304–311.

Roth, M. (2006). Validating the use of Internet survey techniques in visual landscape assessment: An empirical study from Germany. *Landscape and Urban Planning, 78*, 179–192.

Schmidt, W. C. (1997). World Wide Web survey research: Benefits, potential problems, and solutions. *Behavior Research Methods, Instruments, and Computers, 29*, 274–279.

Schmidt, W. C. (2001). Presentation accuracy of web animation methods. *Behavior Research Methods, Instruments, & Computers, 33*, 187–200.

Schmidt, W. C. (2007). Technical considerations when implementing online research. In A. Joinson, K. McKenna, T. Postmes, & U.-D. Reips (Eds.), *The Oxford handbook of Internet psychology* (pp. 461–472). Oxford, UK: Oxford University Press.

Schwarz, S., & Reips, U.-D. (2001). CGI versus JavaScript: A Web experiment on the reversed hindsight bias. In U.-D. Reips & M. Bosnjak (Eds.), *Dimensions of Internet Science* (pp. 75–90). Lengerich: Pabst.

Smither, J. W., Walker, A. G., & Yap, M. K. T. (2004). An examination of the equivalence of web-based versus paper-and-pencil upward feedback ratings: Rater- and ratee-level analyses. *Educational and Psychological Measurement, 64*, 40.

Smyth, J. D., Dillman, D. A., & Christian, L. M. (2007). Context effects in Internet surveys: New issues and evidence. In A. Joinson, K. McKenna, T. Postmes, & U.-D. Reips (Eds.), *The Oxford handbook of Internet psychology* (pp. 429–446). New York: Oxford University Press.

Smyth, J. D., Dillman, D. A., Christian, L. M., & Stern, M. J. (2006). Effects of using visual design principles to group response options in Web surveys. *International Journal of Internet Science, 1*, 5–15.

Stegbauer, C., & Rausch, A. (2002). Lurking in mailing lists. In B. Batinic, U.-D. Reips, & M. Bosnjak (Eds.), *Online social sciences* (pp. 263–274). Seattle, WA: Hogrefe & Huber.

Stieger, S., Reips, U.-D., & Voracek, M. (2007). Forced response in online surveys: bias from reactance and an increase in sex-specific dropout. *Journal of the American Society for Information Science and Technology, 58*, 1653–1660.

Swan, A. (2005). *Open access self-archiving: An introduction*. Technical Report, JISC, HEFCE. Truro: Key Perspectives Limited.

University of Nottingham. (2006). Publisher copyright policies & self-archiving: The SHERPA/ROMEO list. Retrieved June 23, 2007, from http://www.sherpa.ac.uk/romeo.php?all=yes.

Van Alstyne, M., & Brynjolfsson, E. (1996). Wider access and narrower focus: Could the Internet balkanize science? *Science, 274,* 1479–1480.

Wilhelm, O., & McKnight, P. E. (2002). Ability and achievement testing on the World Wide Web. In B. Batinic, U.-D. Reips, & M. Bosnjak (Eds.), *Online social sciences* (pp. 151–180). Seattle, WA: Hogrefe & Huber.

Wilhelm, O., Witthöft, A., McKnight, P., & Größler, A. (1999). On the psychometric quality of new ability tests administered using the WWW. In U.-D. Reips, B. Batinic, W. Bandilla, M. Bosnjak, L. Gräf, K. Moser, & A. Werner (Eds.), *Current Internet science – trends, techniques, results. Aktuelle Online Forschung – Trends, Techniken, Ergebnisse.* Zürich: Online Press. Available URL: http://gor.de/gor99/tband99/.

# Index